Entrepreneur Development

Dr. Satish Taneja
Director of
Banarsidas Chandiwala Institute of
Professional Studies, New Delhi

First Edition : 2010
Reprint : 2012
Reprint : 2015

Published by : Mrs. Meena Pandey for **Himalaya Publishing House Pvt. Ltd.,**
"Ramdoot", Dr. Bhalerao Marg, Girgaon, Mumbai - 400 004.
Phone: 022-23860170/23863863, Fax: 022-23877178
E-mail: himpub@vsnl.com; Website: www.himpub.com

Branch Offices :

New Delhi : "Pooja Apartments", 4-B, Murari Lal Street, Ansari Road, Darya Ganj, New Delhi - 110 002. Phone: 011-23270392, 23278631; Fax: 011-23256286

Nagpur : Kundanlal Chandak Industrial Estate, Ghat Road, Nagpur - 440 018. Phone: 0712-2738731, 3296733; Telefax: 0712-2721215

Bengaluru : No. 16/1 (Old 12/1), 1st Floor, Next to Hotel Highlands, Madhava Nagar, Race Course Road, Bengaluru - 560 001. Phone: 080-22286611, 22385461, 4113 8821, 22281541

Hyderabad : No. 3-4-184, Lingampally, Besides Raghavendra Swamy Matham, Kachiguda, Hyderabad - 500 027. Phone: 040-27560041, 27550139

Chennai : New-20, Old-59, Thirumalai Pillai Road, T. Nagar, Chennai - 600 017. Mobile: 9380460419

Pune : First Floor, "Laksha" Apartment, No. 527, Mehunpura, Shaniwarpeth (Near Prabhat Theatre), Pune - 411 030. Phone: 020-24496323/24496333; Mobile: 09370579333

Lucknow : House No 731, Shekhupura Colony, Near B.D. Convent School, Aliganj, Lucknow - 226 022. Phone: 0522-4012353; Mobile: 09307501549

Ahmedabad : 114, "SHAIL", 1st Floor, Opp. Madhu Sudan House, C.G. Road, Navrang Pura, Ahmedabad - 380 009. Phone: 079-26560126; Mobile: 09377088847

Ernakulam : 39/176 (New No: 60/251) 1st Floor, Karikkamuri Road, Ernakulam, Kochi – 682011. Phone: 0484-2378012, 2378016 Mobile: 09387122121

Bhubaneswar : 5 Station Square, Bhubaneswar - 751 001 (Odisha). Phone: 0674-2532129, Mobile: 09338746007

Indore : Kesardeep Avenue Extension, 73, Narayan Bagh, Flat No. 302, IIIrd Floor, Near Humpty Dumpty School, Indore - 452 007 (M.P.). Mobile: 09303399304

Kolkata : 108/4, Beliaghata Main Road, Near ID Hospital, Opp. SBI Bank, Kolkata - 700 010, Phone: 033-32449649, Mobile: 7439040301

Guwahati : House No. 15, Behind Pragjyotish College, Near Sharma Printing Press, P.O. Bharalumukh, Guwahati - 781009, (Assam). Mobile: 09883055590, 08486355289, 7439040301

Printed at : M/s Sri Sai Art Printer Hyderabad. On behalf of HPH.

ACKNOWLEDGMENT

I am indebted to the fellow faculty and entrepreneur trainers for their reviews and suggestions. I am thankful to Mr. Rampal for his assistance in the chapter on Intellectual Property Rights for this book. I also thank Ms Sukhmani a fellow faculty for contributing two caselets

Last but not the least; I thank my wife, Renu and sons Kashish and Rajat, who have constantly motivated me to undertake this task.

Dr. Satish Taneja

PREFACE

Entrepreneur is presently at the crest of popularity. In India a large number of people are seeking entrepreneurship as a career option. Increasing number of educated youth, are getting attracted towards entrepreneurship and are setting up their business ventures. The management schools have also focused their attention to entrepreneurship and the art of creating a new venture. While some institutes offer the subject as an elective, other consider it vital for development of managerial talent and teach it as a core subject. Present day youth, particularly management students are attracted towards entrepreneurship as it offers vibrant vision of means to fulfill their highest potential.

The response to my earlier books on the subject has been very gratifying and encouraging. Individuals and organizations, in different parts of the country have made use of these books. People from Chennai to Chandigarh have written to me how my earlier books on entrepreneurship have motivated them to become and entrepreneur or to help them succeed as an entrepreneur. The second encouragement came from the reviews by Entrepreneur Development Institutions like NIESBUD and NSTEDB on one hand and Management Institutes like MDI (Gurgaon) on the other. Though this book was primarily written for helping the individuals aspiring to become and succeed as entrepreneur and to be used as text for conducting entrepreneur development programmes by Government agencies, NGO's and other private organizations, yet it will suffice as a text body for a large number of Business Schools for their courses related to entrepreneurship and creation of new venture. Some of my colleagues teaching the subject in different Universities and business schools have suggested some inclusion so as to make this book compatible to their syllabi. Keeping my focus on the prospective entrepreneur and his needs, I have attempted to include many of their suggestions.

While teaching Entrepreneurship to MBA students, I have observed disinterest among a group of students as they consider entrepreneurship as synonymous with small business.

The management students should realize that in this dynamic, fast changing and competitive environment the corporate organization are looking for business leaders rather than manager of yore years. The managers have to train themselves as 'Intrapreneurs'- Entrepreneurs within the constraint of the organizations. Hence, there is a full chapter on Corporate Entrepreneurship.

"Intellectual Property Rights" Knowledge of intellectual property rights has become essential for all entrepreneurs irrespective of the type of business they may choose. The chapter on IPR deals with Patents, Trademarks, Service marks, Geographical indicators and Copy rights. It will assist the entrepreneurs in being on the right side of the law and developing IPR strategies for their ventures.

I firmly believe that entrepreneurship is gender neutral. There are no special projects for women entrepreneurs to choose from. The choice of business ventures depends upon the knowledge, skills and background of a person. Women as a class do face some additional barriers in undertaking any economic activities including entrepreneurial ventures. The chapter on " Barriers to Entrepreneurship" includes barriers to specific groups particularly 'women' and Minorities.

At the request of some of my colleagues, a separate chapter on women entrepreneurs has been added. It deals with the profile of women entrepreneurs, and difference between the motivating factors for male and female entrepreneurs. So as to assist the women in becoming entrepreneurs, an attempt has been made to categories women entrepreneurs and describe various schemes for promotion of different types of women entrepreneurs.

Following are some of the features of this text book:

- **Case studies**: Real life short cases have been given at the end of some of the chapters. These help the students in application of the concepts. Integrated cases are given in the end for practical and over all comprehension.
- **Success Stories**: The biographies of well known's present day entrepreneurs are added with the aim of stimulating the students to entrepreneurship. These demonstrate the traits and action plans of new generation entrepreneurs.
- **Feasibility Studies**: Two live feasibility reports on "solar panels" and "mineral water" then are there to explain the preparation of project feasibility reports in depth.
- The book is written in a lively, enthusiastic style and is virtually free of jargons. The text is extremely readable for students to learn about entrepreneurship, its promises and opportunities.
- This will also server as a reference guide for those planning to take entrepreneurship as a career.

Dr. Satish Taneja

CONTENTS

CHAPTER 1

WHAT IS ENTREPRENEURSHIP?

CHAPTER OUTLINE

INTRODUCTION

The concept of entrepreneurship has been around for a very long time. In the last two decades it has resurged. The concept of entrepreneurship is an age-old phenomenon that relates to the vision of an entrepreneur as well as its implementation by him. Entrepreneurship is a creative and innovative response to the environment. It is also the process of setting up a new venture. Entrepreneurship is a composite skill that is a mixture of many qualities and traits such as imagination, risk taking, ability to harness factors of production, i.e., land, labour, technology and various intangible factors.

Usually any one who runs a business is called an entrepreneur. The more precise meaning of entrepreneur is one who creates his own business, i.e., a person who organises, operates and assumes the risk of a business venture. An entrepreneur is a person who perceives a need and then brings together manpower, material and capital required to meet that need.

Entrepreneurship implies a set of values, norms and traits that are conducive to the growth of a business enterprise. It is the organisational culture that focuses on new opportunities and creation of an organisation where these opportunities can be perused earnestly. An entrepreneur seeks the opportunities, looks for ways and means to capitalise on the newer opportunities by organising the structure and the resources and gaining control on them. As against this, a manager is primarily concerned with the resources under his control, the structure of his organization and its relations to the market. He is also concerned with matching the opportunities with organisational abilities. The entrepreneurs are driven by the perception of opportunities. They seek changes in the political rules, social values, consumer preferences, technology etc. On the other hand resources like money, manpower and material they control, drive the managers.

ENTREPRENEURSHIP : DEFINITIONS AND CONCEPT

Entrepreneurship is an elusive concept that cannot be defined precisely. However, people having different interests have defined 'entrepreneurship' in a number of ways.

- Psychologists and sociologists are interested in why entrepreneurs act.
- Economists focus on "what happens when entrepreneurs act".
- Management experts focus on how the entrepreneurs act, in the characteristics of entrepreneurs and the manner in which they achieve their goals.

Richard Cantillon

The word Entrepreneur is derived from a French word *entrependre,* i.e., individuals who were 'undertakers' meaning those who undertook the risk of new enterprise. The word entrepreneur was first used in the writings of French economist, Richard Cantillon. He described an entrepreneur as a person who pays a certain price for a product to resell it at an uncertain price thereby making decision about obtaining and using resources while assuming "the risk of enterprise". As per Cantillon, entrepreneur's function is to combine factors of production into a producing organism. Entrepreneurs consciously make decisions about resource allocation. Smart entrepreneurs always look for the best opportunity of using resources for high commercial gain.

Adam Smith

As per Adam Smith, the father of political economy, the entrepreneur has a role of an industrialist. In his book, *Wealth of Nations,* he describes the entrepreneur as an individual who forms an organisation for commercial purpose. He is a proprietary capitalist, a supplier of capital and at the same time a manager who intervenes between the labour and the consumer. Adam Smith also treated him as an employer, master, merchant but explicitly considered him a capitalist.

Entrepreneur is one who has unusual foresight to recognise potential demand of goods and services. He is a change agent who transforms demand into supply. He is one who possesses certain arts and skills of creating new economic enterprises. He is a person with exceptional insight into the society's needs and possesses abilities to fulfil them. He is "Economic Risk Taker" of Cantillon and "Industrial Manager" of

Adam Smith. The British economist *John Stuart Mill* had described entrepreneurs as business founders and thus become fourth economic factor with land, labour and capital.

Carl Menger

Carl Menger of Austria was of the view that economic changes do not arise from the circumstances but from the individual's awareness and understanding of these circumstances. The entrepreneur, therefore, becomes a change agent who transforms resources into useful goods and services, thus, creates the circumstances leading to industrial growth. As per Menger's classic theory of production, resources having no direct use in terms of fulfilling human needs were transformed into highly valuable products that directly fulfilled human needs. He saw the entrepreneur as an astute individual who could envision this transformation and create the means to implement it. He adds value to the original resource and this value is rewarded through profits.

Joseph Schumpeter

Joseph Schumpeter, an economist described entrepreneur as one who seeks to reform or revolutionise the pattern of production by exploiting an innovation or, more generally, an untried technological possibility for producing a new commodity or producing an old one in a new way, by opening up a new source of supply of material or a new outlet of products. Entrepreneurship, as defined, essentially consists of doing things that are not generally done in ordinary course of business routine.

An entrepreneur is one who innovates, raises money, collects inputs, organises talent, provides leadership and sets the organisation.

Schumpeter did not equate entrepreneur with an inventor. An inventor is one who creates a new product while Shumpeter's entrepreneur exists if the factors of production are combined for the first time. To him maintenance of a combination is not an entrepreneurial activity.

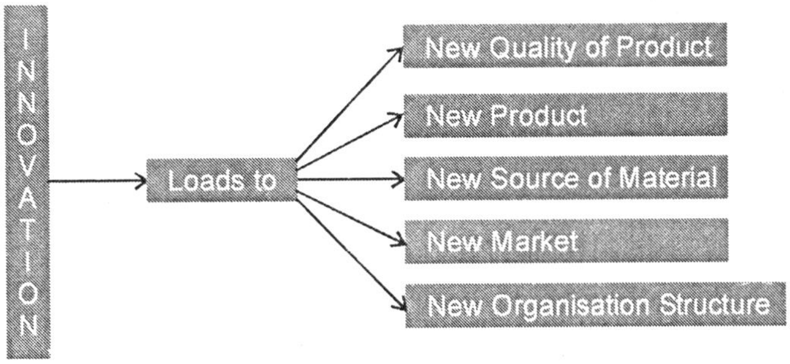

Fig. 1.1 : Innovation

Peter Drucker

As per Peter Drucker, the management *guru*, entrepreneurial role is one of getting and using resources. The difference is that in an entrepreneurial role the resources must be allocated to the opportunities, where as, in the managerial role the resources are allocated to solve the problems. Entrepreneurship occurs when resources are redirected towards progressive opportunities, and are not used for ensuring administrative efficiency. This redirection of resources distinguishes between the entrepreneurial and managerial role.

According to Peter Drucker an entrepreneur is one who always searches for change, responds to it and exploits it as an opportunity. Innovation is an instrument of entrepreneurship. An entrepreneur innovates and creates resources because there is no such thing as resource until someone finds a use for something and endows economic value to it. Drucker considers increasing the value and consumer satisfaction of a resource is an entrepreneurial activity. Entrepreneurs convert a material into a resource or combine the existing resources in a new or more productive configuration. As per Drucker, an entrepreneur need not be the owner of the business. A professional manager who mobilises resources and allocates them to make a commercial gain from an opportunity is also considered as an entrepreneur.

Robert Ronstand

Robert Ronstand had described entrepreneurship as a dynamic process of creating incremental wealth. This wealth is created by persons who assume the major risk, in term of equity, time and/or career commitment of providing value for some product or service. Product or service itself may or may not be unique but value must be infused by entrepreneur through allocation of necessary skills and resources.

Encyclopedia Britannica defines entrepreneur as "an individual who bears the risk of operating a business in the face of uncertainty about future conditions".

FIVE CORE ELEMENTS OF ENTREPRENEURSHIP

From various definitions refered to in previous pages it emerges that entrepreneurship primarily consists of five main elements:

1. Key part of entrepreneurship is to identify opportunities that no one has earlier noticed. Such opportunities need not be large; these can even be small ones. **Creativity and innovation** form the core of entrepreneurship that enables the entrepreneur to think entirely new ways of working. Creative people are receptive to new ideas generated by others.
2. The entrepreneurs have **an ability to apply the creativity** to business problems. They understand the people and environment around them. They can effectively martial resources for the same. It is not enough to think creatively, successful entrepreneurship demands that thoughts be translated into action and result. They need an ability of getting thing done.
3. Entrepreneurs always **take risk**. Their main task is evaluating risk for cutting across accepted boundaries, breaking rules and doing things in a different manner.
4. Thus entrepreneurs **focus on creating value** by doing things in a cheaper, better and faster manner.
5. They have a sound belief in their ability to change the status quo—the way the things are being done presently. With their **drive and passion** to achieve success they change the way things are being performed.

Thus, entrepreneurship can be defined as "*creating of value by people working together to implement an idea through the application of drive and a willingness to take risk.*"

PURE ENTREPRENEURS

Pure entrepreneurs are ones who create a venture from the raw material of their own ideas and hardwork. They nurse them into a successful business with their instinct for opportunity and sense for timing, their hardwork and idea producing ability. It is the pure entrepreneurs who are treated as the celebrities. Dheerubhai Ambani of Reliance and Narayan Murthy of Infosys are modern celebrities at par with Sachin Tendulkar and Shahrukh Khan.

Others who takeover the business after the founders retire, die or sell out and continue to build and innovate, qualify as entrepreneurs, albeit not the pure ones.

ENTREPRENEURS IN A EMERGING ECONOMY

The concept of entrepreneurship is same in developed and developing economies. In emerging economies like that of India the scope and need of non-pure entrepreneur is higher. Here in an entrepreneur need not necessarily innovate, even if he imitates any technique of production/marketing from a developed country, he is an entrepreneur in his own right and makes a contribution to economic development as long as he starts a business, undertakes risk and bears uncertainties. In developing economies entrepreneurship is considered as a form of labour which guides the rest of labour-what to do and how to get things done. Since Schumpeter's entrepreneur only exist if the factors of production are combined for the first time, the entrepreneur in developing economies may not necessarily fit into Schumpeter's model. He definitely fits into Ricardo's theory. Ricardo included the term "entrepreneurial ability" as an independent factor of production and profit as the reward for entrepreneurial ability.

ENTREPRENEURSHIP AS A PROCESS

> The spirit of entrepreneurship is enduring, Says Ashok Soota, CEO, Mindtree Consultancy, one of the most talked about start ups, " Entrepreneurship is the sheer pleasure and enjoyment of putting things together and making sure that you do not letdown the shareholders who have placed their trust in you. Today, I am sure there are people who would love to start their own ventures but are waiting for the right time. We have the right team in place and we knew what it was we were looking for." *Entrepreneurship – Financial Times, New Delhi, 15 Oct., 2002*

In the two decades there has been a resurgence of entrepreneurship in higher education. This revival is not from the traditional discipline of economics but from the discipline of business management. The business schools have instituted new courses in entrepreneurship.

While entrepreneur is a person who sets-up a business, 'Entrepreneurship' is considered as the process or action of setting up of the new venture and the venture so set-up is called the 'enterprise'. Entrepreneurship has been considered as the propensity of mind to take a calculated risk with confidence to achieve a predetermined business objective. It is the risk taking ability of an individual coupled with the correct decision making. Schumpeter described it as a process and the entrepreneurs as innovators who use the process to shatter the status quo through the combination of resources and new methods of commerce.

In brief, the concept of entrepreneurship includes three phases—namely:

- Initial entrepreneurial phase or inception phase which is related to perception of an opportunity to establish the business.
- Operational phase which includes the theory and practice of management functions in the organization of a business unit.
- Managerial phase which includes the profitable application of the mental executive health in taking relevant managerial decisions to run the business unit as a profitable, going and growing concern.

ENTREPRENEURIAL PHILOSOPHY

'To some extent, success of an entrepreneur depends on ones willingness to accept responsibility for ones own work. One must learn a great deal about oneself if one intends to pursue the goals which are compatible with what one wants most in life. Even though the risk of failure is always present, entrepreneurs take risk by assuming responsibility for their actions. Failure must be accepted as learning experience. Some entrepreneurs succeed only after experiencing failure. Learning from past experience helps channelise ones actions to obtain more positive results and success results from persistent efforts.

Pursue goals related to ones skills and abilities. Accept oneself as one is and try to emphasise on ones strengths and play down ones weaknesses. By pursuing ones goals honestly and sincerely, one can achieve positive results. Being goal oriented brings out the best qualities. Acceptable results are more important than perfect results, so do not waste time in achieving perfection.

ENTREPRENEURSHIP—THE DYNAMIC NEED

In general, contemporary economists agree that entrepreneur is a business leader who plays a pivotal role in development and fostering economic growth. Entrepreneurship is one of the most important input in the economic development of a region or a country. The number and competence of entrepreneurs affect the economic growth of a region. It is not wrong to consider entrepreneurship as a panacea of the economic evils in a developing country. In fact, entrepreneurship is the dynamic need of a developing nation.

Entrepreneurship as Career Option

An educated person has broadly two career options. One is called wage or salary employment, wherein people are employed in government service, public and private sectors and get fixed wage or salary. The other career option is entrepreneurial employment under which people set up their new ventures. Wage employment does not generate resources and is organized within the existing wealth. Wage employment is self-saturating. Once availed, it blocks the employment opportunity to others for another 10 years. On the other hand, the latter contributes towards national wealth and has a unique characteristic of self-generation. This starts a chain of activities that create unending employment opportunities. Entrepreneurship promotes small saving amongst middle class individuals for investment into new ventures. It also provides an outlet that creates an urge among individuals to attain excellence in product design and related innovation. Thus, entrepreneurship provides a lasting solution to the acute problem of unemployment.

Table: 1.1

	Wage Employment	**Entrepreneurial Employment**
Nature	Self Satuating	Self Generating
Scope	Limited	Unlimited
Orientation	• Routine Types	• Creative
	• Status Quo	• Innovative
	• Problem Avoiding	• Problem Solving
	• Dependent	• Independent Decisions
Contribution	Consumes National Wealth	Generates National Wealth
Earning	Fixed (Subsistence)	Growing (Generating Surplus)

In the context of employment generation, the three terms, i.e., **Income Generation**, **Self-employment** and **Entrepreneurship** are often used interchangeably. Entrepreneurship refers to identification of innovative ideas, setting up of a new enterprise. Whereas, self-employment refers to full time involvement in ones own occupation. One may or may not be bearing the risk, mobilising inputs, organizing production and marketing the product or service. Income generating activities, on the other hand, are part time, casual and practised with a view of raising additional income. All entrepreneurs are self-employed and income generating persons. But all self-employed and income generating persons may not be entrepreneurs.

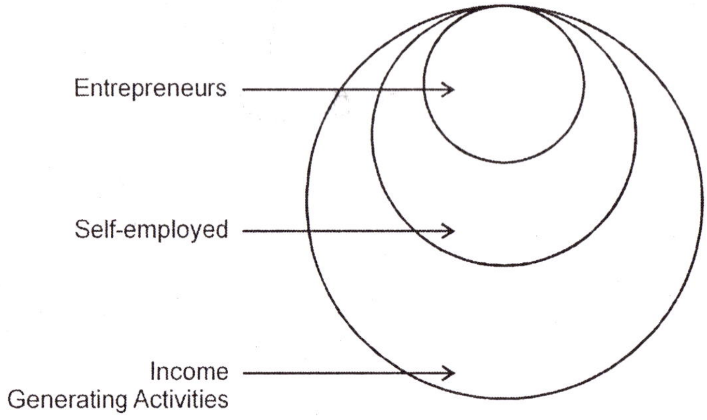

Fig. 1.2 : Income Generation, Self-employment and Entrepreneurship

The three, however, can be considered as initial, middle and final stages of Entrepreneurial Growth Process.

National Income

National Income consists of goods and services produced in the country and imported. The goods and services produced are for consumption within the country as well as to meet the demand of exports. The domestic demand increases with ever increasing population and improving standard of living. The export demand also increases to meet the needs of growing import due to various reasons. An increasing number of entrepreneurs are required to meet this increasing demand for goods and services. Thus, entrepreneurship increases the national income.

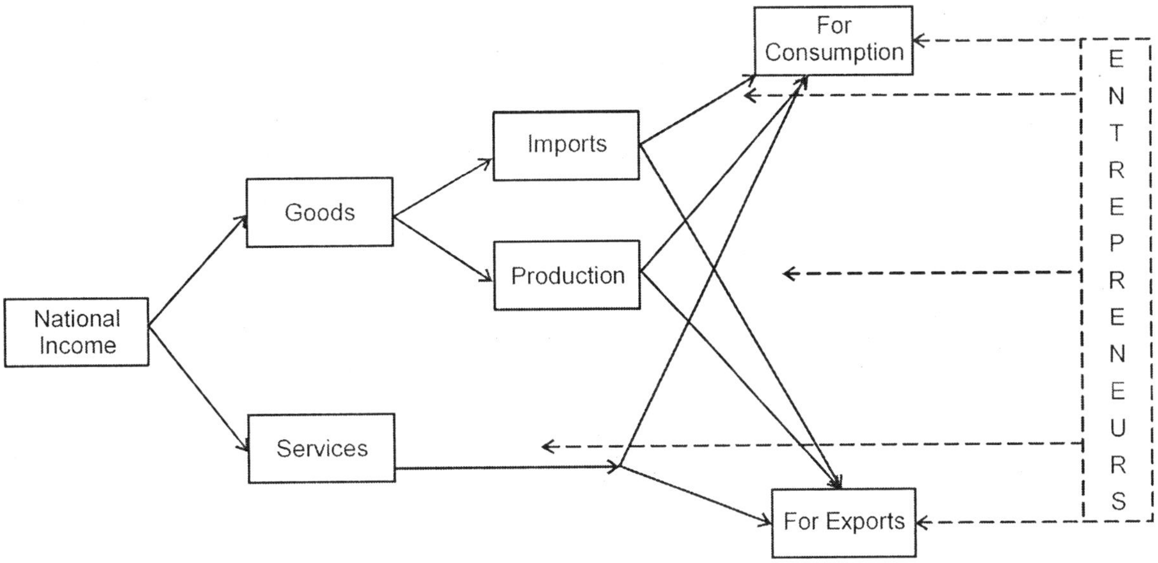

Fig. 1.3 : Entrepreneurship and National Income

Employment Generation

Growing unemployment, particularly educated unemployment is an acute problem of the nation. The available employment opportunities can cater to only 5 to 10 per cent of the unemployed. As discussed, wage employment is a self-saturating. When government creates, say a hundred jobs in various departments, 100 persons get employed and the vacancies are filled for thirty years or so, till these people retire and the vacancies re-emerge. If a hundred persons become entrepreneurs they not only create a hundred jobs for themselves but also provide employment to many more. As the time passes these enterprises grow providing direct and indirect employment to many more. Thus, entrepreneurship is the best way to fight the evil of unemployment.

> Entrepreneurship helps solving problems related to :
> - Employment generation
> - National production
> - Dispersal of economic power
> - Balance regional development
> - Harnessing youth vigour
>
> NIESBUD

Balanced Regional Development

The growth of industry and business leads to a large number of public benefits like road transport, health, education, entertainment etc. When the industries are concentrated in selected cities, the development gets limited to these cities. Till late sixties, 50 per cent of industrial enterprises were located in only six cities of India. A rapid development of entrepreneurship ensures a balanced regional development. When the new entrepreneurs grow at a faster pace, in view of the increasing competition in and around the cities, they are forced to set up their enterprises in the smaller towns away from big cities. This helps in the development of the backward regions.

If a region does not throw up a sufficient number of entrepreneurs, the needs of the local population for the goods and services remain unsatisfied. The entrepreneurs from other places step in and set up enterprises to fulfil the pent up demand of the local people. These alien entrepreneurs do not invest the major part of the profits in the areas in which the unit is located. Usually, the profit is invested at a place, from where the entrepreneurs come from. Such entrepreneurs invest their profits in constructing their houses etc., at the place of their origin. Thus, the backward areas do not get full benefits of business or industrial profits. This drainage of wealth results in further deterioration of the area. The practice of siphoning the profits earned through entrepreneurial activities based on local resources by alien entrepreneurs has been compared with the blood sucking process practised by leeches, and termed as *'leech effect'* by Dr. M.M.P. Akhori.

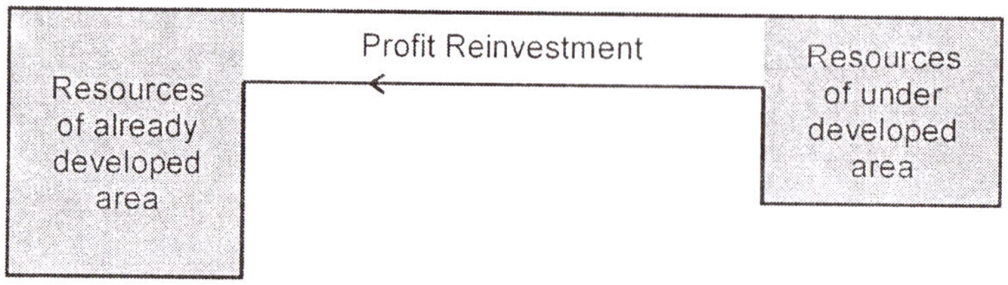

Fig. 1.4 : Siphoning of Profits Through Entrepreneurship Activities by Alien Entrepreneurs

Dispersal of Economic Power

The world affairs have been dominated by power. There have always been two types of power, i.e., muscle power and economic power. In the modern age, the muscle power has lost its relevance and the world is ruled by the economic power. Economic power is the natural outcome of industrial and business activity. Industrial development normally can lead to concentration of economic power in few hands. This concentration of power in few hands has its own evils in the form of monopolies. Developing a large number of entrepreneurs helps in dispersing the economic power amongst the population. This in turn causes hindrance to the growth of monopolies, which exist partly because of lack of sufficient number of entrepreneurs. Setting up of a large number of enterprises for the goods helps in weakening the harmful effects of monopoly.

When a society produces a small number of entrepreneurs, the enterprises due to lack of competition grow into a few big business houses. This results in concentration of wealth in a few families. This can have a serious social and national implication. When the number of enterprises is large national wealth is shared by a large number of entrepreneurs, thus, dispersing wealth. This dispersal of wealth promotes the real socialism and makes the economy healthy.

CORPORATE APPLICATIONS OF ENTREPRENEURSHIP

The major activity of entrepreneurship is to setup and start a new business venture. In fact, besides start-ups there are four other corporate applications of entrepreneurship. According to Aleksander Mandic, CEI.ig.com Brazil these are:

1. The strategic corporation
2. The nimble exploiter
3. The self-sustaining innovator
4. The reawakening giant

Depending upon the role of the leader, each of these involve the five core elements of entrepreneurship with varying emphasis. Entrepreneurial behaviour of a large corporate is often manifested in making bold strategic moves. It is the visionary leader in entrepreneurial role that inspires a *strategic corporation* to develop new ways of creating shareholders value. Such entrepreneurs are often engaged in developing new businesses for their companies.

Corporations fallowing *nimble exploiter* approach pay less emphasis on creativity and innovation than to the drive for executing good ideas and making them success in market place. They capatalise on established ideas on the basis of their strengths.

3M, Sony, Nokia and HP are the examples of *self-sustaining innovators.* They believe in spreading entrepreneurial behaviour throughout their organization by using a different leadership model that helps to innovate in changing markets, developing new product ahead of their competitors. *Reawakening giants* are those large corporations, which are lying dormant on innovation front and with the change in leadership, i.e., getting an entrepreneurial chief executive, have become active. The changed mechanism introduces entrepreneurial behaviour in the industrial giants that have succumbed to cultural inertia.

ENTREPRENEURSHIP IN INDIA

Entrepreneurship is wired into the Indian DNA. From time immemorial Indian entrepreneurs have driven global trade leveraging their intellect, vision and speed of execution. Even today these strengths are driving a new breed of Indian entrepreneurs to emerge as globally dominant forces in their respective industries. Indian entrepreneurs while retaining their Indian strengths, have found a way to overcome traditional orientation imbibed from the family centric value system and domestic market focus.

Indian entrepreneurs operated in a unique environment, characterised by insufficient access to funds, technology and lack of developed knowledge base and support infrastructure. The paucity of capital has driven Indian entrepreneurs to come up with ingenious ways to be more capital efficient and cost conscious. We have a history of enterprises, which have maintained high efficiency levels with lean structures. We clearly see the evidence of this in industries like automotive components, heavy engineering and manufacturing in general. This potent combination of intellect and practical constraints also drives Indian entrepreneurs to adapt mature products and technologies to the needs of the Indian market—essentially process and business model innovation.

This differentiates Indian entrepreneurs from entrepreneurs in developed economies, who mainly play the role of early stage technological innovators. By virtue of Indian Infrastructure being absent or inadequate, Indian entrepreneurs have gone ahead and created it—JRD Tata created an entire township for Tata's employees in Jamshedpur. Entrepreneurs in India frequently operates in isolation, and have to look after every aspect of their business and environment—often merging corporate entrepreneurship with social entrepreneurship. They have frequently come up with unique models of merging business and social responsibility—Dr Verghese Kurian built on the largest and most successful business institutions in India—Amul Co-operative—by organizing rural Gujrat into cooperative units.

Given the political instability in the economy and nascent consumer market, Indian entrepreneurs have developed the agility to respond to the challenge of rapidly changing business environments. The Hero group is the prime example—its evolution from a small bicycle manufacturer to the largest manufacturer of motarised two wheelers and a leading auto component supplier in India is due to the foresight and vision of its founder Dr Brij Lal Munjal. For almost fifty years after India's independence, business focused solely on serving the domestic market. Some of the strengths of our entrepreneurship can be transplanted to other countries. However the ability to work effectively in a global economy is a core skill that needs to be developed. Moreover, while Indian entrepreneurial class is emerging as a strong force shaping India's future, some of our strengths also threaten to impede our efforts in becoming a truly global force. The concept of the family, dominated by patriarch is constraining our horizons. Close monitoring and control can stymie decision making. Lack of diverse workforce outside the family eventually leads to a lack of fresh thinking and innovative ideas.

SUMMARY

Entrepreneurship mainly depends on values, norms and traits that are consistant to the growth of an economy. An entrepreneur always seeks the opportunities, looks for ways and means to capitalise on the newer opportunities by organising the resources. The five core demands of entrepreneurship are creativity and innovation, ability to get things done, drive, focus on creating value, and risk taking. The entrepreneur is one of the most important inputs in the economic development of a country or of regions within the country. The need for a broad-based entrepreneurial class in India arises form the need to speed up the process of activating the factors of production, leading to a higher rate of economic growth, dispersal of economic activities, development of backward areas. A good entrepreneur is one who is capable of inspiring confidence in people and has the ability to motivate them to work with him in fulfilling the economic goals set by him. Entrepreneurship goes beyond creating new enterprises. Today even the large corporations have a scope for entrepreneurship. There are four different applications of entrepreneurship in corporate development. In India entrepreneurs have found a way to overcome traditional orientation imbibed from family centric value system to market focus.

REVIEW QUESTIONS

1. Who is an entrepreneur and what is the entrepreneurship process?

2. How have economist and management experts looked at the entrepreneurs?
3. Analyse critically Schumpeter's views on entrepreneurship.
4. Do you agree that a person who takes over a business from its founder is not a pure entrepreneur? Why and why not?
5. Write a detailed note on linkage between entrepreneurship and economic development.
6. If the government want to solve the unemployment problem, developing entrepreneurship is the right preposition. Please elaborate.
7. Do you find any difference between self-employed person and an entrepreneur? Explain with examples.
8. Entrepreneurship development can go a long way in solving the economic and non-economic problems of a developing country like India. Do you agree? Please explain.
9. Define entrepreneurship and elaborate on its scope and role in developing economies.
10. Explain how the corporate apply the concept of entrepreneurship.

CASE 1.1

RASHMI GARMENTS*

When Arun walked in, he found Mrs. Rashmi Aggarwal sitting in her chair with some papers in her hand, looking around in her shed. She was also watching her children play and quarrel in the gallery near the door of her unit. Arun was a researcher from an Institute of Entrepreneurship Development. He was interested in understanding the processes through which Mrs. Aggarwal had developed her garment business. She told to Arun "See, the orders from my customers are increasing. I wonder how will I manage with the existing manpower in the unit. I also have limited space. I know that I will have to meet the customers demand or, else, I will lose even my old customers. On the other hand, my home also requires more time and attention, especially, my children. Oh! what should I do".

Mrs. Rashmi Aggarwal is a post-graduate in Economics. Since her school days, she had liked the service class women. She was influenced by their way of living, their modern dresses, their status in the family and society. She shared with Arun that while she was still in college, she had made up her mind to do something outside home on her own. She wanted to become economically independent and carve out her own identity in the society.

In 1984, she saw an advertisement in the newspaper for a one month Entrepreneurship Development Programme (EDP) being conducted by the Small Industry Service Institute (SISI), Okhla, New Delhi. She applied and participated in the programme. She learnt how to start her own venture.

Feeling encouraged, she decided to start a garment unit as she had learnt something about garments during her school days. In order to add to her technical know-how, in 1985, she enrolled herself for a two year part time course in Fashion Designing with the Young Women's Christian Association (YWCA). New Delhi. She completed the course in 1987.

In the meantime, on the advice of her husband, she applied for a shed to the Director of Industries (DI), Delhi. The shed was allotted to her in October 1986 at the Flatted Factory Complex (F.F.C.) Jhandewalan, New Delhi.

Mrs. Aggarwal had been living in a joint family at Chawri Bazar with her father and mother-in-law. A year ago, due to the lack of sufficient space, she had shifted to her newly constructed house at Vikaspuri 25 km. away from her unit. She had two school going children—a girl and a boy aged seven and four years respectively. The children were admitted to a school in Karol Bagh near her unit, so that she could herself take care of them after they returned from the school to her unit. Prior to this, her mother and father-in-law used to look after her children. Every Saturday, the children used to stay with their grand parents.

Her husband, Mr. A.K. Aggarwal is M.Sc. in Chemistry. He was working as a Circle Officer with the Delhi Administration, Delhi. From 1978 to 1987, he had also worked with different departments of Delhi Administration and the Ministry of Agriculture as an inspector and an investigator respectively.

He told to Mr. Arun that he had witnessed an event in his neighbourhood, where a young widow had been ill treated by her in laws. This had left a great impact on him and his interest to see his wife do something outside home turned into his determination to make her economically independent.

Both husband and wife told to Mr. Arun that they had never thought about a small scale venture. Indeed, it was by chance and the utilisation of the opportunity of EDP training that had made them embark upon the garment venture. "The Rashmi Garments" was started by Mrs. Aggarwal in May, 1987, by installing two machines—one her own and the other purchased from a local dealer, with a total investment of Rs.20,000/-. Out of this, her own contribution was Rs. 4,000/- (the saving from her husband's salary) and the remaining Rs. 16,000/- she borrowed from her family friends and relatives as interest free loan and without any time limit for repayment. Her husband had suggested her to approach friends and relatives for finance rather than the banks. The banks had a long process and many formalities, like securities, guarantors, certificates etc. to be completed. In addition, there was the burden of repayment at high rates of interest.

During the initial stages, since her unit was not in full production, workers were unwilling to join as they were unsure about the units' survival. After a great deal of effort she was able to hire through her local machine dealer, one worker at Rs. 1000 per month.

She had difficulty in keeping pace with the frequent changes in fashions prevalent in modern society, while maintaining quality and productivity. On the advice of her husband, she started with kurta-pyjamas, night suits and shirts for gents and children only. Her initial strategy was to approach the customers in the local market with sample pieces of her items. The response was not encouraging. Despite her offering 10 per cent less than the market rate the dealers and shopkeepers were unwilling to purchase her items. She then decided to supply the items at cost price. This proved successful to get an entry into the market.

In the next one month, she was approached by three local dealers who placed orders with her. Thereafter, she was approached by three more dealers. She now decided to sell her items at 10-15 per cent profit. This was acceptable to her old as well as new customers. She then employed three more workers and added two more machines to her unit for meeting the demand of her customers. However, in the initial couple of months it was difficult for her to cope with the customer's requirements regarding the types, size and the quantity of the items.

She reinvested more than 70 per cent of the profit into her venture. Gradually, her total invstment rose from Rs. 20,000 to Rs. 40,000. (see exhibit). The turnover also increased from Rs. 5,000 to Rs. 60,000 p.m. during the same period.

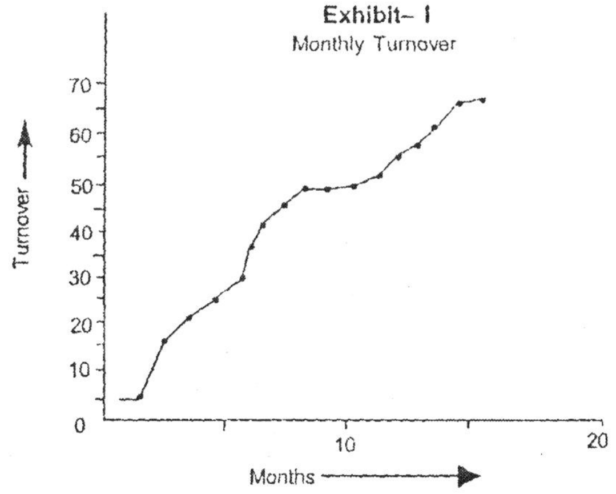

She now had eight workers including one cutting and designing master and eight machines in her unit. There were more than ten customers in the local market. Besides, the cutting and designing master, who was paid Rs. 1500 per month, all others were piece-rate workers. The piece-rate varied from Rs. 6 to Rs. 15. Each worker was making, on an average 8 to 10 pieces per day. The cutting and designing master, in addition to, doing his work used to prepare the items on piece-rate basis. She also employed an accountant on a part time basis at Rs. 200 per month. He used to come once a week for maintaining the accounts and records of her unit.

Mrs. Aggarwal told Mr. Arun that while she always took care of her workers and was ready to help them any time, however, she did not get their help at the time of her need. The workers would always turn up late for work even when the customer's demand was high. This created tension in her mind.

Her workers said that they liked her, due to her good behaviour, soft attitude and cooperative nature. They further said that she was always ready to help them at the hour of their need and that was why they used to work till late in the evenings and some times even on weekly holidays. However, at the same time, they also had their personal problems and limitations.

Both she and her husband due to lack of time were unable to go out of Delhi for marketing the items. She felt the need of a trusted person for this purpose.

To illustrate the problem, she narrated one incident to Mr. Arun. In the month of April, 1988, she was approached by two customers from Jammu & Kashmir and Allahabad, (Uttar Pradesh,) with orders. When the items were supplied through a bank, the customers refused to accept them. Then, her husband had to go to get the items back. This caused great difficulty and wastage of time and money. Recently, her younger brother-enrolled for the company secretary's course, had begun to assist her in local marketing.

She shared with Mr. Arun that her total involvement with the unit left little time for her to look after her children properly. They often slept on her office table. She was hardly able to acompany them once in fifteen days either for visiting the market or for an evening walk. Even her visit to the cinema with her family was considerably reduced. She now saw a movie once in six months instead of her earlier once in fifteen days. She felt that her husband was more cooperative than before. Now, he used to assist her in getting the children ready for school, serving them breakfast and packing their lunch.

The status of their family had been enhanced in the society. Now, some times they received invitations from people who earlier had never given any importance to them. Even distant relatives used to make frequent visits to their house to invite them to attend their ceremonies and functions.

In the initial stages, Mr. Aggarwal used to take all the decisions regarding purchase of raw materials, production of items, marketing, etc. She gained experience by closely watching him. Gradually, she increased her involvement in managing and controlling the production. After five months, she took over full charge of the operation.

In addition, she had taken keen interest in marketing. She used to participate with her husband in the discussions with the customers. This increased her confidence in the marketing activities. In the absence of her husband, she had begun to take the decisions. After getting the telephone connection in January, 1988, it had become more convenient for her particularly in the local market to deal with her customers. She said confidently that now she was able to meet the requirements of her customers in time.

She said to Mr. Arun, "Though, the market demand for my items is increasing, yet I am finding it difficult to cope, due to lack of space and manpower. I need to expand my business. At the same time, I also feel the need to spend more time at home with my growing children. I don't know which way to go".

* **Source:** Prepared by NIESBUD

Appendix - 1.1

ON ENTREPRENEURSHIP
N.R. NARAYANA MURTHY

Founder and Chief Mentor
Infosys Technologies Limited

It is only recently that there is some acceptance in India of the idea that creation of wealth is the only way to solve the debilitating problem of poverty. Mahatma Gandhi's dream was to wipe the tears of every poor person in the country. In my opinion, fulfilling this dream requires a consensus among all political parties on the following tenets:

(a) The only way we can solve the problem of poverty is by creating new wealth legally and ethically; not by redistributing existing wealth.

(b) There are only a few people who can lead the task of creation of wealth, just as there are only a few good surgeons, professors and lawyers.

(c) These people are human beings and they need incentives to create wealth.

(d) The job of the government is not to create wealth but to create an environment where these leaders are enthused to create more and more wealth.

There are two kinds of wealth creators — those that add to existing wealth passed on to them by the previous generation of wealth creators and those that create wealth from scratch. I belong to the latter category and have very little idea of the former. Hence, I will talk a little bit about creating wealth from scratch. Entrepreneurship refers to such a creation of corporate wealth by leveraging sweat equity. In general, entrepreneurship translates to leadership and innovation. Lack of adequate finance forces an entrepreneur to take a path hitherto untrodden and create a niche for himself. A necessary but not a sufficient condition for entry of entrepreneurs into an industry is that it must afford opportunities for innovation executed with sweat equity at least in the initial stages of the enterprise. The software industry world-wide is full of successful entrepreneurs. Rapid advances in technology and the consequent productivity gains have opened great market opportunities for innovation and, thus, ensured a steady stream of entrepreneurs in the American software industry. Whether it is Bill Gates of Microsoft or Larry Ellison of ORACLE, the common factors are; sweat equity, innovation, a brilliant vision, a well thought out strategy and flawless execution.

I have studied entrepreneurship in the Indian software industry for over 20 years and have come to some conclusions. During 1979-1981, ten to twelve entrepreneurs (professionals) started software companies for operating in the domestic and export markets. As of today, only one or two of them have survived, succeeded and been consistently among the top five Indian software export houses. A case study of these ten to twelve companies is a great education. We can draw certain conclusions from these case studies and can define some criteria for success.

The physiology of successful companies and pathology of unsuccessful companies bring out the following criteria for success.

(a) Shared vision : The founders of the company must articulate a clear vision of what they want their company to be in the long run. This vision must be something that provides for a clearly definable synergy between corporate objectives of the enterprise and personal aspirations of the entrepreneurs and the professionals working for the enterprise.

(b) A marketable idea : Unless you have a good idea that adds value to a customer there is no point in proceeding further. Your product or service must provide one or more of the following benefits — reduce cost, reduce cycle time, improve productivity or improve free time — for users of the product. Most failures are due to negligence of this cardinal principle.

(c) A sound strategy and an implementable action plan : Strategy is about making oneself unique in the marketplace. A strategic plan that clearly brings out the competitive advantages of the idea of the entrepreneurs, that masks the weaknesses of the entrepreneurs, that is realistic, and that ensures sustainability is needed. A realistic action plan that has the required resources is needed to put this strategy into action.

(d) A layer of competent management : The bane of most entrepreneurs is that they are primarily technocrats and hardly understand managerial issues in building an enterprise. Indeed, I have come across entrepreneurs who cannot read a balance sheet and hardly distinguish between term loans and working capital. They have a healthy contempt for anything other than technical challenges. Such an attitude is a sure recipe for unmitigated diaster. A successful enterprise will bring together complementary skills in technology and management. Surely, success in an enterprise requires a good understanding of human motivation, finance, leadership, technology, quality, and a host of other skills.

(e) A shared value system : A value system for a group of entrepreneurs is like the rudder for a ship. The temptation to bend your own set of Do's and Dont's is very compelling but the ability to stand firm in the face of an adverse situation is what separates men from boys. I have seen many an enterprise flounder because the entrepreneurs could not come out with a shared value system.

(f) Professionalism : I have seen several budding entrepreneurs criticise their employers and do exactly what they criticised when they start their company. Professionalism is drawing a line between personal needs and company resources, treating all your colleagues with respect and dignity, being issue-based and not personality-based, establishing and following person-independent rules and procedures in the company and showing integrity and honesty in all transactions with your customers, colleagues, vendor-partners, government and the society.

(g) Divorcing control from management : Indeed, if there is one critical issue in succeeding in entrepreneurship, it is the ability to divorce control from management. In the US, any entrepreneur will know that his venture capitalist will put in a management structure independent of his shareholding in the company. You, as the entrepreneur, will be asked to perform the role best suited to the organization's needs. We all know that story of Steve Jobs and how he himself brought in John Sculley to head Apple when he realised the need for professional leadership. You must recognise your strengths and contribute to the organization only in that role.

(f) Spirit of sacrifice : Nothing can ever be built unless there is some sacrifice at least in the initial period. Most entrepreneurs fall prey to the trappings of the so-called "Industrialist syndrome" and end up jeopardising the interests of the enterprise.

(h) Pride in creation of wealth : I have met several entrepreneurs who are very apologetic about creation of wealth. For heaven's sake, there is absolutely nothing wrong in creating wealth by legal and ethical means. Do not ever confuse creation of wealth with charity. First, you create wealth efficiently and only then can you donate your share of the profit to any charity.

(i) Ideology, intellectual arrogance and the enterprise : I have seen several instances where my entrepreneur friends have destroyed their enterprise just because they went on an ill-founded ideology trip. For example, one of my good friends felt that his company must produce compilers and word processors in India and compete with Microsoft's and Borland's even though it was clear to everybody but him that such a strategy was absolutely unwise and disastrous. His whole argument was that we Indians are second to none and that we will prove to the world that we can produce system software better than anybody else. Obviously, he did not succeed as much as his superb intellect should have enabled him to.

(j) R and D and the bread-and-butter stream : It is a truism in any business that the bread-and-butter stream of your enterprise pays for all costs including R and D. A smart enterprise derives its revenues from a bread-and-butter stream, pays for the operational costs and uses a small percentage of this revenue (usually 5 to 10 per cent) to conduct R and D in promising new streams. Some of these new streams will, in the future, become bread-and-butter streams for the enterprise. I have known a couple of entrepreneurs who tried to derive a large part of their revenues from R and D and, I am sad to say they are in serious trouble.

(k) Leadership-by-example : In enterprises dominated by white collar and knowledge professionals, you must lead by example. Today's professional has global level skills and opportunities and he is aware of it. Any discrepancy between what you preach and what you practice will be easily analysed by your younger colleagues and articulated well enough to create a dissonance. After all, Mahatma Gandhi was not wrong.

- Let me close by saying that speed and imagination are the two hallmarks of any successful entrepreneur. Those who leverage these two attributes will survive and succeed in the coming millennium of intense competition.

Source: The Fourteenth Anantharmakrishnan Memorial Lecture delivered at Bangalore on 8th Feb., 99.

CHAPTER

2

ENTREPRENEURIAL VALUES AND ATTITUDES

CHAPTER OUTLINE

ENTREPRENEURIAL VALUES AND ATTITUDES

Entrepreneurial Values

Values are generalised and organised conception influencing the behaviour and nature of human beings. It is a set of beliefs about various aspects of the world. Values provide standards that guide behaviour. Values are also reflective of a culture and are widely shared by those belonging to that culture. Accordingly, values are the inner-most layer of the self which provides the goal and direction to an individual. In terms of entrepreneurship, it means the cognitive functioning of entrepreneurship. Values are also responsible for the selectively organised perception and inter-action which an individual has with his outside world or the environment.

Akhorie and Mishra (1988) considered the following four values prominent among entrepreneurs. These are directed towards :

(a) Innovativeness

(b) Independence

(c) Outstanding performance

(d) Respect for work

These values are important to distinguish between entrepreneurs and non-entrepreneurs. We can develop entrepreneurship in the society by introducing these values and strengthening them through organised training.

(a) Innovativeness

Entrepreneurship essentially means doing things that are not generally done in ordinary course of work. Entrepreneurs do different things and in different ways, they weave old ideas into new patterns and tend to tackle the unknown. Scholars like Schumpeter further describe an entrepreneur as an "ideas man" and a man of action who possesses the ability to inspire others and who does not accept the boundaries of structured situation. He is a catalyst of change, able to carry out new combinations; instrumental in discovering new opportunities, which is the uniqueness of the entrepreneurial functions. Innovation is the process of putting new ideas into action. Innovations may also be repetition of the same idea but at different places and settings.

An innovator is different from an inventor. While the latter sees the possibility of new relationship between aspects of existing world, the former makes the relationships. In respect of entrepreneurship, innovations may be in the area of new product; new methods of production; opening of new markets; new source of supply of raw-material and creation of new type of industry and enterprises. They may also be in the area of attributes or qualities of a product, integrating several usage into one product; and optimum utilisation of resources.

Entrepreneurs tend to be mavericks, and it is often the mavericks who extends the frontier of knowledge. Ideas are their stock in trade. In fact as much significant innovations are likely to come from small business or from individuals as from big business. The need to innovate is greater, not only because of the prospects of generous financial rewards but also because of entrepreneur's creative drive and need for peer recognition as an over achiever.

An entrepreneur likes to experiment with new ideas and thus face uncertainty. It involves imagination, intuition and risk taking. Innovations can be seen through in the following actions.

(i) Enjoying change

(ii) Experimenting with new ideas

(iii) Facing uncertainty in order to try new ideas

(iv) Finding problems to solve

(v) Exhibiting originality

(vi) Looking for unstructured work assignments

(vii) Valuing unconventional behaviour

(viii) Working on a problem which causes great difficulty for others

(ix) Appreciating and contributing to new ideas being developed by others

(x) Using the existing methods or existing equipment or existing services for unconventional services.

The manager's career anchors on competency and efficiency, and the entrepreneur's career is anchored in creativity and innovation. So to promote entrepreneurship, innovative values are to be introduced and strengthened.

amazon.in

Tax Invoice/Bill of Supply/Cash Memo
(Triplicate for Supplier)

Sold By :
EVERY BOOK SUPPLIERS
4263 A/3 1ST FLOOR, ANSARI ROAD DARYA GANJ
NEW DELHI, DELHI, 110002
IN

PAN No: EEJPR0379A
GST Registration No: NotApplicable

Billing Address :
Sumana
No. 191,sri rangadhama, Jai maruthi layout
kumbarahalli siluvepura main road
BENGALURU, KARNATAKA, 560090
IN
State/UT Code: 29

Shipping Address :
Sumana
Sumana
No. 191,sri rangadhama, Jai maruthi layout
kumbarahalli siluvepura main road
BENGALURU, KARNATAKA, 560090
IN
State/UT Code: 29
Place of supply: KARNATAKA
Place of delivery: KARNATAKA

Order Number: 402-7745884-4613105
Order Date: 21.02.2021

Invoice Number : IN-223
Invoice Details : DL-1159546185-2021
Invoice Date : 21.02.2021

Sl. No	Description	Unit Price	Qty	Net Amount	Tax Rate	Tax Type	Tax Amount	Total Amount
1	Entrepreneur Development | 9350971992 (9789350971994)	₹575.00	1	₹575.00	0%	IGST	₹0.00	₹575.00
					0%	IGST	₹0.00	
	Shipping Charges	₹117.00		₹117.00	0%	None	₹0.00	₹117.00
					0%	IGST	₹0.00	
					0%	IGST	₹0.00	
					0%	None	₹0.00	
TOTAL:							₹0.00	₹692.00

Amount in Words:
Six Hundred Ninety-two only

For EVERY BOOK SUPPLIERS:

Authorized Signatory

Whether tax is payable under reverse charge - No

(b) Independence

Freedom of expression a ... controlled
by others. They want to ... initiatives
from others, an entrepre ... inner urge
to make his enterprise a ... *motivation'*
in the entrepreneurs. W ... l guidance,
only if asked for, one is ... uring early
stages often inhabits the ... onsiderably
influenced and encour

(c) Outstanding

Performing routine ta ... ntrepreneurs
since this does not con ... . Outstanding
performance and disp ... ntrepreneurs.
They firmly believe t ... ther forces of
power. They value a ... . They accept
the mistakes and im ... n of the task.
This leads to systema ... l management.
There are a number ... g performance
among prospective

(d) Respect fo

The value given to ... lture from non-
entrepreneurial cul ... more frequently
as entrepreneur as ... eir own hands.
Entrepreneurs valu ... rough work. For
them work is work ... eurs to pursue a
path where the re

Many big b ... by their desire to
excel, seem to pu

Results of s ... as under :

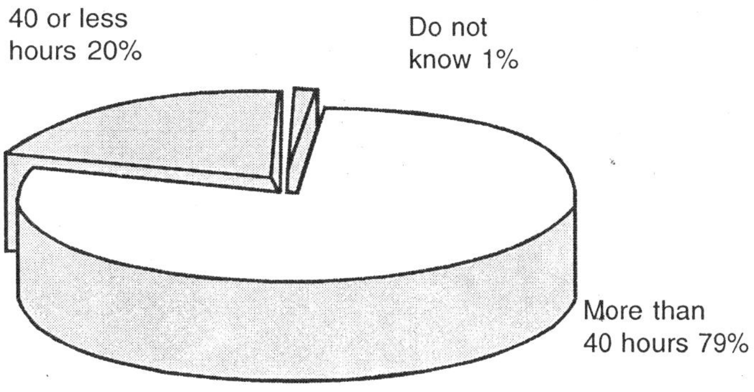

Fig. 2.1: Average Number of Hours a Small-Business Owner Works in a Week

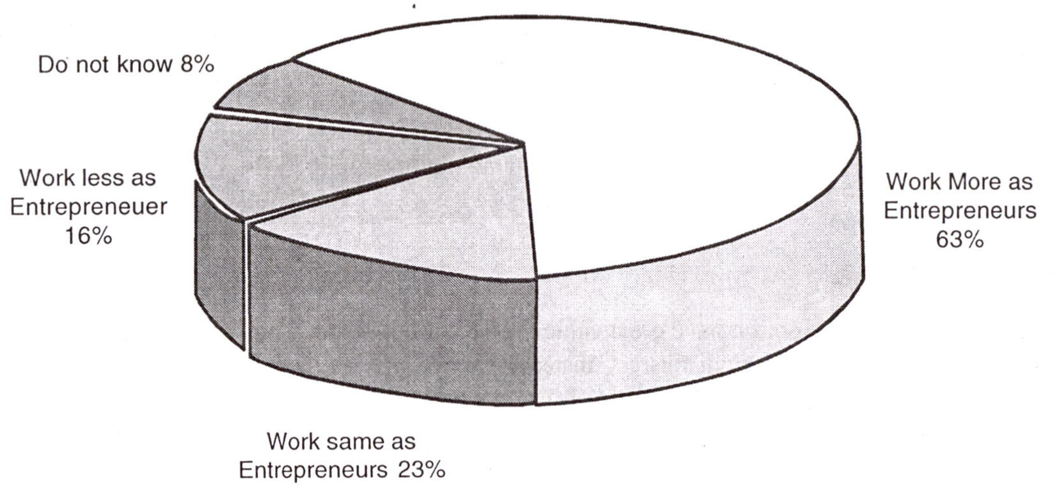

Fig. 2.2: Comparison of Work Load Before and After Becoming an Entreprenur

Source: John B Hinge, "Small Business Big Numbers" The Wallstreet Journal (Nov. 1991)

ENTREPRENEURSHIP VALUES

Shiv Nadar is head of Rs. 4000 crore HCL group. Nadar and his team had the courage to gamble on exponential growth in infotech industry, and the foresight to anticipate the road ahead. He became the fifth richest man in India and 126 in the world. His views on entrepreneurship are as fallows:

Do today's entrepreneurs have the same drive as you had in 1973?

Entrepreneurs will always be the same the world over, all the time. Anyone who seeks excellence will be the same. But excellence and perfection are two different things, Excellence is a standard that you set. We have imbibed the culture of entrepreneurship every where in our company. It is very good to see a large number of young people venturing out on their own. Their chances of success are the same as that of anyone in the Silicon Valley. Typically, a mega success happens one in thousand. In terms of an idea seeing the light of the day, it is one in four.

When children grow up, you must let them go. If they have grown wings, they must fly. Controlling mechanisms, which are protective in nature, are not necessary today. Finally, let them succeed or fail on their own merits. Don't give them any handicaps. We have an ancient culture in which trade and industry flourished. We must have confidence in our roots.

What do you aspire as an entrepreneur?

I aspire for excellence. I am like an athlete who is never satisfied whatever he has done. As an individual, my dominant personality trait is entrepreneurship. Entrepreneurs set out to create things. They see opportunity where the rest do not. Entrepreneurs are fewer than businessmen. Sometimes they turn out to be successful businessmen, but entrepreneurship exists in any endevour. It is characteristic. It exists in sports and music. Even a painter is an entrepreneur.

What were your aims when you started HCL?

I was not alone. We were a group that ventured into this business. Demand for computers in India was growing. (When HCL was set up, it is said that India had a mere 250 computers.) We thought this business would boom because IBM decided to withdraw from India. All of us had similar aspiration. The goal was eminently reachable and we reached it. There was enough creativity. We had 60 people in software R & D in 1978, when Microsoft had only 20. I think we could have been much larger than we are today. We did similar things compared to organisations the world over did. But they became global organisations. This happened because at that time our target was small. Our target was limited to the Indian market. We never thought beyond the shores of India. In 1989 we did 100 crore. But in the last ten years, our turnover has crossed 4000 crore. We are thriving.

What does money mean to you today?

To me, money is not primary objective: the goal is. To an athlete or an entrepreneur, the goal is primary. Money may be one of points in the matrix. I will give you an illustration, I have asked Kapil Dev what is it that he sees when he is watched by 100,000 people facing a bowler, or bowling at someone. He told me that all he tries to do is outthink the opponent. That is his goal. Like that money is only one element; the goal is what I strive for.

Source: Financial Times, 27 Feb, 2001.

PRATIBHA IYER — WOMEN ENTREPRENEUR

For Pratibha Iyer, sales manager, the nine to six ordeal at Windsor Manor was getting a little too much to handle. She wanted to do something which she could call of her own. Something that gave her enough time to run her life the way she wanted and at the same time enough money to take care of her needs. Pratibha is churning out a business of over Rs. 6 lakh at her housekeeping company, 'Personal Touch'. Having run the business for 10 years, Pratibha has bigger agenda for the future. She wants to become a consultant in the house-keeping industry.

ENTREPRENEURIAL ATTITUDE

Those who have imbibed the above mentioned values generally develop common 'tendencies' to act in any given situation. For example, those who value innovativeness develop tendency to use imagination for sensing opportunities. In selecting a goal or line of action or means of tackling a situation they show a tendency to take certain amount of risk. The tendencies to act in response to stimulus is called attitude. A group of persons may decide similar or different course of action for a given situation depending upon similar or different attitudes. Accordingly, the attitude is defined as "*an enduring organisation of motivational, emotional, perceptual and cognitive process with respect to some aspect of individual's work*". Attitudes that show the entrepreneurial pre-dispositions play a significant part in making a successful entrepreneur. The genesis of such attitudes, however, can be traced to the value system.

Akhori and Mishra have considered the following attitudes as closely related to entrepreneurship:

(a) An eye for economic opportunity

(b) Tendency to take moderate risk.

(c) Initiative.

(d) Imaginative

(e) Enjoy freedom of expression

(f) Believe that they can change the environment.

(g) Analysing situation and planning action.

(h) Satisfaction from successful completion of task.

(a) An eye for economic opportunity : Entrepreneurs are highly perceptive and keen in locating business opportunities for economic exploitation in a given situation. What may appear to be a situation of a crisis, festival, social, or a recreation to many, entrepreneurs have an ability to look for economic opportunities in such situations. This tendency makes them stand apart from non-entrepreneurs.

(b) Tendency to take moderate risk : There is a tendency among entrepreneurs to set goals that have certain amount of risk, not a common goal as pursued by others. They take up tasks that have an element of uncertainty in it. Because of this tendency to take risk, an entrepreneur is tempted to try something new in terms of ideas, activity, location, time, etc.

(c) Initiative : Entrepreneurs worship work and they believe that for achieving anything they have to work, hence they have a natural tendency to take initiative. Entrepreneurs prefer to act and do not remain as onlookers. They have a tendency to act and perform as leaders. They are not mere dreamers but they act for converting their dream into a reality. An entrepreneur has the tendency to define task for himself. He is a source of origin for an activity and thus tends to be proactive.

(d) Imaginative : Under a given situation, the common tendency is to take a course of action based on obvious and observable facts. On the contrary some people have a tendency to use imagination for perceiving the not so apparent aspect of a given situation. They also apply intuition in assessing the future course. This tendency is common among the entrepreneurs.

(e) Enjoy freedom of expression : Entrepreneurs have a tendency to enjoy freedom of action and. expression. They don't enjoy getting instructions and then acting upon them. They enjoy fallowing their own dictum. Due to this tendency they often give up their job and start their own ventures. As they value independence and ownership they prefer to think on their own and act accordingly.

(f) Believe they can change the environment : Entrepreneurs value their work and it makes them believe that everything can be achieved through their own efforts. Thus they believe in their capacity to influence the environment. They prefer to change the environment rather than leave everything to luck or forces that are beyond their control. Being influenced by this value, they think that in any given situation they can change and influence the environment.

(g) Analysing situation and planning action : Entrepreneurs respect work and they perform all activities with due seriousness. Due to their respect for work, they develop a tendency to analyse situations and then plan their action accordingly. They respect the work they are involved in, thus cannot afford to neglect the same. Analysing situation into its parts, assessing pros and cons, weighing against resources; foreseeing alternatives; and planning action before actual commitment of the task; are some of the things which distinguish entrepreneurs from others. The work may be simple or complex, significant or insignificant to the outsiders but to an entrepreneur the task at hand calls for a total commitment.

(h) Find satisfaction from successful completion of task : Entrepreneurs always value outstanding performance. Successful completion is an indicator of their performance. They like to complete their task against all odds by mobilising resources and availing help from all available sources. They appreciate feedback on the quality of their performance and enjoy its successful accomplishment.

The biggest asset to sustaining entrepreneurial ability is a positive attitude. In addition, determination, experience, persistence and just plain hard work are essential for being a successful entrepreneur.

CHARACTERISTICS AND ROLL DEMANDS OF ENTREPRENEURSHIP

The wide range in the nature of the business and the entrepreneurs who have started and run them, make generalisations about their characteristics at best, risky and at worst, somewhat misleading. For example, product-oriented businesses are significantly different from service-oriented ones. Technical entrepreneurs have been found to have different educational backgrounds than non-technical and service entrepreneurs. Further, the requirements to build a large enterprise are different and more demanding than the personal requirements needed for setting up a small scale enterprise or even a franchise.

Entrepreneurial Characteristics

Entrepreneurial characteristics such as goal-setting can be developed and certain role requirements such as knowledge of particular business can be learnt. A person in his twenties launching his first venture may start a small proprietorship or partnership concern. Early success in such enterprises provides a valuable learning experience. The experience thus gained provides a platform to build a larger and more complex business venture on a latter date.

For the entrepreneur as well as prospective partner and investor, the question of the nature and extent of one's entrepreneurial potential is paramount. The criteria identified here can be a useful guide to help identify major shortcomings or a fatal flaw that could make pursuit of an entrepreneurial career a failure, rather than a success. It can assist in determining if there is a reasonable chance of launching a successful venture to suit an individual's goals, values and needs or not.

In developing these entrepreneurial characteristics, I examined the available research and theory about the behavioural and other characteristics of entrepreneurs of successful new ventures I also researched the current practices of investors particularly venture capitalists, in assessing the personal characteristics of entrepreneurs in whom they invested. I found there was considerable effort to determine if persons wanting to start a new venture, (an applicant for capital) did in fact, possess the behavioural and other characteristics of successful entrepreneurs. Investigations have identified fourteen dominant characteristics of successful entrepreneurs.

Need to Achieve Desire to be a Winner

Competitiveness by itself can be a misleading attribute. It is most important to distinguish between competition directed toward others, without any objective measure of performance, and competition with a self-imposed standard. Competition directed toward beating the other person (as in boxing) can have in it seeds of self-destruction, for example, price war below variable costs. This kind of competition has an externalised standard (the opponent) or no objective standard at all. This orientation tends to be more reactive to what others are doing, than being proactive in figuring out what to do before-hand based on your goals, capabilities, resources, etc.

Competition with self-imposed standards is an internalised kind of competition. The most obvious example of this kind of competition is the world class swimmer or runner. They repeatedly indicate that they perceive the clock, rather than other swimmers or runners as their opponents.

Similarly, high performance entrepreneur also possess this internalised competitive spirit, in which he continuously engages in competition with himself to beat his last best performance. He has a burning desire to excel.

Moderate Risk Taker Prefer Middle of the Road

The successful entrepreneurs are not high risk taker, they are not gamblers. They prefer to take moderate, calculated risks where the chances of winning are neither so large nor so small as to be a sure thing. Rather, risks are preferred which provide a reasonable and challenging chance of success, and a situation whose outcome is influenced as much by one's ability and effort and not by mere chance. This entrepreneurial characteristic is one of the most important, since it has such significant implications for the ways decisions are made, and thus, for the success or failure of the business.

They seem to be very much aware of "no risk-no return, high risk-high return" continuum. They take moderate challenging risk where moderate returns are attainable and the same are influenced by their abilities and decisions. Several studies have identified or confirmed the importance of this achievement motivation characteristic.

> Venture Capitalists, who finance the new generation entrepreneurs, are not only looking for business ideas but professionals with domain expertise and fire in their belly. They are out for professionals with an appetite for risk.
>
> *Corporate Dossier, The Economic Times, 22 March, 2002*

Perseverance Quality to Stick to it

Entrepreneurs who successfully build new-enterprises possess an intense level of determination and a desire to overcome hurdles, solve a problem and complete the job. Once committed to a goal and a course of action, entrepreneurs become absorbed in it. They are not intimidated by difficult situations. In fact, their self-confidence and general optimism seems to translate into a view that the impossible just takes a little longer. Interestingly enough, if the task is extremely easy or perceived to be unsolvable, the entrepreneur will actually give up sooner than others. While entrepreneurs are extremely persistent, they are also realistic in recognising what they can and cannot do, and where they can get help to solve a very difficult but necessary task.

Use of Feedback Knowing How They Perform

Entrepreneurs are very much concerned about their performance, especially about doing well. This concern is responsible in part for this entrepreneurial characteristic : "use of feedback". Without information or feedback about performance the entrepreneur cannot know how well or poorly he is doing. Successful entrepreneurs demonstrate a capacity to seek and use feedback on their performance, in order to take corrective action and to improve. They like prompt and accurate data and it does not make any difference whether the information they get is favourable or unfavourable. Infact they are stimulated by unfavourable news to pour more energy into attaining their objective.

At an early age this tendency shows itself in the preferences children have for sports and hobbies. For instance, entrepreneurial types like competitive sports, and building things with their own hands. These, provide excellent opportunities for a sense of personal accomplishment, where feedback is readily available. In a similar vein, natural mechanical ability and inclination often are associated with an entrepreneurial type person, and is related, in part, to this characteristic.

Facing Uncertainty Tolerance for Ambiguity and Unfamiliar Situations

Entrepreneurs have long been viewed as having a special tolerance for ambiguous situations and for making decisions under conditions of uncertainty. Achievement oriented people tend to be optimist even in unfamiliar situations. The odds may not be clear but the circumstances may be appealing; the entrepreneurs see no reason why they cannot win through their abilities. They present a picture of boldness in the face of the unknown and prudence in the face of the familiar. They usually win by applying their special insight and skill. In contrast to the professional manager, entrepreneurs are able to live with modest to high levels of uncertainty concerning job, career decisions and security. Job security and permanency are considerably lower on the entrepreneur's hierarchy of preferences compared to his managerial counterpart.

Stress Takers Possess Drive and Energy

Entrepreneurs have a tremendous amount of personal energy and drive. They possess a capacity to work for long hours and in spurts of several days with less than normal amount of sleep. Research confirms drive and energy as a characteristic very frequently observed in successful entrepreneurs and desired by the investors. They have to cope up with many situations, at the same time make right decisions which may involve a lot of physical and emotional stress. They have the capacity to work for long hours and keep cool under tension.

Self-Confidence Faith in Their Abilities

There is an agreement that successful entrepreneurs have a high level of self-confidence. They tend to believe strongly in themselves and their abilities to achieve the goals they set. They do not accept status quo, and believe that events in their lives are mainly self-determined; they have a major influence on their personal destinies, and have little belief in fate. The financial community also looks for a strong sense of self-confidence in the entrepreneurs on whom they place their money. But, they are negative about entrepreneurs being over-confident and arrogant, which suggest a lack of realism.

Initiative Seeking Responsibility

The entrepreneur has always been considered as an independent and highly self-reliant innovator, the champion of the free enterprise economy. Modern research and investigation into the entrepreneurial personality have not only confirmed some of these earlier generalisations, but have also considerably refined the ways of focusing on this self-reliant aspect. Entrepreneurs actively seek and take initiative. They willingly put themselves in situations in which they are personally responsible for the success or failure of the operation and thus take full credit for their success or assume full blame for their failure. They like to take initiative to solve a problem or fill a vacuum where no leadership exists. They always like situations where their personal efforts on problems can be measured.

Positive Self Concept Aware of One Self and Internal Locus of Control

The entrepreneur does not believe that the success or failure of a new business venture depends mostly upon luck or fate or external uncontrollable factors. The entrepreneur tends to believe that one's personal accomplishments as well as set backs lie within one's personal control and influence. This sense of holding oneself responsible for one's success or failure is linked to the entrepreneur's achievement motivation and his preference for moderate risk-taking. This is based upon the awareness of his strength and weaknesses. He uses positive knowledge to support his thinking. He is rarely negative. There is a positive correlation between one's entrepreneurial activity and the entrepreneur's belief that the locus of control over these entrepreneurial events is internal rather than external or just a matter of luck or circumstances.

Motivators Possess Interpersonal Skills

Entrepreneur is a person who, during the course of his activities, comes across many types of people with whom he has to deal. He has to make them, work for him and help them attain the objectives. He should be a person who likes working with people and has skills in dealing with them.

Entrepreneur is required, in many situations, to influence people and make them think in his way and act accordingly. He has to motivate people to act.

Flexibility Flexible in Decisions

Most successful entrepreneurs after weighing pros and cons of a decision, tend to change if the situation so demands. They do not hesitate in revising their decisions. They are people with open mind and are not rigid

Analytical Ability Unaffected by Personal Likes and Dislikes

Entrepreneurs are realistic. They have a specific approach about business undertakings. They are not likely to let personal likes and dislikes stand in their way. When they require assistance, they select experts rather than their friends and relatives to help them. Normally they do not take an emotional attitude towards their business or a problem.

Independence Dislikes Working for Others

It is found that most entrepreneurs start off on their own because they do not like to work for other people. They like to be their own masters and want to be responsible for their own decisions.

Ability to Find and Explore Opportunity

Entrepreneurial persons are quick to see and seize opportunities. They show an innovative turn of mind and convert difficulties into opportunities. But they are realistic too. They plan and anticipate carefully how to achieve their goals in realising an opportunity.

ROLE DEMANDS AND REQUIREMENTS OF ENTREPRENEURS

It is not enough to possess a large and intense level of these entrepreneurial characteristics. In addition, certain conditions, pressures and demands are inherent in the role of entrepreneurship. These role requirements have important implications for a person's suitability to entrepreneurship and for the eventual success of a new venture. While successful entrepreneurs may share several characteristics in common with successful persons in other careers, their preference for and tolerance of the combination of requirements, unique to the entrepreneurial role, is a major distinguishing feature. There are seven important role requirements of an entrepreneur.

Accommodation to the Venture

The entrepreneur lives under a constant pressure—first to survive, then to stay alive and always to grow and withstand competitors' thrusts. The ventures demand top priority for the entrepreneur's time, emotions and loyalty. Entrepreneurs must be prepared to 'give all' to the building of the business, particularly in the early start-up years. On the other hand, research of small business owners shows that there is a room for accommodating family and community priorities without causing harm to the business. In fact, some writers indicate that owners of small business are probably dominated as much by personal and family considerations as by the profitability of the business.

Total Immersion and Commitment

Launching and building a business is not a part-time proposition. Building a high-potential business requires a total immersion in and commitment to that end. The managerial role in business could be delegated, but the entrepreneurial role could not.

The commitment required for entrepreneurship is measured in part by some of the expectations the investor has for gauging commitment : a willingness to invest your life savings, a substantial portion of your net worth, to reduce your income by as much as one half for the first year or two, to second-mortgage your home, not to mention long hours and neglected family life. Building a new business is a way of life for them, it can be intolerable if one is unable to adapt to this style.

Creativity and Innovation

The entrepreneurial role has long been recognised as a prime source of innovation and creativity. It has been observed that career patterns of entrepreneurs follow paths that afford opportunities to be creative and innovative. Different 'career anchors' are associated with different roles. The entrepreneur's career anchor is creativity and innovation and managers have their career anchored in competance and efficiency and college professors prefer autonomy, i.e., having control and discretion over one's time as a career anchor.

Knowledge of the Business

Investors stress the importance of the track record—business experience and accomplishment—of the entrepreneur and the team they invest in. Most strongly prefer that a potential venture be headed by an entrepreneur who has a thorough and proven operating knowledge of the business he intends to launch. Hindsight has made even more investors wish they had insisted upon this requirement, and several studies support this view. Formal education has not been a distinguishing requirement for successful entrepreneurship. But when it comes to technical and scientific based entrepreneurship, formal education related to the kind of business one intends to start, is considered a necessity.

People and Team Building

High-potential ventures are rarely sole-proprietorships. Venture capitalists place considerable emphasis on the demonstrated capacity of the lead entrepreneur to attract, motivate and build a high quality entrepreneurial team. Aspiring entrepreneurs, who are averse to having partners, must recognise the significant implications of a decision to go alone. First, they will generally be unable to raise capital from conventional sources. They will have to rely on personal net worth, friends and family for seed capital. Second, their business, with rare exceptions, will not be able to grow much without a supporting management team.

Economic Values

Business entrepreneurs must share the key values of the free enterprise system : i.e., private ownership, profits, capital gains, responsible growth. These dominant economic values need not necessarily exclude social or other values.

Personal values can have a profound effect on the development of the team and the business itself. Area of high technology entrepreneurship appears to have an exception wherein aesthetic and theoretical values are strongest.

Integrity and Reliability

Not to be confused with situational ethics, integrity and reliability are a must for an aspiring entrepreneur to raise conventional investment money and debt financing. An early eliminator of a proposal is the discovery by an investor that the entrepreneur has not been straight forward and honest in reviling past dealings or even failures. A reputation for dependability, reliability and honesty is a must.

These fourteen entrepreneurial characteristics and seven role requirements are based upon the study of literature on entrepreneurship, and our practical experience. The dimensions comprise what we currently believe are the most important aspects of entrepreneurial behaviour. The biggest gap in existing knowledge is how to measure accurately and consistently the psychologically oriented characteristics. It is emphasized that we have yet to see a single entrepreneur who possessed all of these fourteen characteristics. In principle, more are better than fewer, but weaknesses can be complemented by building on the other strengths. Thus, it is important for entrepreneurs, investors and advisors alike to know thoroughly the entrepreneur's strengths and weaknesses with respect to each of these characteristics. The seven role dimensions comprise what is believed as the most important demands of entrepreneurship.

Potentially, these criteria have implications on at least three fronts. Teachers and counselors can help would be entrepreneurs make a more candid and systematic evaluation of their suitability for an entrepreneurial career. Second, other practitioners, investors, loan officers, etc., can supplement and cross-check their own thumb rules with these criteria. Third, would be entrepreneurs, as well as entrepreneurs who are re-evaluating their careers, may find these criteria useful in sorting out capabilities and attributes.

SUMMARY

Entrepreneurship essentially means doing things that are not generally done in ordinary course of work. Entrepreneurs do different things and in different ways, they weave old ideas into new patterns and tend to tackle the unknown. An entrepreneur likes to experiment with new ideas and thus face uncertainty. It involves imagination intuition and risk taking. Entrepreneurial characteristics such as goal-setting can be developed. Certain role requirements such as knowledge of a particular business can be learnt.

Innovation implies doing new things or doing things that are already being done in a new way. It includes, introduction of new products, creation of new markets, application of new process of production, discovery of new and better sources of raw materials and developing a new and better form of industrial organisation. Entrepreneurs have a tremendous amount of personal energy and drive.

REVIEW QUESTIONS

1. Who is innovator? What are the principles of innovation?
2. Who is an innovating entrepreneur?
3. Explain the various types of entrepreneurs giving examples.
4. Define the concept of entrepreneur. What are the nature and characteristics of entrepreneurship?
5. "Developing Countries need imitative entrepreneurs rather than innovative entrepreneurs"? Do you agree?
6. Is it necessary that entrepreneur should also be a manager/technician?
7. Explain the behavioural patterns of entrepreneurs.
8. What attitudes distinguish entrepreneurs from others ?
9. Describe the characteristics which the investors seek in an entrepreneur.

❑❑

CHAPTER

3

CREATIVITY, INNOVATION AND IDEA GENERATION

CHAPTER OUTLINE

- — Creativity and Innovation
- — The Creative Process
- — Components of Creative Performance
- — Qualities of Creative Person
- — Creativity, Innovation and Entrepreneurship
- — Creative Enterprises
- — Sources and Selection of Business Ideas
- — Project Identification Dynamics

CREATIVITY, INNOVATION AND IDEA GENERATION

Entrepreneurs bring about changes in the use of resources in a society. They setup new ventures, which shift the resources into areas of higher productivity and greater yields. In fact, entrepreneurship is a process of wealth creation and not wealth accumulation. As defined earlier, pure entrepreneurs depend upon innovation to setup new ventures. Innovation helps in development of new ideas through which the opportunities are identified and new ventures, that add value to the society, are established.

CREATIVITY AND INNOVATION

Creativity

There is a popular notion that creativity is a mysterious process performed by a gifted or brilliant mind. D.T. Campbell argued that creativity is largely a product of sweaty trial and error. To be creative a person must work long hours and hard to generate multiple solutions. Creativity is a prerequisite for innovation and it can be developed in any individual especially when there is a concern for excellence. It is an accepted fact that concern for excellence is a common trait for most of the entrepreneurs. Hence, to become an entrepreneur one should develop creativity in oneself. Creativity is development of novel solution to a perceived problem. It is defined as *the ability to bring some thing new into existence*. The emphasis is on the "*Ability*" and not the activity of bringing something new into existence. A creative person must conceive of something new and envision how it will be useful to the society. The action for putting the conceived idea to use is immaterial. Even if no effort is made to follow up the conceived new idea, the person is a creative person.

Innovation

Innovation is the process of doing new things. This distinction is important. While creativity relates to the ability to conceive, the innovation is doing new things. Ideas have little value until they are converted into useful products or services. Innovation transforms creative ideas into useful applications. Hence, creativity is a pre-requisite to innovation. As per Schumpeter a person is an entrepreneur only when he is engaged in innovative behaviour. This innovative behaviour is an entrepreneurial function.

The Creative Process

Entrepreneurs need ideas to setup new ventures. Key to creativity is to persevere and use a diverse set of alternatives. Brilliant ideas do not come out of blue, they evolve through a creative process wherein ideas are germinated, matured and developed by the imaginative persons. The creative process involves six stages as described below.

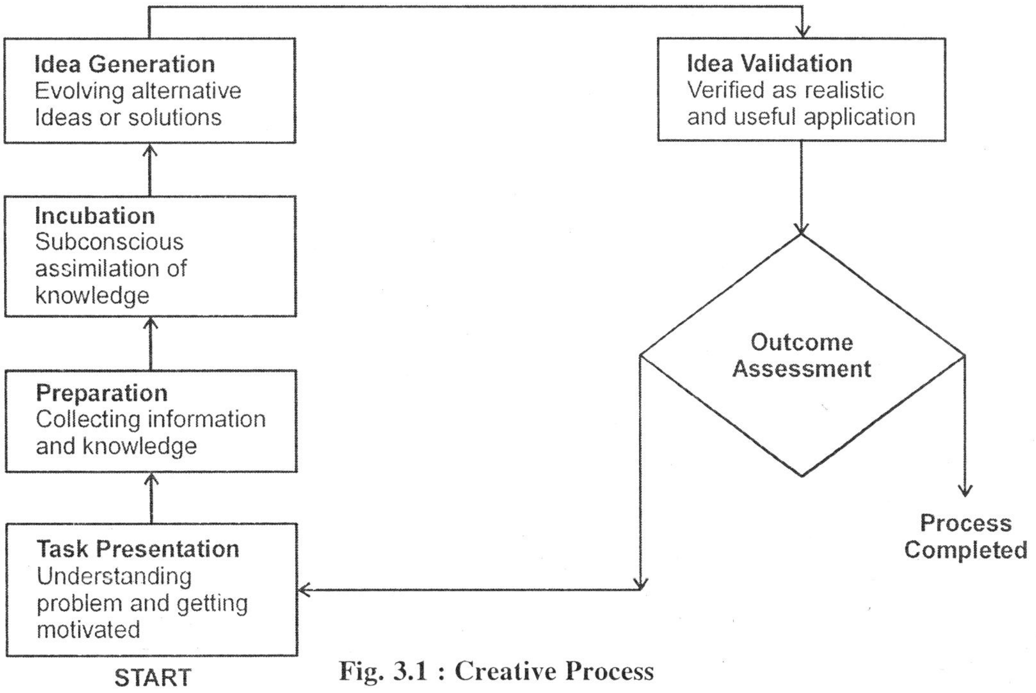

Fig. 3.1 : Creative Process

Stage I – Task Presentation. This stage is akin to germination or seeding process. The creative ideas emerge from deep interest in or curiosity about something, i.e., a specific problem or an area of study. A person should have a burning desire to discover something. He needs to be internally motivated to learn about an issue or he may himself be in a situation that demands a difficult problem to be solved. Hence, *the seed of curiosity takes the form of a focused idea.* If the perceived problem in motivating enough to capture the individual's attention, it leads to stage II.

Stage II – Preparation. It deals with a conscious search for the solutions, seeking information about the problem and how others have tried to solve it. This stage builds up and activates information that is relevant of the problem. It includes any tricks, shortcuts or algorithms that might be useful for the task. At this stage a market research is often conducted for a new product or service. This stage generally does not produce the results. However, *the effort of gathering information and knowledge* is useful for the final solution. Activation of knowledge leads to stage III.

Stage III – Incubation. It is the stage of subconscious assimilation of information. Instead of intensively concentrating on the problem it is put on the back burner. It is *the stage of mulling it over.* Herein the subconscious intellect assumes the control of the creative process and the limitations of human logic do not effect the solutions. Human fantasies are pressed and unusual knowledge and information that is difficult to assimilate rationally is used by the subconscious mind. This leads to the fourth stage.

Stage IV – Idea Generation. Multiple ideas and solutions are generated at this stage. Herein *ideas resurface as realistic creation*. Various approaches to the problem are attempted using individual's reserves of previous experiences, insight and fears. Ideas are recognised as being feasible. It gives one sense of realisation. Idea generation is normally triggered by an opportune incidence. Most creative people after going through the phases of preparation and incubation remain in search of that incident which helps giving full meaning to their ideas.

Stage V – Idea Validation. Ideas generated in the previous stage needs to be verified as realistic and useful. Entrepreneurial effort is required to translate the generated ideas into verified, realistic and useful application. It is the stage that *refines knowledge into application.* Herein each potential solution is tested against the problem.

Stage VI – Outcome Assessment. An assessment of the creative process can lead to either the achievement of the goal wherein a creative idea or solution to the problem is located or no progress in this direction is achieved. In either case the creative process ends. There is also a possibility that the outcome is in-between the two extremes described above. Herein the individual returns to stage I of the creative process.

COMPONENTS OF CREATIVE PERFORMANCE

Creative performance consists of three distinctly identifiable components. A person needs different types of skills to be creative. As one proceeds with the creative process different stages demand separate skills.

Intrinsic Motivation

First component of the creative performance is Intrinsic Motivation to do the task. This provides the initial stimulus for the problem. It is more conducive for :

(a) Processing diverse information

(b) Seeing non-obvious side of an issue

(c) Exploring alternative solution paths

This creative component influence state I and III of the Creative Process.

Skills in the Task Domain

Second component of the creative performance is Skills in the Task Domain. This includes knowledge of the problem area and the technical skills required in solving it. Talents that provide necessary background to solve the problem are also essential. In the absence of necessary skills and talents no attempt to solve a problem is likely to succeed. This component influences stage II, IV and V.

Skill in Creative Thinking

Third component of the creative performance is Skills in Creative Thinking. Creative thinking provides an ability to :

(a) Make random association between ideas.

(b) See divergent uses of a single idea.

(c) Access one's subconscious.

(d) Visualise potential solutions.

(e) Generate a number of diverse alternatives.

(f) Hold back critical evaluation till full range of possibilities is explored.

This component influences stages III and IV of the Creative Process.

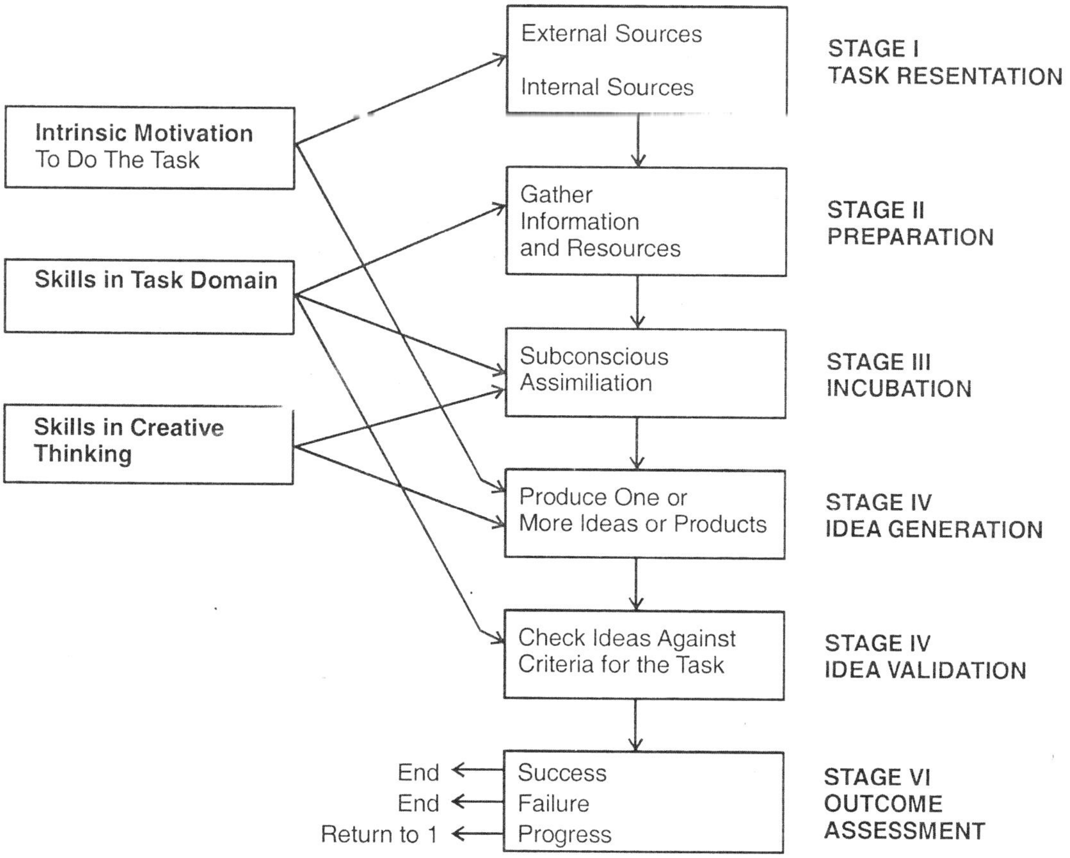

Fig. 3.2: Model of Creative Thinking

QUALITIES OF CREATIVE PERSON

The research studies conducted by Lowerfield and Guilford identified eight characteristics of a creative persons.

1. ***Sensitivity***: The creative individual is sensitive to problems, needs, attitudes and feelings of others. He has an acute awareness of anything odd, unusual or promising in a person, material, or situation with which he is dealing.

2. ***Fluency***: This refers to the ability to take continuous advantage of a developing situation–to use each completed step as a new advantage point from which to assess the problem and move on.

3. ***Flexibility:*** People with high creative ability adjust quickly to new developments and changed situations. Unforeseen obstacles in a problem solving situation are often used to advantage by the creative person.

4. *Originality*: This refers to uncommonness of individual's responses to problematic situations and number and diversity of solutions given.

5. *Redefinitional Skills:* They have unusual ability to rearrange ideas, concepts people and things—to shift functions of objects and use them in new ways.

6. *Ability to Abstract*: It refers to the ability in analyzing a project component, i.e., getting details from the whole.

7. *Ability to Synthesise:* It means ability to combine several components to arrive at a creative whole.

8. *Coherence of Organisation*: The ability to organize a project, express an idea, or create a design in such a way that nothing is superfluous.

Creativity, Innovation and Entrepreneurship

J.A. Timmoans has defined entrepreneurship as "*the ability to create and built something from practically nothing*". Fundamentally it is a creative activity manifested by initiating and building an enterprise or an organisation. It is a knack of sensing an opportunity where others see chaos, contradiction, and confusion. *Entrepreneurship can be viewed as a creative and innovative response to the environment and an ability to recognise, initiate and exploit an economic opportunity.*

According to *Shumpeter*, entrepreneurship is a creative activity. An entrepreneur is an innovator who introduces something new in an economy. Entrepreneurship is doing things that are generally not done in the ordinary course of business. Innovation may be in :

- Introducing a new manufacturing process that has not yet been tested and commercially exploited.
- Introduction of a new product with which the consumers are not familiar or introducing a new quality in an existing product.
- Locating a new source of raw material or semi finished product that was not exploited earlier.
- Opening a new market, hitherto unexploited, where the company products were not sold earlier.
- Developing a new combination of means of production.

Peter Drucker argues that "innovation is specific function of entrepreneurship, whether in an existing business, a public service institution, or a new venture started by a lone individual". Moreover Drucker suggests that "innovation is the means by which the entrepreneur either creates new wealth producing resources or endows existing resources with enhanced potential for creating wealth. Thus, entrepreneurship and the innovation resulting from it are important for large and small firms as well as for start up ventures, as they compete in the present day competitive landscape. Therefore we can conclude that entrepreneurship and innovation are central to the creative process in the economy and to promoting growth, increasing productivity and creating jobs.

Innovation involves problem solving and an entrepreneur is a problem solver. An entrepreneur does things in a new and a better way. A traditional businessman working in a routine manner is not entrepreneurial.

Shumpeter makes a distinction between an innovator and an inventor. An inventor discovers new methods and new materials. It is an act of developing new product or process. On the other hand an innovator is one who utilises or applies inventions and discoveries to produce newer and better quality goods that give greater satisfaction to the consumers and higher profits to entrepreneurs. Innovation is the process of creating a commercial product from an invention. An inventor produces ideas and an innovator implements them for economic gain. An inventor adds to the knowledge of the society while an innovator adds to their satisfaction by means of newer and better products and services. Thus an invention brings something new onto being while an innovation brings something new into use. Hence, technical criteria is used to determine the success of an invention, while commercial criteria is used to determine the success of an innovation. It is an innovator who commercially exploits an invention.

	Activity	Result
Invention	Creation of a New Product	New Knowledge
Innovation	Economic Exploitation of New Idea or Resource	New Product Service Process–Market

Fig. 3.3 : Invention vs. Innovation

Creative Enterprises

In the competitive environment growing enterprises are required to constantly innovate new products and processes. Not only the individuals, even the enterprises are required to be innovative. Creativity can easily be designed into the enterprises by a few simple steps.

(a) Having open channels of communication and allowing contact with outside world promotes creativity in an organisation. Creative organisations allocate overlapping territories to its employees and lay emphasis on normal group activities. Brainstorming and suggestion systems are useful tools that promote creativity in an enterprise.

(b) Using teams for solving the problems is more likely to yield creative solutions. Teams that allow eccentricity and have non-specialists participating as team members usually find more creative solutions.

(c) Decentralised organisation structure with loosely defined positions and loose controls are more creative. Enterprises that promote risk taking and allow mistakes to be made by its employees promote creativity.

(d) Playful culture, freedom to discuss ideas and long term horison of an enterprise is conducive to promotion of creativity in an enterprise. Organisations providing employees the freedom to choose and peruse problems make them more creative.

(e) Enterprises are made creative when resources are allocated to creative personal and projects without caring for immediate payoff. When organisations reward and encourage creative ideas and absolves its employees of peripheral responsibilities it makes the enterprise more creative.

Characterstics of Creative People

- Conceptual Fluency – Openness
- Originality
- Less Authoritairian – Independent
- Playfulness, Undisciplined Explotation
- Persistent, Committed, Highly Focused

THE BUSINESS IDEA

The starting point of an innovation is the generation of an idea that is new and appears to be worthwhile for further use. This is a creative act of fundamental importance for the final result of the innovation, i.e., 'a business idea'.

The business idea arises from an opportunity in the market. It originates from any need or wants for any product or service that an entrepreneur can identify. Entrepreneurs should have a keen and open mind to look for opportunities and generate business ideas.

Selecting a Business Idea

The business idea must be relevant to the entrepreneur. It should be based on a fact that the entrepreneur should be able to sell the product/service at a profit. The business idea should be selected so as to:

1. Enable entrepreneur to utilise the skills. An entrepreneur may have technical, market or any other skills. This gives much greater confidence in entering the market.
2. Enable the use of locally available raw materials for product or service. As compared to imported materials local materials are easy to procure and convert.
3. Help entrepreneurs make products that have a demand, but are not freely available in the market. It is potentially a good idea to start with a product that can be sold. In this case the entrepreneur has only to learn production technology and locate the sources of raw material.
4. Enable use of any technical know-how of the entrepreneur or some specific machines, the entrepreneur is familiar with. If an entrepreneur has knowledge of some special manufacturing techniques, because of previous experience or otherwise it is easier for the entrepreneur to manufacture the product.
5. Enable the entrepreneur to solve a current problem existing in the market. Products may be available in the market but do not meet the demand fully or in a satisfactory manner. Some times an existing product is used in combination with another, which is not available. Attempts to solve such market problems do give rise to business ideas.

SOURCES OF BUSINESS IDEAS

When a person wants to setup an enterprise the first action is to generate ideas for products or businesses. Initially it seems difficult to be able to think of many ideas. The entrepreneurs should use as many sources as possible for scanning product ideas from the environment.

Sources of Business Ideas

- Discussion with other people
- Looking through books
- Visiting shops and attending trade shows
- Information from Research institutes
- Brainstorming

Generating Ideas

When an entrepreneur explores different sources of business ideas like talking to others, visiting shops etc. he should use different approaches like :

Brainstorming : It helps in generating a large number of product ideas. It should be conducted by an expert and none of the ideas mentioned be evaluated or judged. At this stage one should not worry if the ideas is suitable or not.

New ways of doing old things : A large number of products are being made and provided in the market using traditional methods and practices. One approach can be to examine if these can be made by a different and newer method that gives the entrepreneur an advantage over the older method.

Converting hobby into business : Some people are adept at doing something or the other as a hobby or for use in the house only. It is possible to use such skills to set up an enterprise. Hobbies like photography, interior decoration, fashion designing etc. are often developed as business ventures.

Utilising waste material : Conservation and environment protections are presently getting a lot of attention. Recycling waste or turning them into useful products are good product ideas. Presently energy conservation products also have good potential.

Improving an existing product : An existing product can be improved by using old techniques with more care or using newly developed technology.

PROJECT IDENTIFICATION DYNAMICS

Identifying opportunities in a dynamic and uncertain environment requires an entrepreneurial mind set that entails the passionate pursuit of opportunities. A mind-set can be a source of competitive advantage because of the actions resulting from its focus.

After identifying opportunities, entrepreneure must act to develop capabilities that will become the basis of their firm's core competencies and competitive advantages. The process of identifying opportunities is entrepreneurial, but this activity alone is not sufficient to create maximum wealth or even to survive over time. To successfully exploit opportunities an existing firm must develop capabilities that are valuable, rare, difficult to imitate, and non-substitutable. When capabilities satisfy these four criteria, the firm has one or more competitive advantages to exploit the identified opportunities.

Entrepreneurship Product Match

After short listing a number of product/business ideas, it is important to match these ideas with the entrepreneur. One should check the investment required for a given business idea and see if it matches the resources of the entrepreneur. It is necessary to match the requirements of the business idea with what is available with the entrepreneur. Besides finances this matching must consider the entrepreneur's own personal qualities.

There should be a match not only with the entrepreneur's behavioural competencies but also about other resources with regards to finance, skills etc. Using SWOT (Strength, Weakness, Opportunity and Threat) analysis an entrepreneur makes an inventory of his own strengths and weaknesses and also what he sees as opportunities and threats. These may be personal, economic, social, psychological or cultural. A similar analysis for the product is also carried out.

The two SWOT analysis are examined and matched such that :

1. Skills needed for the business idea (product/service) are available with the entrepreneur.
2. Funds available match the funds needed for the business idea.
3. Entrepreneur's weakness does not badly effect making and selling the product.
4. Ensure that the opportunities sought by the entrepreneur are the opportunities offered by the business.
5. Ensure that the threats to the entrepreneur do not cause problem to the business.

IDENTIFICATION DYNAMICS

A sound business opportunity is the resultant of appropriate interaction between the need of the society, capability of an entrepreneur and resources available in the environment. The idea thus generated (in the previous part) needs its conversion into exact entrepreneurial/business opportunities by the interaction of the need, capability and resources.

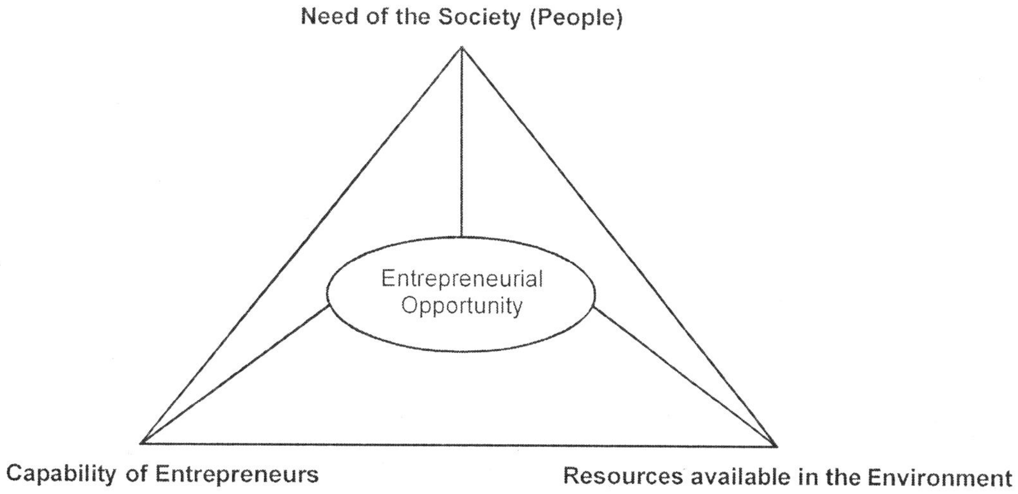

Fig. 3.4 : Dynamics of Project Identification

(i) Need of the Society (People) : An idea may be very good but for converting it into an entrepreneurial opportunity, people must feel its need. If the need has not been felt, the idea will remain dormant till efforts are made to convert this need into a felt need in the society. In case such felt needs already exist, the job of the entrepreneur is comparatively simple. But before finalising the project such needs of the society should be ascertained through various means.

(ii) Capability of Entrepreneurs : Prospective self-employed persons may possess a variety of capabilities and potential due to different family background, previous experience, exposures and personality traits. These varied capabilities make an entrepreneur more suitable for certain projects and less capable for others. This requires careful matching of the existing and desirable capabilities of the entrepreneur to pursue the given business opportunities).

(iii) Resources Available in the Environment : In order to convert ideas into business opportunities, certain resources are required. These may be in terms of finance, raw-material, technology, infrastructural facilities, physical features, climate and skills. For final identification of the project, it is necessary to list the type of resources required and also the kind of resources available in the environment and which can be procured.

A Special Case – The Carpenters

Not every aspiring entrepreneur wants to start up a business that is simply a continuation of what he had been doing before. The Carpenters Workshop, a company that supplied wooden kitchen and bathroom accessories to such leading stores as Marks & Spencer, was founded by three former directors from the food industry. None of them had even so much as nailed two pieces of wood together before. But they were motivated by the challeng of starting up in a sector of the market of which they had no previous experience. It proved no handicap in creating a business which was soon enjoying an annual turnover of millions of pounds.

'Our lack of expericence was probably our greatest asset' suggested Richard Martin, one of the founding directors. 'In an industry that is noted for its conservatism and backward thinking, we have managed to carve out a bit of a success for ourselves, because we have tended to take a different approach to the way manufacturers have historically operated.

SUMMARY

Entrepreneurs bring about changes in the use of resources in a society they setup new ventures, which shift the resources into areas of higher productivity and greater yields. Innovation involves problem solving and an entrepreneur is a problem solver. An entrepreneur does-things in a new and a better way. An inventor produces ideas and an innovator implements them for economic gain. An inventor adds to the knowledge of the society while an innovator adds to their satisfaction by means of newer and better products and services. It is an innovator who commercially exploits an invention.

A sound business opportunity is the result of appropriate interaction between the need of the society, capability of an entrepreneur and resources available in the environment. The idea generated needs its conversion into exact entrepreneurial/business opportunities by the interaction of the need, capability and resources.

REVIEW QUESTIONS

1. Define creativity and innovation and distinguish between the two.
2. Explain the stages of creativity and the importance of each stage.
3. Comment on the statement that creativity is a pre-requisite to innovation and explain the creative process.
4. Emunerate the characteristics of creative persons and discuss what makes an entrepreneur creative.
5. Enlist major qualities of a creative person.
6. How would you select a business idea?
7. A product that may be suitable for one entrepreneur may not be suitable for all. Do you agree? Please explain with examples.

Activities

1. Conduct a brainstorming session to improve the employment potential of your classmates.
2. Select a new course to be introduced in your institute. Do the SWOT analysis for the same.

3. Write five creative solutions to improve the sanitory conditions of your town.
4. Suggest the strategies you would like to adapt to make the environment of your organisation creative. Give reasons for selection of a particular strategy.

Annexure 3.1

Questions An Entrepreneur Can Ask Onself

About the Market

- Is the product choosen available in the market?
- Is the product choosen out of date/style?
- Is the product choosen not easy to use?
- Does the product choosen not exist in the market?
- Does the product choosen has better quality than existing ones?
- Is the product choosen too expensive?

Self Analysis

- Do I really want to do this?
- Can I provide what the customers want?
- Can I get across my ideas to the customers?
- Do I have the resources needed to convert the idea to a business?

Entrepreneur Product Match

- Will I feel happy doing this business?
- Do I really want to work on this idea?
- Do I want to deal with sort of people who would be my customers?
- Do I have ability and attitude to convert the idea into a business?
- Will my family accept my idea and support me?
- Is this idea more important to me than other ideas?
- Will this leave a feeling of guilt in me?

Annexure 3.2

Test Your Creativity

Over time, as one crosses childhood and begins to conform to social pressures, perceptual, emotional or cultural blocks hinder creativity. The barriers to your psyche could relate to:

Your concept of self — i.e., your self- esteem, self-confidence, handling rejection, and the ability to confront differing opinions.

Your need for Conformity — i.e., your inclination to break away 'from tried patterns, to take more risks, to express ideas and scrutinise traditional values.

Your ability to handle the abstract — i.e., your tendencies to use the unconscious mind, to abstract, to view things in holistic ways and to rely on gut feelings or intuition.

Your ability for Task Achievement — i.e. your work patterns, persistence, attitude towards others, and resourcefulness.

Following quiz helps you to assess the barriers in your psyche that hinder your creativity:

Read the statements of the quiz and refer to the following scale and decide which numbers correspond to your level of agreement with the statement. Then write the number in the blank to the left of the statement.

1. Strongly agree
2. Agree
3. Agree somewhat

4. Disagree somewhat
5. Disagree
6. Strongly disagree

- I evaluate criticism to determine how it can be useful to me.
- When solving problems, I attempt to apply new concepts or methods.
- I can shift gears or change emphasis in the abstract.
- I always give a problem my best effort, even if it seems trivial or fails to arouse enthusiasm.
- It is not difficult for me to have my ideas criticised.
- In the past I have taken calculated risks and I would do so again.
- I dream, daydream and fantasist easily.
- Ocassionally I try a so called "unworkable" answer and hope that it will prove to be workable.
- I feel at ease with my colleagues even when my ideas or plans meet with public criticism or rejection.
- I frequently read opinions contrary to my own to learn what the opposition is thinking.
- I translate symbols into concrete ideas or action steps.
- In the idea — formulation stage of a project, I withhold critical judgement.
- I would modify an idea, plan or design, even if doing so would meet with opposition.
- I feel comfortable in expressing my ideas even if they are the miniority.
- I enjoy participating in non-verbal, symbolic or visual activities.
- I keep a file of discarded ideas.
- I would feel no serious loss of status or prestige if management publicity rejected my plan.
- I frequently question the policies, objectives, values or ideas of an organization.
- I deliberately exercise my visual and symbolic skills in order to strengthen them.
- I seldom reject ambiguous ideas that are not directly related to the problem.
- I feel uncomfortable making waves for a worthwhile idea if it threatens the inner harmony of a group.
- I am willing to present a truly original approach even if there is a chance it could fail.
- I can recognize the times when symbolism or visualization would work best for me.
- In the past I have determined when to leave an undesirable environment and when lo stay and change the environment (including self-growth).

Now transfer your inventory responses to the appropriate blanks provided below, and then add the numbers in each column, and record the totals in the blanks provided:

A	B	C	D	
1	2	3	4	
5	6	7	8	
9	10	11	12	
13	14	15	16	
17	18	19	20	
21	22	23	24	
–	–	–	–	Total

Plot the scores from your scoring sheet onto the following graph. The vertical axis which represents your numbered scores, range from 6 to 24. The horizontal axis, which represents the columns on your scoring sheet, ranges from A to D. The key at the bottom identifies the barriers in each column. Connect the points you have plotted with a line. The high points represent your barriers. So try and work on those areas to eliminate their hindrance to your creativity.

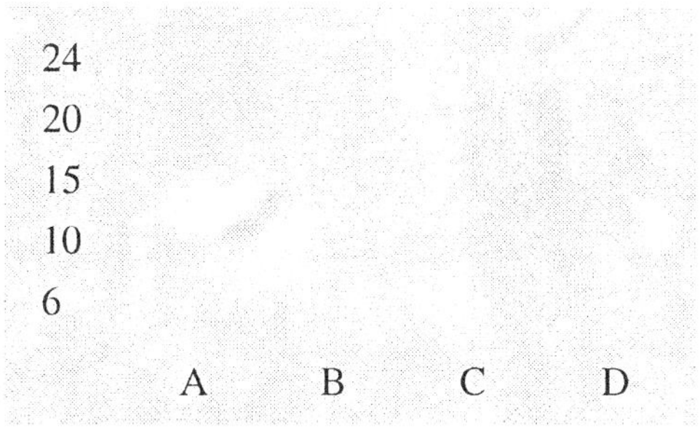

KEY TO BARRIERS

A = Barriers related to Self-confidence and Risk Taking

B = Barriers related to Need for Conformity

C = Barriers related to Use of the Abstract

D = Barriers related to Task Achievement

(Developed by Aparna Chattopadhya of IARI)

CASE 3.1

ANITA RODDICK, FOUNDER OF BODY SHOP

The Body Shop International, named, 'Company of the Year' at the 1987 Business Enterprise Awards, has 300 branches in 31 countries around the world. It has created almost 3000 new jobs and 98 per cent of its products are made in Britain. The inspiration for it all has been its livewire founder and managing director.

"Unemployable" is how Anita Roddick describes herself — but as head of the largest British-owned retail chain overseas, she needn't worry. A former student teacher and United Nations employee in Geneva, she is now the supreme entrepreneur — with a highly unorthodox view of what that means.

"I believe people are confusing entrepreneurship with opportunism", she said in a lecture at the City University Business School. "They measure success by the profit and loss sheet."

"In reality, entrepreneurship consists of three things : first the idea one wants to get across; second, oneself — the person promoting it; third, the money that's necessary to make it happen. The third is the least important of all; the first is what matters — the integrity of the idea. You just have to believe in what you're doing so strongly that it becomes a reality".

"Logically anybody who starts a small business with no money (as I did) can't succeed. But sometimes you do. Because you know if you don't succeed, you don't eat".

Anita Roddick started her first shop in Brighton 21 years ago, with a loan of £ 4,000 and some revolutionary ideas. She wanted to sell simple herbal and plant-based cosmetics, many of which she had seen, used to great effect during her travels abroad. She intended to use the minimum amount of packaging and advertising; and she was determined to sell products that were developed with concern for the environment and were not tested on animals.

She now has a range of over 300 products. The Body Shop still uses the cheapest bottles. "The Sunday Times called them urine sample bottles, and perhaps they are", Mrs Roddick said. There are now five sizes of each product. "Because we had so few products at first, we originated the idea of five sizes; then we could fill a whole wall of the shop". Customers have taken to the idea of a wide range of sizes; they can try the small one first, before splashing out on the more expensive sizes.

Today's Body Shop is a franchise operation, each individual shop being "almost a licence to print money" in Mrs Roddick's words. The franchising came about almost by accident.

"All our 'unique' marketing features happened because we had no money. Because it cost £ 3,000 - £ 4,000 to open up a shop about two decade ago, my husband Gordon and I dreamed up what we called the 'self-financing' idea; we didn't even know the word 'franchising'. Now we have a network of marvellous franchisees".

Community Project Undertaking

She selects her franchisees with extreme care. She looks for franchisees who share her aims and ideals — and insists that each should undertake some kind of community project.

"This is not only altruism — it's survival. We have community projects which are riveting. They range from running drug dependency groups and visiting elderly and handicapped people, to setting up street theatre. Most of our shops are run by women, who are enthusiastic about community work. And it's all done during working hours, not in their own time".

Anita Roddick has an enormous fund of ideas — "drawers full of them", she said.

And she's an expert communicator. The Body Shop publishes a bi-monthly 'Talksheet' for all members of staff, which contains — amongst others — a swap-a-job feature; staff are encouraged to exchange jobs for a few months, so a girl working in Bondi Beach can sample life in Aberdeen, and vice-versa.

Every month a video magazine, 'Talk Shop' is produced by the Body Shop's own video and film production company, and distributed to the franchisees worldwide. It includes reports on the various community projects and on Mrs Roddick's overseas trips: she travels for two months of every year, to find out how people in other cultures take care of their skin and hair, and to visit the various third world projects which produce products — for example, cosmetic sponges — for her shops.

There is also a series of leaflets published for individual customers and for schools, containing detailed product information; and newsletters posted up in the shops. Customers' opinions are actively sought. "Can you imagine", said Anita Roddick, "that we are the only high street retailer which has suggestion boxes in its shops? Why spend billions of pounds on market research if you can do it yourself?"

She sees customer education as a major role. " We reckon that about 25 million people must pass our shops at one time or another, so we use our windows to promote environmental community issues. Every one of our shops is like a major poster site".

She is super-confident about the future, predicting "we will become a major communications company and within two years we plan to have a magazine".

"We think following the route of promoting health is vital for the cosmetics industry — it will not succeed by any other route. In the past it has often tried to create needs that don't really exist. We do things differently. It's so easy to break rules".

Her advise to young potential entrepreneurs is simple : "Never stop annoying people, and never stop asking questions, it is knowledge that gives you strength".

QUESTIONS

1. Is Anita Roddick an entrepreneur? Explain your answer.

2. Discuss the innovative ways adapted by Body Shop.

3. Will this recipe for success work throughout the World?

❑❑

CHAPTER

4

ENTREPRENEURAL MOTIVATION

CHAPTER OUTLINE

- — Motivation
- — Motivation Process
- — Entrepreneurial Motivation
- — Factors for Entrepreneurial Motivation
    - • Entrepreneurial Ambition
    - • Compelling Factors
    - • Supportive Factors
- — Internal and External Factors
- — Types of Entrepreneurs

ENTREPRENEURAL MOTIVATION

Why do people go in for business and become entrepreneurs ? As a simplistic explanation some may think it is greed for money that motivates people to take to entrepreneurship. But this does not apply in most of the cases, as entrepreneurs are not motivated by money alone. There are several other factors that drive people to become entrepreneurs. For this it is important to understand the motivation process.

Motivation

Every individual acts in a distinct manner. Since people act differently, the basic question is 'why they do what they do'? The answer to this question lies considerably in the explanation of motivation. The term, 'motivation' comes from the Latin word '*movere*' which means 'to move'. Motivation, as the base-building block of human action has been studied extensively. Studies on motivation broadly refer to two areas (a) motivating self, and (b) motivating others. Available literature suggests that it is imperative to understand the underlying concept of motivation in order to formulate a theoretical base for both the aspects. Motivational theories are based on the fact that behaviour is essentially purposeful and directed towards the attainment of a goal. Thus, the concept "motive" refers to the purpose underlying all goal directed actions. All motives, however, may not be equally important to the context of the goal. Some actions arise from a biological or physiological need, over which people do not have much control. Such motives are common to the entire animal kingdom. But there are certain crucial and other higher order needs which are common to human beings. The distinctly human motives are largely unrelated to biological and survival needs. These are related to feelings of self-esteem, competency, social acceptance, etc.

Psychologists have described the term motivation as :

- The immediate influence on the direction, vigour and persistence of action;
- The process of arousing action, sustaining the activity in progress and regulating the pattern of activity;
- An inner state that energises activities and directs or channels behaviour towards goal;
- How behaviour gets started, is energised, is sustained, is directed, is stopped and what kinds of subjective reactions are present in the organism while all this is going on;
- Steering one's action towards certain goals and to commit a certain part of one's energies reacting to them.

These descriptions help in answering any or all the following questions :

(i) What energises human behaviour?
(ii) What directs such behaviour?
(iii) How is this behaviour maintained and sustained?

UNDERSTANDING MOTIVATION PROCESS

Motivation is essentially a process. It may be illustrated with the help of a generalised model. The important aspects of the model are (i) needs or expectations, (ii) behaviour, (iii) goal, and (iv) some form of feedback as:

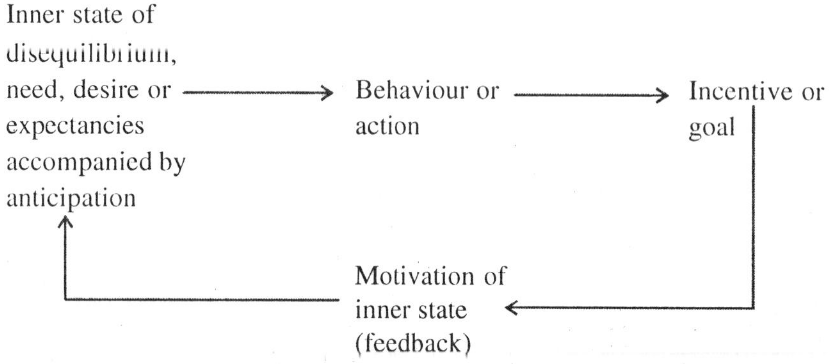

Fig. 4.1 : Motivation Process

Basically, this model indicates that an individual possesses in varying strength a multitude of needs, desires and expectations. These activators are generally characterised by two phenomena. *First,* the emergence of such a need, desire or expectation generally creates a state of disequilibrium within the individual which he will try to reduce. *Second,* the presence of such needs, desires or expectations is generally associated with an anticipation or belief that a certain action will lead to the reduction of this disequilibrium, which becomes the incentive or goal for the initiation of action. In theory, the sets of variable involved, in the motivation process are presumed to be a chain of events. Moved by the desire to reduce the internal state of disequilibrium, with the anticipation or belief that certain action would help achieve that, the individual would initiate the action (behave) in a certain manner that he believes will lead him to the desired goal. The motivation of this action then sets up a series of events, environment, which feeds information back to the individual concerning the impact of his behaviour, such cues may lead him to modify (or cease) his present behaviour, or he may presume that this present course of action is correct.

The model offers three postulates :

(i) Behaviour is caused (need)

(ii) Behaviour is motivated (drive)

(iii) Behaviour is goal-directed.

A state of need is a motive, the action initiated or the drive behaviour is known as motivated and attainment of needs and reduction of drive by the achievement of goal is known as the "process of motivation".

ENTREPRENEURIAL MOTIVATION

Motivation in general is an important determinant for entrepreneurial growth and development in society. However, under the broad spectrum of motivation, certain social motives have been found to be significantly related to entrepreneurial behaviour; such as the need for achievement, power, affiliation, dependency, extension, personal achievement, social achievement, influence, etc. Among all these motives, three categories of social motives seem to be extensively explored. These are the need for achievement, power and affiliation.

These categories of social motives differ from each other in terms of satisfaction desired in undertaking activities as well as in terms of thoughts, feelings and actions of the individual.

Entrepreneurial motivation, therefore may be viewed in terms of a set of motives of varying strength such as a high need to achieve, moderate need for power and low affiliation motive. Apart from the motivational profile, other behavioural dimensions like tolerance to ambiguity, problem solving, creativity etc., adds in building entrepreneurial motivation in a larger perspective. Among these motives, the achievement motive acquires a strategic and important position, and for this reason it is often equated with entrepreneurial motivation which is quite close but is not the same.

People create enterprises in order to grow and fulfill themselves, i.e., for **Self Fulfilment**. Abraham Maslow has referred to this need as "*Self-actualisation*", a need to maximise one's potential, whatever it may be. It is a desire to become what one is capable of becoming. A person normally does not become an entrepreneur for affiliation or recognition, but to achieve what he thinks he is capable of. This urge to self-actualisation is common to all human.

The drive for self-actualisation is frequently more apparent in children than in adults, probably because as adults we have learned to contain our desires. To some extent we have blocked off our innate drives and urges. Maslow went further and distinguished between "*special talent creativeness*" and "*self-actualising creativeness*". While special talent creativeness might be focused on, say, musical or artistic activities, self-actualising creativeness can just as easily be displayed in innovative and entrepreneurial pursuits. We all have a capacity to expand, extend, explore, express, activate, develop and mature.

Human beings are naturally creative and innovative. However, all successful innovators have to learn to overcome the emotional, perceptual and cultural barriers, which prevent them from testing and implementing their ideas.

Maslow's findings indicated that creative people shared certain common features. Their behaviour seemed to be less inhibited and their ability to "express ideas and impulses without strangulation and without fear of ridicule turned out to be an essential aspect of self-actualising creativeness. They are either less fearful of failure or less aware of its consequences".

McClelland found that achievement motivation was lower among people of underdeveloped countries than among those of developed nations. It is the low level of aspirations or ambitions that explains the lack of enterprise in developing countries. Ambition is the lever of all motives. Ambitions motivates men, activates them, broaden their vision and make life meaningful. Ambition is an index of one's resourcefulness. Ambition builds up achievement pressure in the individual and provides the basic for NcClelland's n-factor. The initiative and intentions of an individual are directed by his ambitions. It is the ambition that electrifies man's actions. Therefore, what matters is not merely the people but their aspirations and the means to achieve the goals. However, ambition differ from greed and windfall. Greed results in disaster and windfall makes one a speculator. Unfulfilled ambitions are on to the next generation who may chase the goal with redoubled effort and vigour.

Thus, ambition nourishes achievement motivation and brings economic growth. The biggest obstacle to economic progress in countries like India is perhaps the limited ambition of people. The initiative of an individual is directed by his ambitions. Hence, what matters is not merely the people and their talent but their aspirations. Galbraith has also attributed the backwardness of many Asian and African countries to lack of ambition.

According to Robert W. White, one of the main springs of action in a human being is *desire for competence*. **Competence** implies control over environmental factors — both physical and social. People with this motive do not wish to wait passively for things to happen; they want to be able to manipulate their environment and make things happen. It is natural for people with competence motive to opt for entrepreneurship as a career. The competence motive can be identified in young children and the prospective entrepreneurs can be located at an early age. The feeling of competence can be closely related to expectancy. Whether a child's sense of competence is strong or weak depends on his successes and failures in the past. If his successes overshadow his failures, then his feeling of competence will be high. He will have a positive outlook towards life, seeing almost every new situation as an interesting challenge that he can overcome. Since expectancy tends to influence motives, people with low feelings of competence will not often be motivated to seek challenges or take risk. Such people will always shy away from innovative and entrepreneurial pursuits.

According to White, the competence motive reveals itself as a desire for mastery and professional growth. An individual's job is one arena where he can match his abilities and skills against his environment in a contest that is challenging. In entrepreneurial pursuits such a contest is possible and the competence motive in an individual is expressed freely and significant personal rewards are gained.

Achievement Motivation

Achievement motivation is also termed as "n Ach", the need to achieve, the "urge to improve" in common parlance. If a man spends his time thinking about doing his job better, accomplishing something unusual and important or advancing his career, the psychologist says he has a high need for achievement. He thinks not only about the achievement goals but also about how it can be attained, what obstacles or blocks might be encountered and how he would take help to overcome the obstacles in achieving his goal.

Significance of Achievement Motivation

There are a number of empirical evidences which suggest that the need for achievements is :

— responsible for economic growth and decline of a nation;

— essential ingredient of entrepreneurship leading to economic development;

— one of the most important characteristics of the entrepreneur;

— important contributing factor towards entrepreneurial activity;

— major factors in assessing entrepreneurial awareness and entrepreneurial supply in a social system;

— a psychological characteristic in nature and manipulative through appropriate training programme;

— found to be significant even for successful managers, executives, salesmen, etc.

— viewed as an intervention for organisational development.

These findings conclusively establish the importance of achievement motivation, especially in entrepreneurial development. This is further highlighted if we take into consideration the main characteristics of a person with high need for achievement.

Characteristics of Persons with High Need for Achievement

1. A person with high n Ach. likes to shoulder responsibility.

2. A person with high n Ach. likes to take moderate risks.
3. A person with high n Ach. wants to know the results of his efforts.
4. A high n Ach. person tends to persist in the face of adversity.
5. A high n Ach. person tends to be innovative.
6. The high n Ach. person usually demonstrates some inter-personal competence.
7. A high n Ach. motivated individual is oriented towards the future.
8. A person with high n Ach. shows tolerance to ambiguity.
9. A person with high n Ach. tends to be mobile.
10. A person with n Ach. is adventurous.

FACTORS FOR ENTREPRENEURIAL MOTIVATION

A number of factors have been found to be responsible for the growth of entrepreneurship. These factors can be grouped in three categories namely Entrepreneurial Ambitions, Competency Reasons and Facilitating Factors.

Entrepreneurial Ambition

Earning money and getting rich seems to be the obvious reason for people to set-up their own ventures. Seeking self-employment or continuing family business had been a motivating factor with most of the entrepreneurs. Several people have the ambition to gain social prestige and start their enterprise. However as per a study by James T McCrory "Getting Big" and not "Getting Rich" had been the dream of the entrepreneurs.

Factors That Motivate Entrepreneurship

A. Entrepreneurial Ambition

(i) To make money
(ii) To gain social prestige
(iii) To secure self-employment or independent living

B. Compelling Reasons

(i) Unemployment or dissatisfaction with existing job or occupation
(ii) To use technical or professional knowledge and skills
(iii) To put the idle funds of the entrepreneur to use

C. Facilitating Factors

(i) Previous knowledge, experience or association with same or similar line of activity
(ii) Influence and encouragement by family members, friends and relatives
(iii) Imitation of successful entrepreneurs

Compelling Factors

There have been a large number of causes wherein, it was not the ambition but the compulsion of life that prompted individuals not only to take to the career of entrepreneurship but also succeed in it. A large number of ex-servicemen become entrepreneurs out of compulsion of being retired and becoming unemployed at an early stage of life. During the recent restructuring of economy a large number of professionals and skilled workers, who were not fully satisfied with their job profiles, were compelled to set up their own ventures taking voluntary retirement from their existing jobs. These entrepreneurs wanted to capitalise their skills and knowledge for themselves than working for others. These individuals had always perceived that they possessed higher abilities than those required by their jobs and had higher aspirations about their career. A large number of technically qualified people after gaining initial experience and confidence and not being satisfied by their growth in the profession have a compulsive reason to try entrepreneurship.

Supportive Factors

Ambition or compulsion alone does not make a person an entrepreneur. The moral support from the family and friends, personal experiences and availability of funds are also important factors directing people to entrepreneurship. The previous experience or knowledge of that business, gained either as an employee or in an associated profession imparts confidence to an individual. This helps in reducing the risk perception for that type of business and thus generates a level of confidence to take a calculated risk. The process of becoming an entrepreneur becomes easier if one is encouraged and provided moral support by the members of the family, friends and relatives. Provision of risk capital by the family not only encourages the individual to start his own enterprise, but also enhances the entrepreneurs trust worthiness in the money market and relieves him from the fear of business failure. In Indian society entrepreneurship can not be considered as an individual phenomenon and strictly intrinsic to the person involved. Rather it is the extension of the family aspirations and ambitions that are ultimately realised by an individual.

The success of other entrepreneurs in the region and the recognition and status awarded to them by the society is an important factor inspiring the prospective entrepreneurs. The wealth, fame and prestige earned by the new generation entrepreneurs like Bill Gates of Microsoft at international level, Patels of Nirma, Chauhans of Parle (Thums up) and more recently Mr. Narayan Murthy and Mr. Premji of Infosys and Wipro and many more local entrepreneurs are the inspiration for the modern youth. The media is creating celebrities out of successful entrepreneurs. They are considered as heroes and role models by the present generation youth. All this motivates them to entrepreneurial activities.

INTERNAL AND EXTERNAL FACTORS

R.A. Sharma has studied the factors that prompted new entrepreneurs to enter industry and has classified them in two major categories : the factors that are internal to the entrepreneur and those external to the entrepreneur. The internal factors make the personality of an entrepreneur and induce the person to adopt entrepreneurship. Without the presence of internal factors entrepreneurial activity in a person cannot start. However once the entrepreneurial tendencies germinate in a person, the external factors start playing an important role in the person becoming an entrepreneur and starting his own business venture. External factors like availability of financial assistance, technology, infra-structural facilities, training and guidance form the necessary support systems. Such facilities and assistance form the important external factors motivating and directing people to entrepreneurial career.

Occupational experience is considered as an important internal factor. It provides confidence to the prospective entrepreneur and reduces the uncertainty associated with product demand and manufacturing technology. Thus the traders having knowledge and competence in marketing become industrial entrepreneurs and take up the manufacturing activity with a lower degree of risk. Like wise people employed in manufacturing process, who have mastered the manufacturing technology and have knowledge of raw material suppliers are motivated to set up their independent industrial ventures. In Sharma's study, the relationship between the occupational experience of the entrepreneurs and nature of the industry set up by them highlights that the occupational experience is an important motivating factor.

Educational and technical qualification is the prime motivating factor for educated entrepreneurs. Technically qualified persons normally set up their ventures in the field of their specialisation. A textile engineer will generally set up an enterprise associated with textiles and a system manager will venture in IT related field. Desire to work independently without interference from others in their field of specialisation is another internal factor that motivates people to become entrepreneurs. This factor is more common among the skilled and technically qualified entrepreneurs.

Factors Promoting Entrepreneurship

Internal Factors

- Desire to work independently
- Occupational experience
- Technical/Trade/Qualification and knowledge

External Factors

- Supportive government policies
- Availability of financial assistance
- Ancillary support
- Availability of infrastructural facilities like industrial plot, electricity, technical facilities etc electricty, technical facilities etc.

Government policies and assistance from Financial Institutions are the most important external factors that promote entrepreneurship. Availability of industrial sheds or developed plots in an industrial estate, ancillary support or encouragement from big units, technical and advisory support from government and other agencies are other important external factors.

People become industrial entrepreneurs because of three main reasons:

1. Desire to do something independently in life.
2. Availability of technical/manufacturing or trade knowledge and skill with prospective entrepreneur.
3. Support from government and other agencies.

While studying entrepreneurial motivation, Murthy et al. studied and classified the motivating factors on a different bases. According to them, entrepreneurs are motivated to start business ventures due to the three types of factors.

1. Ambitious factors
2. Compelling factors
3. Facilitating factors

This study reconfirms the classification of motivating factors given by Sharma.

THE RECTEATORS, PATH BREAKERS, PIONEERS AND GAMBLERS

Business Today has divided Indian entrepreneurs in four sections the Recteators, Path Breakers, Pioneers and Gamblers. Infact the four represent four different types of entrepreneurs who have flourished under changing economic conditions.

The Recreaters are the entrepreneurs who have the foresight to adapt their old family business for modern era. These include likes of Kumar Manglam Birla, who changed a stodgy old group into a modern giant; and has taken the commodity driven – cement, aluminum, fertilizer – group of Birlas to apparel, software services, cellular services etc; SalujjaFirodia – Matwani who with her skills brought back Kinetic to its lost glory; Sanjay Genka who moved away from the traditional chemical business to retail and entertainment; Azim Premji who diversified an oilmill to a software empire, etc.

The Path Breaker: They are the sons of austere middle class, including bankers, professionals and even farmers. They challenged the existing business families and created new markets from housing finance to television sets to private airlines. They include likes of, Dhirubhai Ambani, son of a school master, who came from nowhere and build a business empire during licence raj; Brij Mohan Munjal, a bicycle part maker, converted his company to a Rs. 500 crore group with largest selling motor cycle company in the world; Narayan Murthy, a person with middle class ethics and global ambition created Infosys, India's best employer.

The Pioneers: The entrepreneurs who by passed the government and made money by adhering to new life style demands, to occupy market niches – in India and across the world. They found opportunity in newer areas of call centre, health management, and vast innovative markets. They include likes of, Dalip Chhabria, a sultan of car design with international recognition; all centre veteran Raman Roy of Spectramind eServices, Ekta Kapoor of Balaji Telefilms whose soaps caused an explosion of cable TB in India; Rajinder Mudaliar, whose Colour Plus is an answer to legendary western clothing brands, etc.

The Gamblers: We know now that the dotcom era was a burst. But it did a great service by releasing a flood of entrepreneurship. I last several years we have seen entrepreneurs willing to take all manner of gamblers in their quest for not just fortune but achievements. They are not in quest for money alone but for a sense of achievement. The gamblers includes the likes of, Sanjay Reddy of GVK Industries who instead of running the family business of particle boards ventured into bio informatics; Ms Suhag Khemlani who established Techno Clean India – a company to clean steel and glass of high rise structures.

TYPES OF ENTREPRENEURS

As discussed a number of factors are responsible for driving a person to entrepreneurship and his becoming an entrepreneur. However, in case of every individual some factors play a greater role than others. Based upon their motivating factors entrepreneurs can easily be classified into three types as Spontaneous, Motivated and Induced entrepreneurs.

Spontaneous Entrepreneurs: These entrepreneurs are motivated by their desire for self-fulfilment and to achieve or prove their excellence in job performance. They are the natural entrepreneurs in any society and generally do not need any external motivation. They are the Pure Entrepreneurs discussed in the first chapter. Their strength lies in their creative abilities, which leads them to set up innovative business ventures. Such entrepreneurs can normally be identified while they are young and are fired by an ambition to be their own boss.

Motivated Entrepreneurs: These entrepreneurs are motivated by their desire to make use of their technical and professional expertise and skills. They have confidence in their abilities, posses initiative and boldness, are highly ambitious and are normally not satisfied by the slow progress in their jobs. A small dose of any of the compelling reasons discussed above and a little support motivates them to start their enterprise. They come into being because of the possibility of providing some new product or service to the consumers. If the customers accept the product or service, the financial rewards further motivate the entrepreneurs. However, they are equally likely to setup innovative or imitative business ventures.

Induced Entrepreneurs: Induced entrepreneurs are those who are induced to take up entrepreneurship due to policy measures of the government promoting entrepreneurship. Generally, governments provide assistance, incentives, concessions and other facilities like infrastructure support to people setting up new ventures. Some times prospective entrepreneurs are induced or even forced by their special circumstances, such as loss of job or inability to find a job suitable for their talent, to adapt to entrepreneurship. Till a few years back, import restrictions and reservation of certain products for Small Scale Sector induced a large number of entrepreneurs to set up their small scale units. Presently venture funds are inducing the successful IT professionals to become entrepreneurs.

According to some studies, on the basis of their motives, entrepreneurs have been classified into three categories :

- Managing entrepreneurs whose chief motive is security ;
- Innovative entrepreneurs who primarily look for excitement.
- Controlling entrepreneurs who become entrepreneurs to fulfil their desire for power

SUMMARY

Motivation in general is an important determinant for entrepreneurial growth and development in society. Self-actualisation, competence, achievement and motivation are very close to entrepreneurial motivation. A number of factors have been found to be responsible for the growth of entrepreneurship. These factors can be grouped in three categories namely entrepreneurial ambitions, competency reasons and facilitating factors. Earning money and getting rich seems to be the obvious reason for people to set-up their own ventures. Seeking self-employment or continuing family business had been a motivating factor with most of the entrepreneurs.

Ambition or compulsion alone does not make a person an entrepreneur. The moral support from the family and friends, personal experiences and availability of funds are also important factors directing people to entrepreneurship. The previous experience or knowledge of that business gained either as an employee or in an associated profession imparts confidence to an individual. Government policies and assistance from financial institutions are the most important external factors that promote entrepreneurship. Desire to be independent, and occupational knowledge and experience induce a person to be an entrepreneur. Government policies and other factors suppliment the same.

Based on the motivating factors there are three types of entrepreneurs, namely spontanous, motivated and induced entrepreneurs.

REVIEW QUESTIONS

1. Explain the motivation process.
2. What do you understand by entrepreneurial motivation? Discuss its role for a successful entrepreneur.
3. What are the factors that motivate people to become entrepreneurs?
4. What is achievement motivation? Is it an essential ingredient for entrepreneurship?

5. Comment on competence and self-fulfilment as entrepreneurial motives.
6. What factors motivate the growth of entrepreneurs?
7. "Many a times it is compulsion rather than ambition that makes successful entrepreneurs." Critically examine the statement.
8. It is said that "ambition is the lever of all motives". Do you agree? Describe the ambitions that lead to entrepreneurship.
9. "Ambition and compultions may not be enough to make a person an entrepreneur." What other factors are necessary so that people may become entrepreneurs?
10. Classify the entrepreneurs on the basis of their motivation and describe the type of enterprises preferred by them.

CASE 4.1

RANI SINGH THE EXPORTER

Rani Singh is a women who owns her own business. Like many other women entrepreneurs she is torn between her role of a women, i.e., a wife, a mother, a home maker and most import a daughter in law of a middle class Indian house hold and an entrepreneur. While she has been a successful business women, she often wonders if she had been a successful person too.

Background

Rani caught entrepreneurship fever from her father. He owned and managed a company, a travel agency and a furniture store in an industrial town of U.P.

Her father was a compulsive achiever. Besides managing three businesses at once, he served on the school board. Rani said so about her father. "He expected us to achieve, so we all did" one of her brother is an MLA and the other is the Mnaging Director of a sugar mill. "If we got 'B' grade in some subject in stead of 'A', father wanted to know how come. He never talked about money, but he talked about integrity and character.' She started her first venture at an age of 15 when she organised an excurtion trip of her school students and earned Rs. 2000/- besides a free trip to Mussorie. In the college, she formed a musical group and financed her college education till her father found out and stopped her. Rani says "I had no shortage of money during my college days. It was the sense of independence which was more important. I wanted to start my own business and wanted to create my own seed capital for the same."

She competed her B.Com. (Hons.) from Shri Ram College of Commerce, Delhi University and a short term course on export documentation. She joined an export house as a junior executive and become merchandising manager in three years time. Within six months of her promotion she resigned to setup her own business of leather garment export.

As per Rani, there is nothing more exhilarating than owning your own business, and for her, the fun was in the challenge of making the firm grow from a small business straggling for existence. Today more and more women are making this choice rather than pursuing traditional career. Development Commissioner (small scale industries) notes that for the past five years, the number of women starting new ventures is three times more. There are several reasons for this trend. "Some women find that owning a business is the only way to combine a decent wage with time for their children by having the flexibility to control their schedules. Others see themselves as unlikely corporate managers and recognizing the gender problem that exist for achieving success, choose the entrepreneurial route. Still others see entrepreneurship as a way of controlling their lives, pursuing interest that would be impossible in corporate jobs.

Rani has travelled through the world. Every year she spends atleast two months abroad visiting the buyers, and participating in trade fairs. Today at the age of 35 she is the managing director of a export house with the turn over of Rupees Twenty crores.

The women entrepreneurs have to pay a price that men do not have to consider. In case or a women there is often a conflict between the role of a "women" as a home maker and a business owner. Often husband and wife develop separate career tracks which cannot be reconciled. Rani had to pay this price through her divorce. She says that her business played a significant role in dividing her loyalties. "My in-laws were very conservative, they did not like my meeting with my clients. My husband accompanied me on first two foreign trips. These turned out to be more of pleasure than business trips. His own priorities prevented him to accompany me each time. In spite of all my efforts, I found it difficult to satisfy my in-laws particularly Rakesh's (my ex-husband) mother and sister. Though I never neglected the household work and always tried to present myself as a dutiful "Bahu" of the household. There was a strange coincidence that my husband's guests would arrive only when I was busy with my important clients or arranging an already delayed shipment. Women often find it lonely in the business world, especially if the business clients are only men, it was a problem for me". Many women however have a business that fits well with their interest and have women customers. These include services in beauty care, women's clothing, education, entertainment etc. "In order to over come this loneliness and to win over Shalini, my sister-in-law, I made her a part of my business and took her along on all meetings especially outside Delhi. But this did not help, rather my mother-in-law and Shalini started poking their nose in my routine business matters. Ultimately I could not tolerate Shalini's interference as it effected not only my independent working style but also the reputation and growth of my business, which I had nourished at a great cost of time and effort."

Nevertheless, being in business often extract a double price from women, yet for those who are determined, the rewards are plentiful.

QUESTIONS

1. Do you consider that Rani's family had a role in her taking entrepreneurship as a career? Yes or No. Please explain.
2. What were the motivating factors that prompted Rani Singh to choose entrepreneurial career.
3. Discuss the specific motivational factors and hurdles faced by women in entrepreneurial pursuits.
4. Identify and describe opportunties that women might find rewarding as business ventures. Discuss the advantages and disadvantages of non-women specific business enterprises.

CHAPTER 5

ENVIRONMENTAL BARRIERS

CHAPTER OUTLINE

— Economic Barriers
- Capital
- Labour
- Raw Material

— Non-economic Barriers
- Cultural Block
- Practical Values
- Respect for Entrepreneurs
- Tradition Binding
- Emotional Block

— Internal and External Factors

— Personal Barriers To Entrepreneurship

— Entrepreneurial Barriers For Specific Groups

— Minority Entrepreneurs

ENVIRONMENTAL BARRIERS

It has been observed that some societies are more entrepreneurial than others. These societies promote and encourage entrepreneurial behaviour and as a result they throw up more number of entrepreneurs as compared to other societies. In the previous chapter we have seen the importance of entrepreneurship to the society in general and its economic development in particular. All governments encourage and promote entrepreneurship in all sections of the society. In spite of all their efforts some societies are unable to produce sufficient number of entrepreneurs. There are certain factors which either support entrepreneurship or act as barriers to entrepreneurship. Such factors are economic, social, political and psychological. Their negative influence create inhibiting milieu to the emergence of entrepreneurship.

ECONOMIC BARRIERS

There are primarily three economic factors whose inadequacy is the primarily course of lack of entrepreneurship in certain regions.

Environmental Barriers to Entrepreneurship

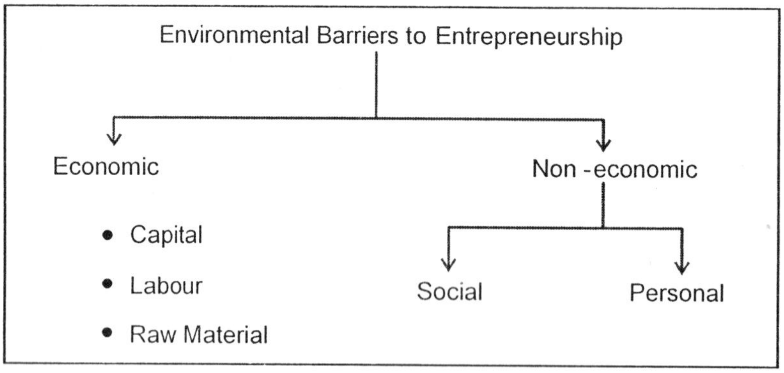

Capital

Capital is the most important pre-requisite for setting up the new enterprise. Capital is a lubricant to the process of production. Money is the resource that helps mobilise other resources like men, materials and machines. Entrepreneurship in any society increases with the increase in the supply of capital. Thus, lack of availability of capital with any society or nation acts as a serious barrier for promoting entrepreneurship in that society.

Labour

It is the poor quality of labour rather than inadequate quantity of labour force that acts as a real barrier to entrepreneurship. Cheap labour of a developing country may *primafaci* appear to be strength in promoting enterprises, but the fact is that cheap labour is often unproductive or has a low level of productivity. This unskilled and low productive labour acts as a barrier in setting up the modern enterprises. However, by using labour saving innovations, the innovative entrepreneurs have been able to over come the disadvantage of high cost labour in developed economies.

Raw Material

In the absence of raw material no enterprise can be established and in the absence of enterprises the entrepreneurs do not emerge. The lack of raw materials is normally the greatest economic barrier for growth of entrepreneurship. Japanese society has been able to over come the problem of lack of raw material through innovative management systems.

Non-economic Barriers

A large number of sociological and psychological factors act as non-economic barriers. Many societies and regions endowed with skilled labour and natural raw material have remined entrepreneurially backward because of such factors. The factors which prevent the emergences of entrepreneurs can be classified as *environmental* and *personal barriers*. The environmental barriers are rooted deep in the society and are also known *socitial barriers*. In some societies such barriers are stronger than in others. However, with time many changes take place in the society. Some of the societies are able to overcome these barriers easily while others may find it difficult to change the factors acting as barriers. Some of the important **environmental barriers** are as follow:

Cultural Block

People are bound by their cultural values. Every society lays down some unwritten norms of acceptable behaviour. All members of that society are required to follow these norms. If such norms are broken, the society does not approve of the resultant behaviour and exert direct and indirect pressure on the individual to conform to a particular way, purely because it is customary. Ground rules of social behaviour are learnt from the parents at a very early age. During school days, the support and approval of others is conditional on certain standard relating to good behaviour, good exam-results and so on. Even at home and office, the conformity is at a premium. As against this, an entrepreneur is required to be innovative, thus, conformity and enterprise seldom go hand-in-hand. Enterprise needs the status quo to be investigated, challenged and if necessary changed. The dilemma for the would be entrepreneurs lie in balancing the creative urge to 'improve' something with the natural human need for the 'acceptance by others'.

Most people do not like to be too unlike their peers. They are sensitive to the reaction of those around them. There is a latent desire to conform to an accepted pattern. Such desire and cultural block prevent persons from setting up their own ventures in non-entrepreneurial societies.

Practical Values

Most of progressive societies, discourage day dreaming, playfulness and fantasty by their adult members. Such behaviour is considered childish and unsuitable for grown up persons. The adults are required to be functional in their thinking. Psychologist agree that children are more creative than adults, as adults are more aware of their practical constraints. As a person grows and matures, more and more stress is placed on practical aspects of the achievement as a result mental playfullness, fantasy and reflectiveness are driven out. Hence, instead of finding innovative alternative solutions adults normally end up with 'derivative innovations' that are based on logic, existing systems and products. When the new system is close to the existing one, it is easier to understand and work with, and people feel more secure as compared to the more imaginative innovations. The preponderance of practical values as a part of cultural blocks prevent innovation and act as a barrier to entrepreneurship.

Importance of Logic

Many people give higher importance to reason and logic as compared to intution and subjective evaluation. Number of alternative patterns of logic are in conflict, the consumers and sellers can have conflicting logics. People have a tendency to see logic as fixed and this stems from historical background of our culture. Pragmatism and logic are considered associated with masculinity while intuition, imagination, poetry, music and tenderness are associated with feminity. Males and females have their preferred methods of thinking. Males use more of the left brain, the logical part. As men have dominated the society for long, it is this type of thinking which is identified as most valuable. The right brain thinking, where women tend to excell is not given importance in the society. We have already established that entrepreneurship requires high level of creativity, an area in which the right brain dominates. Thus, over importance of logic, the left brain, is a barrier to entrepreneurship.

Respect for Entrepreneurs

The socio-cultural setting of any society determines the degree of approval or disapproval of the entrepreneurial activities. Schumpeter calls it appropriate social culture for entrepreneurship. The social status of the entrepreneur in a society is an important factor that has a direct bearing on the emergence of entrepreneurs in a society. The societies which tend to view the entrepreneurs as role models and heros, accord due status to the entrepreneurs, encourage their people to choose entrepreneurial carriers. In most of the Indian societies, businessmen and entrepreneurs are not accorded a high status. Rather business is considered as profession of lower hierarchy. This lack of legitimacy to entrepreneurship and lower social status of entrepreneurs in a society is a major barrier to entrepreneurship.

Tradition Binding

Some people take pride in their traditional culture and preserve their dress, dance, architecture and traditional ceremonies. This provides emotional support to the individuals and shared interests and values to their society. Binding tradition represent a substantial block to change and progress. Social movements, attitudes, entertainment and dress styles are continuously changing. Many people dislike such changes either because of fear or distrust or some unpleasent past experience. People prefer to live in good old days. Some cultures place a great deal of emphasis on the preservation of traditional ways of life at the expense of innovation and development. Such societies resist introduction of any change. Thus, tradition binding cultures are a barrier to entrepreneurship.

Emotional Block

Entrepreneurship involves risk, besides financial risk it involves emotional risk. Every entrepreneur runs a risk of making mistakes and incurring losses in his venture. People usually understand two situations, i.e., either a person is right or wrong. Through out one's life one is trying to find right answers to the problems and avoid the wrong solutions. Right answer is considered synonymous to success and being wrong is considered as failure. A fear of being wrong leads one to construct elaborate justification for own judgements and actions.

At work, people use a number of productive tools like sales forecast, market research, budgets etc., so that in case of failure their decisions are perceived as rational. In case the decision proves to be wrong one can defend it by claiming that high level of prudence was exercised. People are afraid of not only making mistakes but more so appearing foolish because of such mistakes. This emotional fear is the barrier to entrepreneurship.

Environmental / Social Barriers

1. Cultural Barrier
   - Conformity
   - Practical Values
   - Logic
   - Social Status
   - Traditionalism
2. Emotional Barrier
   - Fear of Failure

PERSONAL BARRIERS TO ENTREPRENEURSHIP

In a give environment few people take up the career of entrepreneurship. Even among the societies which are considered entrepreneurially progressive only selected few venture to set up their own enterprises. This indicates that personal barriers prevent people from launching their enterprises.

As per various studies the following factors act as a personal barrier to entrepreneurship.

1. Lack of sustained motivation
2. Difficulty with ambiguity

3. Inability to dream
4. Impatience in solving problems
5. Risk Avoidance
6. Lack of clean perception

1. Lack of Sustained Motivation

Most people enjoy initiating a new product. People generally have a need for new experiences and involvements. Being a part of new development furthers their status need. They appreciate the idea of being a part of something new. Thus, it is easy to attain a high level of commitment, enthusiasm and motivation at the initiation stage of an enterprise. However, when the project is off the ground or faces first obstacle the initial level of interest gradually wanes off. The entrepreneurship requires a sustained level of motivation and commitment and it is often difficult to sustain this motivation against the initial hurdles. Maintaining a pace for entrepreneurship requires emotional qualities of toughness and persistence which are normally at odds with enthusiastic or manic type of personalities that are best suited for the initial phase.

People normally lack motivation to initiate a new venture and take the risk of setting up an enterprise. Those who cross this hurdle have a more difficult task of maintaining this motivation while facing different obstacles in setting up the new enterprise.

2. Difficulty with Ambiguity

Most people are at ease with certainty than with uncertainty. We all like to live having an order around us. Thus, one tries to impose a controlled orderliness in various aspects of ones life. One also develops strategies to cope up with inevitable uncertainties that crop up in our lives. Some people are very compulsive and become upset if the order of their physical life is violated. Such people prefer every thing to be at its right place. This is also true to mental processes and in certain cases ability to create a new structure or sequence may also be impaired because of lack of orderliness. Although orderliness provides the advantage of aesthetics and functionality, yet it is important to have an ability to cope with asymmetry. When a new method of working is initiated, it not possible to foresee every eventuality and predict the exact outcome. Some of the things can not be simulated and have to be tested only by experience. In many situations the data collected will be hazy or imperfect and ultimate decisions will be based upon opinion and value judgements. People who excessively depend on order will find it a hindrance. Entrepreneurs do need an ability to bring order to chaos and their first requirement is "*to be able to tolerate chaos*".

3. Inability to Dream and Use Subconscious

It is general experience that when a deadline is fixed for an assignment, the initial progress is slow and gains pace when the last minute approaches. Most people do their best work immediately prior to the final deadline as they allocated enough time in the early stages of the assignment to store up the information in their sub-conscious. This is because one needs time for ideas to 'incubate'. That is why when one faces a difficult problem, one is advised to "sleep on it". This recognises the power of subconscious, the under-used part of ones intellect. The entrepreneur needs to use both parts of his intellect, the sub-conscious for incubation of ideas and conscious for resolution of problems. A balance between reflection and activity allows an entrepreneur the opportunity to consider alternative and more productive methods of operation. The sub-conscious intellect facilitates day dreaming. As discussed earlier entrepreneurs are day dreamers and a few in our society have ability to day dream and use their subconscious intellect.

4. Impatience in Solving Problems

When people face difficult problems generally they grab the first available solution and try to implement the same. People sometimes act so because of their emotional insecurity or with a view of hiding their incompetence. As a result only the most important aspect of the problem is addressed that too inefficiently by an inadequate and unimaginative solution and the rest of the problem remain unattended. This solution mostly lacks imagination, creativity, enterprise and is normally less sustainable.

The entrepreneur has to find more creative, imaginative and sustainable solutions. Thus, setting up an enterprise needs a lot of patience and an eye for details by the entrepreneur. This attitude of finding quick solutions prevent people from setting up the enterprise and acts as a barrier to entrepreneurship.

5. Risk Avoidance

Ned Heizer, who founded Heizer Centre for Entrepreneurship Development at Northwestern University's Kellogg School, believes that business schools teach students to avoid risk and that big companies build the avoidance of risk into their management structure. He says that analysis of both are limited to risk analysis and the belief that "no one is paid to take risks". Entrepreneurs are less risk averse than the traditional managers and spend more time analysing how to get something done, rather than worrying about what to do if they fail.

To entrepreneurs, risk is merely one factor of risk-reward equation; risk is a flashing yellow traffic light that you glance at as you whiz by on the road. To (managers) others, however, risk is a barrier; risk is flashing red traffic light that you keep your eyes on and that makes you stop. Risk is real, but perception varies.

6. Lack of Clear Perception

An entrepreneur is one who can easily identify an opportunity and exploit it for commercial gain. Most people will agree that number of times they have failed in seeing an opportunity or an obvious solutions to a problem. When the opportunity is exploited by others, they realise how their perception was biased in some way or the other. Normally one is swayed by irrational prejudice and try to impose one's pre-conceived ideas as a solution. This behaviour is a major barrier to entrepreneurship.

People often have "*stereotyped*" ideas about particular groups of people. Such stereotypes are generally based upon past experiences with a few individuals and certain specific situations concerning such groups. Thus, people tend to prejudge certain types of people and situations. Their judgement seems irrational to others as they do not share or understand their experiences. Although prejudgeing based on very limited experiences normally leads to confusion and misunderstanding yet prejudging can sometimes prove to be useful. People need to be careful in distinguishing between casual and serious factors on which to base their judgement. Mostly they are misled by their memories because their attitudes, opinions and beliefs affect their perception.

As the memory does not store every detail of each experience, the mind normally only stores the framework of an event. Hence, even when the new experience varies in detail from the previous one the stereotype prevails as there is a similarity in the framework. This leads to an inaccurate understanding of experience and is thus a barrier to entrepreneurship.

Tunnel Vision is another case of unclear perception. This limits the way people look at the things. Our cultural barriers prompt us to conform to set pattern and this tendency of conformity limits our field of imagination and restricts our ability to innovate.

Let us consider an example. Try to join the nine dots given below by using four continuous lines without raising pencil from the paper.

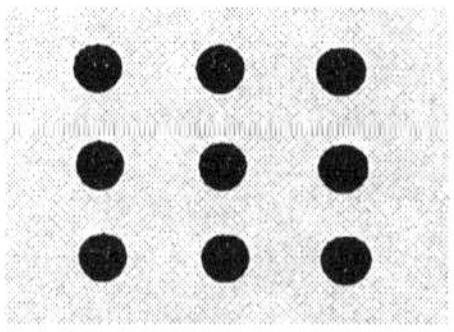

Nine dots Problem

Many people find it difficult to solve this puzzle as most of us think inside rather than outside. We create our boundaries and try to find the solution of our problems within these boundaries. We refuse to look beyond these set boundaries. This is a case of tunnel vision.

A favourite trap for the professionals in all fields is "*to ignore the obvious*". They are used to look into all problems in correct professional way and as a result often ignore the obvious. Newton, the greatest scientist and mathematician of his times, had two cats one was big and the other was a small one.

He built a cage for these two cats and provided two doors in it. He told his friend that smaller door was for the small kitten while for the bigger cat there was a big door. His friend asked if one door would not suffice. At this Newton replied how the big cat can come out from the smaller door. The friend remarked that the smaller kitten can definitely use the bigger door. At this Newton realised that he had ignored the obvious.

ENTREPRENEURIAL BARRIERS FOR SPECIFIC GROUPS

Women Entrepreneurs

The greatest barrier to women entrepreneurs is their being a women and their tendency to keep away from highflying economic activities. Our society regards business as a preserve of men. On one hand bankers attach higher risk to women entrepreneurs as compared to men and often look for men behind the women applicants. On the other hand families including parents and husbands show reluctance for providing seed capital to female members for their business ventures. Banks and financial institutions show unwarranted inquisitiveness towards women applicants and scare them away by asking embarrassing questions and insisting on stiffer and sometimes, unreasonable security considerations. Women from rural and sub-urban areas face greater difficulties, as social setting there is non-conducive. Not only men but also even elderly women are less understanding and less co-operative. They are opposed to economic independence of women in general and entrepreneurship in particular.

Besides personal and environmental barriers discussed above the woman entrepreneurs face the following additional barriers.

1. **Family Ties:** In most of the societies, looking after children, husband and other members of the family is regarded as the first duty of a woman. Women especially the married one are required to make a fine balance between their household and business activity. The joint family system rather than supporting the entrepreneurial activity of women by providing support by way of taking care of the children is often a major hindrance. It has been noticed that traditional *mother-in-law* syndrome prevails and they are not supportive of their daughter-in-laws taking up entrepreneurship as a career. Occupational backgrounds of the families and educational levels of the family members, particularly the husbands, have a direct bearing on women entrepreneurship. Family ties may cause initial hurdles to a woman in starting an enterprise, but once she achieves initial success and develops a rapport with the family members these hurdles are overcome and the family ties become the source of support. (Ref. Case of Ratna Enterprise for detailed discussion).
2. **Social Attitude towards women:** It had been the most important stumbling block in the development of women in general and women entrepreneurship in particular. Despite, equality for sexes granted by the constitution a wide spread discrimination is practised against women. With increase in educational level of public, particularly the women, better communication and the success stories of a number of women entrepreneurs like Ms. Eakta Kapoor of Balaji Telefilms, the society's perception in this regard is changing fast.
3. **Low Mobility:** An entrepreneur is required to travel from one place to another for business reasons. Besides, their normal business callings entrepreneurs in India have to travel to district and state capitals to liaison with various government agencies like labour officers, pollution control boards, district industries centers, excise and sales tax authorities. Women entrepreneurs are greatly handicapped by the inability to travel from one place to another and visit various government agencies not only at the time of setting up their enterprises but in the course of their normal business routine. This makes their life miserable.

On one hand simplifications of work processes in government agencies has reduced the frequency of travel, on the other hand the improved communication, better travel facilities and road conditions have made it easier for women to undertake business travel thus improving their mobility.

In addition some of the barriers for general entrepreneurs are more severe in case of women entrepreneurs. On the economic front women find it difficult to raise capital (loan as well as risk capital) not only from banks and financial institutions but also from the family sources. Women normally do not have large capital of their own. Besides, they are normally not free to invest their own money. Even to invest her 'Istri Dhan' an Indian woman needs the consent not only of her husband but entire family including her in-laws.

On non-economic front, the cultural block is greater for women as compared to men. Women in India have been leading a protected life. This reduces their ability to bear the financial risk. The lack of sufficient social support adds to their emotional block and are saddled with a higher degree of 'fear of failure'. On personal front, because of our social set-up, lower education levels etc. a larger number of women lack the necessary initiative, suffer from inferiority complex and are easily disheartened by the failures.

Minority Entrepreneurs

The barriers to entrepreneurship by minority groups relate to understanding the difference in the behaviour of various ethnic groups in context of the environment and the economic opportunities available in the societal context. Several studies have looked at the ownership rates and trends among minority groups. As per an American study Asians have the highest rate of small business ownership fallowed by Hispanics, while the American-Africans have the lowest participation in small business. In India Parsies, which are, miniculous minority communities are among the most vibrant and successful entrepreneurs. Sikhs are born entrepreneurs, not only the Indian industrial towns of Ludhiana, Jullunder, Batala and Amtitsar but Manchester in UK pay a tribute to their entrepreneurship. Similarly Gujraties are considered good entrepreneurs in India and Patels of Gujarat are the largest owners of motel business in USA. This proves beyond doubts that their minority status of these communities in UK and USA is not a hindrance in their becoming entrepreneurs. Our study reveals that there are no specific barriers to minority entrepreneurship. Members of minority face the same economic, non-economic and personal barriers as faced by the majority community. However the social and cultural barriers vary for different ethnic groups and specific hindrances in taking to entrepreneurship depend on the socio-cultural background rather than minority status.

REVIEW QUESTIONS

1. What factors prevent the emergence of entrepreneurs in Indian society?
2. Discuss the economic barriers to entrepreneurship.
3. Cultural traditions and inhibitions prevent the emergence of entrepreneurs in the older societies. Do you agree? Please discuss.
4. In a given society some people are unable to avail the entrepreneurial openings in spite of various incentives. Discuss the personal factors which prevent them.
5. You realise that most people are concerned with earning more money yet few have considered working for themselves. Few people make much money being employed. Identify and evaluate the barrier to self-employment.
6. Some economies are seen as more enterprising than others. What factors are responsible for the same and what measures might government take to encourage the entrepreneurisation of economy.
7. Do Indian women face additional difficulties in starting their enterprises? Explain.

Solution to Nine dots problem

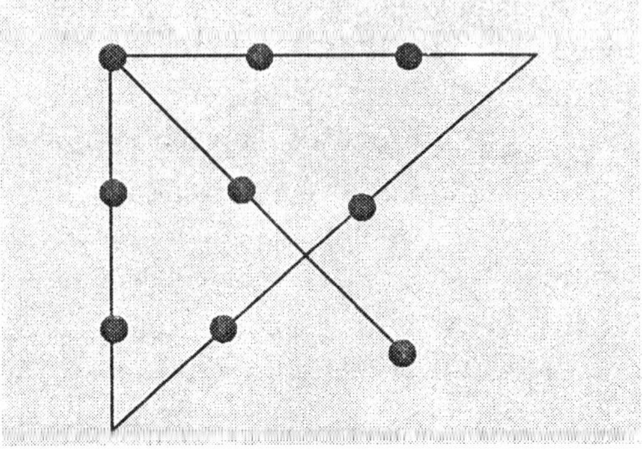

CHAPTER

6

WOMEN ENTREPRENEURSHIP

CHAPTER OUTLINE

— Profile of Women Entrepreneurs

- Hero the differ poem Male Entrepreneur
- Difference between motivating factors for men & women Entrepreneur
- Definition of women Entrepreneurs

— Three Categories of Women Entrepreneurs

— Developing Women Entrepreneurs

— Financial Assistance

WOMEN ENTREPRENEURSHIP

Entrepreneurship among women has been a matter of recent concern. In India, men generally take the lead in the entrepreneurial world. With the change of time as well as cultural norms and increase in literacy, women are increasingly entering the field of entrepreneurship. There has been a significant growth in female self-employment with women starting new ventures at a faster pace. The myth that women lack entrepreneurship or entrepreneurial motivation has been exploded. What they lack is not innate will and inclination nor motivation but the supportive climate where their motives to excel is charged, their vision for action sharpened. The hidden entrepreneurial potential of women has gradually been changing with the sensitivity to their role and economic status in the society.

PROFILE OF WOMEN ENTREPRENEURS

Women entrepreneurs represent a group of women who have broken away from beaten track and are exploring new ventures of economic participation. Women look at entrepreneurship from a different perspective depending upon their education. The women who have higher educational qualifications are looking at it as a challenge, ambition and doing something fruitful while other women with moderate qualifications can not think of it beyond a tool for earning money. The factors that favour women in running organised industries are their skill, knowledge, their talents and abilities in business and compelling desires to do something positive. Although the characteristics of both men and women entrepreneurs are generally same, women entrepreneurs differ in terms of motivation, business skills and their occupational background. There is a difference in the factors, which propel men and women to become entrepreneurs. Men are more often encouraged by their dissatisfaction with present goals, motivated by their drive to control their destiny and an urge to make thing happen their way. As against this women are motivated by need to achieve arising out of job frustration that is caused by lack of growth opportunities. The need for achievement or excellence was present amongst the women on a relatively moderate pace as compared to the trend of entrepreneurs in general. Women prefer to combine their need for excellence with emotional bond so that they can influence people around them and nurture the world they lived in. Thus they are found keen to strike a balance between their business and home life. The other important motives for women are flexibility and control over their work environment that allows them to fulfil the dual role of family and business. The reasons of becoming an entrepreneur can be multifarious but establishing their creative idea along with a sense of economic independence is perceptible. As per a study by Dr. N. P. Singh and Ms. Rita Sen Gupta 'Economic Gain' is ranked as the reason of greatest importance followed by "keeping one self busy". 'Fulfilment of own ambition' ranked third followed by "want to become independent". A large number of women take to entrepreneurship at a later stage of their lives, after they are married and are having school going children. Their family expenses are increasing and at this stage of life it is difficult to start afresh in wage employment. Thus educated and dynamic women get motivated to start their own enterprises. Men and women have similar reasons for starting their business ventures. Both have some experience and strong interest in the area of their business. For men, their business ventures often are an outgrowth or sideline of their existing occupation. Women on the other hand start their business because of high level of frustration with their existing jobs, outgrowth of a hobby or just an enthusiasm to start a new venture to supplement family earnings. They generally lack practical experience thereby making transition somewhat difficult.

The personalities of women are similar to those of male entrepreneurs. Researches and experiences have indicated that women entrepreneurs in comparison with men are not different in terms of their personality, cognition, achievement, motivation, dependency and other selected attitudes.[1] However, women still needed a 'pull' and 'push' because they were still hesitant to put forth their ideas. Though, like men they are energetic, goal oriented and independent, yet they are more flexible and talented than men.

Without moral support of males or any other members of the family the venture seemed impossible. The married women get direct or indirect help from their husband. This help may be financial, physical or moral in nature. Hence more of married women start their ventures. The bankers have greater confidence in financing a married lady. Behind every successful woman entrepreneur there is a likelihood of a man

---

[1]Vishze MD, Women entrepreneur in India, Mittal Publications, 1996.

who would have paved the way either with money, business knowledge or moral support. Unlike men who have their own information sources, women entrepreneurs depend entirely on trade associates and women groups.

Most women start their business ventures at the age of 35–45, when they have settled in family life as against men who start their ventures at a younger age of 25–30 before they settle down for raising family. As per a study by NIESBUD, 75 percent of women entrepreneurs were married at the time of starting their enterprise. 58 percent of women were working and 33 percent of them were housewives, remaining were unmarried and unemployed.

There are no special businesses, which are more suitable for women entrepreneurs. Basically, women entrepreneurs are found in all types of business. However, they are more likely to start a business in service related areas such as retail, public relations or educational services and shy away from manufacturing and high tech ventures. As a result women enterprises are generally smaller with lower earnings.

Women Entrepreneur Defined

The National Level Standing Committee on women entrepreneurship (Ministry of Industry) defines women entrepreneurs as those who operate and control an enterprise, and whose holding in the enterprise is at least 51 percent.

The following two cases[2] help us in understanding the women's psychological need and provide a deeper insight into their motivational trends. These typical cases provide us an insight into what drives women to entrepreneurship.

Renu: Persistent but to be nurtured

We met charming Renu at a women entrepreneurs training course. She was vibrant, smiling and always enthusiastic to respond to the questions of the classroom. During the selection interview her responses were striking and discriminating from others. "My husband has many things to own. I have hardly anything except my hobby to own. I would like to have something different for myself", she told firmly during selection.

Renu the wife of a young industrialist and daughter-in-law of a renowned industrialist looked confident of herself. "It was love at first sight at the age of 16 when I chose my husband", she told us with a sweet and loud smile.

She was put in a boarding school, as her father was in a transferable job, at the age of 7. She did not like it in the beginning, but gradually made a number of friends and started enjoying a very independent life. She could not pursue higher education nor she desired strongly. She went to UK with her husband immediately after marriage. "I loved my stay at UK as I did some very responsible job and grew with it". After 2 years she came back to India while her husband stayed back there itself.

Her father-in-law was a leading industrialist in Calcutta. It used to fascinate Renu when her father-in-law used to discuss with her about his production, his development in marketing scheme and how he faces the labour problems. At times she used to visit his factory along with him but did not actively participate. Her husband came back from UK and joined his father in industry. It was a fascinating experience and she found the task quite challenging. She started taking little responsibilities – she was aware of the techniques, strategies and marketing area. By then she had achieved her own goal by becoming a mother of a daughter but achievement in her career remained unfulfilled. Her husband shifted to Delhi. She stayed back along with her daughter. Her father-in-law groomed her and she was almost managing the company.

She becomes shaky when her father-in-law expired. Company was facing labour problems. She was not sure of her direction. Somehow she was managing the show. "I did not get any physical support from my husband", she told with a sense of pride.

The time was not favourable to her. Her six years old daughter suddenly expired. The union leader threatened her life in an encounter—it was difficult for her to take any more traumas—she had a nervous breakdown. The management of her company declared a lockout. "If I retrospect at this stage, I feel that

[2] Adapted from Potential women entrepreneurs, a NIESBUD publication

management was doing all kinds of injustice to the workers and I was also not sure how to handle it", she confessed authentically.

She came to Delhi. Her husband had almost settled in the new industry at Delhi. Time being the best healer—she was recovering gradually but all along she felt, "I have to 'win' somehow or the other. I just cannot accept defeat". "My husband was sympathetic and encouraged me throughout and made me aware of the facts for which I had a 'defeat'. All dark clouds have a silver lining and I want to start my life afresh", she told emphatically in a tone of determination.

Renu at 29 is a mother of one and half year old son. She is starting an industry of an electronic item. She is determined and hopeful of starting her new project.

Let us analyse and understand Renu. Renu thinks that she has become wiser through her experiences. Her need and desire of achievement remained unfulfilled and she has been trying her best to gratify it by proving her self-worth. She wants to achieve something of her own by herself. Her traumatic experience still haunts her, at times, and she is trying her best to overcome it. These incidents have not made her pessimistic, on the contrary it has given more courage to face it. Her need for achievement and courage to take risks may help her to fulfil her ambitions.

Why she cannot accept 'defeat'. It appears that she has been fighting with herself-her beliefs, values and with proven sense of competence as told by the world during her early period of growth. Is her persistent need to excel and achieve linked with her equally strong desire to be nurtured, loved, cared and fondled. At one stage it was her father-in-law, today it her husband and tomorrow it may be somebody else. It is the unsatisfied need for her nurturance that she is hankering for in her concern to excel.

Vijaya: In Search of Significance

I always had a feeling that women are being dominated by men, but was convinced when my brother was allowed to go for his medical course whereas I had to sacrifice my studies, sit at home for economic reasons (although I was more intelligent than him). That was the time we had just come to India after partition and our economic condition was in a bad shape. I consoled myself by saying that his studies are more important than mine. I being a woman should silently suffer. I would always feel that my place was behind somebody. I would ask a question to myself.

I spent my childhood at Sind. I was the 4th child of my parents amongst 10 children. My father was in Govt. Service. I did not like the way he dominated my mother. My mother on the contrary was much liberated in her outlook and treated me and my brothers in a similar way.

I took up a job on my own in a post office in Delhi after my intermediate when I could not pursue my studies. I was hurt but felt at least I can stand on my own feet. The job gave me confidence and fulfilment. I also felt in my heart that my brother would be doctor one day and would always be obliged to me for my sacrifice. I refused to marry when the proposal came, because I felt that I would lose my independence and would be dominated. I wanted to be on my own, without any interference.

Certain stark realities impinged upon me because monthly bills had to be paid. I can take care of myself, to utter those words, and mean them, would be like putting a pox on myself.

Finally, I was married at the age of 27. My son was born after a year and problem started when my old servant left. Because of my son I resigned from my 7 year old job. We suffered a lot economically (because I was earning as much as my husband) and moreover a sense of vaccum occupied my mind. I felt I am becoming a load on my husband.

During my job I understood the difficulties and tension of working mothers. At the age of 34, I opened a 'crèche' with whatever money I had in my provident fund. It served me two purposes, my child could get company and I could earn money as well as satisfaction. 'Crèche' was of a tremendous success, gradually the number of children were more, I had to employ two "ayahs", and subsequently we shifted to bigger house. Financially, I was not gaining much but in turn had a sense of fulfilment and achievement and satisfaction. I was feeling on the top of my world.

After two years, we had to vacate the house and shifted to government accommodation. The space was not enough to run a 'crèche'. With a great pain I had to discontinue. I wrote to government to take over or to give me space to run it but somehow it did not work.

I had knowledge of cutting and stitching clothes and therefore, started doing a piecemeal job. Gradually two or three ladies joined me. I was working with Red Cross Society also as a voluntary worker. To me money was not so important, but as a human being I wanted to contribute something.

Even at this stage of my life, I still feel I must do something important which would be used mainly by women even when I would not be there. I am, therefore, planning to open a readymade garment factory and want to utilize ladies from weaker sections of the society who can supplement their family income. I am sure, I would achieve my goal and succeed.

Let us analyse the case now. Vijaya was very independent and determined individual from the beginning. She wanted to excel in life with recognition and appreciation. Her need for significance was so high that even at the fag end of her life, she wanted to be someone and fulfil the social demands and to be known and respected for what she had done and been admired. Is she searching for her significance, importance and recognition. Her venture of starting 'crèche' is basically reflective of her affiliative concern. Her social needs are seemingly great; recognition for service to humanity, popularity and affiliations. A very mixing social person attracted attention of friends and peers around. She would find very difficult to cope with her personalised need in her entrepreneurial world, particularly in the beginning without any social status, importance and social recognition. Nevertheless, her need to achieve coupled with her need to relate was dominated by her own need for popularity and fame-essentially the need for power. Her driving force was the power need, therefore, her entrepreneurial venture was also people related (crèche). Her constant comparison with her own brother, speaking for the cause of women reflects her power and affiliation concern.

THREE CATEGORIES OF WOMEN ENTREPRENEURS

Women entrepreneurs can be categorised in three groups. The *first group* consists of women who are educated and professionally qualified. They take initiative and manage business as well as men do. Women entrepreneurs with basic managerial training and educational qualification usually head medium and large units. As per a study 45% women were found to be graduates, 25% post-graduates and 7% professionally qualified.

The *second group* consists of women who may not have educational or formal training in management but have developed practical skills required for small scale or tiny enterprises. They choose the products they are familiar with, e.g:, handicrafts, garments, retail, beauty saloons etc. Some may be in the business of biotechnology, furniture, printing etc. In their initial period these women entrepreneurs even need certain special privileges to overcome the practical handicaps they face.

The *third group* of women entrepreneurs works in cities and slums to help women with lower means of livelihood. Their's is a service-motivated organisation to assist economically backward section of society. Such entrepreneurs like promoters of "Lizzat Papad" and "Sasa Detergents" need government support in marketing and getting finance at concessional terms.

DEVELOPING WOMEN ENTREPRENEURS

It is said that when a man starts a business venture he only becomes the entrepreneur while when a women takes to entrepreneurship the whole family becomes entrepreneurial in its behaviour. Hence, if the aim is to 'entrepreneurise the society' one should promote entrepreneurship among women. Either because of this reason or just to raise the economic level of the women folk or to raise their social status in the society various government agencies and NGOs are working to promote and develop entrepreneurship amongst women. Small Industries Service Institutes (SISIs), State level Institutes of Entrepreneurship Development (IEDs), Technical Counselling Organisations (TCOs) and Entrepreneurship Development Institutes of India (EDI) and various NGO regularly conduct 4 to 6 weeks training programmes to develop women entrepreneurs. Since its inception Small Industries Development Bank of India has sponsored more than 400 Entrepreneurship Development Training Programmes exclusively for women.

FINANCIAL ASSISTANCE

As discussed earlier women face difficulties in getting loans from Bank and Financial Institutions for starting their business ventures. To overcome this difficulty Financial Institutions and banks have specialised schemes where in finance is available to women entrepreneurs on concessional terms. Two of such important schemes are Mahila Udyog Nidhi (MUN) scheme of Small Industries Development Bank of India and Stree Shakti Package of State Bank of India.

Mahila Udyog Nidhi

This is a special scheme for the purpose of meeting the gap in the equity when women with inadequate resources venture come out to set their units. The scheme is re-finance scheme operated through State Financial Corporations and Scheduled Commercial Banks. Funds provided under the scheme are treated as equity for calculation of Debt Equity Ratio to satisfy the needs of the lending Institutions. The scheme provides a soft loan up to 25 percent of cost of Project subject to a maximum of Rs. 2.5 lakh per project at zero interest but a service charge of only one percent is charged to meet expenses of the lending institutions. To avail this assistance the cost of project should not exceed Rs. 10 lakhs. The assistance is available to women entrepreneurs setting up new projects, expansion, modernisation, technology up gradation and diversification of an existing unit and also for rehabilitation of viable sick units in manufacturing or service sector.

Stree Shakti Package

It is a unique scheme run by State Bank of India, aimed at supporting entrepreneurship among women. It is available to enterprises where women own more than 50 percent of the share capital. The following concessions are offered under Stree Shakti Package:

1. The margin is lowered by 5 percent as applicable to that type of industrial unit.
2. When the loan amount exceeds Rs. 2 lakhs the interest rate is lowered by 0.5 percent.
3. In case of tiny sector units no security is required for loan up to Rs. 5 lakhs.

In addition women entrepreneurs receiving assistance under this package are also eligible to get financial assistance by way of interest free loans under the *Equity Fund Scheme of SBI* to fully meet their share of equity.

It is clear that women entrepreneurs have much in common with their male counterparts. Although some of the background and personality traits are quite similar, there are differences between sexes in terms of motivation activities engaged in wide starting business venture and business skills they bring to their enterprises. Difference in type of business started can be attributed to a large part to difference in education and work history. Government has started a number of schemes to promote women enterprises and success rate of entrepreneur training programs for women is better.

Women and Men - A Comparison		
Characteristic	**Women Entrepreneurs**	**Men Entrepreneurs**
Occupational Background	• Housewife • Service related occupational background	• Experience in line of work • Competence in managing business
Sources of funds	• Family and personal funds • Personal loans	• Personal savings • Bank finance • Investors
Reasons for becoming an entrepreneur	• Earning extra money for the family • Keeping oneself gainfully occupied • Inability to seek wage employment • Lack of growth in the present job	• Job frustration • Side activity of present job • Grabbing an opportunity
Motivation	• Flexibility in working hours • To be independent • Achievement – accomplishment of a goal	• Self image as it relates to status • Desire to grow faster • Achievement – strive to make things happen
Personality	• Flexible and Tolerant • Goal oriented • Adequate self confidence • Enthusiastic and energetic • Creative and realistic	• Goal oriented • High level of self confidence • Enthusiastic and energetic • Innovative and idealistic
Support group	• Close friends • Family and husband • Women organisations	• Professionals • Family • Business associates

Table 6.1. Women and Men Entrepreneurs – A Comparison

SUMMARY

Women entrepreneurs are defined as those who operate and control an enterprise and their holding in the enterprise is at least 51 percent. Their skill, knowledge, talent, ability in business and a compelling desire to do something positive are the factors that favour women entrepreneurs. Flexibility and control over their work environment is the major motivating factor for women. Men and women entrepreneurs differ in terms of valuation, business skills and their occupational background. Women have a moderate need for excellence which they combine with emotional bond to strike a balance between their business and home needs. They take to entrepreneurship at a later stage in life at the age of 35–45 years when they are settled in their family and are looking at economic gains or ways to keep themselves busy. Women entrepreneurs are there in all types of businesses and there is no specific list of business suitable for women. However, they are more likely to start ventures in service related areas and sky away from manufacturing.

There are three categories of women entrepreneurs namely educated and professionally qualified, not well qualified but having practical skills and the third group is those entrepreneurs who set up their enterprises to assist other women or backward sections of society. Thus there are more of social entrepreneurs amongst women. In order to promote women entrepreneurship various government agencies, and NGOs conduct specialised training programmes exclusively for potential women entrepreneurs. Small Industries Development Bank of India, State Bank of India have special schemes to provide financial assistance to women entrepreneurs on concessional terms.

REVIEW QUESTIONS

1. Define women entrepreneurship.
2. Discuss and differentiate between the motives of men and women becoming entrepreneurs.
3. Should women take entrepreneurship as a career? Comment.
4. Draw a profile of women entrepreneur.
5. Women should only start enterprises dealing with women items. Do you agree? Give reasons.
6. Describe different categories of women entrepreneurs and what are their motives for becoming an entrepreneur?
7. Explain the source of concessional finance to women entrepreneurs.

CHAPTER

7

INTRAPRENEURSHIP

CHAPTER OUTLINE

— What is Intrapreneurship
— Strategic Entrepreneurship
— Social Entrepreneurship
— Intraprenurial Activities
— Types of Corporate Entrepreneurs
— Corporate Versus Intrapreneurial Culture
— Barriers to Intrapreneurship
— Intrapreneurial Characteristics
— Intrapreneurial Climate
— Fostering Intrapreneurial Culture
— Promoting Intrapreneurship

INTRAPRENEURSHIP

The fast changing business environment coupled with sociological conditions has created a new era in business. The established corporations worldwide are being threatened by smaller, aggressive entrepreneurial driven firms, who are developing more and more of newer products/ services and capturing the markets. This business era can aptly be termed as an *era of the Entrepreneur*. In this era only the business ventures that innovate fast succeed. This requires the corporate not only to have fast decision-making but also an ability to take risk as the business managers cannot afford the luxury of collecting the relevant information as is needed for an informed decision-making. To grow or even to survive in this highly competitive business environment the existing business organisations are required to be innovative. Their managers are to assume the role of entrepreneurs so that their companies can expand, diversify and grow by innovations. Thus in short the existing corporate, especially the large ones, have to be entrepreneurial in nature. In a large corporate house the organisational culture thwarts creativity and innovation, particularly in activities that do not constitute the corporate's main mission. This reduces the flexibility and inhabits diversification and growth.

WHAT IS INTRAPRENEURSHIP

This resistance against diversification, growth and innovation can be overcome by developing a spirit of entrepreneurship within an existing organisation. This spirit of entrepreneurship within an established organisation is better known as *Corporate Entrepreneurship* or *Intrapreneurship.* There is no consensus about the term and several authors refer it as '*Intra Corporate Venturing*' All these terms are used for entrepreneurial activities that are explicitly supported within established organisations, provided with resources and are accomplished by company's employees.[1]

There is no clear definition of Corporate Entrepreneurship or Intrapreneurship. In general it is agreed that innovative employees disrupt the organisation in constructive ways to instigate new product or services. These persons often work independently, or with some degree of autonomy, and although they are given latitude to explore new ideas, there is no presumption of business ownership. In general such entrepreneurial employees are at odds with their companies and often leave to pursue their own ideas. Shiv Nadar and friends left DCM to start HCL. However progressive and growth oriented organisations are finding ways and means not only to retain but to encourage such intrapreneurial persons. Corporate entrepreneurship is a process where by an individual or a group in an existing organisation creates a new venture or develops an innovation.

There is a stubble difference between managers and intrapreneurs. A manager who creates something new as part of his job (for example, a design engineer or a product manager) may or may not have the commensurate responsibility for taking a personal stake in their creation. He does not assume a personal risk; there is no sharing of profit or loss. This does not qualify for an entrepreneurial activity and the manager is not an intrapreneur. The employees stop being employees and start being intrapreneurs when they are charged with the responsibility of championing their innovations. More precisely the individuals are expected to create an entrepreneurial team that could evolve into a new operating division or a subsidiary.[2] These intrapreneurs or corporate entrepreneurs as they are often called, have no direct investment and bear no financial risk. They act to create new ventures, and their reward is limited to promotions or bonus.

STRATEGIC ENTREPRENEURSHIP

Strategic entrepreneurship is taking entrepreneurial actions using a strategic perspective. More specifically, strategic entrepreneurship involves engaging in simultaneous opportunity seeking and competitive advantage seeking behaviours to design and implement entrepreneurial strategies to create wealth. These actions can be taken by individuals or by corporate and are of increasing importance in present day competitive environment.

1. Rosabeth Mass Kanter, Cynthia Ingots, Erika Morgan and Tobias K Seggarman "Corporate Entrepreneurship" Management Review, April 1987.
2. Hans Schollhammer, "Internal Corporate Entrepreneurship" Prentice Hall, 1982.

The competitive environment has resulted in a global marketplace with significant complexity and uncertainty. This uncertain environment makes it difficult for the firms to predict the future. Thus the firms have to develop strategic flexibility with a range of strategic alternatives to be implemented as per the evolving needs. Hence they need to acquire resources and build capabilities necessary to fit into the dynamic environment. In short the firms have to be proactive to succeed in the competitive environment. In this competitive environment entrepreneurs and entrepreneurial managers design and implement actions that capture more of existing markets from less aggressive and innovative competitors while creating new markets. In effect, they are trying to create tomorrow's businesses.

In other words, firms must be entrepreneurial and innovative, yet strategic in their thinking and actions. Innovations are critical to firms' efforts to differentiate their goods or services from competitors in ways that create additional or new value for customers. Thus, entrepreneurial competencies are important for corporate to achieve and sustain competitive advantage.

SOCIAL ENTREPRENEURSHIP

Increasingly, entrepreneurship is viewed by some as a means of bringing about changes that have implications for broader societies. Called social entrepreneurship, different interpretations of the term and the actions associated with it remain. Social entrepreneurs share some if not all the traits associated with entrepreneurs as discussed earlier

INTRAPRENURIAL ACTIVITIES

Intraprenurial activities move beyond new business venturing and include four key elements.

Intraprenurial Activities
- Corporate venturing
- Innovativeness
- Self-renewal
- Pro-activeness

Corporate Venturing includes creating new businesses for an existing organisation. It refers to creating something new of value either by redefining the company's current product or service or by developing a new market or by forming autonomous units under the same organisation. Formation of new corporate ventures is the most salient manifestation of Intrapreneurship. ***Organisational Innovation*** means a technological innovation affecting a product or service. It is manifested in product improvement, new product development, a new method of production or a new procedure of business operation. ***Self-renewal*** means transforming an organisation by renewing the key ideas that form the basis of an organisation. It is a strategic renewal that redefines the business concept and includes reorganisation of the business culture through organisational change. ***Pro-activeness*** is initiative and complete aggressiveness of the top executives. It includes risk taking boldness. Pro-active organisations believe in experimentation and take risk in pursuing bold and aggressive opportunities. The pro-active organisations tend to be leaders by innovations rather than fallowing their competitors.

TYPES OF CORPORATE ENTREPRENEURS

Hans Schollhammer describes five types of corporate entrepreneurs. Each has a distinctive role as innovator and a strategy for corporate sponsorship, requiring different supportive environment.

Classification of Corporate Entrepreneurship

1. Administrative Entrepreneurship
2. Opportunistic Entrepreneurship
3. Acquisitive Entrepreneurship
4. Imitative Entrepreneurship
5. Incubative Entrepreneurship

Administrative Entrepreneurship: Here in the corporate moves beyond formal Research and development activities and encourages greater degree of innovation to commercialise the new inventions.

The corporate philosophy, that enthusiastically supports the researchers and provides them with adequate resources for the commercialisation of new ideas, forms the base of administrative entrepreneurship. The implementation relies on the formal structure of entrepreneurial teams led by the champions where in the R & D personnel along with people from production, marketing, finance etc. also contribute.

Opportunistic Entrepreneurs: In this model the formal structural ties are loosened but the champions are allowed the freedom to pursue opportunities within and outside the organisations. For example, the commercial banks give their fund managers responsibility to invest in high risk high yield opportunities. Such fund managers enjoy a higher degree of autonomy in their work environment, manage their own budgets and report to top executives.

Acquisitive Entrepreneurship: The model moves away from traditional dependence on research and development for growth and diversification. Here in the corporate managers seek external opportunities in other firms and entrepreneurial start ups. The expansion is through joint ventures, licensing arrangements, mergers and acquisitions. Instead of developing ideas internally the corporate prefer to tie up with others having promising products and proprietary knowledge. Hindustan Lever acquired Modern foods to diversify into bread business and General Motors has created joint ventures for expanding their business in India.

Imitative entrepreneurship: Here in a corporate takes advantage of other company's idea and uses its corporate muscle to control the market. In the period just after Second World War, Japanese did not recognise world patents and developed cheaper versions of American goods. Indian pharmaceutical industry did not recognise the product patent and developed an alternative method to manufacture the same drug and export it. This method sometimes borders on corporate espionage. Imitators are there in all parts of the world. Imitation is considered as a way of shaking out the inefficient producers as more capable ones take the initiative. On several occasions the imitators have helped the society by making commercial success of the products that the inventors failed to produce and market.

Incubative Entrepreneurship: Here in instead of developing the new business venture upto a stage of commercial feasibility internally by a dedicated entrepreneurial team, the task of commercial development is assigned to a team outside the organisation. Such teams, though supported by the corporate sponsoring it, bear the risk for its success or failure. Such teams are established as semi-autonomous new venture development units with seed capital and access to corporate resources, freedom of independent action and total responsibility for implementation of the project. Xerox has set up Xerox Technology Ventures (XTV) for investing in the promising technologies of the company. The $30 million fund has supported a dozen start-ups as Incubative entrepreneurships and only two of these have failed.

CORPORATE VERSUS INTRAPRENEURIAL CULTURE

Corporate have realised the beneficial results that occur when their employees are effected by the entrepreneurial bug. Presently more and more companies are trying to emulate the spirit and culture of entrepreneurship in their organisations by creating the suitable culture and reward system. Corporate need employees who think entrepreneurially. Thus they should try to establish an entrepreneurial culture that inspires the employees to engage in intrapreneurship. Apple Computer's Steve Job was committed to help Apple become more entrepreneurial. Apple had introduced some innovative products, such as i-pod, portable digital music player. Hence it is important to study the difference between corporate and entrepreneurial cultures.

A typical *corporate culture* lays emphasis on gathering a large amount of information that forms the basis of rational decision-making. In cases where the decision proves to be incorrect the information collected is used to justify the decisions taken. As a result no one in the organisation suffers for a wrong decision. Risky decisions are often postponed till enough hard facts are gathered. Thus corporate culture promotes conservative decision-making. The organisational climate is such that for any large project very many executives are involved and the responsibilities are so shared that no individual can be personally held responsible for any failure. In this culture you are not permitted to make any mistake and are required to guard against any kind of failure; no experimentation but adhere to the given instructions; no initiative but keep waiting for the instructions; stay within your turf and protect your back. This restrictive environment suppresses creativity, openness, independence and risk taking.

The organisations with traditional culture have hierarchical structure and reporting system. Here lines of authority and responsibility are strictly fallowed; you are not allowed to deviate from the established procedures and instructions. The general climate and control mechanism discourages the creation of new ventures.

Intrapreneurial culture is quite different from the traditional corporate culture. Here in employees are motivated to be flexible and independent. Creativity and risk taking behaviour is encouraged. The goal of intrapreneurial culture is very different: to develop vision, goals, and action plans; to be rewarded for action taken; to suggest, try and experiment; to create and develop regardless of area; and to take responsibility and ownership. As against hierarchical structure the organisations with Intrapreneurial culture tend to have flatter organisational structure with developed teamwork and networking. There is an atmosphere of trust where employees develop close working relationship. People enjoy their work and do not hesitate in putting extra effort or time to complete the tasks. Instead of building barriers to protect their turfs, individuals make suggestions within and across functional areas and divisions, resulting in cross fertilisation of ideas.

Table 1. Comparison Entrepreneurs, Intrapreneurs and Managers

Intrapreneurs verses Traditional Managers and Entrepreneurs			
	Traditional Managers	**Intrapreneurs**	**Entrepreneurs**
Motivation	Corporate rewards- promotion, better office, more	Independence and career advancement staff, power etc.	Independence, money and achievement orientation
Risk Profile	Cautious	Moderate risk taker	Moderate risk taker
Activity	Delegates, more of supervision than self involvement	More of direct involvement than delegation	Direct involvement
Time Prospective	Short term	Medium term	Long term
Decision Making	Generally in accordance with the likes of senior managers	Able to get other to agree	Follows dreams with decision

Source: Adapted from G. Pinchot, Intrapreneuring, Harper & Row. 1985.

Different types of management styles succeed in corporate and intrapreneurial cultures. A corporate manager delegates and supervises the subordinates while having least direct involvement. The intrapreneurial managers have more of direct involvement than delegation. The entrepreneurs believe in direct involvement with least delegation. In their risk profile the corporate managers are careful (risk avoidance), while like entrepreneurs the intrapreneurial managers take moderate risk. Besides an intrapreneurial manager works with a longer time prospective as compared to a corporate manager.

The traditional managers are mostly concerned about the likes and dislikes of their senior managers, the intrapreneurs serve themselves and their sponsors in the organisation. Like entrepreneurs the intrapreneurs build strong relations with those around them, where as managers usually follow the relationship as per the organisation chart. Another important difference between the two is related to their motivation. Managers are motivated by salary raise, promotions and other corporate rewards, while independence and scope of working creatively motivates the intrapreneurs. However intrapreneurs expect suitable rewards for their performance.

To enhance the entrepreneurial competence of an enterprise, knowledge must be transferred to others in the organisation. The transfer is likely to be more difficult in larger firms. Research has shown that units within an enterprise are more innovative if they have access to new knowledge. Transferring knowledge can be difficult as the receiving party must have adequate absorptive capacity to learn the knowledge. This requires new knowledge to be linked to the existing knowledge.

BARRIERS TO INTRAPRENEURSHIP

There are definite reasons why large corporations have trouble staying entrepreneurial.

(a) The Inherent Nature of Large Organisations

As a company grows larger addition layers of management are added in order to keep the organisation manageable. Once the entrepreneur looses contact with workers, it is difficult to ensure that appropriate level of entrepreneurship exists within the organisation. Multiple layers of management also create too many levels of approval between the innovator and the person incharge of resources. Each level has the potential to kill the project before it gets funded. As the business grows, need to control performance also grows and rules and standards become more important than entrepreneurial behaviour.

Another problem is the corporate culture. The guiding principles in a traditional corporate culture are: Fallow the instructions given; do not make any mistakes; do not fail; do not take initiative but wait for instructions and stay within your turf. This restrictive environment is, of course not conducive to creativity, flexibility, independence and risk taking which are essential for intrapreneuring.

(b) Need for Short-Run Profits

Apart from those characteristics inherent to large corporations that make entrepreneurship difficult is the need of most publically held ventures to show short-run profits. Established corporations thrive on short-run profits, they are an organisation's measures of success. Corporations must also secure short-turn profits in order to keep stock prices up and attract investors. Thus there is constant pressure on top management to devise strategies for short-run performance rather than long-run investment. Entrepreneurial ventures, on the other hand, may lose money for some time. Their key to survival is cash-flow. They need to attract money into the venture without guaranteeing the investors a sure return.

(c) Lack of Entrepreneurial Talent

There are very few true entrepreneurs in large organisations. Typically, they are not attracted to large organisations in the first place. Large organisations do not encourage them. They see the entrepreneur as loner rather than a team player and as an eccentric who is interested in pet projects rather than in getting corporate work done. Entrepreneurs are often viewed as cynics, as rebels, or as free sprits, who are late and do sloppy work that does not conform to standards set by the corporations. This forces the entrepreneurial person to leave the big corporations and look for alternatives.

(d) Inappropriate Compensation Methods

Most organisations have few methods to compensate creative employees. Wages for the employees are based on productivity by input/output measures rather than by innovation in products or processes. Even though monitory rewards may not be especially important to entrepreneurial individuals, some mechanism of rewarding innovation must be evident if innovation is to be continued. Non-monetary rewards are also typically missing from corporate structures.

INTRAPRENEURIAL CHARACTERISTICS

Various researchers have identified the following characteristics that help intrapreneurs to succeed.

- Being visionary
- Creativity
- Encouraging teamwork
- Build a group of supporters
- Persistence

A person capable of establishing a new venture in an existing company has to be a *visionary leader*. He ought to have great dreams to be converted into reality. He has the ability to dream great things and communicate these to his colleagues in such a fashion that they would like to be a part of the dream. An intrapreneur is a leader, with dreams, who overcomes all obstacles in selling and achieving the same. To be able to have his vision shared by others he needs a through understanding of the environment. This requires a high level of *creativity* and the same is lacking in larger organisations. Intrapreneurs challenge the beliefs and assumptions of their organisations and this creates an opportunity of doing something new. Creativity and understanding of the internal environment of the organisation and external business environment help in setting up the intrapreneurial ventures.

Intrapreneurs are flexible and open to change. This characteristic helps them in creating various management options that lead to new business activities. They have an ability of *encouraging team work*. Any new venture needs multi disciplinary skills ranging from finance, operations to marketing and legal. Intrapreneurs prefer creating multi disciplinary teams where open discussions are supported. Though this generally goes against the management concept of specialisation and routine departmental structure of the corporations and their reporting system, yet the freedom to disagree and to critique an idea helps in reaching the best solution. The constructive disagreement and diverse skills of a multi disciplinary team helps in pre-thinking and elimination of possible causes that may lead to the failure of a new venture.

The degree of openness in the team depends upon the openness of the intrapreneurs. This openness helps in *establishing a strong group of supporters* within the organisation. The intrapreneurs are required to take extra pains in building this support base by continuously encouraging the team members. As the usual motivators of career path and job security are absent in intrapreneurial ventures, a good intrapreneurs makes every one a hero and thus survives by cultivating a base of supporters.

Last but not the least, is *persistence*. One is most likely to face obstacles and frustrations in intrapreneurial activity of starting some thing new. Only the persistence of a leader will take you through.

INTRAPRENEURIAL CLIMATE

Having understood the difference between intrapreneurial and managerial cultures, the question arises, how to develop the intrapreneurial climate in an organisation? Good intrapreneurial climate is identified by ten characteristics as follows:

1. Intrapreneurial organisations have a climate of encouraging new ideas. As research and development is the key source of new products, such organisations often *operate on the frontiers of technology*. Most organisations, looking after high sales volumes and growth in return on investment, discourage new ideas as these tend to hinder immediate increase in sales and ROI. However intrapreneurial climate supports or rather encourages new product and process ideas.

2. Such organisations *encourage trial and error and experimentation*. It is expected that any new product will require sufficient amount of trial and errors. A new product is rarely a success at the first attempt hence experimentation is encouraged and in the process failures tolerated. Intrapreneurial climate allows mistakes and failures in implementing innovative ideas. Such failures do not have a serious impact on the career prospects of intrapreneurial managers as failures are considered a part and parcel of establishing successful new products or ventures.

3. The organisation should *not insist on any pre-conceived initial parameters*, as this inhibits creativity for developing new products or processes. Protecting various turfs in an organisation may frustrate the potential intrapreneurs to establish new ventures. Consider a case when a manager's initiative for a new product is rejected on the ground that the said project falls under the preview of a different department or a subsidiary.

4. The organisation should be able to allocate sufficient resources to the new projects without much of red tape. The *resources* should not only be *available* for intrapreneurial activities, but the same should be *easily accessible*. Allocation of insufficient resource for a new venture is the sure way of killing the same. Even when the resources are available some times the reporting requirement become obstacle in obtaining them and it can be a very frustrating experience.

5. Intrapreneurial environment *encourages multi disciplinary team approach*. Cross functional teams facilitate efforts to integrate activities associated with different organisational functions, such as design, manufacturing and marketing. In addition, new product development processes can be completed more quickly and the products more easily commercialised when cross-functional team work effectively. Using cross-functional teams, product development stages are grouped into parallel or overlapping processes to allow the firms to tailor its product development efforts to its unique core competencies and to the needs of the market. Team leaders are encouraged to include members with different background of knowledge and skills. An employee's contribution in different multi disciplinary teams is considered as an asset and valued favourably for promotions and career advancement.

6. The corporate environment must establish *long term time horizon for evaluating the success* of the overall program as well as the success of each individual venture. The company should be willing to commit funds for a longer period of 5 to 7 years for setting up intrapreneurial ventures. Intrapreneurial investment by the corporate has the same time horizon as that of venture capital in a start up project or any other risk financer of an entrepreneurial venture,

7. Spirit of *intrapreneurship comes voluntarily* and cannot be forced upon the employees. There is a difference between a corporate leader and an intrapreneurial leader. One cannot be a substitute for another. It may be difficult to select an intrapreneurial manager based upon his performance as a traditional manager. Organisations should allow the intrapreneurs to emerge by a self-selection process and allow them the latitude to carry a project through its completion. Instead of delegating responsibility to different specialists for different stages of a product, an intrapreneur who has fallen in love with his newly created internal venture is, supported by the multi disciplinary team of specialists, and allowed to carry on with the project.

8. The organisational reward system has to be different from that of a traditional organisation. It should be one that explicitly supports innovation. Intrapreneurs need to be *appropriately rewarded* for their extra effort and risk taking in setting up new ventures. The reward should be explicitly based on achieving the pre-determined goals.

9. The corporate climate that encourages intrapreneurs has *sponsors and champions* in the organisation who support the creativity and resulting failures. They also provide flexibility in planning to such an extent that if needed the organisational objectives are modified or new ones added. Normal corporate cultures evaluate managers on their ability to come close to the corporate objectives while intrapreneurial climate allows them the flexibility of changing the corporate objectives to include the proposed new ventures.

10. Last but not the least is that any intrapreneurial activity must be whole heartedly *supported by the top management.*

3M-A Self-sustaining Innovator

3M is a large living organisation with 50,000 products and a turnover of $15 billion. Its management believed that the business is best served when management trusted those with direct knowledge of market the operations or the technology. The philosophy is summed up in the statement, 'Mistakes will be made, but if a person is essentially right, these mistakes are not nearly as serious in the long run as the mistakes management makes, if it is directional and tells those under its authority how they must do their jobs.'

Adapted from Ghoshal and Bartlett, Changing the Role of Top Management: Beyond Structure to Processes, Harvard Business Review, January 1995.

Fostering intrapreneurial culture

If the large companies want to be entrepreneurial, they are required to develop the organisations such that the employees can, want and know how to be intrapreneurs. A four point program is suggested to achieve the same.

1. Corporate strategy should aim at developing intrapreneurial confidence

The corporate strategies should be formulated so as to inspire confidence in the employees to undertake innovative and entrepreneurial activities. If employees have to feel comfortable in taking initiative and acting independently, they should have shared values and a common purpose. Having the clear picture of corporate objectives and strategies gives employees a confidence to drive towards their ideas. It ensures that they are creating value for the organisation and thus feel comfortable in taking appropriate risk. The familiarity with the common purpose and value system gives general direction and confidence to the intrapreneurial leaders.

In developing the corporate strategy and shared values an intrapreneurial leader involves employees and ensures that the strategy is properly communicated to all concerned. Using their everyday experiences employees gather information about the market place and thus help in responding to events at a faster speed. So employers at all levels are encouraged to provide inputs to strategic process.

2. Big corporate to learn to act like small enterprises

Intrapreneurial organisations ensure that strategic decisions are executed swiftly. Present businesses are embedded in a complex system of networks, where traditional hierarchical behaviour patterns do not suffice. Organisations are to act on a global scale and yet maintain nimble and flexible structures, and maintain the ability to react quickly to the changing environment. Large corporate should capitalise on its giant size yet maintain the focus of a growing small enterprise by maintaining the right balance between investment and risk, long and short-term development, global and local operations. Big organisations should realise that drive is the essential to intrapreneurial behaviour. If the staff has a greater sense of teamwork and responsibility, they develop higher creativity and collaboration where by the ideas easily get fructified. Creating the feel of a small organisation without sacrificing the benefits of size is not just about structure. It is the responsibility of the leader to delegate authority to encourage this type of initiative, and thus providing freedom to managers to think and act like entrepreneurs. Large organisations are often broken down to smaller units by dividing their constituent businesses. This promotes the key managers to the top positions in the subdivided businesses and it is the greatest incentives to make them perform with greater zeal. ABB has incorporated some 1400 units as companies in their own right.

3. Assure intrapreneurship is valued

Intrapreneurial organisations create an environment that assures the employees that intrapreneurship is appreciated and valued. They should be convinced that intrapreneurial behaviour does not carry a very high risk. The organisations, in their value system, should inspire a desire for change, a mindset of break through thinking and a culture of creativity and innovation. The performance appraisal and reward system should be modified to include intrapreneurial activities. Many companies have introduces an appraisal system that includes change and innovation as a key element. They have build measures of innovation along with financial and market results. It is equally important how this change is communicated to the concerned employees.

4. Encourage diverse thinking

Intrapreneurial culture becomes more creative and innovative when the organisation has people with diverse viewpoints, perspectives and experience. It is a proven fact that diversity of thought enhances creativity and ability to generate not only a larger number of solutions but even better solutions. In an organisation people, who are continuously dissatisfied with the way the company is running, add to the diverse thinking and are hence a valuable asset. Organisations must recognise and protect these *germs of dissatisfaction,* as they are source of continuous improvement.

A diverse work force with varied background helps the companies to recognise and respond quickly to the needs of a complex market. Recruiting people with variety of ethnic backgrounds often increase the diversity in an organisation. Some inject young blood for this purpose and others seek out perspectives from outside their state or even national borders. For this reason Bharati Enterprise continuously hires new people at the highest levels: "We believe that new faces are good around the decision-making table," says the group Chairman Sunil Mittal. Another approach is to make use of the diversity present in a company's virtual network of alliance partners, other organisations and people connected with these. The forms of collaborations like joint ventures, partnership with university also add to diversity in thinking. To infuse diversity of experience and thinking amongst the existing employees, instead of working in a single department and specialising on one function alone, many organisations make them work on a series of diverse assignments. In India senior IAS officers are trained in this way. It keeps employees exposed to fresh challenges and environments.

Finally an intrapreneurial manager should always be ready to receive new ideas and view points.

Coca Cola – Promoting Intrapreneurship

Coca Cola is a highly centralised company. Of late it has taken an initiative to dismantle command and control culture at its head office in Atlanta. It is now empowering the regional managers with sufficient authority so as to respond faster to the changing tastes of respective local customers. Realising that non-fizzy drinks are taking market share from traditional sodas, it expects the regional managers to boost the growth by responding to the changing consumer taste, innovation and thinking besides acting local. The approach has worked well in Asia where Coke now sells over 250 different drinks. Regional managers are required to use their imagination to launch new short cycle brands. If in the process the short-term financial targets suffer, it is taken supporting. In the process the company is taking a huge risk of cannibalising the existing products by the ones, leading to lack of focus to the main product – Coke and thus thinning the brand. However, the company considers the renewed innovation and rejuvenated business model as the best bet to grow further.

PROMOTING INTRAPRENEURSHIP

Apparently there are only two ways by which Intrapreneurs emerge in an organisation. Intrapreneurship either emerges as a spontaneous team or is created by a formal venture team.

The Spontaneous team/Autonomous Strategic Behaviour: This normally happens in organisations where there is a poor intrapreneurial culture. When an organisation lacks a policy and a formal system to encourage innovation and empower teams for developing new ventures, enterprising mangers may form informal relationships. A few close associates work together on new ideas. The same at a later stage develop into a new venture within the organisation. Autonomous strategic behaviour is a bottom up process in which product champions pursue new ideas, often through a political process, by means of which they develop and coordinate the commercialisation of a new good or service until it achieves success in the market. Pinchot[3] has identified four stages of developing such spontaneous teams.

Stage 1 It is the solo phase where an adventuresome individual works alone, conceives the idea and mulls over it till he develops a confidence in the practicability and use of the idea to the extent to share the same privately with one or two close associates. During this phase the innovator is not seen mixing with others, he may be working alone in the laboratories; workshops even after office hours or may be carrying the files home. A product champion is an organisational member with an entrepreneurial vision of a new good or service who seeks to create support for its commercialisation. Product champions play critical roles in moving innovation forward. The person is very secretive about the idea in the solo phase.

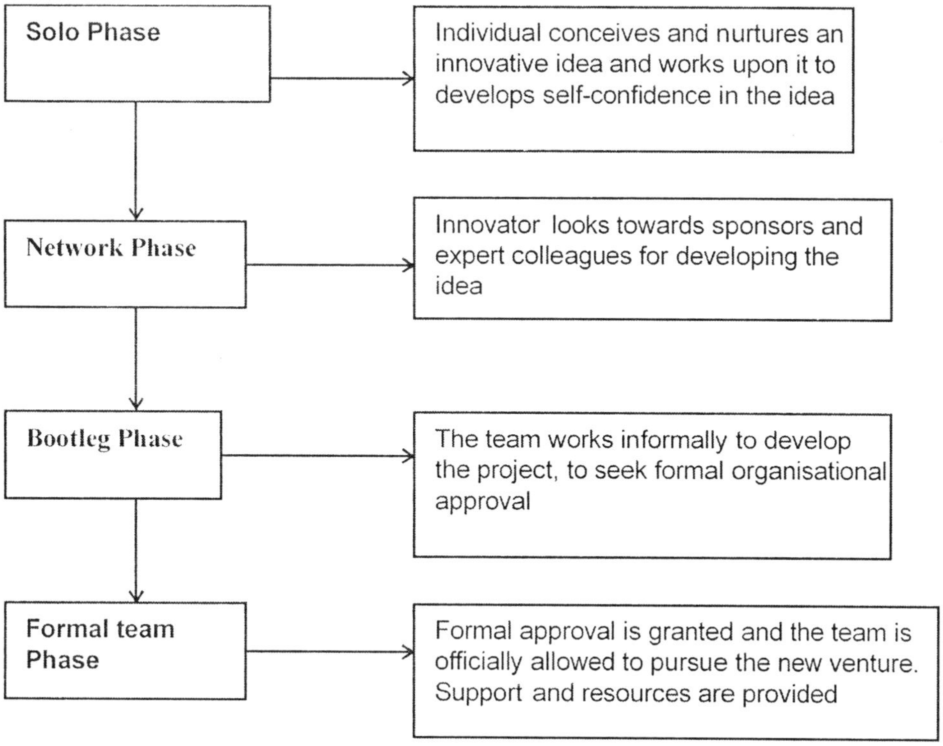

Fig. 7.1. Four Stage Model of Spontaneous Team

Phase 2 In the second phase the innovator after he is convinced of his idea discusses the same with friends and seeks support and advice from experts. He looks for the sponsors in the organisation who may back his idea and provide resources. It is the networking phase to find sponsors and allies. The preliminary reason for this "no business idea takes root purely on its own merit; it has to be sold."

Phase 3 The third phase is called bootleg phase. When an informal team begins to form. The team works on developing the idea without any approval or sanction from the organisation. The innovator is no longer ploughing a lonely furrow. The team works to gather market information, lines up production resources, and prepares a prototype. After gathering the required information the team prepares a project feasibility report also called business plan. This report is similar to the one submitted by an entrepreneur to the financers of his venture. The business plan is put up to the corporate management for a formal approval of the project and allocation of resources. Thus a firm's technological capabilities and competences are the basis for new products and processes

3. Pinchot Giggord, Intrapreneuring, Harper & Row, 1985.

Stage 4 It is known as the formal team phase and starts with the formal corporate approval for the project. The resources are allocated and the team members get a formal authority to manage the project within the specified budget. To be effective, an autonomous process for developing new products requires that new knowledge be continuously diffused throughout the firm. In particular, the diffusion of tactic knowledge is important for development of more effective new products. The Japanese culture is high on uncertainty avoidance. As such, research has found that Japanese firms are more likely to engage in autonomous behaviour under conditions of low uncertainty.

Formal Venture Units/ Induced Strategic Behaviour: Induced Strategic Behaviour is a top down process where the firm's current strategy and structure foster product innovations that are closely associated with that strategy and structure. In this form of venturing innovation is filtered through the firms structural hierarchy. This normally happens in organisations with a well developed intrapreneurial culture. Such organisations have a formal mechanism that allows creative persons to build legitimate teams in the beginning of the innovative process. The initial teams are not unofficial. However the innovation process starts with a solo phase where the individual conceives a creative idea, mulls over it and matures the idea to what is known as a pre-feasibility stage. As in the spontaneous team innovator does not operate in a clandestine manner, but with the due knowledge and permission of the corporate management. The pre-feasibility reports lacks the details of a business plan but gives enough information to the management to take an informed decision to support the idea or not.

The second phase starts with the formal recognition of the idea. An intrapreneurial team is established to develop the idea to the project stage and implement the same. The team is responsible for the market research, development of the prototype, testing and preparing the detailed project report or the business plan. The budget is sanctioned for these activities and funds are provided as seed or risk capital. The intrapreneurial team often reports to a sponsoring manager who tracks the effort. A review committee critically evaluates the detailed business plan and if satisfied sanctions resources for the implementation of the project. In case the idea does not find favour at this stage the seed money provided till now is written off. The funds are now provided as development budget for final development of the new venture.

Stage 1 Initiation

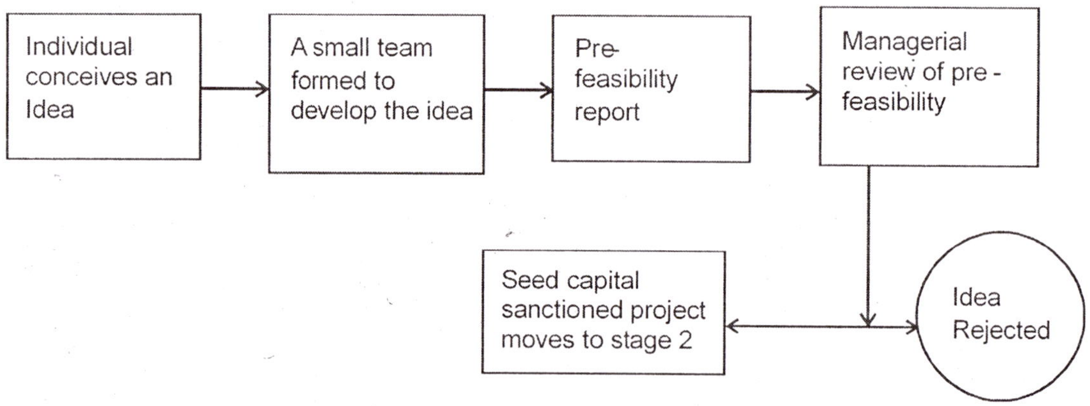

Stage 2 Feasibility Study

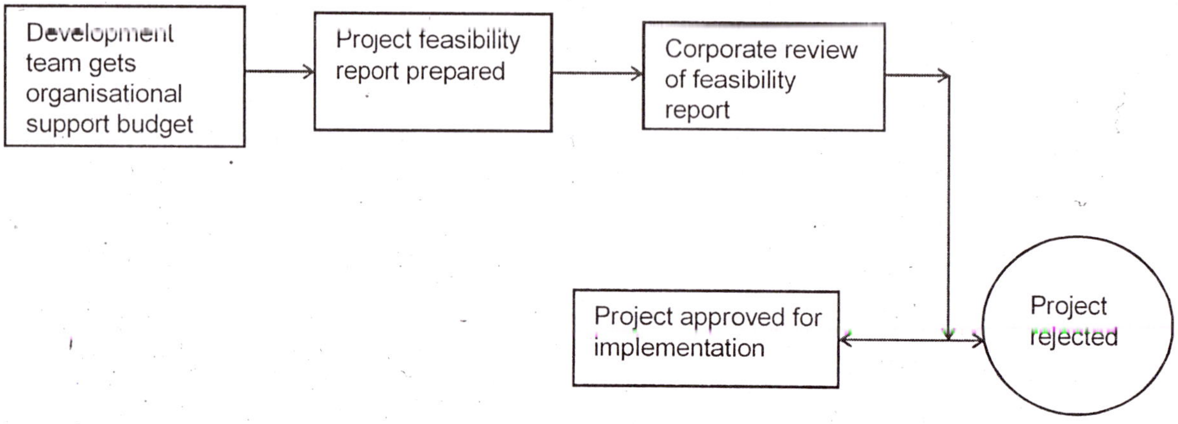

Stage 3 Implementation

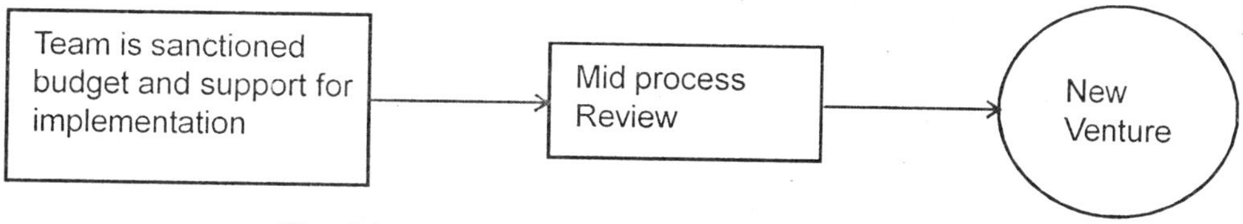

Fig. 7.2. Three Stage Model of Formal Venture Team

The third phase is the implementation phase where the team once again refines the proposal to implement the project. The team is bestowed with all the required authority and budgetary support is sanctioned for setting up of the new venture.

Establishing Intrapreneurial Ventures

Irrespective, how the intrapreneurial ventures are developed, by the spontaneous or the formal process, the corporate have three distinct methods of establishing the new units. These are setting up of a new division, integrating the new product in the existing operation, or spinning of the new project into a subsidiary of the existing company. Setting up of a new division leads to the horizontal expansion with diversification and causes least disruption to the existing operations of the company. Integration of the new product in the existing operations is often a painful process and is adapted only when there is a great similarity with the old products or when the old products are to be phased out. There are two reasons for going the subsidiary route:

(i) the objectives of the new venture are different from the existing corporate objectives;

(ii) the intrapreneurs are offered an equity stake in the project.

SUMMARY

In order to survive in the highly competitive market even the large business establishments have to innovate continuously. To have a steady growth the existing companies need to be entrepreneurial in nature. The managers are required to innovate and take risk. Intrapreneurship or corporate entrepreneurship, also called inta-corporate entrepreneurship, is the process of encouraging innovation within the existing companies through motivated employees who are supported by company resources. Some people view corporate entrepreneurship as a contradiction in terms, that is, entrepreneurship does not exist because salaried people who innovate take little risk and are seldom rewarded for their achievements. Other consider intrapreneurs as leaders who change the course of the organisations they work in and risk their career in smashing the status quo.

Intrapreneurship is not limited only to setting up of new business ventures. It includes activities like organisational innovation, self renewal by aging companies and pro-activeness by business leaders. Four approaches to intrapreneurship have been suggested.

(i) Administrative intrapreneurship, where Research and Development department acts as a base for new products and ventures and the researchers creating new ideas are charged with the responsibility of commercialising the same.

(ii) Opportunistic intrapreneurs, where managers work on an ideas generated outside their organisation and use their corporate strength in adapting and commercialising the same.

(iii) Imitative intrapreneurship implies copying others, including competitors, ideas. It borders on industrial espionage.

(iv) Incubative intrapreneurship where a large corporation acts like a venture capitalist and provides seed capital and support services to employees or even outsiders for developing their brilliant innovative ideas. It involves intensive in house efforts to establish new methods of innovation.

A successful intrapreneur should have the appropriate leadership characteristics. In addition to being creative, flexible and visionary, an intrapreneur must be able to work within the corporate structure. He needs to encourage teamwork and work diplomatically across the organisational structure. Open discussions and strong support of team members are required. Lastly the intrapreneur must be persistent so as to overcome the inevitable obstacles.

To develop successful innovation, the corporate is required to develop a suitable organisational culture. Traditional managers are supporters of the established hierarchical structures, have low risk taking ability, and emphasise short-term results. These characteristics inhabit creativity, flexibility and an urge to new ventures. To promote intrapreneurship, the organisational climate should encourage experimentation with newer ideas and provide them encouragement and resources, promote team work. Organisations should tolerate failures and enlist the support of top management for voluntary intrapreneurship.

Employee, who develops commercial ideas for new ventures, is often rewarded by spinning of the new venture as a separate company with innovator as its chief executive. When, the organisational culture is not supportive of intrapreneurial activities, spontaneous teams champion innovative ideas in bootlegging manner. In supportive companies employees are encouraged to put forward their creative ideas and the feasible ones are screened and supported

REVIEW QUESTIONS

1. What is Intrapreneurship and why is it required?
2. Discuss the conflicting view points on corporate entrepreneurship?
3. Identify and discuss how the organisations promote intrapreneurial cultures.
4. How would you classify Corporate Entrepreneurship?
5. Intrapreneurial activities go beyond creating new business ventures. Discuss and suggest intrapreneurial activities,
6. What is the difference between an entrepreneur and a manager? Can a manager become a successful entrepreneur?
7. How does intrapreneurial culture differ from traditional corporate culture?
8. Discuss the similarities and differences between traditional and intrapreneurial managers.
9. List the steps you would undertake to promote intrapreneurial activities in your organisation.
10. What qualities should you possess to be a successful intrapreneur?
11. Explain how intrapreneurship develops in organisations with different cultural background.

Annexure 7.1

WIPRO'S FLEXIBLE APPROACH AND INNOVATIVE IDEAS

At Wipro innovative ideas have to pass through six stages before they make the grade, Go - No go decisions are taken at each stage. Initial stages are easy to pass but not the later ones. Any one can bring ideas, but once they start persuing it further, they have to satisfy the concerns of the potential customers and draw up fool proof business plans.

Stage 1. Any employee gives his idea for consideration.

Stage 2. Questioning process begins when the idea is received. The person with idea is asked to indicate how the idea is likely to work and its market angle. At this stage the person is made to think more about the idea.

Stage 3. Idea is put to the innovation council to take a look at the idea and consider if the idea has a market potential and falls in line with the corporate business.

Stage 4. If the innovation council consider it a promising idea, if required, it sanctions manpower and resources for evaluation the market potential of the idea. This is the first stage of the company funding the employee's initiative.

Stage 5. Once the basic business idea is reasonably researched and accepted by the innovation council, the company starts becoming more rigorous. People from various disciplines are co-opted for further processing the idea and business plans with revenue projections are formulated.

Stage 6. The project is monitored clearly during initial incubation period. After first 3 to 4 months go - no go decision is taken. There after the progress is monitored regularly every 6 months.

Annexure 7.2

STORY OF AN INTRAPRENEUR

From selling Voltas refrigerators to PCs, Shankar Iyer, CEO of Silverline Technologies, has come a long way. His CV today is likely to say more about his business development, people management and investor relations expertise than hard selling.

Though Iyer holds a US driving licence, he claims to live in India. "I was born and brought up in Bombay and graduated from Bombay University. Subsequently, I did my MBA from the same university and landed up with a job in Voltas." Iyer, who wanted to be in the US without battling the GMAT or GRE, saw great opportunity in selling PCs for Silverline Technologies in the late 80s.

Says Iyer : "Silverline needed someone to manage people who were in the US on projects. And we started our first company from a basement. Gradually, from a body shopping company we became a services company." Today, as the 14th largest software services company, Silverline's cost-effective solutions cover all areas related to e-business, CRM, legacy transformation and integration systems, application development maintenance and outsourcing.

Iyer attributes Silverline's rapid growth to its business model. "We manage by our objectives. Our model is that of an Indian company with international business. We want to be where our customers are. Our delivery organisations are based in India and sales in the US as it's a very important market. From a management perspective, it is not important where I am based. I travel back and forth," says Iyer.

Talking of market dynamics, Iyer is of the opinion that India is leaps and bounds ahead of other emerging countries. He cites two reasons for this. "Our strongest points are language (English) and superior education. Also the critical mass is missing in other countries." Though some of these other emerging countries have an edge over India in terms of infrastructure, IT-enabled businesses will grow due to the availability of trained professionals in India, he believes.

However, this is no indication that India has captured all there is in the overseas soft-ware services market. Of all the Fortune 500 companies, only 80 are currently sourcing from India. And the remaining are not spending more than 10 per cent of their budget on India. This segment can certainly be expanded, feels Iyer. Like a lot of other software companies, Silverline too is exploring other markets like Europe and Japan. But each of these markets is different, says Iyer. "Japan is a different market from the US. In the US, you first get business and then build relationships. While in Japan, relationships come before business. For instance, we did a project for NEC and we were termed the most preferred solution provider."

Another area that Silverline is aggressively getting into is e-consulting. Commoditisation of information and technology has made it impossible for any organisation to ignore it. "Companies are increasingly realising the importance of using IT as a weapon to become successful. IT today comes under the portfolio of a CEO and not CTO. Business processes are all about IT."

After the boom in the software services sector, companies are graduating on to the second phase of e-integration, which will be the next wave of spending. And Silverline is well armed to cash in on this phase, which will include integration of web and backend processes of organisations. Its acquisition of Seranova was the first step in that direction. "What worked for IT companies in the 90s will network now. Customers are looking for complete solutions. Business intelligence front-end is what others don't have. The others are still to get it, Acquisition is one way to do it," says Iyer.

When asked about his vision for Silverline, Iyer says the ambition is to become a company that is sought after." In an industry where people are important, it's not enough to be a good IT company. The aim is to be an employer of choice. The IT industry is not just about stock options. The industry has changed the culture of workplace in recent times because a good working environment empowers people."

But Iyer's task does not end with keeping his employees happy. Investor relations is an area which gives him sleepless nights. As CEO, he ends up spending a lot of his energy in interacting with overseas investors. Says he: "Market perception has to be managed. Industry captains in the US don't spend the kind of time on investor relations as Indian CEOs do. Companies like Infosys have set certain standards in the market. We also deliver services of the same quality. But they make shareholders an important part of business."

Living up to standards set by heavyweights like Infosys and Wipro cannot be easy. But from what's apparent, Silverline's determination is not waning in the least.

CASE 7.1

DEVELOPING INTRAPRENEURSHIP

Many corporations are turning to a form of "new venture" creation in an effort to revive their organizations. The objective is to emulate the behaviour of smaller, lean and mean, entrepreneurial ventures that are innovative and nimble. Many of these efforts are highly successful, but corporate executives find they cannot always change their behaviour. Several examples are noteworthy.

In the 1990s, Shell had around 100,000 employees – mainly long-standing – across 130 nations, and was in danger of becoming bureaucratic and slow-moving. Shell needed both to cut costs and to create new engines for growth and innovation. Steve Miller, head of Worldwide Oil Products, decided to cut through the existing bureaucracy by engaging members of the front line organisation directly in the challenges Shell faced. Local managers were given the chance to approach business problems in a new entrepreneurial way, with direct coaching and sponsorship from the senior executive team. As part of this adaptive leadership approach, Miller reallocated over 50 per cent of his available time to work directly with front line personnel, fostered many local initiatives in groups, and conducted intensive 'action labs' and 'fishbowl review' with local teams. He used wave after wave of retailing 'boot camps', releasing what change guru Richard Pascale calls 'capacity for self-organisation and emergence'.

This approach generated hundreds of informal connections between headquarters and the field and the infectious optimism, energy and commitment of many employees had a major impact on more senior staff. This new leadership style was initially very hard for the established Shell, but as Miller found, 'The leader becomes the context setter, the designer of a learning experience – not an authority figure with solutions. Once the folks at the grassroots realise they own the problem, they also discover that they can help create and own the answer and they get after it very quickly, very aggressively, and very creatively, with a lot more ideas than the old style leader could ever have driven from headquarters'.[2]

Within the financial services industry, Swedish company Skandia stands out as an example of how entrepreneurial culture and innovation can be made a real differentiator. With operations in 23 countries, by 1997 Skandia had made it into the Fortune 500, with outstanding financial and stock market performance. It won international and industry awards for innovation and customer service, and demonstrated a real focus on intellectual capital. By 1998 CEO Lars Eric Peterson pronounced Skandia 'an innovative growth company rather than a traditional insurance company .... the group's identity lies in our ability to achieve innovative renewal'. Over the past 10 years, investment by the top leadership group in entrepreneurial levers for change has resulted in culture and approach almost unique in the industry. This has included the creation and stimulation of 'futurising', with team chosen for their diversity from all parts of the company, to quest6ion the future, conduct 'future café' conversations throughout the organisation, and work with 'Future Centres' aimed at making innovation a core competence. The former Director of Intellectual Campital Leif Edvinsson said of one Centre, 'The place is for futurising. It is about prototyping new behaviour – very agile, moving at high speed new connections and new possibilities, streching'.[4]

In spite of having 170, 000 employees around the world, Sony maintains what Yoshihide Nakamura, currently leading one of the four major divisions, describes as a 'Small Venture capital spirit that can be brought into management'. This is done through the organisational freedom given to different business divisions, investment in R&D (6-7 per cent of revenue annually invested in R&D), and encouragement of diversity in styles and backgrounds of management – including many non-Japanese. There is a highly effective and systematic approach to the take-up and incubation of new project ideas. When Nobuyuki Idei became president in 1995 he used the slogans 'Regeneration' and 'Digital dream kids', aiming to revive the spirit of being young and small that had made Sony successful, Sony's unique culture has been key, Nakamura says. 'Sony's culture is a mix of very Japanese thinking and not very Japanese thinking. In a sense we are very free. We are not forced to do anything as long as we are doing a good job. You really have freedom in Sony. If you're innovative, you are given new opportunities – to realise your dreams'.[5]

---

1. Quotes from Centrica annual report 1999.
3. Quotes taken from Richard Pascaleet al, Surfing the Edge of Choos, 2000.
4. Taken from London Business School case study, 1999 – Michael Earl and Janine Nahapiet.
5. Quotes taken from Academy of Management Executive interview conducted by Paul Beamish, Director of the Asian Management Institute, University of Western Ontario, 1999.

In 1996, Centrica started as the retailing and supply arm of British Gas, inheriting around 20 million customers. The market was being opened up to competition and Centrica's business was under threat from price-cutting. Its market share could only go down. A new management team and corporate centre were created, giving Centrica the opportunity to de-merge from British Gas and go for a strategy of growth rather than retrenchment. Under Chairman, Sir Michael Perry and Chief Executive Roy Gardner, the corporate centre has masterminded a number of strategic entrepreneurial moves, often criticised for being risky and diverging from Centrica's industry competence.

The company moved into electricity, capturing an estimated 4 million customers, started a credit card and financial service business, with 1 million cardholders and 1.6 million insurance policy holders, extended home services and bought the Automobile Association. Most recently it has launched into home telecommunications, Internet and mobile phone services. These moves have been enabled by innovations in alliances, joint ventures, acquisitions, and value. The value created for share holders has been considerable, with the share price up 400 per cent over four years – out – performing the average share index by 100 per cent. Gardener sees a world of opportunity that goes well beyond the UK: 'We are in an era of deregulation in our core energy-supply business, liberalisation of energy markets and rapid expansion of e-Commerce. International boundaries will become less significant and opportunities for developing relationships with consumers will accelerate. We believe our model for our consumer services businesses positions us well for the future'.

Questions

1. Explain each of the example in terms of different approaches to achiving corporate entrepreneurship.
2. Describe the advantages and disadvantages of the different approaches taken by each company to encourage innovation or to introduce new products.

❑❑

CHAPTER

8

STAGES FOR STARTING A NEW VENTURE

CHAPTER OUTLINE

— Scanning The Environment
— Product Development and Selection
— Project Report Preparation
— Project Appraisal
— Resourcing

Once an entrepreneur becomes aware of the concept and role of new venture, he could make up his mind and proceed toward taking concrete actions to establish the unit. The entrepreneur could for that purpose, draw a plan of action so as to suit his requirement of setting up a new venture.

To be a successful entrepreneur it is necessary to have the foresight and an ability of sensing opportunities. It is an important entrepreneurial function which calls for the ability and eagerness to perceive and receive the curious signals, sieve and process them for arriving at a final decision in favour of an idea/enterprise. An entrepreneur searches for and identifies an opportunity before working energetically to convert it into a business reality. Opportunity is a result of interaction between the need of the society, capability of the entrepreneur and resources available in the environment. He does this by being alert to the world around him. The process of 'opportunity sensing' involves five steps :

(*a*) Scanning the Environment
(*b*) Product Development and Selection
(*c*) Preparing Project Report
(*d*) Project Appraisal
(*e*) Resourcing

SCANNING THE ENVIRONMENT

Scanning of environment refers to the understanding of socio-culture, economic, technological, fashion and even the changing life style and aspirations of local people. It is not a matter of just observing the obvious in the environment but sensing the emerging opportunities out of the interaction of such futuristic/emerging needs of goods and services which otherwise are not perceived by general masses. Scanning of environment is done by collecting information from various sources.

Personal Informal Sources :

(*i*) Family
(*ii*) Customers
(*iii*) Friends
(*iv*) Colleagues
(*v*) Salesmen
(*vi*) Social Contacts
(*vii*) Employees

Personal Formal Sources :

(*i*) Bankers
(*ii*) Business Councillors

Impersonal Written Sources :

(*i*) Magazines
(*ii*) Journals
(*iii*) Books
(*iv*) Newsletters
(*v*) Newspapers
(*vi*) Catalogues

Impersoanl Oral Sources :

(*i*) Trade Shows
(*ii*) Seminars / Workshops
(*iii*) Professional Organisations
(*iv*) Small Business Organisations
(*v*) Suppliers/Dealers

One should use as many sources as possible for the purpose of scanning the environment.

PRODUCT DEVELOPMENT AND SELECTION

The environment scanning as described earlier will result in the location of a variety of situations out of which product/service can be selected. There are a number of ways of selection and development of new product and service.

Solving people's problems

Listening to a housewife wishing for a water filter which should be attached to the faucet to give direct supply of filtered water gives a business idea for a new water filter.

A German lingerie company, Triumph International AG, has come out with a line of "Frequent Flyers" brass with special wires and claps that do not trigger metal detector alarms at the airports.

Combining two or more ideas :

Selling different items in one-shop presents the "new" idea of a departmental store.

New ways of doing old things :

Popularising gas lighter as substitute for match box for lighting gas oven gives the idea of a new product. Instead of selling pizza in a bakery shop the sale through mobile vans at different locations gives a "new idea" for business.

Improving the product/service :

Milk which was usually supplied in bottles when packed in sachet or tetra-packs was seen as 'new idea'.

Gerry Calaprese of Florida, is in the business of high-end custom aquariums. When he saw the news about the anthrax contamination, he took a look at his aquariums and decided to adopt his normal construction process to build a sealed glass case for people to open their mail in.

Extending somebody else's successful idea to other settings :

The successful introduction of a new product service gives ideas for repeating to catch growing market in other places, e.g., electric mosquito repellent in most of the developing countries.

Adding new value to an old product :

Ball point pens used for writing to have printed name of customers become a "new idea" for its use as publicity material.

Doing market research :

Determining demand-supply gap through market research gives 'new idea' for products and services.

Use of 'hobby' :

Hobby of collecting flowers may give rise to a business idea of 'dried flower' art objects.

Building up the skills :

Skills very often give ideas of skill-based enterprises. Typing skill can be used for starting a typing school.

Turning waste materials into something usuful :

Availability of waste paper gives an idea of an enterprise making paper products.

Bringing ideas home from holidays:

Difficulties faced in arranging accommodation during holidays/visits may give rise to an idea of starting a travel agency, providing these facilities.

Brain storming :

A group of persons sit together and generate as many business ideas as possible. One idea leads to another. Ideas that appear to be crazy may prove furture boon.

Checking published lists :

Several publications list down business opportunities. Scanning such lists gives business ideas.

Talking and listening to people :

By being a keen listener, one can find out what people need or what new suggestions they have to offer for setting up new ventures.

Day dreaming and fantasing :

This may sound funny but can be very useful for generating business ideas. Variety of video games are an example.

Understanding what things do rather than what they are :

Attractive glass container has a function of carrying wine but often used as decoration piece.

Thinking of product use with change in size and shape :

Take the case of a plastic paper weight. Reduction in size gives an idea of a dice ; whereas an increase in size may lead to the idea of plastic stool for drawing room.

Commercialising inventions :

Inventions in the laboratories may gives ideas for their commercialisation.

Yellow Page Diretory :

Yellow Page Directory often describes products and services. This may also help in generating ideas of repeating or evolving substitutes for these items in different locations or combining many of them under one venture.

Changing fashion and life style :

Changes in fashion require new products and services-short hair style of ladies leads to the need for more 'ladies hair cut saloons'.

Pratibha Iyer – The Housekeeper

Pratibha is churing out a business of over Rs. 6 lakhs at her housekeeping company, 'Personal Touch'. In fact her entry into housekeeping business, ten years ago, was not a planned one. A friend told her that Hong Kong Bank was looking for some one who could maintain their guest house, and suggeted her to take a look at that. It made sense, since she was planning to get out of her routine job. She did not have a clue about housekeeping.

Pratibha, however, knew how a guest house should look, thanks to her exposure to the hotel industry. The rest fell in place once she took up the assignment. In the last ten years, the number of Pratibha's clients have gone up. Personal Touch now caters to the needs of Oracle, HSBC, Mascot Systems etc.

PROJECT REPORT PREPARATION

Having decided upon the product and organisation, the entrepreneur has to put his ideas and other information sought in black and white. This should be so well presented that it provides all relevant information in reference to the project.

Accordingly, the task or project report preparation encompasses information under various heads. Necessary documents, quotations and enquiry should be attached with the details under the given heads to form a project report. It may not be out of place to emphasise that the project report should be prepared by the entrepreneur himself. This, not only would save his money, but also clarify many doubts, thereby, making him more optimistic of the success of the project. A project report should normally cover following points in detail :

1. Brief introduction of the proposed project.
2. Brief History : Why did the entrepreneur(s) decide to set up this particular project?
3. The Unit : (Attach relevant documents)
   (*a*) Constitution of the unit (proprietorship, partnership, private limited company etc). Share of each partner in case of a partnership concern should also be mentioned.
   (*b*) Nature of unit : Whether ancillary to some large unit or not.
   (*c*) Details of associate concerns, if any.
4. The promoter(s) and key personnel (viz, Proprietor/Partners/Directors)
   (*a*) Brief detail of background with special reference to any experince in related fields and how it will help the promoter(s) in successfully running the unit.
   (*b*) Enclose bio-data (data-wise details of education, jobs held and business/industrial activities undertaken).
5. Product :
   (*a*) Description of the product to be manufactured.

(*b*) Where is the product used or consumed?

(*c*) Product range : Various types of products to be manufactured.

6. Marketing and Competition :

   (*a*) General market trends.

   (*b*) Estimated overall demand.

   (*c*) Segmentation of estimated demand, the proposed share of the unit and projected sales for first three years.

   (*d*) Region or segments proposed to be covered by the unit.

   (*e*) Competition and how does the unit propose to meet the competition?

   (*f*) Price and quality : How the unit's product will compare with those of its competitors?

   (*g*) Marketing strategy :

      (*i*) If selling directly to customer, then details of showroom, sales force etc.

      (*ii*) If selling through agents their details, period of contaract, commission payable, scurity etc, to be offered by them and terms of payment.

   (*h*) Value of orders in hand (already recieved by the promoters) and expected shortly (correspondence going on).

7. Manufacturing process :

   (*a*) Process flow chart, giving the manufacturing flow from one process to the next; from one machine to the next.

   (*b*) Various operations for each item, sequence of operations and time taken for each operation.

   (*c*) Input/Output ratios between raw material and finished products.

   (*d*) Any special techniques involved.

8. Machinery and plant capacity :

   (*a*) Details of machinery required for the project.

   (*b*) Capacity of each machine and power required for them.

   (*c*) Technical details and specifications of machinery.

   (*d*) Details of suppliers.

   (*e*) Price of each machine.

   (*f*) Procurement time and availability in market.

   (*g*) Spare parts required and their availability.

   (*h*) Reasons for selecting a particular supplier, alongwith quotations for each item from at least 2 or 3 different suppliers (not different firms under same control).

9. Raw material :

   (*a*) Details of various raw materials required.

   (*b*) Specifications of each type of raw material.

   (*c*) Availability (where available, how easily available etc.).

   (*d*) Names of suppliers.

   (*d*) Source.

   (*f*) Whether quota, non-quota or imported items.

   (*g*) Price at which raw material is available.

   (*h*) Procurement time from time of ordering to receipt of material.

   (*i*) Minimum order quantity.

   (*j*) Whether any credit is available from suppliers.

   (*k*) Details of consumable item (such as oil, lubricants, cleaning material etc.)

10. Land and Building (in case own building is to be constructed) :

   (*a*) Total area and cost of land required.

   (*b*) Cost of land development

   (*c*) Covered and uncovered area.

   (*d*) Estimate of building including utilities (water, electricity, etc.).

11. General management and technical staff :
    (*a*) Duties of promoter(s).
    (*b*) Indirect staff such as sales-cum-purchase assistant, accountant-cum-storekeeper etc.
    (*c*) Direct labour strength such as skilled workers, unskilled workers, semiskilled workers.
    (*d*) Salary or wages, incentives, bonus etc., of each worker.
12. Cost of the project :
    Land, building, plant and machinery, furniture and fixture, pre-opeative expenses, contingencies, working capital required. Supporting details should be given in annexures. Discuss each item in detail.
13. Means of Finance : (Discuss each item in detail)
    (*a*) Term loan from bank.
    (*b*) Government subsidy (if available),
    (*c*) Deferred payments.
    (*d*) Promoter's contribution.
    (*e*) Loans from friends and relatives.
    (*f*) Equity assistance.
14. Working capital required :
    (*a*) Anticipated monthly sales.
    (*b*) Cost of raw material consumed per month.
    (*c*) Total monthly production cost.
    (*d*) Average raw-material stocking level for various raw materials and consumable items.
    (*e*) Average period of processing or work-in-process.
    (*f*) Finished goods stocking level.
    (*g*) Cash sales.
    (*h*) Credit sales and period of bill realisation.
    (*i*) Average credit available from market.
15. Cost of production and profitability :
    (*a*) Details of raw material content for each item.
    (*b*) Details of monthly expenses.
    (*c*) Bifuraction of monthly expenses into fixed and variable expenses.
    (*d*) Itemwise cost of production and total annual cost of production.
    (*e*) Itemwise annual sales turnover.
    (*f*) Total annual profit.
    (*g*) Total cash accruals.
16. Profitability and Break Even Point (BEP)
17. Project implementation schedule.
18. Repayment schedule as desired by promoter(s).
19. Internal rate of return.
20. Security offered.
21. Any other details.

PROJECT APPRAISAL

A final view on the proposal is taken which is based on combination of factors like technical, financial, commercial, managerial and operational. Weakness or deficiency in any project does not prepare a ground for its rejection but care is taken to initiate action to minimise its impact on the project. In order to overcome or minimise the deficiencies in a project, promoters are advised to revamp the project or take necessary precautions. Suitable conditions are stipulated to ensure that these suggestions are implemented.

Banks and financial institutions are required to examine the viability of a project before deciding whether to provide financial assistance or not. It is essential for a financial institution to ensure beforehand that the project will generate sufficient return on the resources invested. The surplus available from the project should be sufficient to pay interest on term loans and repay the principal amount within a reasonable period, depending upon the nature of the project. Moreover, highly capital intensive projects require higher repayment period vis-a-vis small and medium projects. The viability of a project depends on the technical feasibility, marketability of the products at a profitable price and management of the unit. Alongwith, the project should also be within the framework of natioal priorities based on social cost benefit analysis.

Objectives of Project Appraisal

Project appraisal is a tool for an ex-ante analysis of a designed scheme. It identifies and estimates the expected costs and benefits to a project. It is a conscious scrutiny which helps to design a conceptual framework that helps monitor and evaluate the actions.

Project appraisal undertaken by the financial institutions furnishes necessary information on the following aspects :

- The specific and predicted results of a project.
- The information necessary to determine the success or failure of a project.
- The standard yardsticks to be applied while determining the rate of success or failure of a project.

> We had to work our projections, and change our business plans several times. But we were still on the right track and gave our customers and stake holders the kins of commitment they looked for." Says Soota the CEO of Mind Tree councelling. *Financial Times, New Delhi 15 Oct., 2002*

Aspects of Project Appraisal

A comprehensive apprraisal of a project can be performed by covering the following perspectives :

- Technical appraisal
- Financial appraisal
- Economic appraisal
- Management appraisal
- Operational appraisal
- Organisation appraisal

It the proposal is prima facie satisfactory, the entrepreneur may be advised to submit the necessary information in the prescribed application form for detailed appraisal to be done by the bank. The appraisal of a small project may need less information as compared to larger projects. The task of the banks and financial institutions does not end with the proper appraisal and sanction of financial assistance. Prompt disbursement, close supervision and follow up is necessary during the project implementation and afterwards as well.

RESOURCING

The implementation statge comprises all spade work required to set up the business venture. This covers procurement of land, construction of building, erection of machinery, obtaining necessary licenses and registration of the enterprise etc.

To set up a business venture, particularly a manufacturing enterprise, an entrepreneur needs to develop a network of individuals/organisations who can help him in various stages of setting up an enterprise and running it. Typically, assistance may be sought from the following :

– Small Business Club

– Bankers

– Solicitors

– Suppliers

– Technical Consultants

– College/University Business Departments
– Resarch Laboratories
– Exhibitions, Trade Fairs .
– Chamber of Commerce
– Entrepreneurs' Association
– Trade Association
– Relatives/Friends
– Technical Training Institutes
– Small Business Dedvelopment Organisation

Categories of Resources

Resources may be further categorised as :

Physical Resources – premises, supplies of raw materials, tools, equipments, machinery, etc.
Technical Resources – technical know-how, prototypes, designs, technical training, etc.
Financial Resources – funds needed for physical, technical facilities and inputs for the enterprise.
Human Resources – workers/managers.
Marketing Resources – dealers, wholesellers, stockists, agents, salesmen, marketing organisations, etc.

Before tapping any of the resources, it is necessary to assess the requirements.

Ask yourself.

• Do I really need it?
• Can I get it now?
• Can I get it for nothing?
• What is the associated cost?
• Can I arrange it on hire?
• Can I obtain it on credit?
• Where can I buy it cheapest?

Resourcing Fund : Without money, no progress can be made. The start-up cash will include

• Fixed Capital
• Working Capital

Fixed Capital is the money required to buy premises, furniture and fixtures, machiney, tools, equipments and vehicles-assets that last long.

Working Capital is the money required to buy raw material and for turning it into finished goods for sale to customers—such sales may be on credit basis.

Fixed capital and working capital give the total start-up funds required and can be raised as

– Equity (including own funds)
– Loan
– Risk Capital
– Grants

Men and Material Resourcing – A lot of resourcing is needed to organise appropriate work-force at a work place. Determine the organisational chart for managing various critical areas. Such critical areas are :

– The whole business (seeing how various areas are managed)
– Purchases and supplies
– Manufacturing
– Inventory
– Marketing and sales
– Accounting and finance
– Personnel

- Legal aspects
- Public relations

Also decide the firm's constitution regarding :

- Proprietorship
- Partnership
- Company (public or private)
- Cooperative society

Resourcing for Premises : Look out for a location that suits your business requirement. The space should be sufficient to take care of today's and tomorrow's requirements. Probably you need reprographic equipment, telephone, specialised machiney and services. Are you going to own them? Or else, arrange easy access to each of your requirements?

SUMMARY

Scanning of environment refers to the understanding of socio-culture, economic, technological, fashion and even the charging life style and aspirations of local people. The task of project report preparation encompasses information under various heads. Necessary documents, quotations and enquiry should be attached with the details under given heads to from a project report. It may not be out of place to emphasise that the project report should be prepared by the entrepreneur himself.

A final view on the proposal is taken which is based on combination of factors like technical, commercial managerial and operational. Weakness or deficieny in any project does not prepare a ground for its rejection but care is taken to initiate suitable action to minimis its impact on the project. Banks and financial institutions required to examine the viability of a project before deciding to provide financial assistance.

REVIEW QUESTIONS

1. Describe the various steps to be taken by an entrepreneur to start a new venture.
2. Outline the guidelines to be followed while preparing a project report.
3. What are the main contents of a project report?
4. Discuss the licensing and other legal formalities to be completed before starting a new venture.
5. State the different stages in the registration of a company.

Annexure : 8.1

FORMAT OF FEASIBILITY REPORT

Ministry of Industry
Small Industries Service Institute
Okhla, New Delhi-110020

I. The Enterprises and The Enterpreneurs

Project Report for the nanufacture of

(*i*) Name of the Item/Items____________________________________

(*ii*) Name of the Unit and Address________________________________

(*iii*) Telephone No., Office ________________ Factory__________________

(*iv*) Name(s) and Address of the
Promoteres in (Block Letter)__________________________________

____

(*v*) Constitution of the Firm : ___________________________________
(Proprietory/Partnership)/____________________________________
Pvt. Ltd., Coop. Society_____________________________________

(*vi*) Qualification both Academic/Professional of the Enterpreneur(s)
Name ____
Qualification____

(*vii*) Production/working experience of the entrepreneur(s)
Name of the Organisation ____________________________________
Items Manufactured_______________________________________
Period____

(*viii*) Family background (please give details of your close relations who are in industry and business)
Name and Address of the unit, items manufactured____________________

____

____

(*ix*) Location / Proposed Location__________________________________

(*x*) Name and Address of the Bank with which you want to deal with____________

____

II. Economic Viability and Marketability

(*i*) Introduction____
(Basic and Presumption)______________________________________

(*ii*) Scope____

(*iii*) Marketability (please give proposed selling arrangements and list of places where the product will be mainly sold and likely buyers)

III. Technical Feasibility

(*i*) Manufacturing Process (please give process flow chart).

(*ii*) Please indicate the processes which will be got done from outside.

(*iii*) Specifications (whether proposed to adopt ISI specifications or some other)

(*iv*) Components to be purchased from outside.

Name of The Component	No.	Specifications
(*v*) Installed capacity	Qty. ______________	Value________________
(*vi*) Proposed Capacity to be utilise.	Qty. ______________	Value________________

(*vii*). Motive Power requirements (HP) Approx.

IV. Financial Projections

A Fixed Capital

(*i*) (a) Land, Area and Value

(b) Building area, value owned / rented or leased

(c) Please mentioned if some arrangements have been made in this respect. (please append the proposed layout plan)

(*ii*) Machinery and Equipment

S.No.	Description and Specification	Indigenous/ imported	Qty.	Price	Sale Tax	Int.	Total	Name and Address of supplier
1	2	3	4	5	6	7	8	9

(*iii*) Testing Equiupment (with details as above).

(*iv*) Electrification and Installation Charges.

(*v*) Cost of Tools Jigs/Fixtures/Mould/Working tables etc.

(*vi*) Cost of office equipments.

(*viii*) Pre-operative expenses (cost of project preparation, technical know-how expenses royalties' etc.)

(*viii*) Total non-recurring expenditure

(B)Working Capital (per month)

I.

Staff & Labour	Designation	No.	Salary	Total
Technical				
Office				
Sales				
Others				
Salaries P.M.				
(Technical + Office + Sales + Others)				
Prequities (2020 to 25% of Salaries)				
Total Salaries				

(*ii*) Raw Materials (per month including packaging materials)

Name with specifications	Indigenous/Imported	Qty.	Rate	Total

(*iii*) Other items of expenditure

(per month basis)

(a) Utilities

Power.........KWH unit @........... per unit cost, Rs. ....

Fuel (coal/furnance oil........ tonnes @ .... per tonne Rs. ....

Water .... kilo litres .... per KL .... Rs. ....

Total Cost of Utilities...........................

(b) Advertisement and publicity.

(c) Transport

(d) Commission to distributors / agents.

(e) Consumable stores.

(f) Rent
(if any where cost of land and building is not given)
(g) Taxes (other than income tax)
(h) Insurance.
(i) Stationery.
(j) Postage, telephone etc.
(k) Repair and maintenance.
(l) Sales expenses.
(m) Other miscellaneous expenses (not given above).
Total overhead (a + b + c + d + e + f + g + h + i + j + k + l + m)

(*iv*) Total recurring expenditure (per month)
(i + ii + iii)
Working capital for two/three months
(depend upon need or worked out on the
bank system of assessment of working capital needs).
2/3 × recurring expenditure.

B. Total Investment

(*i*) Fixed Capital
(*ii*) Working Capital

Total ___________________

____

C. Cost of Production (per year)

(*i*). Total recurring expenditure (per year)
(*ii*). Depreciation on building
(*iii*). Depreciation on machinery and equipment
(*iv*). Depreciation on fixtures/jigs/tools/moulds
(*v*). Depreciation on office equipment
(*vi*). Depreciation on furnances
(*vii*). Interest on total investment

Annexure : 8.2

A Sample of Feasibility Report
Juicer Mixer Grinder (Electric)

INTRODUCTION

Electric Juicer Mixer Grinder and Food Processor and Motor Driven appliance, which have come to stay not only with Uraban housewifes but also among Rural working class.

The mass electrification programs of our rural areas and village are the basic reason for the outstanding popularity, these wounderful household gadgets have attained in recent years.

It is indeed an indispensable collection in setting a modern kithchen especially for working housewifes

Since it is electrically operated consumer durable item. Utmost care has to be exercised to provide 100% safe operating system to customers.

An effective after sale service plays a vital role in making a brand more popular.

Electric motor driven appliances used for processing/cooking food, can perform functions like :

- Mixing
- Wet and Dry Grinding
- Whipping
- Blending
- Liquidising
- Kneeding
- Mincing
- Juice Extraction

It has become an indispensable gadget for an urban housewife and specially for working women. As it is a consumer durable item it should be very safe in operation, must be very efficient, should give trouble free services.

Good after sales services plays a vital role in product differentiation and hence improving the brand image of the product.

Basis and Presumption

It is not feasible to manufacture all the items in the unit itself. Especially such items, which require sophisticated technology, such as for manufacturing universal high speed motor having low size, output ratio.

Hence, it would be procured from reputed manufacturer of such motors, similarly the injection molded plastic items, aluminum die casting, rubber items and hard wares will be bought out or sub-contracted.

The blade sets, its heat treatment and gear cutting are also to be given on sub-contract.

The cost of producing these facilities in-house will be a very costly affair, besides dies and moulds for these items would cost a huge amount. Therefore, for the start of the project only those parts whose design and dies that are easily available in the market and do not require any fundamental change in the design will be manufactured.

Product Description

Product Model	:	"Kitchen's Pride" Juicer Mixer Crinder
Power Consumption	:	400 W (Full Load)
Voltage	:	240 V AC 50 Hz
Motor Type	:	Universal 400 W
Rating	:	30 Minutes
Basic Unit	:	High Quality ABS plastic
Flex Cord plug	:	PVC Approx. 2 mtrs, long, with 5A3-pin
Juicer Body / Spout	:	High quality ABS plastic
Juicer Top Cover	:	SAN plastic
Filter Mesh	:	Dynamically balanced electric from Nickel mesh moulded in ABS plastic
Locks	:	CRCA Sheet-Power coated.
Blender/Mixer Jar	:	Stainless Steel Polished
Material of Dome	:	Polycarbonate
Grinding Cap	:	Polypropylene
Blades	:	Hardened stainless steel, polished
Speed Control	:	5 speed with rotary type switch + 1 inching speed
Capacity	:	Dry Grinding—200 to 300 gms Liquidise/mix 0.5 to 1 ltrs
Net Weight	:	5.2 kgs
Carton	:	49 cm × 24 cm × 31 cm
Overload Protection	:	Hand reset type overload protector (Located under the body)
Safety Switches	:	Mocro switches provided on both Blender/ grinder and food processing sides to prevent accident during use.

Market Demand

The product, which is chosen by me, is Juicer, Mixer and Grinder.

The product has witnessed the following demand by volume :

Year	No. in Millions
1993	1.53
1994	1.68
1995	1.75
1996	1.87
1997	2.07
1998	2.10
1999	2.25

The Mechanics of Market

- Consumption, net income, differentiates consumer setments.
- A six million strong super rich class has emerged at the top.
- The amorphous middle class comprises 3 different setments.
- Upto 90 million households are buying non-durable.
- Comfort and personal choice are the two most important priorities.

Demographic Distribution

- The number of high income household is growing rapidly.
- The proportion of lower middle income earners has stabilized.
- The top three income brackets accounts for a sixth of the population.
- The high income group is growing fastest in the north and the south.
- The high income households are growing much faster in rural India.
- High income earners are growing much faster in mini metros.

Demographic Distribution

- The expansion of the rural market has started gaining.
- The number of household of the low-income groups is rising.
- Rural and Urban share of purchases of watches and TV is higher.
- Rural and Urban shares of purchases of many consumable are equal.
- Urbanisation is creating rural demand for urban products.
- Slow pase of rural electrification is choking the rural demand

The Purchasing Patterns

- Ownership of portable radios has troubled between 1986 and 1994.
- Penetration rates for the most products remain flat despite higher ownership.
- The rural share of purchases of toiletries has risen sharply.
- Purchases of Rs. 6000 plus products have grown by 25% in one year.
- Low income households are buying more of low priced variants.
- Functional products are the least price sensitive products.

The Rise of the Rich

- The undeclared incomes make many households richer.
- Between 6,00,000 to one millions household earn more than Rs. 10 lakh per annum.
- Between 88,000 and 1,39,000 rural households earn over Rs. 10 lakh p.a.
- Between 4,24,000 and 4,89,000 urban homes earn over Rs. 10 lakh p.a.
- Consumer for the highest priced product numbers 3.36 million.
- Almost 6.8 million to 16.2 million household earn Rs. 1 lakh to Rs. 5 lakh p.a.

Definition as per 1991 Census

Urban Areas

They include all places with a municipality/corporation and cantonment board or a notified town area, and all other places satisfying following criteria :

- A minimum population of 5000.
- At least 75% of male workforce has no agricultural pursuits.
- A population density of over 400 per square km.

Household

It is defined as a person or a group of persons, related by blood, marriage or adoption, sharing the same kitchen. Servants and related members are treated as members of households if they eat from the common kitchen.

Income Groups

Household has been classified into 5 income groups on the basis of total annual household income for 1993-94 at 1993-94 prices.

- Low : Up to Rs. 20,000
- Lower Middle : Rs. 20,001 — Rs. 40,000
- Middle : Rs. 40,001 — Rs. 62,000
- Upper-middle Rs. 62,00 — Rs. 86,000
- High : Above Rs. 86,000.

Penetration Rate :

For consumer durable penetration is defined as ownership of a product per thousand households with reference to purchases. For consumer expendable as the number of households purchasing the product per thousand households.

Pricing Strategy

Price Objective :

- To have stable profit
- To meet competition

The company will follow the strategy, whose the sales price is an independent variable, is not result of cost calculation, but is a value given by the customers.

The competitors in the organized sector are :

Name of Competitor	Rate per Unit	No. of Unit per Year	Production Base
1. Sumeet	3200	3.0 Lakh	Mumbai
2. Gopi	2300	2.5 Lakh	Jalandhar
3. Maharaja	2600	2.0 Lakh	Delhi
4. Philips	2800	2.0 Lakh	Mumbai
5. Lexus	2775	1.5 Lakh	Delhi

The company expects a net sales realisation of Rs. 2000 per unit.

Distribution Channels

The firm has chosen direct marketing channel by selecting an agency that specialises in similar products. The agency has expertise in making goods widely available and accessible to target markets.

Marketing intermediary, through its contacts, experience, specialisation and scale of operation will offer the firm more than it is likely to achieve on its own.

Technology Selection

Manufacturing Precess :

Manufacturing process of Electric Juicer Mixer Grinder include manufacture of following items, asseemble and testing. The parts to be manufactured are :

1. Shafts and other bar components.
2. Machining of die cast components.

Shafts and other bar components are Manufactured from stainless steel bar with help of precision automatic lathes, grinding machines etc. Die cast items such as housing for gearbox and cover are obtained from outside parties and finished in the unit. The major machining operations are turning, drilling of shaft, tapping the cover holes etc. Gear hub blanker are turned in the unit and are sent outside for gear cutting and hear treatment.

Quality Specification :

Product shall conform to BIS series standards. Routine and acceptance tests are to be done in the unit premises itself. Type test will have to be carried out on 5 samples of mixer from the production line at random. Sample testing will be done at the Regional Testing Center.

Process of Manufacturing Mixie Body

The major operations are as follows :

Turning

Turning of mixie body, that it takes the desired shape as per the design of different models.

Drilling :

Holes are drilled on the body to fix

- rest pads
- rest plates
- silver switch
- handles

Rest Pad Fitment :

Rest pad fitment is done for creating a space between lower sockets and mixie body.

This rest pads are fitted for longer life of lower socket and mixie body so that they don't wear out easily. When the mixie operates, it creates a cutting action between the plastic surfaces and the rubber pad prevents the direct impact

It is also fitted to help in proper fitment of lower socket to the body of the mixie.

Metal cap Fitment :

Metal cap fitment is done for the positive locking of jars. A person need not stand by the mixie while it is operation.

Rest Plate Fitment :

Rest plate is fitted to improve the appearance and also to provide a base for holding something like glass or bowls.

Handle Fitment :

A handle fitment is provided for carrying the mixie body, from one plance to another so that it is easy for housewives to carry this product. Hence, it acts a USP of this product as no other mixer grinder provides handles to carry it from one place to another. Normally a mixie is lifted from its base in this case handle will be used for holding it.

Silver Switch Sleeve :

A silver switch sleeve is provided in the mixie to prevent the spill over which usually occurs in house due to carelessness on the part of the housewives. This will ensure that mishapps will not occur if child is trying to play with this gadget while the gadget is on.

Incher Switch :

The product also has the provision for the incher type of switch which helps in providing the whipping action to the blade and hence useful in making froth for lassi, milkshakes etc.

Terminal Block :

Thimbles are used for proper locking of connection between motors and switches. It is a USP of the product. This will help in keeping the connecting wires intact inspite of vibrations.

Motor Mounting Gromet : Motor mounting gromet is press fitted to absorb the vibrations.

Main Switch Assembly :

A diode is used for reducing the wattage of motor thus generating 5 speeds from a 3 speed motor.

Cord :

Cord of 1.8 m is soldered to the terminals.

Flow Chart of Assembly Line

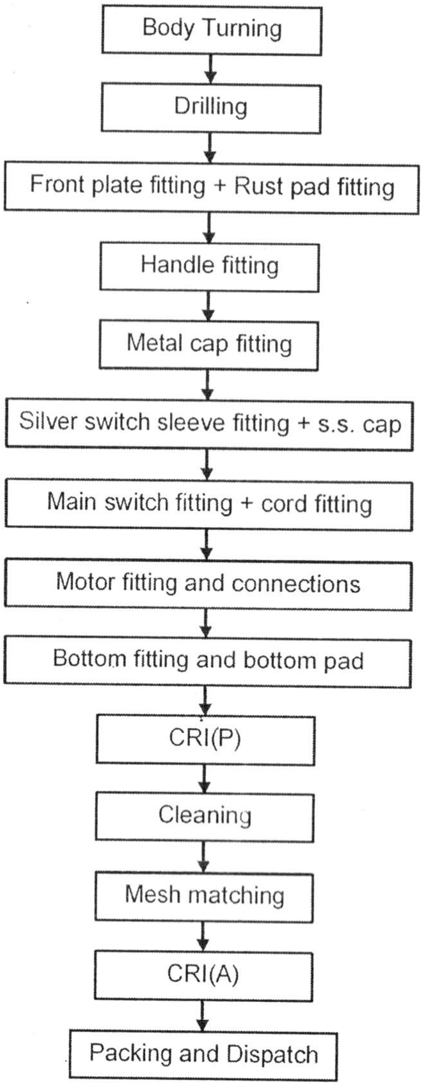

Fig.

Land Location and Site Selection

The site Okhla Industrial Area in Delhi has been selected because of the following reasons :

1. Easy availabilty of raw material.
2. Availability of skilled labour.
3. Availability of labour from nearby locations.
4. Transportation network is strong.
5. 85% of the suppliers are located nearby.
6. Strong infrastructure.
7. Site in any other area outside Delhi incurs a 4% CST.
8. Nearness to the market.

Layout Plan

A layout plan was prepared by the industrial engineer. The shed area is 20% more than the area required by the layout plan prepared. This is considered sufficient for future expansion

Cost of Projects :

Particulars	Amount (Rs. in MIllion)
Land and Site Development	9.6
Building and Civil Works	2.0
Plant and Machinery	2.0
Other Fixed Assets	0.5
Preliminary Expenses	0.1
Preoperative Expenses	0.2.
Contingency	0.2
Working Capital Margin	1.4
Total	**16.0**

Capacity Utilisation and Income Estimate

Desdcription	1 yrs	2 yrs	3 yrs	4 yrs	5 yrs
Installed capacity (units)	50.00	50.00	50.00	50.00	50.00
Capacity utilisation (%)	50.00	60.00	70.00	70.00	70.00
Production p.a, (units)	25.00	30.00	35.00	35.00	35.00
Net sales realisation Rs. @ Rs. 2000/- unit	50000	60000	70000	70000	70000

Working Capital Requirements

ITEM	Norm in months	1 yr.	2 yr.	3 yr.
1. Raw Material	1	2.33	2.80	3.27
2. Stock-in-progress	0.05	1.17	1.40	1.63
3. Finished Goods	0.05	1.46	1.75	2.04
4. Book Debts	1	4.17	5.00	5.83
Total Current Assets		9.13	10.95	12.77
Less : Margin for Working capital (25% of total current assets)		1.40	2.74	3.19
Less : Trade credit for Raw material		1.17	1.40	1.63
Bank finance for working		6.56	6.81	7.95
capital Interest @ 16%		1.05	1.09	1.27

Interest on Term Loan

(Rs. in Millions)

Year	Loan o/s at the beginning	Loan o/s at the end of the first half of year	Loan o/s at the end of the year	Int., for the first half of year	Int., for the second half of year	Total annual interest for the term loan
1.	12	12	12	0.9	0.9	1.8
2.	12	12	11.92	0.9	0.894	1.79
3.	11.92	11.84	11.76	0.89	0.88	1.77
4.	11.76	11.68	11.60	0.88	0.87	1.75
5.	11.50	11.52	11.44	0.86	0.85	1.71

Depreciation Schedule :

(Rs. in Million)

1. Depreciation Schedule for company law purpose (straight line method)

Building @ 4%	:	0.08
Plant and Machinery @ 8%	:	0.16
Misc. Fixed Assets @ 5%)	:	0.025
Annual Depreciation	:	0.265

2. Depreciation schedule for income tax purpose (written down value method)

Year	1	2	3	4	5
Building (10%)	0.02	0.18	0.16	0.15	0.13
Plant and machinery and misc fixed assets (30%)	0.75	0.53	0.37	0.26	0.18
Total	**0.77**	**0.71**	**0.53**	**0.41**	**0.31**

Profitability Estimates : (Rs. in Million)

Particulars	1 Year	2 Year	3 Year	4 Year	5 Year
Installed Capacity	50000	50000	50000	50000	50000
Production	25000	30000	35000	35000	35000
Capacity Utilisation (%)	50	60	70	70	70
A. Sales realisation	50	60	70	70	70
B. Cost of Production					
• Raw Material	28.0	33.6	39.2	39.2	39.2
• Power	2.0	2.4	2.8	2.8	2.8
• Wages and Salaries	4.0	4.8	5.6	6.4	6.8
• Factory Overheads	1.0	1.2	1.4	1.4	1.4
C. Administration and Selling Expenses	4.0	4.8	5.6	5.6	5.6
D. Gross Profit Before Interest	11.0	13.2	15.4	14.6	14.2
E. Total Financial Expenses					
• Interest on term loan	1.8	1.79	1.77	1.75	1.71
• Interest on bank borrowing	1.05	1.09	1.27	1.27	1.27
F. Depreciation	0.265	0.265	0.265	0.265	0.265
G. Operating Profit	7.88	10.15	12.09	11.31	10.95
H. Preliminary Expenses Written of off	0.01	0.01	0.01	0.01	0.01
I. Profit / Loss Before Tax	7.87	10.14	12.08	11.30	10.94
J. Provision for Tax	3.314	4.365	5.125	6.187	6.057
K. Profit after Tax	4.556	5.675	6.955	5.113	4.883

Project Balance Sheet : (Rs. in Million)

Liabilities	1 Year	2 Year	3 Year	4 Year	5 Year
• **Reserve and Surplus**	4.56	10.24	14.56	20.28	25.39
Secured Loans					
Term loan	12	11.92	11.76	11.67	11.44
Working capital adv.	6.56	6.83	7.95	7.95	7.95
• **Current Liabilities**					
Trade credit	1.17	1.51	1.63	1.63	1.63
Total	**24.29**	**30.37**	**38.83**	**41.46**	**46.41**

Assets :	1 Year	2 Year	3 Year	4 Year	5 Year
Fixed Assets					
Gross block	14.50	14.50	14.50	14.50	14.50
Less : Accumulated depreciation	0.26	0.53	0.80	1.06	1.33
Net Fixed Assets	14.24	13.97	13.70	13.44	13.17
• Current Assets, loans and Advances					
Raw Material	2.34	2.8	3.27	3.27	3.27
Stock-in-Progress	1.17	1.4	1.63	1.63	1.63
Finished Goods	1.46	1.75	2.04	2.04	2.04
Book Debta	4.17	5.00	5.83	5.83	5.83
Cash and Bank Balance	1.40	4.83	9.36	15.99	21.22
• Preliminary Expenses	0.09	0.08	0.07	0.06	0.05
Total	**24.29**	**29.83**	**38.90**	**41.46**	**46.41**

Tax Calculations : **(Rs. in Million)**

Particulars	1 Year	2 Year	3 Year	4 Year	5 Year
Profit/loss before depreciation	7.87	10.15	12.09	11.31	10.95
Add : Dep. for com. law purpose	0.265	0.265	0.265	0.265	0.265
	8.135	10.41	12.35	11.57	11.21
Less : Dep for tax purpose	0.77	0.71	0.53	0.41	0.31
Gross Income	7.365	9.70	11.72	11.16	10.90
Income tax @ 45%	3.314	4.365	5.27	5.022	4.905
Income after Tax	4.050	5.335	6.45	6.138	5.995

Projected Fund Flow Statement : (Rs. in Million)

Particulars	1 Year	2 Year	3 Year	4 Year	5 Year
Sources of Funds					
• Profit before taxation With interest added back	10.72	13.02	15.12	14.32	13.92
• Depreciation	0.265	0.265	0.265	0.265	0.265
• Preliminary Expenses	0.01	0.01	0.01	0.01	0.01
• Increase in bank (wc) borrowing	6.56	.25	1.14	–	–
Total (A)	**17.53**	**13.55**	**16.54**	**14.60**	**14.20**

Particulars	1 Year	2 Year	3 Year	4 Year	5 Year
Disposition of Funds					
• Increase in working capital	7.96	1.59	1.59	–	–
• Decreased in term loan	–	.08	0.16	.01	6.16
• Interest on term loans	1.8	1.79	1.77	1.27	1.27
• Interest on bank (wc) borrowing	1.05	1.09	1.27	1.27	1.27
Taxation	3.31	4.37	5.12	6.19	6.06
Total (B)	**14.12**	**8.92**	**9.91**	**9.37**	**9.20**
Opening Balance of	1.40	4.83	9.36	15.99	21.22
Cash-in-Hand / Bank	–	–	–	–	–
Net Surplus / Deficit (A – B)	3.43	4.53	6.63	5.23	5.00
Closing/Balance of Cash-in-Hand/Bank	**4.83**	**9.36**	**15.99**	**21.22**	**26.22**

Limitations

The time limit available for conducting the study was limited, therefore only selective sources of information could be exploited.

The study is based on certain assumptions. However, an attempt has been made to keep the assumptions as realistic as possible. The case relates to year 2001.

CASE 8.1

SUBHASH CHANDRA OF ZEE TV

Subhash Chandra is the first self-made media billionaire. He has thus made a mark, as today Zee is a household name not just in India and Asia but also across large swatches of the Non-Resident Indians (NRIs) population in the U.K., U.S.A., South Africa, with more than 200 million viewers.

He has reached the position, starting from scratch. Starting the life as a rice trader in Hissar, he went into packaging because of the shortage problem caused by the bumper harvest of the early 1970s. He acquired a lamination plant and began making laminated covers for Food Corporation of India under the name Essel Packaging Ltd. Later Essel packaging went into laminated tubes. The trading business brought in a lot money which Chandra invested in land. Essel World, the amusement park, was outcome of his efforts to find a use for the land.

Then the Iraq-Kuwait war broke out and it was telecast live by CNN, Chandra wondered whether it would be possible to have such a channel in India. Zee was a natural corollary. He saw the opportunity in brodacasting created by satellite technology which allowed signals to be uplinked from outside India, bounced off a geo-stationary satellite almost 36,500 kms. up in space and then received by an inexpensive dish antenna all over India. First slowly and then rapidly Zee's programmes drew viewers away from the government-run Doordarshan. Advertisers quickly followed. Soon Zee became one of the most powerful brands all over India.

But Chandra is not the one to sit happy after winning laurels. Today, he has not only taken open the competitors successfully, but, thanks to his vision and foresight, created a global Zee network consisting of programme /software supply companies, broadcasting companies, world-wide multi-media companies and distribution companies. His fingers firmly on the pulse of the Government, viewer's tastes, competitors and emerging technology, he has been quick to come out with befitting reply, with his yearning for combat still in tact.

QUESTIONS

(*i*) Explain how good Subhash Chandra has been successful in identifying business opportunities as an entrepreneur.

(*ii*) A mention has been made about the vision and foresight of Subhash Chandra. Discuss the importance of these qualities for an entrepreneur.

Enterpreneurial Development, MBA, Pune University, Dec. 1999.

CHAPTER

9

FRANCHISING

CHAPTER OUTLINE

— The Attraction of Franchise
— Franchise Relationships
— Master Franchise
— Selecting A Franchise

Entrepreneurship is more often described in terms of setting a new venture, not buying an existing one. These days buying into a business is probably just as common as starting a new one. Many people rather buy out a ready-made business than take pains to setup their enterprise from a scratch. Over the past few years buying into the business through franchise contract is becoming more and more popular.

As the service economy grow in India the opportunities for franchising are going to be multiplied. As per a study by Anderson Consulting, franchising in India accounts for 4 per cent of the nations gross domestic product. In US the global franchise economy accounts for 17 per cent of the world's business. A look at the growing number of franchise in different sectors like Healthcare, Food, Entertainment, Education etc., indicates that franchise economy has arrived in India.

While traditional franchise business such as petrol, auto dealers and soft drink bottlers continue to grow in India, the most rapid expanding industries for franchise are service business involving education, training, recreation and leisure activities. It could be a catalyst to give a forward push to entrepreneurship.

In franchising the entrepreneurs play a role both as franchiser as well as a franchisee. The franchiser creates a business concept and its replica are sold to others. The franchise is also an entrepreneur who buys a venture which is a part of a chain of similar business units. The entrepreneurs have a major role in developing as well as buying the franchises.

"Franchising" is the transfer of rights to sell a trade marked product or service through a system prescribed by a "franchisor" who owns the trademark.

"A Maruti franchisee has a contract with the Maruti Udhyog Ltd., the manufacturer of Maruti cars, to serve as its representative. The dealer sells only Maruti cars and provides necessary maintenance and repair service to Maruti cars."

The word franchising comes from the French word "*franchir*" which means "to free". It originally meant "to free from slavery". Today franchise is an agreement between a buyer and a seller. This agreement permits the franchisee, i.e., the buyer to sell the product / service of the franchiser, i.e., the seller. The *International Franchise Association defines franchise as a continuing relationship between the franchiser and the franchisee in which the sum total of franchiser's knowledge, image, success, manufacturing and marketing techniques are supplied to the franchisee for a consideration.*

THE ATTRACTION OF FRANCHISE

Since franchise is a ready made business available to an entrepreneur, it is an attractive proposition as compared to setting up an enterprise from the start. The franchisee gets a semi established business from the day one. The business is akin to the other enterprises of an established chain. The franchiser is required to provide the franchisee with all the assistance in starting and establishing the venture.

Normally the franchiser is expected to assist the franchisee in :

1. Advertising and providing a strategy for marketing
2. Training the manpower
3. Selection of the equipment
4. Office design, layout etc.
5. Standardised policy and procedures
6. Assistance in site selection and logistics
7. Assistance on legal matters.

In addition to the professional help, the franchisee also get lot of intangible benefits. Like all other things the franchise also has some disadvantages as they lack independence, individual identity, and have continuous obligation that is difficult of cancel. Franchises normally combine personal ownership with the systems of big business.

Franchising is also advantageous to the franchiser who grows rapidly using other peoples money. It helps him in expanding the business geographically into various location including the remote one. He can manage with less number of people and hence is saved of many a labour related problems. Franchisee being independent owner of various chain stores are more committed and work longer hours than managers.

Besides other benefits discussed above franchising provides an entrepreneur the ability to penetrate the market rapidly with limited finances. Even larger companies are being attracted to franchising, thus, making franchise a mere lucrative business for the franchisee. Franchise is becoming popular as it is regarded as a promise of instant success and is considered to be least risky way to become an entrepreneur. However with the mushrooming of franchising these benefits are limited to franchisee of a few reputed franchisers.

Yet, franchising has it own risks. When a large franchiser folds up, the effects on the rest of the network can be crippling. A few years ago an apparel company 'Stencil' had to close shop. Well over 100 franchisee found themselves out of business overnight. The same was the fate of Mothercare franchisees when it pulled the stutters. The franchise relationship is an unequal one. A franchiser gets to call the shots. In US the law of franchise protects the interest of the franchisee while in India there is no law regulating franchising business and buyers of the franchise have the be extra cautious.

As per a study in USA, of the retailers who were in business in 1987, 45 per cent of young franchised retailers had failed by 1991 as against 23 per cent young independent retailers. A good number of established entrepreneurs are still shying away from franchising. The perception is that franchising adversely affects the quality of service. They are afraid of negative effect on their business because of inability on the part of some of the franchisee to maintain the quality standards. VLCC a fourteen crore chain of personal grooming and fitness clinics, appointed franchisees eight years ago. Realising that their business was about people's health and well being, they were not very comfortable with the standards maintained by their franchisee. VLCC opted out of franchising to setup joint ventures with interested partners, keeping 60 per cent stake and the management control in their hands.

The other hurdle for the franchiser is that few entrepreneurs are willing to take on a new franchise without a guaranteed amount of sales. Minimum sales guarantee means that if the franchisee is unable to reach the anticipated sales level, the franchiser will compensate him for the balance amount. Some people feel that in our economy it is still a case of too many franchisers chasing a few potential franchisee. The scenario is yet to change as the franchising industry matures.

Another factor which restricts the franchising is that mostly the franchisee who are small businessmen, are unwilling/unable to grow with the franchiser. This puts a break on the pace of growth of the franchiser. 'Archies' have realised the need for up grading the quality of their outlets in line with changing customer needs. The franchisee are required to invest more in upgradation. The franchiser is facing serious resistance from its 400 franchisees.

FRANCHISE RELATIONSHIPS

The most common franchise relationship is between a retailer and a manufacturer or sometime a wholesaler, e.g., Car showrooms, Bata and Liberty shoes showrooms, Haldiram franchise etc. In India manufacturer-manufacturer franchise relationship is the oldest. Here one manufacturer produces goods for the other under licence. A large number of items are reserved for manufacture in SSI units. These franchise SSI units manufacturer the items as per the design, specifications and quality control of the franchiser. They use the logo and trademark of the franchiser who is responsible for sales and marketing

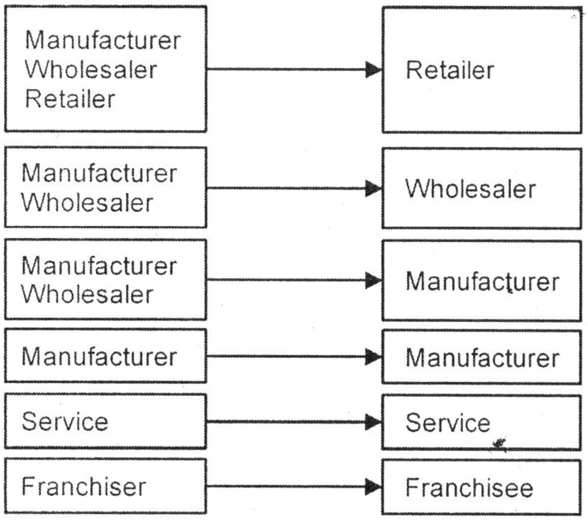

Fig. 9.1. Franchise Relationship

e.g., Singer Sewing Machines have three franchise manufactures in Ludhiana besides one in Hapur. Road Master Industries and Dewan Rubber are the franchise manufacturers of TI cycles for bicycle tyres and rims, Colgate and Hindustan unilever use franchisee for production of tooth brush as the item is reserved for manufacture in SSI sector. It also includes sub-contractor producing goods as per the design and technical specifications of the mother units, who provide them with all technical assistance.

Exclusive dealership is an example of manufacturer-wholesaler franchise relationship. The retail and service franchise are comparatively new relationships in India and differ widely from manufacturer-retail franchise system already prevalent in India. Retail-retail relationship tries to duplicate one retail outlet. It can vary from the Kwality chain of restaurants, wherein the franchisee have a lot of independence and pay a royalty for using the name, to Wimpy or Pizza King wherein all decisions including recuritment and training are reserved for the franchiser. Here the franchisee is an extension of the franchiser. Each franchise outlet clearly resembles that of the franchiser. It is akin to company outlets but with different owners and investors.

The franchise is like a marriage. The stakes are high on both sides. The franchiser gives up his precious asset, the brand and the franchisee forgoes his independence and right to operate alone. The implicit trust is the corner stone of the relationship between the franchisee and franchiser

Franchise arrangements are usually either :

(*i*) Product or trade name franchises, or

(*ii*) Business format franchises

The former involves product-distribution arrangement within a specialised geographic territory. For example, a petrol pump is a product and trademark franchise. A business format-franchise includes not only a product and trade name, but also operating procedures such as design facilities, accounting procedures and practices, employee relations, quality assurance standard, and over all image and appearance of business, e.g., restaurants, convenient stores are often a business franchise.

MASTER FRANCHISE

Franchising values uniformity and consistency. The entrepreneur is required to conform to the franchise agreement, this normally restricts the franchisee's growth. Depending upon the potential the location offers, the franchisee's growth potential gets limited. An enterprising owner often expands by purchasing franchise for additional territories or maturing in to a master franchise.

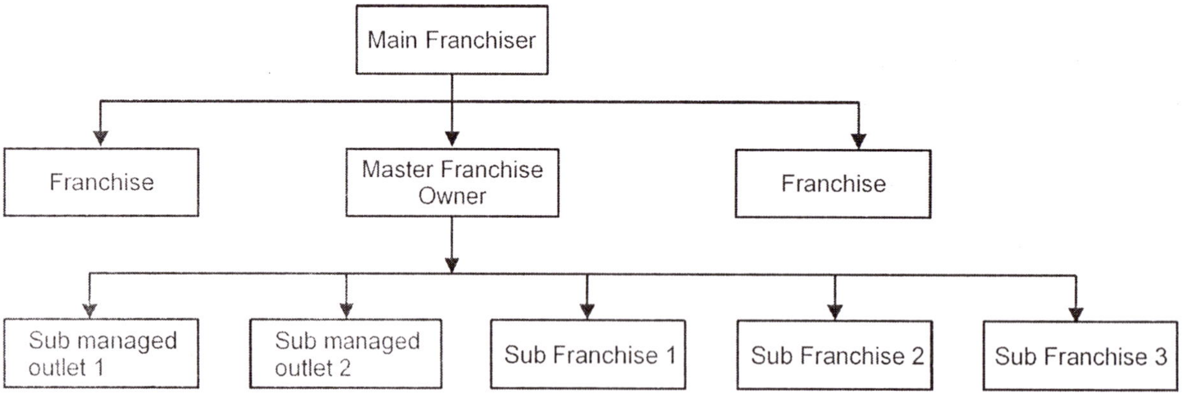

Fig. Franchise Structure Involving a Master Franchise

Franchise opportunities hand book (US Department of Commerce) defines a master franchise as a contract that allows an entrepreneur to establish multiple outlets within a given territory or geographic area. Herein the franchisee has the rights of a regional franchiser and can either open multiple outlets in the region or act as a sub franchiser who can contract independently and appoint franchisee for different locations in his territory.

Master franchisee are provided for several regions/countries. These master franchisee create regional management that takes into account the local requirements and diffuses distribution and decision-making control. Master franchisees are selected from well established entrepreneurs (often existing franchisee) who have the ability to manage growth and resources to expand rapidly.

SELECTING A FRANCHISE

Before an entrepreneur selects franchise he should ensure that he wants to be a franchisee rather than setting up his independent business from the scratch. He should seriously view the pros and cons of a franchisee vis-a-vis an independent business. He should also identify and define his skills and desires and ensure that these suit the requirements and role demands of a franchisee. After ascertaining the market potential for the same he should choose the product or the service he is interested in and search for a suitable franchiser. The information about the franchisers can be obtained from various business and trade journals or from an existing franchisee. As the franchise territories are normally protected, most franchise owners will be willing to give information about the business and the people to be contacted for obtaining a franchise.

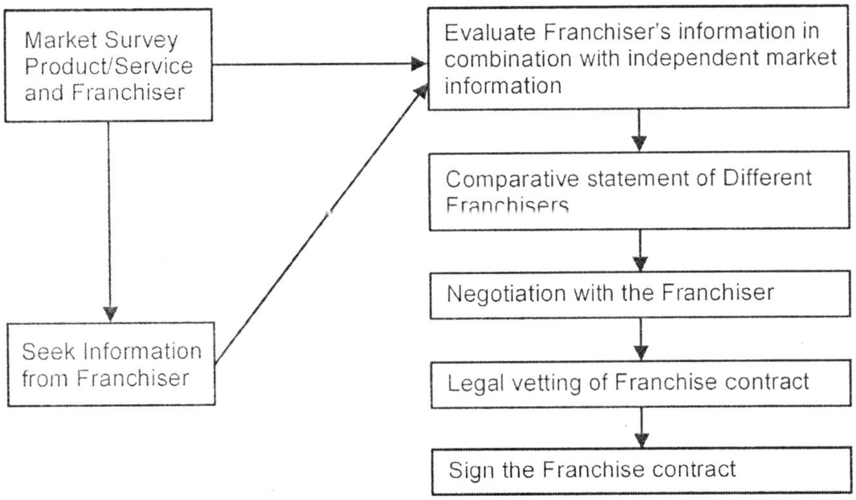

Fig. 9.3. Steps in Starting a Franchise.

On approaching, a franchiser, the prospective franchisee will have to prove his bonafides as well as abilities and seriousness to the franchiser. A franchiser normally prequalifies a prospective franchisee before proceeding further and provides the sensitive business information only after evaluating the prospective franchisee.

The franchisee then seeks from the franchiser information that is suitable and sufficient for a through evaluation of the business. As per US federal law every franchiser is required to provide its "Uniform Franchise Offering Circular (UFOC)", a disclosure statement to all prospective franchisees. This is to enable them to take an informed decision about the franchise. In India there is no law governing franchising. However, an entrepreneur contemplating to buy a franchise should ask for the information that would enable him to evaluate the prospects of the franchise he plans to buy.

Important Information an Entrepreneur Should Seek From a Franchiser

1. Financial statement of the franchiser for at least three previous years.
2. Information about the initial franchise fee and other payments including security deposits that may be payable.
3. An itemwise estimate of franchise's initial investment, i.e., opening inventory, working capital, fixed assets, real estate expense, furnishing, docor etc.
4. Royalities and profit sharing arrangements.
5. Audited performance data, e.g., sales volume, costs and profits.
6. A list of names and addresses of other franchisee.
7. Support services to be provided by the franchiser, i.e., training of staff, merchandising and advertising programmes, equipment purchase or lease options, on site constancy etc.
8. Detailed copies of all agreements including legally binding documents that the parties are required to sign.

The entrepreneurs proposing to buy a franchise should thoroughly study these documents and critically evaluate the franchiser. The information provided by the franchiser though essential for evaluation of the business proposal, yet is generally not sufficient for singing the contract. The entrepreneurs are advised to conduct their own market survey to satisfy themselves about the soundness of the business prospects. It is advised that where ever the entrepreneur has a choice to choose between two or more franchisers for similar product/service, the comparative data be studied and used for negotiations with the franchisers

Armed with all these evaluations the entrepreneurs negotiate with the franchiser. Many entrepreneurs prefer to handle activities like accounting, purchasing, training of employee, leasing etc., themselves. They may prefer to make the location decision jointly with the franchiser. However, the negotiations provide very little latittude for the decisions about facilities and unique designs. Some terms like franchise fees, royalty, inventory, brand management, use of patents, trademarks etc., are general not negotiable.

The final step before signing the franchise is to get the negotiated proposal vetted by a chartered accountant or an attorney experienced in due dilligence research. It is a standard practice with the franchisees in USA and is even more important in India where there is no law on disclosures by a franchiser or any other legislation governing any aspect of franchising. The lawyer should inform the entrepreneur about his legal rights before he signs the agreements which are normally prepared by the franchisers. All contractual agreements are based upon exercise of good faith and fair dealing by both parties. "It is the duty of each party to any franchise to act in a fair and equitable manner towards each other, so as to guarantee each party's freedom from coercion, intimidation, or threat of coercion".

A Caution

During negotiation of the franchise agreement the entrepreneur should consider and pay due attention to the following.

1. Total Investment in the Franchise :

An entrepreneur should estimate the total investment needed in setting up the franchise. He is required to estimate the hidden costs of franchise, e.g.,

- Lease deposits.
- Modifications and refurbishing of the real estate.
- Franchise fee which is payable up front for purchase of the franchise.
- Working capital, i.e., money needed to buy stocks pay salary and wages to employees.
- Funds to make lease payment.
- Fund to finance credit sales.
- Equipment and furnishing costs. Whether these costs are to be born by the franchisee or the franchiser will provide the same against regular payments to be made by the entrepreneur.
- Royalities as percentage of sales to be paid to the franchiser.

He should carefully prepare a feasibility report and calculate all the costs involved in buying and running a franchise. The entrepreneur has also to consider if the investment required is within his budget. He has to examine the assistance if any that the franchiser if to provide for raising the necessary financial resources.

Franchisers normally have a better clout with the banks and financial institutions. They can assist in negotiating a loan. Nationalised banks like State Bank of India and Canara Bank are providing debt finance to VLCC and Archie franchisees. ICICI Bank also extends loan to reputed franchisee if the franchiser agrees to be the guarantor. Some times the franchiser also assist by taking a minority stake in the equity of their franchisee.

2. Conditions and Cost of Pulling Out a Franchise Contract :

Entrepreneur should explicitly know what they may gain or lose if they decide to pull out of the franchise or if the franchiser opts to cancel the contract. He should understand the conditions under which the franchise contract can be cancelled. Such conditions normally include :

- Unability to meet the sales targets.
- Unability to meet the service standards set up by the franchiser.
- Misuse of patents, trademarks and name of the franchiser.
- Deficiency in providing the franchiser with reports, financial statements and documents as agreed.

3. Freedom to Sell Out the Franchise Before the Contract Runs Out :

An entrepreneur should explicitly negotiate about the right to sell or transfer his franchise, back to the franchiser or to any other person. The franchiser can protect his patents, trademarks and other uniquely developed services but should not deprive the franchise from selling and transferring his business.

He should also ascertain if he can sell the business at the market price or at the price to be determined by the franchiser. In case he sells the business at market price to the highest bidder, is he required to share the proceeds with the franchiser or not? In case the price is to be determined by the franchiser, the entrepreneur should know whether he will get the book value in full or not, also how the goodwill be evaluated and the proportion in which he would be required to share it with the franchiser.

4. Support Services Offered by the Franchise :

An entrepreneur should evaluate the support services provided by the different franchisers to choose the best. One of the crucial item of support is the type of training the franchiser provides. Some franchisers run special training programmes for the franchisee and their staff in their office, others arrange on the job training of new franchisee staff at one of the existing franchise while some send their team to the new franchisee for initial period (say a month) to train their staff. An entrepreneur should check if the franchiser has a regular training schedule to upgrade the skills of the franchisee's managers and workers.

Besides, the entrepreneur should evaluate the support he is likely to receive in building sales. New franchisers often guarantee a certain level of sales which means if a franchisee is unable to meet the anticipated sales level, he will be compensated for the balance amount.

SUMMARY

Franchising is also advantageous to the franchiser who grows rapidly using other peoples money. Franchisee being independent owners of various chain stores are more committed and work longer hours than managers. The most common franchisee relationship is between a retailer and a manufacturer or a wholesaler, wherein a retailer sells the product of a manufacturer or sometime a wholesaler.

The retail and service franchise are comparatively new relationship in India and differ widely from manufacturer-retail franchise system already prevalent in India. The franchise is like a marriage where the stakes are high on both sides. The franchiser gives up his precious asset, the brand and the franchisee forgoes his independence and right to operate alone. It is the implicit trust that is the corner stone of the relationship between the franchiser and franchisee.

Before an entrepreneur selects franchise, he should ensure that he wants to be a franchisee rather than setting up his independent business from the scratch.

REVIEW QUESTIONS

1. Define the concept of business franchise.
2. Franchisee is a smarter entrepreneur. Do you agree? Please explain.
3. How does a franchiser profits by enrolling the franchisee?
4. How would you evaluate a franchise option?
5. Explain what a franchisee can expect from buying into a franchise.
6. Franchising is a growing concept with varing franchise arrangements and multiple types of relationships between the franchiser and franchise. Explain with suitable examples.
7. Explain the concept of Master franchise and how it helps the entrepreneur in fullfilling their need for growth.
8. In the absence of any Law governing franchising in India what are the pitfalls of becoming a franchisee and what precautions you recommend to a potential franchisee.

ACTIVITIES

1. Visit a local franchise service business with a pre defined lists of questions about the requirements for owning a similar franchise. These should be used for discussion and comparison in class.

Annexure 9.1

DR. LAL'S PATH LABS

Business concept : national pathological grid
No. of labs planned : 10-15 every year
Company investments : Rs 2 crore
Frenchisee investments : minimum Rs. 50 lakh
Frenchisee's ROI : 25-30 per cent

Try getting a relatively complicated virus test in any non-metro town in India. Chances are you won't find a lab which can do it. That's because other than in metropolitan towns, such facilities are simply not available.

Now, that would seem like a great business opportunity-especially for Dr. Lal's Path Labs, Delhi oldest Pathological lab. But expanding the network is fraught with great risk. Even if one test-tube gets exchanged, there is every danger of getting a wrong diagnostic result. So, the question is : how do you expand without impairing the quality of service?

The key is the degree of control. Lal's national pathological grid—which is in the process of being rolled out in the near future—has found a way to do just that. Dr. Lal is appointing master franchisees in large towns. These will act as collection centres, where patients can walk in to deposit their samples. With the help of global management consultants Arthur Andersen, Lal has invested Rs. 2 crore in a diagnostic software. So, when a patient walk into one of his franchised collection say in Patna, the software generates a bar code which is affixed to the sample and also registers him at the Delhi read by the lab's computers. Then it is sent to the diagnostic machine where it is tested and revaildated. Following this, the data is transferred to Patna—all in less than 24 hours. A large franchise network allows Lal the necessary economies of scale to invest in expensive equipment to carry a battery of specialised tests, which are normally available in select hospitals.

To carry his business idea forward, Lal is enlisting in a the support of his community of pathologists. Dr. Praful Amin, a successful pathologist in Mumbai, is already a part of the pathological grid, and a partner. The way it works; Lal invites experienced doctors to be franchisees. They must have minimum turnover of Rs. 2 crore, and also Rs. 50 lakh to invest in the software. Once they sign on, Lal and the franchisee will together invest in an electronic network to pass on data. With the infrastructure in place, the franchisee then looks at expanding his network. For instance, Amin is talking to doctors with pathology labs in towns like Surat, Vadodara, Kolapur and Sholapur.

But would a successful doctor fancy himself as a mere franchisee? Lal realises the gravity of the issue. So, he envisages that two-three years down the line, most of his franchisees will be offered a stake in his company. "Once we have developed a good working relationship and got used to this kind of business operation, I expect most franchisees to own small stakes in the company". says Lal Once a pathologist evinces interest, Lal will carry out a due diligence of the franchisee's operations. The stake, he is offered, will depends on the kind of value he generates and service he provides.

Source : Business World, 28th Feb., 2000

CHAPTER

10

ENTREPRENEURIAL BUY-INS

CHAPTER OUTLINE

— Buy-out Selection
— Searching for Buy-Ins
— Evaluating the Existing Business
— Seller Motives
— Business Valuation
— Business Assets
— Operational Performance
— Business Environment
— Fixing the Price
— Assets Approach
— Earnings Approach
— Buying-in for Expansion

ENTREPRENEURIAL BUY-INS

Of late it has become a common practice by the entrepreneurs to buy-out a business as against setting up a new one from scratch. Corporate mergers and acquisitions were always there, these were associated with the buy-out of one corporate or a part of it by another established business corporation. As against this entrepreneurial buy-out means that a new or a budding entrepreneur buys out an existing, mostly a profit making business. This is purely an entrepreneurial decision and uses a specific set of tools leading to such a decision. The sound reasons are needed for an entrepreneur to buy-out an existing business. As entrepreneur should first define the kind of product/service that suits his temperament before he selects a buy-out.

BUY-OUT SELECTION

Before one embarks on selecting a suitable business for buying in, it is important to evolve a criteria for such selection. Normally five major issues are addressed while selecting the business.

1. **Special Product/Service :** The entrepreneur defines the business in terms of the business of auto part or an ethnic restaurant. This criteria is set up in line with the skill and temperment of the entrepreneur. Experience relevant to the proposed venture is often an asset. An automobile engineer may decide to buy a motor workshop as it helps him to use his skills. A marketing executive having experience in software merchandising may buy out a software developing business with the expectation to use his market knowledge for its growth. An aspiring software developer who has no experience is starting a new venture is likely to benefit by selecting a product / service suitable to his technical skills for buying in and thus avoiding pitfalls of creating a new enterprise.
2. **Available Financing :** It could be an important criteria for selecting a suitable business. The entrepreneur knows how much funds he can marshal as equity including his contribution as well as what he can collect from other sources, besides the debt he can arrange from the banks and financial institutions. On the other hand the capital expenditure of acquisition as well as the operating expenses are to be accounted for. The selection criteria, herein, means that total funds required for acquisition and successful operation should be well within the available budget of the entrepreneur.

   The cost of purchasing new assets in normally much higher then buying them as a part of a business. However, it is important to be vigilant about the usefulness and service ability of these assets when they are purchased as a part of the business.
3. **Ideal Sales Range :** Different businesses have different operational requirements. The managerial work increases with the range of sales, so also the potential profit and reward to the entrepreneur are a function of the turnover. Even the scope of expansion depends on the present sales. Most entrepreneurs have sufficient idea about the time and effort they would like to put in the business they may buy in. Besides their own vision about its growth, they have a clear perception about the profit and reward they might expect from the buy in. Hence, it is important to lay down a criteria about the turnover of the business one may be interested to buy in. A person looking for a business with a turnover of Rs. 1 crore per annum will neither be interested in small family restaurant with turnover of 30-40 lakhs per annum nor in a hotel with a turnover Rs. 5 to 6 crores. The ideal sales range should fit in the buyer expectations and availability of the finances with him.
4. **Location :** While selecting the proposed buy-ins, entrepreneurs normally have their personal preference for certain geographical locations. Most of them would like to limit their choice to the city/town where they live in or where they would like to settle down. On one hand this choice of location is governed by the business prospects, on the other, the location is also affected to a great deal by personal reasons, like its suitability to the family needs. Most of the up market areas in smaller towns are over crowded and it is difficult to find a suitable location to start up a new venture in these areas. Hence, buying-in is a easier route to set up the establishment at these places.
5. **Risk :** All buy-in's are subjected to two types of risks, i.e., Business risk and Personal risk. The entrepreneur should account for these risks. The business risks are a function of economic

conditions, market potential and management. Depending upon the pace of changes in environmental, some business are more risky than others. Further, the buyer often changes the business policy and operates the acquired business in a different manner. This increases the risk. The personal risk is associated with the changes in the management. The new entrepreneur take time to understand the nitty grilly of the business. Often this risk is reduced by insisting that the seller be present during the change-over phase till the new owner understands the business and settles down. Though laying down such criteria normally limit the selection process yet it is useful for the entrepreneur who is buying-in a business about which he has little experience.

SEARCHING FOR BUY-INS

After laying down the criteria for the business to be bought by an entrepreneur the logical next step is to search for the businesses available for sale that meet the buyers criteria. Normally the search can be done through one of the following two routes.

- Using business brokers, consultants.
- Through bankers, state financial corporation, venture capitalist or chartered accountants.

Business brokers and consultants are often engaged in making a match between the buyers and sellers of business ventures. Brokers engaged in this business maintain a list of prospective sellers and help the buyers locate the business that meet their criteria. They charge an upfront fee for introducing the interested parties and brokerage if the deal is struck.

Consultants normally provide added services like market information, financing arrangement, loan syndication etc. They also help the clients in negotiations.

Bankers, financial institutions, and venture funds normally are privy to the business information of their clients. They also have a financial stake in their clients business and would like to have a say in the selection of the successor, in case the business is sold. Chartered Accountants are professional advisors to the entrepreneurs and often the entrepreneurs utilize their services to sell their business. These institutions are a natural source of prospective sellers and are normally helpful to the prospective buyers since they expect further business from the entrepreneurs buying in these ventures.

Venture capitalist are another source for buying a business. Venture capital firms, as a policy, like to get out of the ventures financed by them when the same have matured. If the existing entrepreneur is unable to buy the venture capitalist's stake the venture capitalist sells the venture to highest bidder amongst the prospective buyers. However, this source has not yet become popular in India.

EVALUATING THE EXISTING BUSINESS

An existing profitable business is less risky as compared to a new start up venture. An existing business always possesses a performance track record. This forms the objective data for deciding a buy-in. An existing business has a pattern of profits and sales over the past period besides the assets employed are also known and their usefulness can be easily evaluated. For evaluation of an existing business track records of its profits, sales and even labour problems are studied in details for their consistency and growth patterns. However, the past records do not necessarily eliminate the business risks. These risks are a function of the ability of the new owner as well as are dependent upon changes in the environment. Thus, it is important to know and understand the sellers motive in parting off with his venture.

Seller Motives

Normally, sellers have one of the following reasons to sell their business.

Changes in Career : Personal and Career reasons are often responsible for the owner to convert the holding of a family held business to cash. "Paramount Tailors" was a tailoring venture setup by a Punjab University Graduate in late fifties. By mid seventies Paramount Tailor was one of most prominent men's tailor in Old Delhi and was employing about 25 skilled tailors and two master cutters. He sold his business as he wanted to change his profession from a tailor to more respected one, say a watch dealer. Now Paramount Times is one of leading wholesaler in watches at New Lajpat Rai Market in Old Delhi. Many a times a person sells his business either to start a new venture or change his career. Some even do so to take to a relaxed life.

Management Succession : Many a times when the entrepreneur grows old, he may not have a family member who is willing to continue with the family business. Sometimes owner may have the successors but he may doubt the ability of the successor in the family. In such circumstances the owner is motivated to sell of the business.

One Person Management : Most enterprising people start their venture on a small scale and then the business grows gradually. In few cases the business grows up rapidly and it becomes difficult for the entrepreneur to handle it independently. The options before the owner is to corporatise the business or to sell it. Many people, because of their temperament, may not like to share their business with others and choose to sell it off.

However, seller often hide the real reason for the sale of their business. One may be inclined to sell off his business because of technological obsolescence resulting from the product / services getting outdated and may give different reason for the sale.

PT Computaerage was a successful computer training institute in Faridabad near Delhi. It had a goodwill of ten years'and was providing specialised training in CAD/CAM. When prohibition was removed from Haryana, a liquor shop was opened just next this computer training institute. The owner apprehending decline in business because of this location problem put the business on sale.

Besides the good reasons for setting their business there are also the negative reasons for entrepreneurs to sell their ventures. These are as under :

- **Product of Service Outdated :** The owner is often the first person to know that the product or the service he is offering is becoming obsolete. He is normally the first to notice the emerging competition from substitutes being developed. For example, coir foam matteresses replacing the rubber foam mattresses. Some time setting up of an modern plant based on the contemporary technology or entry of a large corporate house in the niche market of a small player may have a potential of making the product or service outdated.
- **Technological Changes :** Presently the technological changes are taking place at a very fast pace. Often the technology for a product or a process develops so fast that a small entrepreneur may face difficulties in assimilating the same. ICIM a computer manufacturing company at Pune wound up its business as it could not keep pace with the rapidly growing technology. In certain cases the present owner may not be able to arrange resources for purchase or development of the new technology. However, the venture can be a good buy for one who has an access to the technology and by buying in the unit he gets the instant infrastructure to manufacture and market the product.

SELLERS MOTIVES

- Entrepreneur Changing the Career
- Entrepreneur has Succession Problem
- One Person Faces Management Problem
- Outdated Product / Service
- Fast Moving Technology Changes
- Converting Business Wealth into Personal Wealth

- **Converting Business Wealth into Personal Wealth.** Of late a large number of 'Dot com' ventures were sold out as their valuation had increased so much that the owners were lured to convert the riches of their business into their personal fortune.

  The other reasons like a carrier shift, difficulty in managing the growing business, a fear of technological obsolesce or increasing competition in certain cases might have contributed to their decision of transferring wealth from business to oneself. Sabber Bhatia sold Hot mail to Microsoft and in the process transferred the wealth of Hotmail to his personal account. Sanjay Jha and Pallavi Jha of Walchand Netsoft, who promoted the portal "Cricketnext.com' sold 33% of their business to convert company wealth to personal wealth.

BUSINESS VALUATION

Once an entrepreneur short lists an enterprise for buying in, it is important to correctly evaluate the business financially as the success of buying-in will depend upon the proper valuation of the business.

The important task is to answer the question : What is the worth of this business? This requires accurate information about three aspect of the business to be acquired;

(*i*) Business Assets,

(*ii*) Operational Performance, and

(*iii*) Business Environment.

Business Assets

Every business has two types of assets : **tangible and intangible.** Tangible assets include land and buildings, plant and machinery, facilities, vehicles, inventories, accounts receivable as well as patents and trademarks. Integrable assets include goodwill and experience, knowledgeable and experienced work force. It is easy to evaluate the tangible assets and is discussed in the later part of this chapter. Intangible assets are a bit difficult to evaluate as these are subjective assets. Goodwill is a business's ability to produce earnings more than that of its competitors. Premium is normally added to the value of a business based upon its ability to generate income in excess of the average income generated by the similar business enterprises. Goodwill is valued considering the reputation, image, credit rating, consumer base etc., of the enterprise, which are more likely to benefit the entrepreneur buying in the business. The valuation of intangible assets should be fair both to the buyer and the seller

Operational Performance

The buyer should analyse the operations of the target enterprise to know about the health of the target business as well as how profitable it had been in the hands of the existing owners. For this the buyer is required to analyse the sales from a different prospective. The present level of sales as well as the rate of growth of sales are important. The buyer is not only interested in the absolute sales figures but is keen in knowing his market share and the changes in it. He is concerned about the seasonal variation and consumer profile of the business and carefully studies the sales pattern. In certain cases it may be noticed that an enterprise with an impressive sales data is dependent upon only on a few customers and some of them are the close associates of the owner and may not remain with the new entrepreneur. Further, the sales are the close associates of the owner and may not remain with the new entrepreneur. Further, the sales are a function of the credit policy and any changes in the credit policy directly effect the sales value. Factors like after sales service, distribution channels, warranty policy and selling skills and the dedication of the sales force also directly affect the sales volumes. The buyer has to be confident of his abilities to increase or at least maintain the sales.

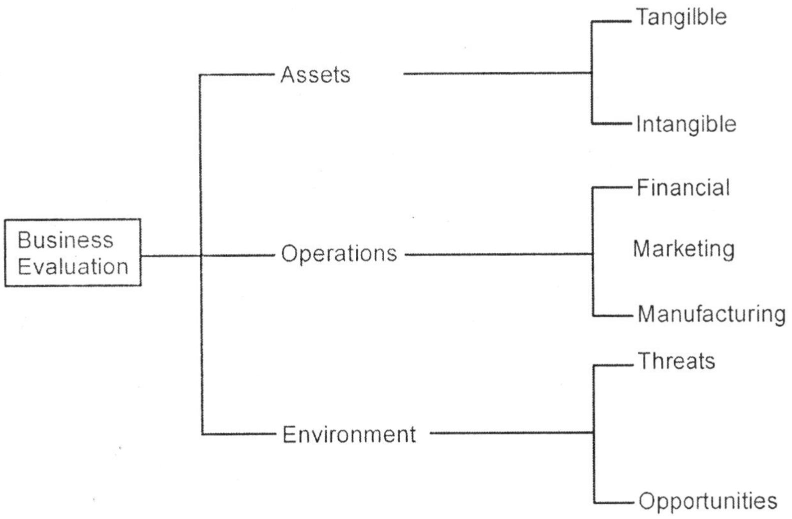

Fig. 10.1. Components of Business Evaluation.

Besides the sales, the **operations** relating to the production aspects of the business needs to be evaluated. All manufacturing aspects, like choice of technology used, process engineering, production system, plant utilisation factor, product design, quality and reliability, inventory policy, raw-material supply etc., need to be evaluated for their strengths and weaknesses. Operational aspects like conformity to the legal labour practices, environment pollution norms safety records of the production unit, are to be given due importance in the evaluation of the business. Minor negligence in any of these areas can lead to a disaster. If the buyer slips up in technical evaluation of the wastage disposal treatment plant which fails to meet the requirements of the pollution control legislation, he will face huge cost of plant modifications which he had not earlier planned while deciding to buy the given business. Besides obsolence of production process, the maintenance of plant and equipment and the residual life of the important machines are to be considered. It is advisable to use the services of professionals like chartered engineers, surveyors and consultants for this.

The **financial aspects** of the business are the other aspects of the operational performance. Analysis of the financial statements forms the basis for evaluation of the financial performance of any venture. The routine analysis of the balance sheet and profit and loss statements of a business can at times be misleading. It is an unpleasant fact that business men can more or less select the profit level of their business and a few owners juggle their account books. They inflate or deflate their profits mostly using means that are on the right side of the law. For example :

- Different methods are used for treating the depreciation of the assets thus affecting the profits.
- Cost of assets such as buildings, plant, equipment etc., can easily be inflated or deflated.
- Different methods of inventory valuation can have a direct bearing on the profits.
- The reliability of the account receivable is an important factor directly affecting the profits.

It is a known fact that in case of smaller business enterprises, especially the proprietary and partnership firms the accounting practices vary widely and these are not required to conform to any particular norm. Normally the professional accountants are hired, who, through their due-diligence research, bring out the financial deficiencies to light. They are required to audit the Balance Sheets, Profit and Loss Accounts, comment on the accounting practices and in the process set the price for the acquisition.

The investigation of the operational performance of the target business is a team effort involving financial deficiencies ot light. They are required to audit the Balance Sheets, the buyer, his lawyer, accountant and chartered engineer.

The services of lawyers are required in the end to sort out the legalities of buying the business. The lawyer drafts the buy out agreement to be executed by the sellet and the buyer. Before that he checks all the records to ensure that the tax lien against the property, outstanding product warranties and other payments due under contract. The leases, the licenses, franchises and contracts are also examined to ensure their transferability and other suitable clauses are added in the sale *deed*.

Business Environment

The entrepreneur buying in any venture has to conduct a market research in the same manner as for starting a new venture. This should include a study about the potential customers and competitors. He

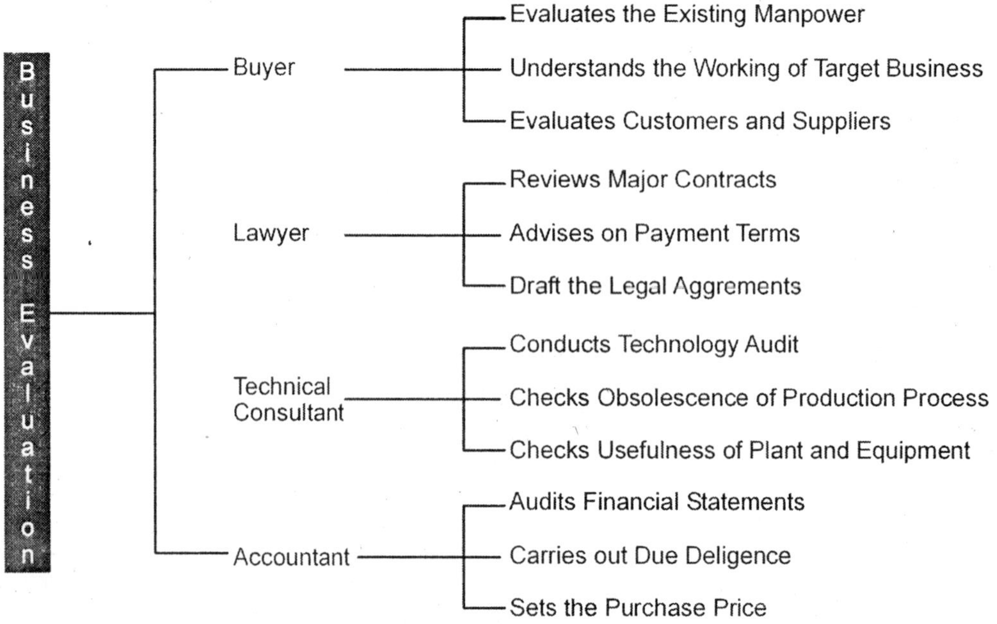

Fig. 10.2. Buy-In—A team effort of Buyer and Professionals.

should project the marketing strategies and estimate the expected sales based upon these strategies. The buyer should confirm if after the take over he can improve or in certain cases maintain the existing markets. He is concerned about the market, the growth and its pace. He is required to acquaint himself with the actual competition in the market; the strategies followed by the existing owner and their effectiveness. He is to be concerned with the changes in the business environment. He is to ensure if the past trends will also be valid for the future. The effect of substitutes and changing consumer preferences are to be looked into before finalising the proposal to buy-in any venture.

The business environment extends beyond market consideration. Includes demographic changes in the society, legislative changes and changes in tax laws which intimately effect the business operations and profits. The opening up of the economy has altered the competitive forces and the way the business was being conducted for years. For example, the changes in the enforcement of pollution laws has changed the automobile industry in India and also led to the closure of a large number of industrial units in Delhi.

Fixing The Price

The price of a business venture is influenced by many factors. As such there is no fool proof way to price a business that will satisfy both, the buyer and the seller. The best option is one wherein the buyer in addition to his own view point also looks at the business from the point of view of the sellers. There are two approaches for pricing a business.

- The **asset approach :** It focuses on the assets of the target enterprise without any reference to their earning potential.
- The **earning approach :** It focuses on the past or future earnings of the target enterprise.

Assets Approach

The worth of the target enterprise, no doubt depends upon the tangible and intangible assets of the business. The assets valuation of the enterprise to be bought may be based on one of the methods.

(*a*) **Book Value of the assets :** It is also called "balance sheet method" and the "net worth approach". In this method the value of various assets given in the latest balance sheet of the firm are taken as worth of the assets. From the total of book value of the assets, the amount of external liabilities is deducted to find out the net worth of the enterprise. This is the value of the business without considering goodwill. The assets valuation based upon the book values of the assets suffers from a short coming, that is, it is based upon the historical values and costs which may be irrelevant at present. For example, in case of land and building, the present cost may be much higher than the historical values appearing in the balance sheet.

Example

Book Value of Business	
Assets	
Fixed Assets	
Plant & Equipment	50,00,000
Less Depreciation	12,50,000
	37,50,000
Current Assets	
Inventory, Receivable and Cash	25,00,000
Total Assets	**62,50,000**
Liabilities	
Long term liabilities (Term Loan)	20,00,000
Current liabilities	
A/c payable	5,00,000
Total liabilities	**25,00,000**
Net worth Rs.	**37,50,000**
(Book Value of the Business)	

(*b*) **The Adjusted Book Value Method :** The book value is not a fair value for buying or selling a business. All tangible assets are required to the evaluated so as to correct the inaccuracy in the books of accounts due to unrealistic depreciation, bad debts, obsolescence etc. Accounts receivable may have value less than that indicated in the books of accounts due to bad debts and write off (uncollectable and overdue payments). Similarly the inventories as indicated in the book, may be over valued because of slow moving and obsolete stocks, allowance for poor quality, breakage etc. Even the book value of the plant and equipment needs to be adjusted to reflect their real valuation, e.g., a poorly maintained machine may be worth much less than its book value and an old machine having near zero value in the books may have a useful residual life of several years. Besides facilities like land and buildings that are depreciated in the account book often appreciate in real life. In this method, the book values of assets and liabilities are adjusted so as to reflect their real (realisable) value. In the adjusted book value method the value of total assets is increased by adding the value of intangible assets, namely goodwill. The valuation based on adjusted book value, definitely has an edge over the valuation based on book values, as the former gives a current and close approximation of the worth of the target enterprise.

Example

Adjusted Book Value of a Business	
Unadjusted book value of the business	3,75,000
plus	
Increase in the value of plant eqpt.	30.000
less	
Provision for unsaleable inventory	20,000
Provision for bad debts	2,50,000
Adjusted book value of the business	**3,33,000**

(*c*) **Selected Assets Method :** Herein, the buyer selects only those seller's assets that he believes are needed. The unwanted equipment's and inventories remain with the seller. Similarly only those of intangible assets like particular patents or goodwill that are needed by the buyer are considered. In this way only a part of the target business and not all of it is evaluated.

Approaches for Price Fixing

- Assets Approach
  - Book Value Method
  - Adjusted Book Value Method
  - Selected Assets Method
- Earning Approach
  - Multiplier of Earning
    - Profit Capitalisation Method
    - Personal Return Method
  - Discounted Cash Flow Method

Earnings Approach

The target enterprise can also be valued on the basis of its earning capacity. With reference to the funds invested in the business to be bought, the enterprise value will have a positive correlation with the profits of the enterprise. Here the profits of the enterprise can either be past profits or future expected profits. However, the future expected profits are preferred for obvious reasons. The entrepreneurs interested in buying in an enterprise are interested because of its future potential. Thus, future expeted earnings of buy-in, enterprise gives a better valuation. These expected profits figures and suffer from various limitations and there fore should be converted into future are however accounting figures cash flows by adjusting non cash items.

There are two traditional methods of fixing the price of an enterprise based on the earnings.

(*a*) **Multiple of Earning :** This method is used to capitalise net income by multiplying the net income by a factor. The multiplier factor combines, the risk perception, future earning potential and returns expected by the entrepreneur. The factor is low for the business that are considered risky, and have a low potential for the growth. Herein the entrepreneur wants the pay back in short period.

If valuation multiple is 3 it means that the business has low growth is considered risky and the entrepreneurs expects to recover his investment in 3 years. As against this if the multiplier is say 8, the business is considered as less risky with high potential for growth and entrepreneur will be satisfied if the investment is recovered in period of 8 years. Slight changes in multiplier can result in large difference in the price of target enterprise. The expert analysts and accountants use specialised techniques to fix the multiplier.

Further, an entrepreneur choosing this approach, may use either of two methods. *Capitalising profits* or *Personal returns*. The capitalising profits is a popular earning method for the evaluation of the business. The main problem in this method is after tax profits, which can be estimated in different ways, e.g., consider last year's profit or the average profit of several previous years. The problem here is that such profits are historical and ignore changes in business environment, especially those stemming from the contribution of the new entrepreneur. The other alternative is to use projected profits for next several years. However, there are problems in determining the future profits particularly at a stage when the entrepreneur has not yet taken over and developed a complete understanding of the enterprise and the business.

The capitalising profits method has a weakness. It considers the buying of a venture from an investor's point of view and not that of an entrepreneur. The second method, i.e., personal return method considers the buy in from the entrepreneurial perspective. This method distinguishes between the business earnings and that of the entrepreneur's. It relates the total income which the entrepreneur receives from the buy-in (including salary, dividends, interest, perquisites etc.) to what he personally invested and not the total cost of the buy-in as explained in the following example.

Example

A person buys an enterprise for Rs. 5 lakhs which is financed as under :

1. Equity of Rs. 3 lacs and loan of Rs. 2 lacs. The entrepreneur sells 50 per cent of stock to friends at a premium of Rs. 5 and thus collects to Rs. 2.25 lacs for 50 per cent share capital and is require to put in Rs. 75,000 for personal 50 percent stake.

   The entepreneur also advances a loan of Rs. 2 lakhs to the business at 15 per cent. He earns an salary of Rs. 20,000 per month and avails perks, like provident fund, car, telephone and club membership valued at 50 percent of the salary. His return can be calculated as under

Salary (per annum)	Rs. 2,40,000
Perks (Per annum)	Rs. 1,20,000
Annual interest on term loan of Rs. 2 lakh @ 15%	Rs. 30,000
Total Annual Income	Rs. 3,90,000
Entrepreneur Investment	
Equity	Rs. 75,000
Loan	Rs. 2,00,000
Total Investment	Rs. 2,75,000
Personal return	Rs. 3,90,000
Personal investment	Rs. 2,75,000
Personal return on investment	3,90,000 /2,75,000 = 141.81% a year

Of the two multiplier approaches, the capitalisation of profits lays emphasis on the after tax profit of total business investment and personal return expressed as percent age of personal investment.

(*b*) **Discounted Cash Flow Method :** The method is also called present value method as it use net present value (NPV) technique to set the price of the enterprise based upon its future earnings. The expected future earnings are discounted to reflect their present value. The process involves :

(*i*) Estimating the future cashflow (i.e., profit after tax + non-cash expenses).

(*ii*) Find the total present value of all these cash flows by discounting at an appropriate rate.

(*iii*) The liabilities of the target enterprise, when are a part of the buy-in are treated as outflows at time zero and are deducted from the present value of all future cash flows (as calculated in step (ii) above).

(*iv*) The balancing figure is the NPV of the enterprise and is the maximum purchase price which the entrepreneur should pay for the buy-in.

$$\text{Maximum Purchase Price} = \sum_{i=1}^{n} \frac{Ci}{(1+ki)^{i}} - L$$

where

Ci = Cash flow over different years

L = Current value of liabilities

k = Appropriate discount rate.

The main problem in this method is to estimate the future cash flows and determining the appropriate discount rate.

It is not necessary that the price of the enterprise may be fixed applying only one of the above approaches. Rather all these methods may be considered simultaneously and a fair price based on assets, earnings, capitalised profits, personal returns, cash flows and other relevant factors be arrived at. After arriving at the price of the target enterprise the entrepreneur will get down to the nitty-gritty of negotiating the price with the seller.

BUYING-IN FOR EXPANSION

Once the new venture is established, the entrepreneurs look for the avenues of expanding their business. The expansion improves their customer base and thus expands the sales. The increased sales result in the increased operations and profits. This strengthens the enterprise through financial leverage, improved distribution, consumer services, and economies of scale at various levels of operations, e.g., advantage of bulk purchase automation etc. The two options for expansion include setting up of new additional business ventures or buying into some existing businesses. It has been observed that one-third of small businesses are bought in by the established entrepreneurs.

Most of the time the business are bought for vertical integration. For example, a distributor or a wholesaler may buy-in a set of retail stores or a manufacturing unit. Conversely a manufacturing unit an buy-in a distributor or a retail store and a retail store may buy-in a wholesaler of his region or the manufacturing unit of the product he deals in. Such vertical integration adds to the value chain which results in cost reduction and an increase in the overall profits for the entrepreneurs.

The business are also bought for horizontal expansion. For example, one retail store may buy in another retail store (dealing in the same product) located in the other part of the town. A manufacturer or distributor may acquire products or services that compliments its exists business. For example, Victoria Foods, the manufacturer of Rajdhani Atta bought in a dal mill and then a rice sheller, thus, adding lentils and rice to their flour business.

Three ways of expanding business ventures
- Setting up a new additional venture
- Buying in of an established venture
- Selling / buying-in of Franchise

Expanding vertically into the distribution channel or horizontally with complementary products enables the entrepreneurs to hire and retain professional people. With the financial strengths and increased operation the entrepreneurs, for example, can employ a professional accountant to maintain accounts or a marketing mew business the established entrepreneurs increase their manpower, so offering addition benefits (e.g., medicine policies, retirement benefits, even canteen and transport facilities) become more cost effective.

Thus, there is a routinely for buying into an initial venture and also for expanding an existing business.

SUMMARY

Business brokers and consultants are often engaged in making match between the buyers and sellers of business ventures. They charge upfront fee for introducing the interested parties and brokerage if the deal is struck. Venture capitalist are another source for business buying venture capital firms, as a policy, like to get out of the ventures financed by them when the same have matured.

The entrepreneur buying in any venture has to conduct a market research in the same manner as for starting a new venture. This should include a study about the potential customers, competitors and project, the marketing strategies and likely sales, based upon these strategies.

The business environment extends beyond market consideration. It includes demographic changes in the society, legislative changes and changes in turn which intimately effect the business operations and profits. The price of a business venture is influenced by many factors. As such there is no fool proof way to price a business that will satisfy both the buyer and the seller. The best option is one wherein the buyer in addition to his own view point also looks at the business from the point of view of the sellers.

REVIEW QUESTIONS

1. What are the advantages and disadvantages of buying in an existing business?
2. What procedure would you recommend to evaluate a target business for buying-in?
3. Write a critique on seller's motives in selling a profit making venture.
4. What are the advantages to an entrepreneur in buying-in an existing business over starting a new one?
5. Describe important considerations for buying-in an ongoing business.
6. Would you consult on accountant and lawyer before buying-in a business? Why or why not?
7. Describe the various methods of asset approach for fixing the price of a target business.
8. How does the personal return method differ from the capitalising profits method?
9. Contrast sellers and buyers perspectives for purchase terms in buying an existing business.
10. Distinguish between considerations for buying to become an entrepreneur and expanding the business by an entrepreneur.

CASE 10.1

WOMEN'S APPAREL SHOP

Urmila Mathur was very excited today. Six months back when her husband joined LML Ltd. as Vender Development Manager, she shifted from Delhi to Lucknow. Urmila did her graduation in Fashion Technology and had worked as a merchandiser with a leading garment exporter and had been a visiting faculty at National Institute of Fashion Technology.

After shifting to Lucknow Urmila spent first three months in arranging her house and settling down in the new city. For the last thee months she had surveyed the city and had been toying with an idea of opening a boutique in an up market area. For the last three months she had not been able to find a suitable location for her boutique. A few days back she was told by an agent that women's apparel shop in Hazratganj area was up for sale. She had visited the shop a couple of times and on each occasion she did buy a dress for herself. She was impressed by its location and considered it very suitable for her boutique. She felt it was an ideal opportunity to buy this running garment shop and convert it into her dream boutique.

Urmila knew the garment business inside out. However, buying a business is a complex matter. Last night she discusses the matter with her husband. They listed the main problems in buying the business as—evaluating the business, fixing the fair price for the same and closing the deal in a safe, legal and equitable way. They decided to work on the project.

Mr. Lalwani the owner of the women's apparel shop told Urmila that he was selling the unit as he wanted to help his son who had set up a yarn mill at Kanpur and needed his assistance. Mr. Lalwani also told her that the business had provided his family a good living and he felt that with her knowledge and experiences in fashion the business would make a good progress. He told her that he expected Rs. 22 lakhs for his business and gave her the latest financial statements of his business for review.

She had returned home very excited and was eagerly waiting for her husband to analyse the financial statements thereby evaluating the prospective business and fixing a price for the business the be bought.

Balance Sheet as on 31st March, 2003

Assets	Amount	Liabilities	Amount
Fixed Assets	3.52,000	Owners Equty	8,48,000
Stocks	11,36,000	Accounts payable	3,36,000
		Other Liabilities	3,04,000
Total Assets	**14,88,000**	**Total Liabilities**	**14.88,000**

Profit and Loos Account for the year 2002-2003

Sales Income	57,12,000
Cost of Goods sold	33,76,000
Gross Profit	23,36,000
Expenses	12.96,000
Operating Profit	**10,40,000**

She was of the opinion that a shop of the same size in any good market is going to cost her not less than Rs. 5.5 lakhs and she would have to spend at least Rs. 2.5 lakhs on the interiors. She had carefully examined the inventories, and had liked the range not more than 5 per cent of the stocks were old or slow moving. Even these could be easily disposed in a sale at their cost price. The business was having an average growth rate of ten per cent for the last three years and she was confident of achieving a growth rate of fifteen percent.

QUESTIONS

1. What steps do you think Mrs Mathur should take before deciding upon buying this business?
2. What do you recommend as fair price for Mrs. Mathur to pay in case she opts to buy the garments shop? Explain.

CHAPTER

11

MARKETING CONCEPTS FOR ENTREPRENEURS

CHAPTER OUTLINE

- Scope of Marketing
- Marketing orientation
- Market Assessment
- Market Segmentation
- Marketing Mix
- Product Management
- Pricing Methods
- Marketing Startegy for New Ventures
- Branding Strategies
- Managing Brand Systems
- Packaging Strategies
- Distribution Strategies
- Pricing Strategies
- Developing the Sales Promotion Schemes
- Product Life Cycle

MARKETING CONCEPTS

Marketing is the basic reason for the existence of a business organisation. In the age of fast changes, marketing is the springboard of all business activities. It works as the guide for all business/non-business organisations. It is a powerful mechanism which alone can satisfy the needs and wants of consumers at the place and price they desire. The success of an enterprise depends largely on the effectiveness with which its marketing strategies are formulated and implemented. Marketing is said to be the eyes and ears of a business enterprise because it keeps the enterprise in close contact with its economic, political, social and technological environment and informs it of events that can influence its activities as per requirements of the market. Marketing helps in having a good range of products in constant demand and suggests the scope for improving and developing new products to satisfy the changing customer needs. Customer is the king of the market. Customers decide what products suit their needs. Therefore, we can say marketing satisfies our needs by providing form utility, person utility, exchange utility, place utility and time utility.

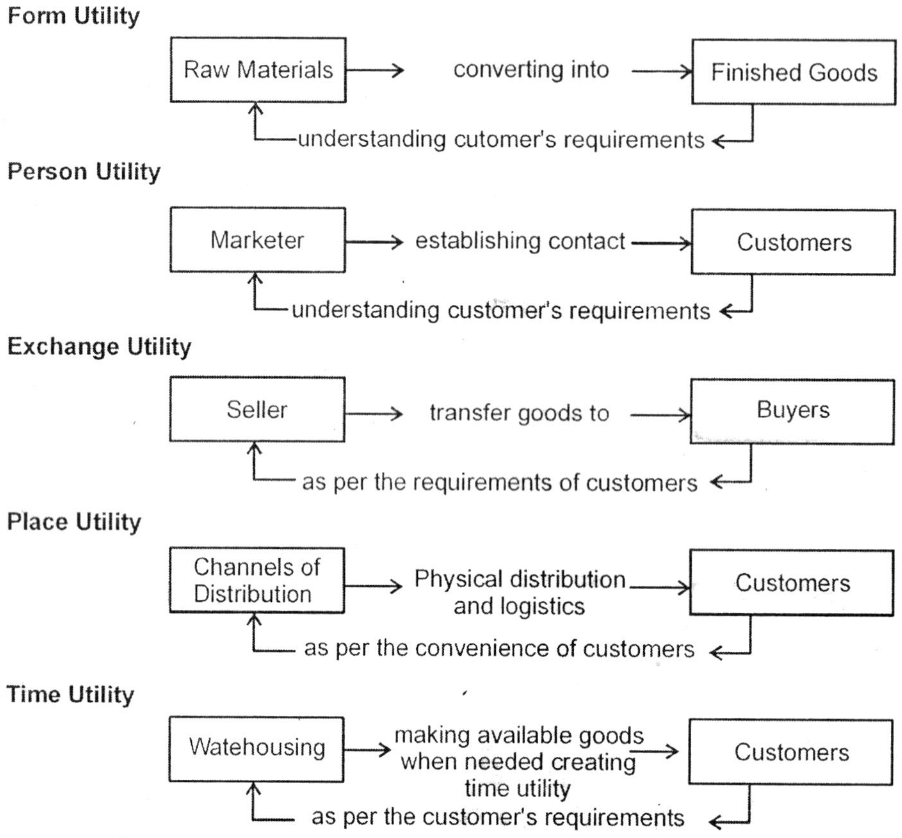

Fig. 11.1

Marketing can be summed up as consisting of:

— Sales in a planned way

— Creation of customers

— Creation of demand and satisfying it.

Selling a product without appropriate pricing, proper packing, need-based promotional inputs and choosing a right market place, would be like firing an unguided missile. Until and unless a product is 'tuned' for a given product-market situation, it will meet its own death.

With the changing business scenario, marketing has taken the shape of value-added activity, wherein the basic pressure of any marketing activity for sales in a planned way is tuning the four Ps, i.e., product, price, promotion, and place. The customer realises that he needs a given product, and at the same time the seller's product itself should speak of its attributes and should be positioned accordingly to have a user-friendly image for itself.

For a business enterprise to realise the full benefits of the marketing concept, the philosophy must be translated into action, i.e., (i) the marketing activity should be fully coordinated and well-managed; and (ii) an important role must be accorded to the chief marketing executive in planning a new ventures.

SCOPE OF MARKETING

The scope of marketing is very wide. It may be analysed in terms of performance of various functions. A number of functions are inherent in every marketing process and these functions are to be performed on the basis of various utilities :

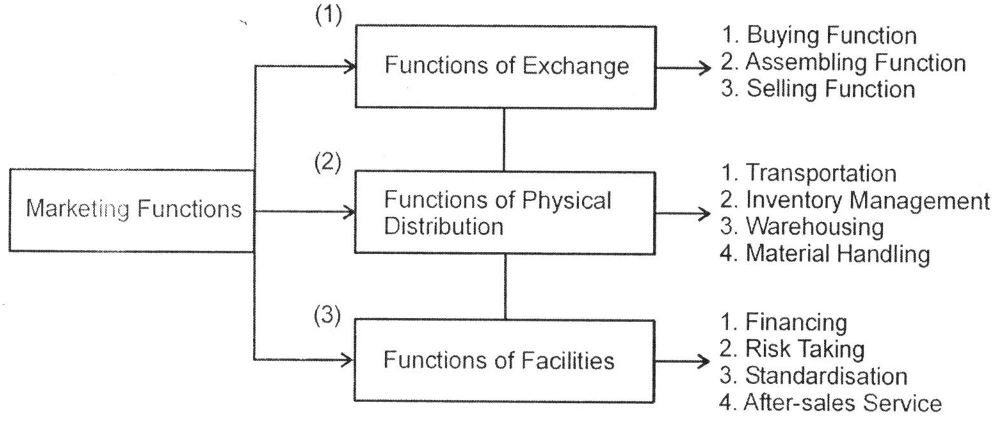

Fig. 11.2: Marketing Functions

Functions of Exchange

(*i*) ***Buying Function.*** A manufacturer is required to buy raw materials for production purposes. Similarly, a wholesaler has to buy goods from manufacturer for purpose of sales to retailer. A retailer has to sell the goods to consumers. Thus, functions of buying has to be performed at various levels.

(*ii*) ***Assembling Function.*** Assembling is different and separate from buying. Buying involves transfer of ownership of the goods from seller to the buyer; whereas in assembling, goods are purchased from various sources and assembled/ collected at one place to suit the requirements to the buyer.

(*iii*) ***Selling Function.*** Selling involves transfer of ownership from seller to the buyer. Selling function is vital to the success of any firm. Its importance has been continuously increasing in all organisations due to the emergence of severe competition. Producing goods is easy but it is very difficult to sell them.

Functions of Physical Distribution

(*i*) ***Transportation.*** It includes decision to be taken on mode of transport, service selection, freight consolidation, carrier routing, vehicle scheduling, processing claims, etc.

(*ii*) ***Inventory Management.*** It includes :

- Short-term sales forecasting
- Product mix at stocking points
- Number, size and location of stocking points
- Just in time (JIT) or push or pull strategies.

(iii) Warehousing. It includes the following functions :

- Space determination
- Stock layout and design
- Stock placements

(*iv*) ***Material Handling.*** It includes the following functions:

- Equipment selection
- Equipment replacement
- Order picking procedure
- Stock storage and retrieval

Functions of Facilities

(i) ***Financing.*** The importance of extending liberal credit facilities as a selling tool cannot be underestimated. This would necessarily involve higher working capital requirements. Hence, arrangement of finance has become an increasingly important function. Therefore, a marketer can plan for various kinds of finance : Short-term Finance, Medium-term Finance, and Long-term Finance. There are various sources of finance, for example, commercial banks, cooperative banks, credit societies, government agencies, etc.

(ii) ***Risk Taking.*** There are innumerable risks which a marketing enterprise has to bear in the process of marketing of goods and services. Risks arise due to unforeseen circumstances. Risks can be insured also. For example, the risk due to fire and accidents may be covered by insurance. But the risks due to changes in government policies, risks due to increased competition, technological risks and business cycle risks cannot be insured.

(iii) ***Standardisation.*** Buyers and sellers always prefer to have standardised goods and services. This will relieve buyers from examining the product and wasting time. That is why standardisation has now been accepted as a convenient and ethical basis of marketing.

(iv) ***After-sales Service.*** The importance of after-sales service facilities as a marketing tool cannot be ignored. Hence, arrangement of after-sales service has become an increasingly important function. Therefore, an entrepreneur has to plan for after-sales service. For example, repairs, replacements, maintenance, etc.

MARKETING ORIENTATION

The first tasks of an entrepreneur is to make correct decisions regarding the kind of goods or services to be produced which can be sold to the customers. Marketing orientation induces thinking about customers and their needs, and assists in creating an appropriate product or service and also in selling it.

Fig. 11.3: Marketing Orientation

As discussed earlier the best way of sensing opportunities for new ideas is to study the benefits that people are buying in a product rather than its physical features.

Why do people go to hill station during summer? What BENEFITS they are seeking?

* Cool atmosphere	* Relaxation
* Green sight	* Fun
* Scenery	* Romance
* Cheap fruits	* Change
* Summer festivals.	

For instance, in India the desert cooler market grew because many people wanted the cool atmosphere for which desert cooler is much cheaper and available for longer duration than a visit to a hill station.

Identifying WHY people buy rather than WHAT they buy is essential for successful marketing.

Marketing means that entrepreneurs manufacture what they could sell to the consumer, and not sell what they could manufacture.

Marketing orientation has become increasingly relevant to low technology industries and services such as :

Apparel	Consumer Durables
Transportation	Grocery
Health/Beauty aids	Cosmetics.

Successful marketing depends on the degree to which resources of the enterprise are effectively mobilised to respond to the current and anticipated consumer needs.

MARKET ASSESSMENT

The market is composed of a wide variety of customers with different backgrounds and spread over a wide geographical areas. As the first step an entrepreneur is required to know the potential demand of the products or services he wants to offer. It may also be necessary to understand the nature and the extent of competition in its market and the prevailing trade practices. Such efforts help assess the market. Depending upon several factors like the availability of resources, the scale of operation, and the impact on profitability, one may decide the customer group, called the market segment, which is of interest to the enterprise.

The marketing assessment involves three major steps —

(a) Analysis of demand.

(b) Understanding the competitive situation; and

(c) Trade practices.

Analysis of Demand

Demand Analysis refers to assessment of the willingness and ability of the customers to buy products or services. Three sources are commonly used to collect information for analysing demand.

(*i*) ***Primary Sources*** – An enterprise may have household as well as institutional demand for its product. The demand from the household customers is usually met through the dealers and, as such, a rough estimate of the total demand from such customers could be made by personally contacting the dealers selling the items. Similarly, a number of institutions using the items may be contacted to ascertain the demand. Such personalised contacts with primary sources are possible only when customers are concentrated in a limited area.

(*ii*) ***Secondary Sources*** – In case the potential customers are scattered over a wide area; published data regarding population, production, economic condition, living habits, census data and development plans of the respective state or country are used to estimate the demand.

(*iii*) ***Sample Survey*** – When the potential customers are spread over a wide area and are large in number, information is obtained by sending a questionnaire through mail to a small but representative sample. It may be necessary to consult an expert in drawing the sample and designing the questionnaire.

Elasticity of Demand: Demand at what price? Demand for some products and services is more flexible than for others. Demand is said to be elastic when a small change in the price affects a large change in the quantum of demand. If a change in price does not substantially change the quantity of demand, the demand is said to be inelastic. For a product, the demand for which is highly elastic, a high managerial efficiency is required to maintain price stability.

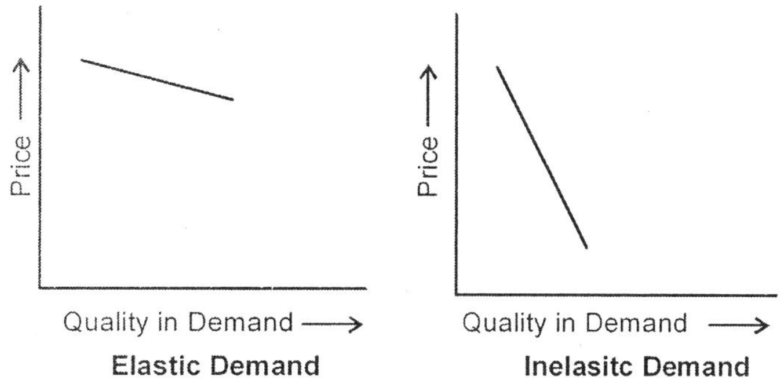

Fig. 11.4: Elasticity of Demand

Understanding the Competitive Situation

Competitive situation demands special attention in the whole exercise of market assessment. To understand it in respect of a given product/service, an entrepreneur is required to answer questions such as :

- How many enterprises are offering the same or similar goods/services?
- What are their market share?
- What are the strengths and weaknesses of their products?
- What kind of consumer image does each product enjoy?
- What trade practices the competitors employ?
- Who are the major customers of each brand?

Table 11.1: Competitive Situation

Competitive Products	Market Share	Product Features	Product's Image	Discount to Dealers	Credit Terms	Major Customers
Brand A Brand B Brand C						

The answers to such questions may be tabulated for understanding the competition. The analysis (SWOT-strengths, weaknesses, opportunities and threats analysis) will tune his marketing efforts to the requirement of the customers and trade by highlighting the areas of opportunities and threat.

Trade Practices

Trade Practices reveal the mode, means and modalities of serving the customers with products/ services. Very often, due to the spread of customers, or their buying habits or even the nature of the products, it is not feasible for an entrepreneur to reach customers directly. A host of middlemen like distributors, wholesalers, retailers, commission agents, brokers, super markets and export houses are employed to provide various types of services on different terms and conditions. A study of the prevailing trade practices in the beginning would enable entrepreneurs prepare a more realistic plan for marketing the products or services.

MARKET SEGMENTATION

The market consists of a large number of individuals having different characteristics. They differ in their education, employment, income, status, preferences, likes, dislikes and opinions. Not all of them are the potential customers for a product.

Through market segmentation, groups of customers are identified sharing some common characteristics and are considered as the target group or segment for the product.

Basis of Market Segmentation

(*i*) *Geographical:* Village, Town, State, Country, Region, Hill, Valley, Rural, Urban, etc.

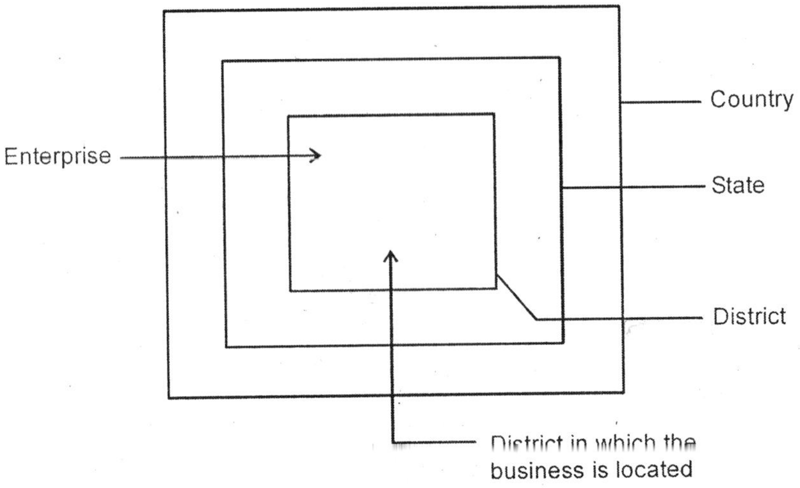

Fig. 11.5: Geographical Segment

(*ii*) Demographic : Age-Children, Youth, Adult, Old
Sex - Male, Female
Income - High, Middle, Low, Below Poverty Line
Occupation - Executives, Professionals,
Farmers Education- Primary, Seconday, Tertiary. :

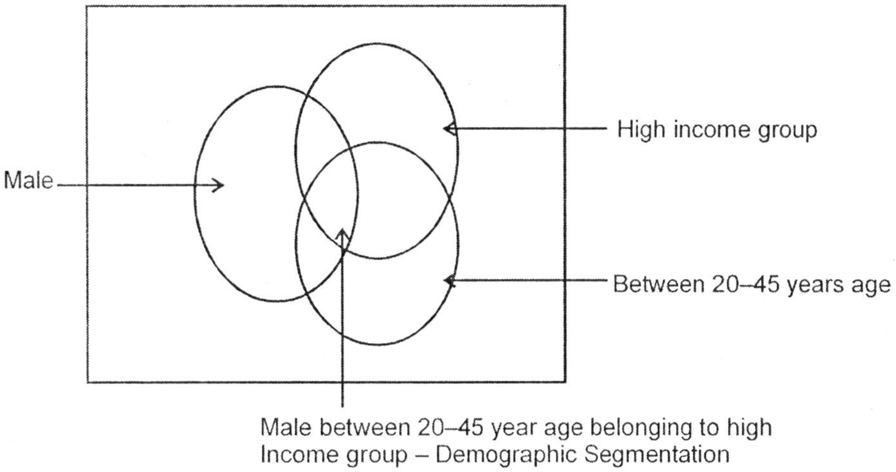

Fig. 11.6: Demographic Segmentation

(*iii*) *Psychographic* : Attitude – Conservative, Liberal, Radical
: Autonomy – Independent/Dependant
: Work Orientation – Hardworking, Fun loving

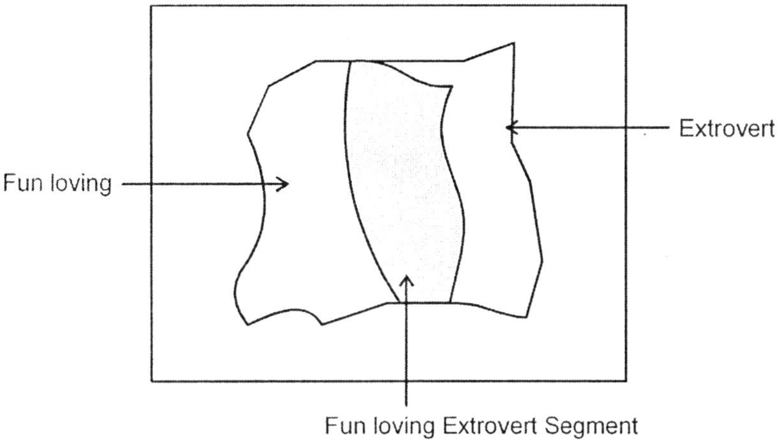

Fig. 11.7: Psychographic Segment

There can be many more basis for segmentation such as habit-smoker, non-smoker, etc. The identified segment must be sufficiently different from the rest to justify calling it a segment. Segmentation is useful and cost effective since it helps selecting appropriate methods of selling, pricing, packing and promoting the product/ service.

MARKETING MIX

The term 'marketing mix', was introduced by Prof. N.H. Borden of the Harvard Business School of America. It describes combination of the four inputs which constitute the core of a company's marketing system — the prouct, the distribution system, the price structure and the promotional activities. According to Mr. Jerome McCarthy, an American expert, "Marketing mix is the pack of four sets of variables, namely product variables, price variables, promotion variables and place variables".

The basic task of the entrepreneur is the successful management of the marketing mix. Success means that the customer is satisfied and that the organisation's resources are effectively deployed to that end.

Marketing mix is the set of controllable variables and their levels that the firm uses to influence its target market. McCarthy popularised a four-factor classification of these tools called the four Ps: **product, price, place** and **promotion.**

Product — What decisions relate to product or service range.

Price — What price should be set for each product/service.

Place — Identification and selection of channels for distribution and deciding what levels of service are appropriate thus defining the logistics involved.

Promotion — How to communicate with the target market and persuade the people concerned to buy.

The concept of the marketing mix is a schematic plan to guide analysis of marketing problems through utilisation of:

(a) A list of important forces emanating from the market which bear upon the marketing operations of the enterprise; and

(b) A list of elements (procedures and policies) of marketing programmes.

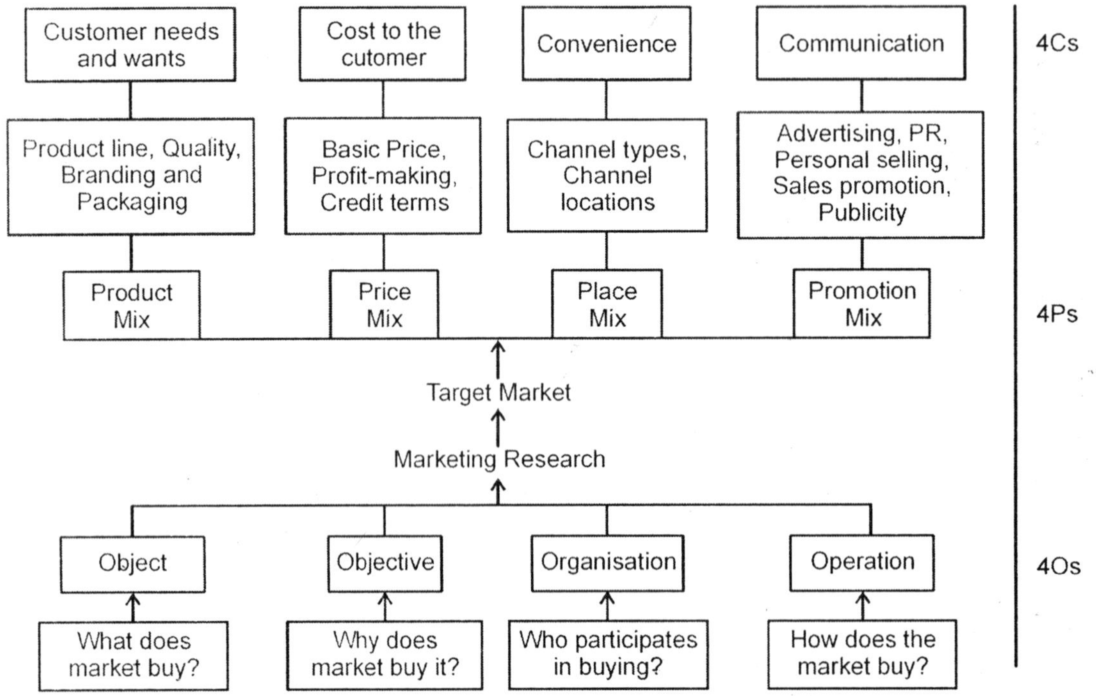

Fig. 11.8: Understannding Marketing Mix

The Four P's of Marketing

Product Mix
— Quality, Technology
— Packaging
— Labelling
— Branding
— Trademark
— Merchandising
— Size, Design, Colour, Features
— Services
— Warranty
— Product Line and Range
— Competition
— Terms of Delivery

Price Mix
— Pricing Policies
— Credit Terms
— Cost and Profit
— Allowance and Discounts

Place Mix
— Distribution Channels
— Transportation
— Warehousing and Storage
— Inventory Level
— Positioning

Promotion Mix
— Advertising
— Sales Promotion
— Personal Selling
— Public Relations
— Publicity
— Direct Responses

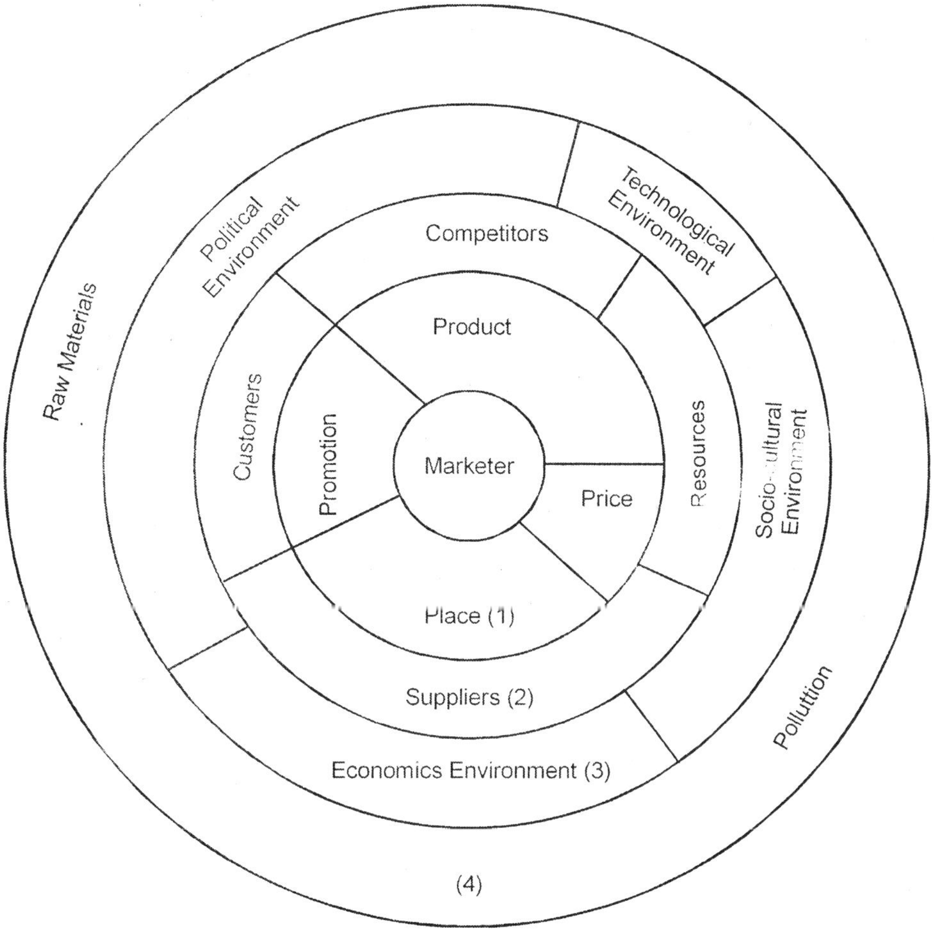

1. Marketing mix
2. Micro environment
3. Macro environment
4. Physical environment

Fig. 11.9: The 4 P's of Marketing Mix Operate Within a Business Environment

Product

A product has both tangible and intangible components. Customers view products as :"bundles of satisfaction" rather then "just physical things".

Product Mix

The word "product mix" is used to describe the assortment of different product types that a company produces and markets. The product line is the number of brands or related products in each product type. Proctor and Gamble, for example, have four major product lines : detergents, toothpasts, soaps and deodorants. For each line, there are a number of brands (DAZ, Ariel, etc.) and the number of different brands represents the length of product line and the number of different lines represents the width of the product mix.

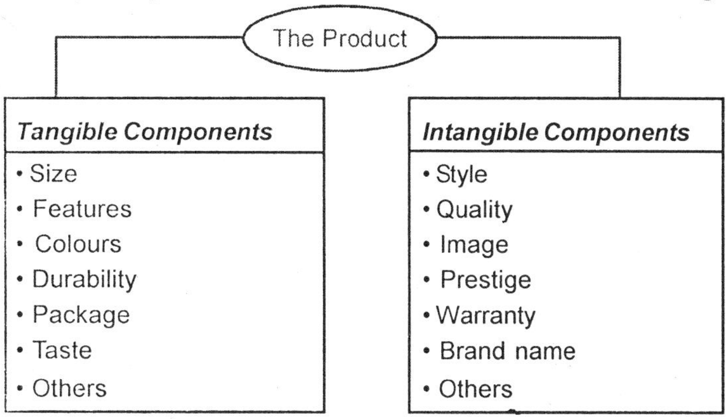

Fig. 11.10: Components of a Product Examples of Product Line and Range.

Examples of Product Line and Range

• Bajaj Auto Ltd. :

Product line	*Product range*
1. Scooters	Bajaj Super, Bajaj Cub, Chetak, Chetak Electronics, Priya, Bajaj Super FE
2. Motor-cycles	Kawasaki Bajaj, KB 100
3. Mopeds	M-80m, Sunny 50 cc
4. Three Wheelers	Various models

- **Hindustan Lever Ltd.** has a product line consisting of vanaspati, soaps, detergents, cosmetics, etc.
- **Philips** has a wide range in audio systems and home appliances.

Price Mix

Price is an important consideration in buying decisions. Price also denotes quality in the consumers' mind a psychological factor. For some products, when many identical brands are competing with each other for consumer preference, the price may be an important influencing factor. Price is the basic vehicle for telling the consumer about the value and associated conditions of a particular product.

Price is an important element of marketing mix. It may be defined as the value of product attributes expressed in monetary terms, which a consumer pays or is expected to pay in exchange. Pricing is a marketing function, which has an important role to play in marketing decisions. Pricing influences the profit level, the operational level, etc. The following factors determine the price of a product:

– Pricing objectives
– Demand for a product or service
– Competition
– Profitability
– Distribution channels

Examples

1. *Price of "PEUGEOT 309"*. The Premier-Peugeot Limited plans to use the market-based pricing where it will exploit the market fully, aiming at charging a price that will be close to Maruti's model 1000, which is priced at Rs. 4 lakhs approximately. The company plans to attack the market of Maruti 1000 by an offer of a better product for a little more.
   Price of "Peugeot 309" in Mumbai: Ex-showroom price - Rs. 4.42 lakhs.
2. *Price of "Accent"*. The Hyundai Motor Company plans to follow the market penetration pricing, initially pricing the car at lower or same price to attract a larger number of customers, preferably permanent ones. It plans to offer a product at a price which the buyer perceives to be an offer of something more for the same price.
   Price of "ACCENT" : Rs. 5.00 lakhs.
3. Prices and positioning of Kwality Wall's icecreams

Price Range (Rs.)	*Brands*	*Product Form*	*Target Segment*
60 to 100	Dairy Classic	Take Home	The Indian women.
20	Cornetto	Novelty	Young, adults and teenagers
16 to 19	Feast, Dairy Classic Cassatta	Novelty	Young, adults and teenagers
11 to 15	Maha Choco Bar, Dairy Classic Range	Mainly cups	Adults
7 to 10	Split	Stick	Children
4 to 6	Hattrik, Fruitline	Stick	Children
2.50	Solo	Stick	Children

Place Mix

The entrepreneur has the responsibility of making his product available near the place of consumption so that the consumers can easily buy it. If the brand preferred by the consumer is not easily available at a convenient location, he may buy some other brand. Thus, an entrepreneur has to ensure that his product is available to the target consumers wherever required. There are two major areas in place mix : (i) Marketing channels, and (ii) Physical distribution (Logistics Management).

It is true that channel decisions affect other marketing mix elements, and involve a relatively long-term commitment of resources. It may take a marketer years to build up relations with the intermediaries and sometimes these are contractual. As we know, intermediaries are independent organisations and, therefore, their needs must be taken into account while evaluating various channel alternatives. In fact, the success of a company's marketing effort depends to a large extent on the soundness of its distribution network. Physical distribution involves transportation, warehousing, material handling, and bulk packaging among others. Some of these activities will also be performed by the intermediaries and a great deal of coordination is required between the various links in the channel in order to get the optimum results. For many years, physical distribution was a neglected area of marketing management, but an entrepreneur has to become conscious of its importance in the overall marketing strategy.

***Examples :* HM-Mitsubishi Cars In India**

The company plan to use both One and Zero level of channls of distribution. The company lanuched "LANCER" in the four metropolitan cities, viz., Delhi, Mumbai, Kolkata and Chennai, besides Cochin also.

The total number of dealers appointed in India is 135.

The dealers will be provided training and help under the corporate identity programme.

The present widespread dealer network of the Hindustan Motors will handle sales, servcies and spare parts acitvities.

The dealers and engineers will be trained under the company inhouse programmes in India as well a abroad.

Promotional Mix

Marketing promotion is a management process through which an organisation develops, presents, and evaluates a series of messages to an identified audience. So, effective promotion depends on :

- The nature of communication
- The target audience
- The environment in which it is received
- The receivers' perception of the source as, e.g., friends, reference groups, etc.
- The medium used to transmit the message.

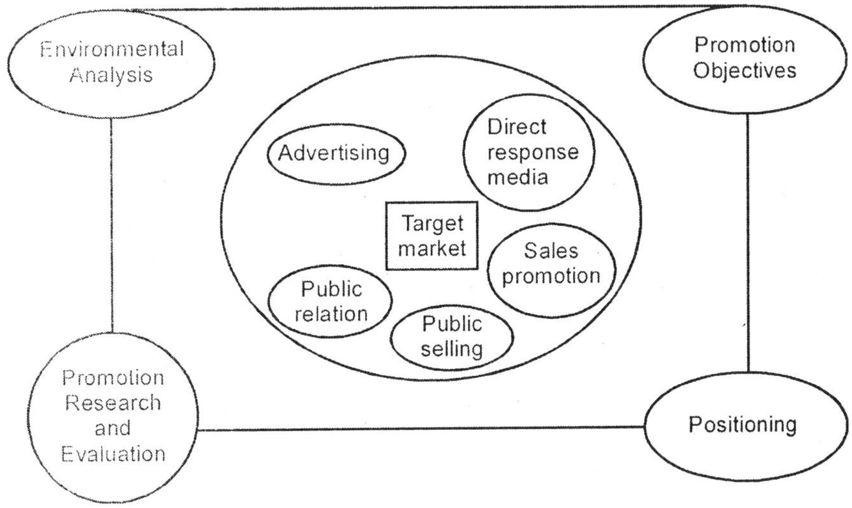

Fig. 11.11: A System of Promotion Mix

A summary of the key characteristics of the tools of marketing communication is indicated in the following table :

	Advertising	*Sales Promotion*	*Public Relations*	*Personal Selling*	*Direct Response Media*
Communications					
Ability to deliver a personal message	Low	Low	Low	High	High
Ability to reach a large audience	High	Medium	Medium	Low	Medium
Level of interaction	Low	Low	Low	High	High
Credibility given by target audience	Low	Medium	High	Medium	Medium
Costs					
Absolute costs	High	Medium	Low	High	Medium
Cost per contact	Low	Medium	Low	High	High
Wastage	High	Medium	High	Low	Low
Size of investment	High	Medium	Low	High	Medium
Control					
Ability to target particular audiences	Medium	High	Low	Medium	High
Management's ability to adjust the deployment of the tool as circumstances change	Medium	High	Low	Medium	High

Source : Marketing Communications Framework, Theories and Anulicatinna hit Chri Fill.

PRODUCT MANAGEMENT

A product is anything that is offered to the market for sale at a price. It can be a physical product like a typewriter or a service provided by a travel agent.

1. Types of Products

A. Consumer Products: Goods which are bought by individual households without requiring further processing, i.e., soaps, television sets, toys, clothes, and furniture are all consumer products. These consumer goods could be further categorised as :

- Durable Goods : Which survive many uses and have a relatively long life (e.g., refrigerators, typewriters, fans, etc.).
- Non-durable Goods : Which are consumed in one or a few uses and last a relatively short period (e.g., soft drinks, soap, cigarettes, etc.).
- Convenience Goods : Which are frequently purchased with minimum of efforts in deciding (e.g., newspapers, tooth brushes, etc.).
- Shopping Goods : Which are bought after comparisons at the retail outlets (e.g., readymade garments, furniture, curtains, etc.).
- Speciality Goods : Which have unique features and, therefore, require special purchasing efforts (e.g., sporting equipment, stereo systems, racing cars, etc.).

B. Industrial Products : Industrial products are goods which are sold to other business firms, either for their own consumption or for producing other goods. They can be further categorised as :

- Capital Goods : e.g., machines and equipments used in factories, offices, or stores.
- Raw Materials and Parts : e.g., steel sheets, nuts and bolts, etc.
- Supplies and Services : e.g., lubricating oils, grease, repair and maintenance services.

C. Services : There are many services like insurance, transportation, tourism, health care, education, entertainment, repairs etc. As distinct from the normal physical products, one important feature of services is their intangible nature. Some services like teaching have very high degree of intangibility while some other like health care have both tangible and intangible components.

II. Product Mix

As discussed in pre pages product mix is the set of all the products offered by a firm for sale. It may consist of a single product line such as different varieties of soap, or more than one product line such as different varieties of soap and toothpaste.

Small firms usually make just one product or a couple of products in a product line. However, as it grows, it has to take decisions in regard to its product mix. The factors affecting the choice of the product mix of a company are :

(a) Profits and sales growth potential

(b) Stability in sales

(c) Better customer service

(d) Utilisation of available know-how and other strengths of the company

(e) Cost reduction

(f) Better capacity utilisation.

III Packaging Concept

Packaging, over the years, has acquired a lot of promotional value for a product. Many products like cosmetics, playing cards, and readymade garments are made attractive to the customers through fancy and elaborate packaging. Packaging performs several functions, including :

(a) Protection from damage during handling, transportation, storage, etc.

(b) Creating a distinctive brand image in the minds of the customers.

(c) Providing information about various aspects of the product like weight, name of the manufacturer, date of manufacture, contents, etc.

(d) Making the product attractive to the customers. Cosmetics are excellent example.

(e) Improving the handling and convenience during storage, transport and displaying.

Many new materials and technologies are now available for packaging of different products. While designing the package for a product, a firm should consider the following:

(a) The functions which are to be performed through packaging;

(b) The practice being followed by the industry;

(c) The availability of any new materials, technologies, or styles;

(d) The tastes, preferences, and convenience of the customers; and

(e) The costs involved.

IV. Branding Concept

The important components of branding are :

A ***brand*** is a word, mark, symbol, or combination thereof used to identify the goods or services.

A ***brand name*** is that part of a brand which can be vocalised (e.g., Gillete, Sony, Titan).

A ***brand mark*** is that part of a brand which can be recognised but not vocalised.

A ***trade mark*** is that part of a brand which has legal protection for exclusive use.

We see that most products that are sold today are branded. Some of the advantages of branding are :

(a) It helps in giving a distinctive image to the product;

(b) It helps in communicating to the customers some desirable features of the product;

(c) It makes it easy for the customers to order and identify the product;

(d) It could help in providing legal protection against imitation;

(e) It helps in building a loyal set of customers;

(f) It helps in earning goodwill for a company which is useful for growth and diversification.

V. Product Service (After Sales Service)

For many products, there is need for service after they are sold and delivered to the customer. In fact, for products like television sets, typewriters, computers, and automobiles, the availability of after-sales services is important criteria for deciding the purchase. Companies manufacturing such items spend large amount of money in making the services available to the customers.

The services include :

(a) Installation, maintenance and repairs of the equipment;

(b) Training of the customers on various aspects of product use ;

(c) Provisioning of spare parts.

Provision of good after-sales service can be used as a strong marketing point in case of many products. It increases the saleability of a product by generating confidence in the minds of the consumers. Moreover, satisfied customers ensure not only repeat purchases but also act as a source of publicity for the firm. Recognising the importance of after-sales services, many firms emphasise this aspect in their advertising.

VI. Product Pricing Concept

The price of a product is the amount of money a consumer must pay to have it.

Pricing decisions are extremely important as they greatly influence the profitability of a firm. Moreover, price is perhaps the most handy tool available to a firm to adopt its marketing strategy to changes in demand, costs, and competitive situation.

Many factors, both economic and non-economic, influence the pricing decisions. These are :

(a) Cost

(b) Demand

(c) Competition

(d) Government regulations

(e) Behaviour of the consumers, and

(f) The objectives of the enterprise.

Pricing Methods

Some methods and policies which are used individually or collectively in taking pricing decisions regarding pricing are :

1. Cost Plus Pricing

The total cost of the product is first determined. (Total cost is the sum of variable costs and fixed costs that are attributable to one unit of output). A margin of profit is then added to determine the price.

Suppose the total cost of making a fan is Rs. 400. If the manufacturer wishes to have a margin of 20% on the sale price, what should be selling price ?

To answer this question let us assume the sale price is Rs. x. The margin of the manufacturer is $x - 400$ (as the total cost is Rs. 400). Since the margin required is 20% of x, i.e., 0.2 x, we have :

$$0.2\,x = x - 400$$

or

$$0.8\,x = 400$$

$$x = \frac{400}{0.8} = \text{Rs. } 500$$

This method has several advantages :

(a) It is easy to operate,

(b) The prices can be adjusted according to the changes in the costs,

(c) The entrepreneurs become cost conscious, and

(d) The profitability is known easily.

There are certain disadvantages as well in using this method, since it does not take into account demand aspects, and other external environmental factors.

II. Variable Price Policy

Some entrepreneurs adopt a policy of charging different prices from different customers depending upon the situation prevailing in the market. This policy is usually adopted when the product is sold in different market segments. Situation under which the variable price policy is adopted are :

(a) Difference in the order size of the product;

(b) Difference in the anticipated business from different customers;

(c) Difference in the bargaining power of the customers ;

(d) Ignorance of the buyers ;

(e) Localised difference in the demand, and

(f) Difference in the ability to pay.

Under this policy, the minimum price is determined by the total cost of the product, and the maximum price by the customer's ability to pay. Bargaining is normally resorted to in finalising a deal. However, the use of this method may affect the goodwill of the company in the long run.

III. Base Price and Discounts

Under the variable price policy, the prices are changed according to the particular situation. Under the base price and discounts policy, a base price or list price is fixed and varying discounts are offered to different categories of customers. The discounts are offered uniformly to all customers and each one of them can avail these on satisfying the stipulated conditions.

Discounts and Allowances

These are the concessions in price offered to traders or buyers in the form of deductions from the list price or from the amount of the bill or invoice. These concessions are meant to reward the parties for certain acts such as early payment of dues, purchase in large quantities, off season buying and so on. Allowing discounts and making allowances tantamount to price differentials in the price actually charged to the customers. The objectives of price differential through discounts and allowances are : (i) accommodate different circumstances of purchases, (ii) to provide incentives to buy, (iii) to meet competitive situations, and (iv) to compensate buyers for the loss of some value satisfaction. Some important price discounts and allowances are briefly described below.

(a) Cash Discount: Most business transactions take place on credit. Hence, cash discount is allowed to encourage the debtors to pay in full by cash or cheque within a short period. It is deduction from the amount of book debt standing in the name of the debtor. The following are the merits of cash discount.

(i) The entrepreneur need not have a larger working capital as his cash is not going to be held up in debts.

(ii) There is a relief in the recovery of debts and there would be no danger of bad debts. Cash discount is calculated on the net amount due after first deducting trade discount and quality discounts from the catalogue price.

(b) Trade Discount: It is offered by the manufacturers to trade channel members viz, wholesalers, retailers, dealers, etc, who perform certain functions such as selling, storing and record-keeping. Hence it is also called *functional discount.* The purpose of this discount is to compensate the channel members for the services rendered by them. If the trade discount is *large,* the retailer may pass on a part of it to the consumer which may result in greater sales volume. Trade discount is calculated on the list price or catalogue price and shown as a deducttion in the invoice itself.

(c) Quantity Discount: In order to encourage a customer to make large purchases at a time or to retail buyer, quantity discounts are offered. Quantity discounts can reduce the prices for bulk purchase order. They are also called *patronage discount.* The following are the advantages of quantity discounts: (i) sales of slow moving items can be stimulated, (ii) entrepreneurs can reap the economies of large-scale production and large-scale selling and, (iii) the producers will be relieved from the burden of accumulated stocks and inventories.

(d) **Seasonal Discount:** It is a discount given to buyers who buy a product in off-season period. It is very common for products like fans, refrigerators and tourist services. It helps the entrepreneur to maintain a steady production throughout the year.

(e) **Allowances :** The entrepreneur may offer promotional allowances like advertising allowance, window display allowance, free samples, free display materials, free training, pre-sale demonstration, etc. It amounts to a price reduction of an equal amount of service expected.

IV. Market Rate Method

If the nature of the product manufactured by a firm is such that it is largely indistinguishable from those of the competitors, or if it is found that all manufacturers are charging more or less the same price for their products, the market rate method of pricing is usually adopted. The price is guided by the prevailing market rate. This method, is quite common in the case of services like courier, tailoring, or car or scooter servicing. The advantage of this method, specially for newly established small ventures, is that they get some immunity from the vagaries of price fluctuations.

MARKETING STARTEGY FOR NEW VENTURES

Marketing strategy is the set of programmes which are matched with the target market opportunities in order to achieve organisational objectives. Drawing up a marketing strategy essentially consists of these steps : target market selection, setting marketing objectives and developing the marketing programme.

Target Market Selection

A firm may choose to market its products to all users or to some subgroups. The startegic decisions that a firm has to make here are :

(*a*) ***'Whether to sell to the entire product market en masse or concentrate on a portion of the market:*** For example, a (readymade) garment/textile manufacturer may have to decide whether to carry the whole range of men's ladies and children's wear or to concentrate on men's wear alone. The company may take into account its product and market synergies before arriving at a decision. 'Vimal' is an example of the former while 'Raymonds' is an example of the later.

(*b*) ***Determining when an existing target market strategy needs to be modified:*** A survey revealed that Dabur India Ltd. was perceived as a small, old fashioned, fuddy duddy outfit in a remote corner near Delhi—while the fact is that it is a giant with huge manufacturing setup covering seven product area, with a strong multi-brand portfolio. To break such an image the company has called for a modification of its marketing strategy: including modernising packaging of its various brands, focusing on its R & D strengths etc.

(*c*) ***Deciding to stop serving a particular target market:*** Products which become obsolete or irrelevant, which are not able to survive against competition and which show slow growth rates because of declining industry growth (sunset industries) force the entrepreneurs to withdraw them from the market.

Strategic Approaches To Segmentation

Approaches to segmentation have their roots in a firm's strategic approaches to cover a market. An entreprener can choose any one of five strategies in the marketplace.

1. **Single Market/Segment Concentration:** This is a one product—One market strategy, also called 'niching'. For example, advertising agencies sometimes concentrate on a 'niche', offering hoarding or billboard sites in various locations of a city.
2. **Product Specialisation:** This is a one product—many markets strategy wherein the firm makes one product, may be with slight variations in model or variety, but sells it to various segments in the marketplace. Taking the same example as in the previous case, an advertising agency specialising to financial advertising (e.g., Sobhaghya) undertakes the advertising task for a public issue, corporate image, financial highlights and such other related services for its corporate clients.

This strategy helps firms build up strong position in their specific product category and establish their expertise in the market.

3. **Market Specialisation :** Offering many products to one market is the hallmark of this strategy. Johnson & Johnson offers almost the entire range of baby care products and has carved out an impressive share in the baby care market. Market specialists can use the insights gained into the behaviour of the market segment to introduce new products.
4. **Selective Specialisation:** This is a 'multiple niching strategy' wherein many distinct segments are chosen and product and market offerings are tailored to suit each segment. This helps the firm spread out its risk but requires a lot of resources to serve the multiple segments.
5. **Full Coverage:** This strategy calls for covering all customer groups with all the products. This is possible only for large firms with abundant resources. IBM, the computer giant, offers all the possible types of hardware and software covering all the segments in the computer market.

An entrepreneur can choose any one of the above strategies for market coverage. The implementation of the strategies can be done through:

(*a*) ***Differentiated Marketing:*** It involves either 'concentrated marketing/niching' or 'customisation'. Niching involves serving a segment with one product and marketing mix, while customisation means treating every customer as unique and designing a market offering to suit individual's needs. A via media approach is termed 'micro marketing' which entails cornering a small neighborhood with one market offering. For example, a satellite cable operator could differentiate his services to predominantly South Indian preferred satellite networks on a selective basis instead of investing on receiver sets for all the available channels.

(*b*) ***Undifferentiated Marketing :*** Also termed 'mass marketing' wherein total standardisation of product and marketing mix elements is one and the entire market is treated as one mass entity. Standardisation minimises costs of promotion as it is uniform in all the markets and also achieves economies of scale due to mass production of a narrow range of products. But it may also lead to neglect of many small segments which could aggregate to a large and attractive market.

BRANDING STRATEGIES

There are Four strategies available to an entrepreneur when he decides to introduce any product in the market place. Philip Kotler neatly sums up these strategies in the following grid:

	Product Category: Existing	Product Category: New
Brand: Existing	Line Extension	Brand Extension
Brand: New	Multibrands	New Brands

Fig. 11.12: Branding Strategies

Line Extension

When additional product items are introduced in the same product category with slight modification in terms of colour, size, form, ingredient and flavour, it is line extension. Companies sometimes use the same brand name for the extended line.

Some of the examples are given below :

- Nirma detergent powder and detergent bar.
- Horlicks and Complan in regular and chocolate flavours.
- Amrutanjan and Amrutanjan Strong
- Rin - Super Power, Triple Power, Shakti etc.
- Cinthol Lime and Cinthol Cologne
- Cologne Clinic, Clinic Active and Clinic Plus.

Line extension seeks to satisfy a customer's variety-seeking tendency and also force retailers to allot more shelf space to a company's product variants.

Even if one unit of each variant is stocked and displayed, a lot of shelf space is occupied at the store.

However, stretching this strategy too far could result in what Alries and Jack Trout call 'the line extension trap'. It can only lead to cannibalisation of sales between items of a company. Moreover, the promotion costs of all the extended items must be adequately covered by their sales.

Brand Extension

An existing brand name is used to launch a product in another category. For example, Ponds uses the same brand name for its shampoo, toilet soaps, talcum powder and cold cream, Dettol for antiseptic liquid and soap. Brand-extension as a strategy capitalises on the goodwill of a popular and well-entrenched brand already existing in the market. This leads to saving on advertising costs and company efforts to introduce a new brand name into the consumer's mind. However, indiscriminate brand extension leads to brand dilution and may hurt both original and the new products. Companies have to consider three important criteria before taking a brand extension decision. There include:

(a) The *'Fit'* between the categories of products — Dettol is accepted as an antiseptic but will it be accepted as a perfume? According to C. Merle Crawford, a 'brand elasticity analysis' has to be done to see how far a brand can stretch itself to other product categories and yet remain acceptable to the consumer.

(b) The *Value Perception* of the new (brand) category must be similar to that of the parent brand. A 'value-for money' perception is different from a 'great quality' perception.

(c) The *Competitive Edge* of a brand might not exist in another product category or might not be strong enough to face the competitors in that category. Which cosmetics company's brand can really make a dent in the baby powder and soap market vis-a-vis Johnson & Johnson?

Multi Brands

This involves introducing additional brands in the same category so that more market segments are covered. For example, the Titan range of watches covers the regular priced jewellery watch segment and the Raga range covers the women's watch segment. The tricky decision here is to weed out weaker brands so that the promotion effort is not diluted by the presence of too many brands.

New Brands

When a company launches products in a new category, it might have to do so under a different brand name. But promoting a new brand name is very expensive and involves as much thought and complexity as much as starting a new business venture.

MANAGING BRAND SYSTEMS

"A house of brands is like a family; each needs a role and a relationship to others",said Jeffrey Sinclair, a brand strategist.

Consider Jenson & Nicholson. This paint company has recently introduced computer-based systems of colour mixing to give householders an infinite range of shades branded as Instacolour. A crucial strategic question is : what will be the relation of Instacolour to several other brands of the company that have been heavily promoted in the past, e.g., Robbialac, Special Effects and the like?

How should they be fitted into a hierarchical structure of their brands as outlined in the box:

Brand Hierarchy
Corporate brand :
Umbrella range brand :
Individual product brand :
Sub brand :
Branded feature :

What should be the weight of the marketing and communication effort behind each? Should Jenson & Nicholson or (J & N) as a corporate brand be given any attention ('Whenever you see colour, think of us') ? Should the brands previously well known to consumers be allowed to languish in favour of Instacolour? What will give J & N's Instacolour a competitive edge when every big paint company is coming out with 'me-too' offerings?

Some brands in a brand system have to play a strategic role. These have given the company long term strength. Lesser brands are either to be considered under the umbrella of a strategic brand or divested.

These are typically some of the problems that may come to the centre stage. In the early stages these are latent problems and are allowed to linger.

Competitive Persuasion

The whole brand management game is, after all, a matter of competitive persuasion — of persuading a segment of consumers that the particular brand is more suitable for them than any other.

But the search for competitive advantage has got bogged down. Those brands which continue to base their strategies on a meaningful and persuasive USP and have won, continue to be market leaders or serious contenders, e.g., Pepsodent.

A modest number or other brands — despite financial parity — have based their success on advertising which is better liked and is more appealing. This liking has, in fact, made the brand well liked as well e.g., Minto.

Successful brands are those that can offset functional parity, when that is inevitable, with value added service. This will hold true for FMCG brands, consumers durables, business products and services, whether banks, hotels or air-lines. Number of examples of this trend can be found in today's market conditions, Farex vs. Cerelac being one of them.

Electronic Commerce

This is no longer a novel idea but is worth emphasising that brand managers must equip themselves to take advantage of what will surely be one of the most rewarding and also one of the most challenging strategies for brands — how to use the Internet to the brand's advantage.

PACKAGING STRATEGIES

The entrepreneur is required to develop suitable strategies for packing their products. This is primarily done keeping in view other P's of marketing. The major strategies involved are listed below:

Family Packaging

Related products are packed in similar packages to take the advantage of easy recognition and noticeability.

Multiple Packaging

Several units of the same product are packed in one container. This increases the total sales of a product.

Package Change

Design and /or materials of the packaging are changed to enhance the atractiveness and to improve the quality of the package. Sometimes the packaging is merely updated to be in tune with the changes in the marketing strategy for the brand.

DISTRIBUTION

W.J. Stanton provides the following guidelines for developing channels of distribution.

(i) The channel analysis should begin with the final customer and worked backwards for the producer because, essentially, channels of distribution are determined by consumer buying habits, i.e., appropriate outlets should be available to the customer.

(ii) Distribution channels finally established must be totally appropriate to the basic objectives of the firm's marketing programmes.

(iii) Distribution channels should provide a firm with an access to a pre-determined share of the market, including a definite level of intensity of market penetration.

(iv) The channels must be adequately flexible so that the use of one channel will not permanently close another.

(v) There is a high degree of interdependence among all firms in the distribution for any given product. To be successful there should not be a weak link in the supply chain.

(vi) Constant evolutionary and sometimes almost revolutionary changes occur, which necessitates that economic forces should be taken into account while formulating changes in the distribution strategy.

(vii) Services of middlemen can be effective only when their existence is economically sound and socially desirable.

PRICING STRATEGIES

One of the important task of an entrepreneur is to develop and implement appropriate marketing strategy. Generally, we find two strategies, viz, high price strategy and low price strategy. In the high price strategy, we can charge high prices till the rival competitors enter. The pricing policy like skimming the cream is a suitable example of the high pricing strategy. Contrary, the low price strategy is a situation of charging low prices. Such pricing strategy is followed with the purpose of entering or penetrating the market. This strategy is suitable particularly in situation where demand for the product is highly elastic. The rising trends in competition also induce a firm to follow this pricing strategy. As a matter of fact, the decision-making practices for the pricing strategies can't be adopted in isolation. While developing pricing strategies, the entrepreneurs must consider production and pricing promotional activities as a whole or as interdependent variables.

Pricing a New Product

The introduction of a new product may involve some problems as there is neither an established market for the product nor a demonstrated demand for it. The entrepreneur may expect a substantial demand for the product, though it still needs to be established. Even if there are some near substitutes the actual degree of substitution has to be estimated. Again, the entrepreneur will not have reliable estimate of the direct cost of marketing and manufacturing of the product.

Moreover, the cost patterns are likely to change with greater knowledge and increasing volume of production. The basic pricing policy for a new product, however, remains the same as for established products — it must cover full cost in the long run and direct cost in the short run. Of course, there is greater uncertainty about both the demand and costs of the new product particularly from a new venture.

Apart from the problem of estimating the demand for an entirely new product, certain other initial problems likely to be faced are :

1. Discovering a competitive range of price,
2. Investigating probable sales at several possible prices, and
3. Considering the possibility of retaliation from products substituted by it.

In addition, decisions have to be taken on target markets, design of the promotional strategy and the channels of distribution. Test marketing can be helpful in solving these problems.

Under test marketing the product is introduced in selected areas, often at different prices in different areas. These tests provide the management with an idea of the amount and elasticity of the demand for the product, the competition it is likely to face, and the expected sales volume and profits it might yield at different prices. Test marketing, however, is not a perfect simulation of full-scale production and distribution. Yet it may provide very useful information for better planning of the full-scale effort. It also permits initial pricing mistakes to be made on small scale rather than on a large scale. Test Marketing does not eliminate risk. It only improves knowledge, and reduces the chances of expensive mistakes.

The next important questions is, "Whether to charge high initial price or a low penetration price?

If a skimming price is adopted, the initial price is very high. This policy may be held for varying periods of time, indefinitely if the product enjoys valid and defensible patent protection. But usually, it is not longer than the time necessary for competitors to study the product's usefulness, to decide what to do about it and to prepare for making a similar product. This requires a period ranging from few weeks to as much as two years. After this period, the price is apt to drop precipitately and over a period of few years to approach the usual or customary margin above cost that is common in the industry.

In case of penetration pricing, the initial price of the new product is apt to be somewhere near what may be expected to be the usual or customary level. Once competitors enter the field, generally it is slightly above this level. If the initial price is properly fixed, only minor adjustments would have to be made as and when the competition develops.

DEVELOPING THE SALES PROMOTION SCHEMES

After deciding the objectives and tools of sales promotion, the entrepreneur has to make a few more decisions to ensure effective results. The following area highlight a few such aspects :

1. Size of Incentive

The entrepreneur has to determine how much incentive should be offered. A certain minimum incentive is necessary if the promotion is to succeed. A higher incenttive level will produce more sale response, but at a diminishing rate. The marketer may usually decide the quantum of incentives on the basis of effectiveness of past promotion plans.

2. Condition for Participation

Incentive should not be distributed to all the prospective buyers indiscriminately. It should be offered only to those who have the innate desire and attitude to purchase products offered by the company.

3. Distribution Pattern

The entrepreneur should also decide the mode and media of distribution of incentives. The cost of distribution should not be more than the results that are expected from the sales promotion efforts.

4. Duration of Sales Promotion

If the sales promotion period is too short, many prospects will not be able to take advantage, since they may not be repurchasing at that time. If the promotion runs too long, the scheme will loose some of its effects.

5. Timing of Promotion

The sales promotion managers have to develop a time schedule for the promotions. The dates must be suitable to production, sales and distribution managers. Some unplanned promotion may become necessary. At that time, the co-operation of the people concerned must be enlisted.

6. Sales Promotion Budget

One can choose the promotion tools, and methods of implementation in advance. On the basis of such a plan, he can estimate the cost of sales promotion activities. The more popular way is to earmark a percentage of the total budget to use for sales promotion.

7. Pre-Testing

Sales Promotion schemes should be pre-tested if possible. The purpose is to determine whether the scheme is appropriate or not. It is also helpful to test the suitability of the size of the incentive in the context of a particular target group.

8. Implementing the Promotion Schemes

Companies should establish implementation plans for each promotion covering lead time and sell off time. Lead time is the time required to prepare the programme before launching it. Sell-off time begins with the launch and ends when the deal closes.

Sales Promotion Schemes

On the Basis of Target Group

Consumers
1. Samples
2. Coupons
3. Premiums
4. Price of promotion
5. Money refund offers
6. Contests
7. Sweepstakes and games
8. Demonstrations
9. Trading stamps

Middlemen
1. Buying allowance
2. Buy-back allowance
3. Count and recount
4. Merchandise allowance
5. Free goods

Sales force
1. Bouns
2. Commission

On the Basic of Location

In-store Promotion
1. Premiums
2. Price reduction
3. In store display
4. Demonstrations

In-house or in business promotion
1. Coupons
2. Samples
3. Contests
4. Demonstrations
5. Public relations

PRODUCT LIFE CYCLE

A product passes through four stages in its life namely, introduction, growth, maturity and decline. With the product passing through these stages the entrepreneur faces varing challenges, opportunities and problems. Profits rise and fall at different stages of the product life cycle. Most product life cycle curves are bell shaped and are divided into four stages.

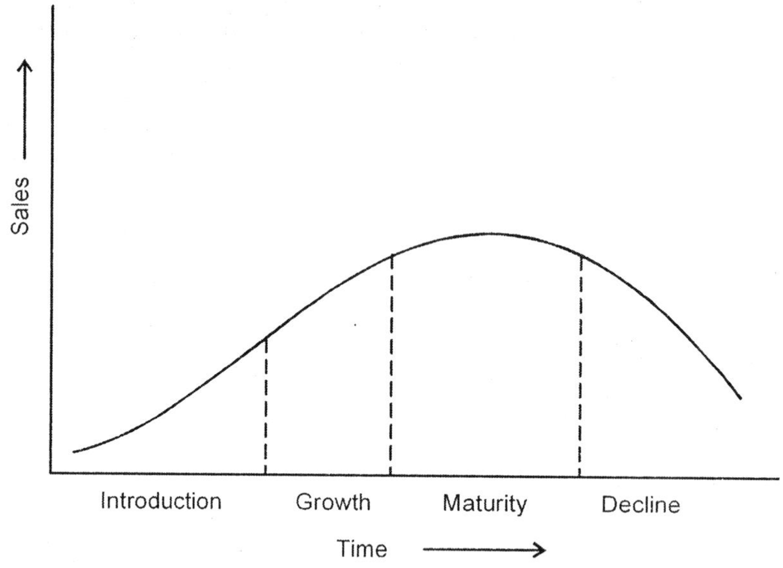

Fig. 11.13

Introduction: When the new product is introduced it starts with a period of slow growth. Profits are usually non-existant as heavy expences are incurred for introducing the product.

Growth : The sales as well as the profits increase rapidly as the product is accepted in the market.

Maturity: This is a period where the sales growth slows down. The product has been accepted by most of the potential buyers. Profits stabilise, may be at a level lower than their previous peak levels . The completition has increased.

Decline: The sales show a downward drift. **Profits erode and substitutes have appeared in the market.**

Products require different marketing, financial manufacturing, purchasing strategies at each stage of their product life. Entrepreneur has to choose a suitable marketing strategy depending upon the products position in its life cycle. The important strategies are as follows :

Introduction Stage Strategies

The main objectives during this stage are to inform the customers about the product, to induce trial of the product and achieve adequate distribution of the product. Marketers can follow strategies as shown below :

Rapid Skimming Strategy : consists of charging a premium price to make as much profit as possible. The firm has to spend heavily on promotion to convince customers to accept the product even at the high price. For example, consider the pricing of many electronic gadgets like televisions, VCRs and music (audio) systems. There is a readiness to buy the product—the marketer creates brand preferences.

Slow Skimming Strategy : uses low level of promotion to market a high priced product. Due to the limited size of the market, the marketer expects to make profits by keeping promotional expenses down. Example—exercise cycles are priced almost twice the price of ordinary bicycles.

Price Level	Low	High
High ↑	Rapid Skimming	Slow Skimming
Low	Rapid Penetration	Slow Penetration

Promotion Level ⟶

Fig. 11.14: Marketing Strategies at Introduction Stage

Rapid Penetration Strategy : is a low price-high promotion strategy designed to capture as much of the market as possible. Nirma washing powder is one such example.

Slow Penetration Strategy : believes in low price to attract consumers to buy the product. Low promotion costs helps keep the net profit position healthy.

Growth Stage Strategies

This is the most attractive stage for competitors who enter the market encouraged by the success of the pioneers in the product category. Here, each firm tries to show its one—upmanship over the competing firm's products. Product quality improvement, addition of product features, introduction of new models and styles, entering new market segments and building brand preference through persuasive advertising are some of the strategies entrepreneurs adopt in order to sustain sales growth volume.

Maturity Stage Strategies

At this stage, companies focus on somehow increasing the sales of their product or decide to abandon it to make way for more profitable products. The firm can pursue some strategies aimed at the market, the product or the marketing mix at this stage.

Market Modification Strategies : are ways to expand the market. These include converting non-users of the product category—example; computers sold to homes; encouraging consumers to switch from competitors brands—Complan versus Horlicks; entering new market segment—portable generator sets in the household segment; increasing frequency of use - example ; toothpaste marketers promoting brushing of teeth after every meal; stimulating more usage per occasion—example : detergent (Surf Ultra) marketers supplying deep spoons for using 'scoopfuls' of powder for every wash; and identifying new uses for the product—example Milkmaid; as dessert ingredient with various recipes.

Product Modification : consists of presenting quality improvements and launching 'New', 'Improved', 'Extra Strength', 'Plus' and 'Super' versions of the product such that the customer sees a perceptible difference between the old and the new product versions.

Feature Improvement: consists of adding features the enhance product performance. For example, twinblade razors promise a safer, smoother shave in comparison to the conventional single blade razors.

The consumer electronics companies too use feature improvements quite often with each company offering an improved technology.

Style Improvement: is done to enhance aesthetic appeal. Introduction of new models of a product and enhancing the attractiveness of packaging leads to style improvement.

Marketing-mix Modification : involves changes in the elements of the marketing mix.

Prices : can be lowered through discounts, easy purchase schemes, credit purchases etc., or prices can be raised to give a premium image.

Distribution : can be expanded to cover more number and types of outlets.

Advertising : changes can be made in message/ media and frequency of advertisement.

Sales promotional measure : like trade schemes, consumer promotions, contests, gifts, rebate coupons etc. can be offered.

However, it is difficult to keep a product going on the strength of promotional schemes alone and the result is often a marketing war among the competitors. A good example of a company attempting at adopting market modification (attracting non-users, entering new market segments), product modification (distribution in 'upper class' outlets also) could be Lifebuoy Gold introduced by HLL.

Decline Stage Strategies

A declining product has to be identified at the right time by using cost and profit information. A declining product would have lost its distinctive position because of too many imitative products available in the market. A technology change could also render the product obsolete and push it into decline.

At this stage distribution strategy gets focused on removing the product from unprofitable outlets and concentrating on a select few outlets. Promotional support becomes almost nil as sales shrink too low. Prices are pushed down in a bid to clear stocks in the market.

Once a declining product has been identified, *a product deletion decision* could be taken. At this stage, the timing of the decision is very crucial. Especially in the case of durables, adequate advance warning has to be given to customers and spare parts and replacement parts have to be kept available for a considerable period of time when the product is phased out. If the entrepreneur develops and introduces a new product to replace the old one, it will be an ideal strategy to maintain customer loyalty.

Product Rejuvention : can sometimes occur if a major product improvement or repositioning is done even at the decline stage. For example, cinema or the movie industry faced a decline the world over due to television, video and satellite channels. But a revival is occurring due to the use of special visual effects, Dolby sound systems and 'multiplex' theatres. Customers have been forced to come to theatres to watch movies like Jurassic Park which would seem toy-like and ridiculous on the small screen.

Summary

Marketing management looks at the environment, while entrepreneur scans the environment in a dynamic fashion to look for potential opportunities as well as threats. Typically marketing management takes a snapshot of the environment. Entrepreneur looks at the environment through a movie camera and scans dynamically.

The decision process adopted by strategic marketing is more bottom-up with participation by many individuals. Marketing allows for greater participation from people who are in direct contact with the customers. Marketing strategy is the set of programmes which are matched with the target opportunities in order to achieve organisational objectives. One of the important responsibilities of an entrepreneur is to develop and implement appropriate market strategy formulation.

REVIEW QUESTIONS

1. "The marketing concept does not imply that marketing executives will run the firm. The concept requires only that whoever is in top management be marketing oriented". Explain the above statement and distinguish how marketing concept is different from product concept and societal concept.
2. What is market segmentation ? Why should a company want to segment its markets ? What are the limitations of market segmentation?

3. List the various types of channels of distribution and also the functions performed by them. Also explain the merits and demerits of direct marketing in the Indian context.
4. What is brand equity ? What are the steps involved for building and managing brand equity ? How do you measure brand equity ?
5. What are the conditions under which you would follow each of the following pricing strategies ?
   (a) Skim the cream-pricing strategy;
   (b) Penetration-pricing strategy.

Illustrate your answer with suitable Indian examples.

6. Identify the key factors which have brought about a marketing revolution in India, especially after liberalisation of the economy. Also identify any five of the major marketing challenges facing Indian firms in the context of integration of the Indian economy with the Global economy.
7. Discuss the psychological and socio-cultural factors that influence Indian consumer behaviour with suitable illustrations.
8. Discuss the role of market segmentation and also explain the steps involved in the market segmentation process with suitable illustrations drawn from Indian experience.
9. List the phases of the product life cycle and examine the product diffusion process.
10. Explain the meaning of price and its role in the marketing mix. Also identify major pricing strategies that could be considered while launching a product that is completely new to the market.

CASE 11.1

THE "SUCCESS" STORY

A distribution house was handling a number of consumer products of reputed companies, acting as their—selling agent. The products were marketed by the company under the brand names of their respective manufacturing concerns. The company lost a profitable agency since the distribution of the products was taken over by the manufacturer himself.

Based on its past experience on similar lines, the company introduced a tooth paste in the market manufactured by itself, under the brand name of 'Success'. At this point of time, 'C' was the brand leader in the tooth paste market followed by 'B' and 'F'. When 'Success' in 'Large' size was launched initially, the distribution was fantastic, in both the rural and the urban markets. The coverage was extensive and the consumer response was very encouraging. The product was much in demand in all the retail outlets, including pan shops. However, after sometime, the company started getting a number of complaints related to packaging. The caps used were unable to withstand the transportation, due to which the contents from the tubes were leaking out. Without fully rectifying the defects the company came out in the market with bigger sizes of tooth pastes like 'Giant' and 'Economy' under the same brand name 'Success'. Simultaneously, the company introduced a new range of product like talcum powder, hair cream, tooth brush and shaving cream. All these products, were manufactured by the company itself. At the time of launching these products, the company was already marketing shaving cream and tooth brush under different brand names with regular trade schemes. But the company did not operate any attractive dealer scheme for the 'Success' range of products and the sudden spurt in the number of products handled did not have the requisite advertising back-up.

The company began to notice a sudden decline in the sales of the newly introduced products. At this stage, the company also introduced the 'Success' tooth powder in two different sizes. During this period the supplies of the brand leader 'C' were irregular and restricted. The other two tooth paste manufacturers, viz., 'B' and 'F' did not have tooth powder. Therefore, the 'Success' tooth powder started moving well in the market.

The company again launched a new series of similar products except tooth paste under a new brand name 'Victory'. This turned out to be an utter failure due to poor marketing strategies, which adversely affected company's image.

The company appoints' a new professional marketing chief, who decided to go in for yet another range of cosmetic products grounding the 'Success' series of products, out of the market. The new venture also proved to be futile exercise, and the 'Victory' range of products also had to be abandoned finally.

QUESTIONS

1. How do you correlate the failure of the 'Success' range of products?
2. Is the company justified in introducing the 'Victory' range of products?
3. What is your reaction to the decisions of the new marketing chief?
4. Do you find any organisational weaknesses in the functioning of the company?

CHAPTER

12

OPERATIONS MANAGEMENT

CHAPTER OUTLINE

- — Operations Management
- — Size and Location of Enterprise
- — Layout
- — Manufacturing Processes
- — Inventory Control
- — Purchasing
- — Quality Control

OPERATIONS MANAGEMENT

In any business enterprise, products are produced or services are provided. For this, certain operations are carried out through a combination of raw material, processing or assembling the various components, using the services of workers, machines, tools and power. In any enterprise the items are produced or service is provided with a minimum waste of raw material and consumption of time and effort while assuring quality.

An operation may be defined as "*the process of changing inputs into outputs thereby adding value to some entity*". Value is added to the entity by one or more of the following ways, i.e.,

(i) Altering the form of inputs, e.g., converting crude petroleum to petrol or converting raw food into a dish.

(ii) Transporting the materials to where they are required, i.e., taking out coal from mines and moving it to power stations.

Size and Location of Enterprise

While establishing the unit, an entrepreneur is required to pay attention to various aspects like size, location and layout as these effect the efficiency of the operations. Such factors should preferably be considered by the entrepreneur at the project planning stage and need to be taken care of at the project implementation stage

Size

The size of the unit refers to the production or *installed capacity*. The size is important as it determines the use of technology and in most cases the layout of the production process. The size of the plant should be fixed with due consideration to economy of scale. Size also encompasses factors like land, building etc. Size of land should be such to take care of storage of raw materials, finished goods as well as construction of factory for processing/manufacturing. The size of the plot of land should be such so as to take care of present and future requirements of expansion. This would also apply to the building which may be constructed or rented.

Location

Proper location of an enterprise is crucial for its success. Raw material, skilled labour, and market are the factors that help production in a manufacturing unit. Location of manufacturing establishments would depend upon their type, which could be :

- Resource based;
- Demand based;
- Skill based, or
- Foot loose.

For resource based units like agro-industry, nearness to the source of raw material is a definite advantage. Thus, a sugar factory should be located near sugarcane growing area otherwise cost of transporting the raw material will be high. Similarly, for demand based industries location near the market is advisable and for skill-based industries like gold embriodery or information technology, locate the units at a place where such skilled workers are available. It is for this reasons, entrepreneurs and corporate from different parts of the world are setting up their software and processing units in India.

A unit to be located in a residential or commercial area has to take note of local bye-laws and should not be a nuisance to the neighbourhood in terms of pollution (including sound), work force, transport bottle neck, etc.

Location Strategy

It is difficult to set down rules, whereby, the problem of location can be programmed but there are a number of factors which should be considered. It is worth differentiating between the problems of location and of site : the location is the general area, and the site is the place chosen within the location.

The decision on selecting, thus, probably proceeds in two stage : in the first, the general area is chosen; and then a detailed survey of that area is carried out to find possible sites. The final decision is made by taking into account more detailed requirements.

1. **Proximity to market :** Organisations may choose to locate facilities close to their market, not merely to minimize transportation costs, but to provide a better service. The closer the plant or facilities are to the consumer, the easier it is to provide just-in-time delivery, to respond to changes in demand and to react to field or service problems. The choice of market promixity is clearly restricted for those providing a pure service which is not easily transported. Customer-based services such as retail-stores, health care, theatres and restaurants clearly must be located close to the market.
2. **Integration with other parts of the organisation :** If the new plant or facility is one of a number owned or operated by a single organisation or group, it should be so situated such that its work can be integrated with that of the associated units. This will require that the group should be considered as an entity, not as a number of independent units.
3. **Availability of labour and skills :** Labour may be more readily available in some places than in others. Certain geographical areas have traditional skills but it is very rare that a location can be found which has appropriately skilled and unskilled labour, both readily available, in the desired proportions or quantities. The choice often has to be made between a location where skilled people exist, but are not readily available, and one where there is a supply of semiskilled labour. Of course, new skills can be taught, processes simplified and/or made less exciting, and key personnel moved.
4. **Availability of amenities :** A location which provides good external amenities — housing, shops, community services, communication systems — is often more attractive than one which is more remote. One important amenity in this connection is good personnel transport — buses and trains. Evidence of good schools, hospital and civil infrastructure is often important to attract knowledge workers.
5. **Availability of transport :** It is important that good transport facilities are readily available. There are five basic modes of physical transportation; air, road, rail, water and pipeline. Goods intended largely for export may prefer a location near a seaport or a large airport, but the choice of transport method and therefore location, will clearly depend on relative costs, convenience and suitability. Mail-order businesses, delivery services, and operations like Disney World tend to make location decisions based very much on availability to a good transportation network.
6. **Availability of inputs :** Good transport facilities will enable goods and services to be obtained and delivered readily, but a location near main suppliers will help to reduce cost and permit staff to meet suppliers easily to discuss quality, technical or delivery problems. Any purchaser who has tried to improve the delivery performance of an inaccessible supplier will bear witness to the considerable difficulties involved. Important supplies that are expensive or difficult to obtain by transport should be readily available in the locality.
7. **Availability of services :** There are six main services which need to be considered :
   (a) gas;
   (b) electricity;
   (c) water;
   (d) drainage;
   (e) disposal of waste;
   (f) communications.

Certain industries use considerable quantities of water, e.g., food preparation, laundries, chemicals, metal plating etc., others use a great deal of electricity, e.g., steel and smelting processes. An assessment must be made of the requirements for these, for as far as possible. Under-estimating the needs of any of the services can prove to be extremely costly and inconvenient. Financial services often require rapid communications throughout the world. Hence, large banks are often located in large, well-developed cities with excellent telecommunication networks.

8. **Suitability of land and climate :** The geology of the area needs to be considered, together

with the climatic conditions (humidity, temperature and atmosphere). Modern building technologies are such that almost all disadvantages of terrain and climate can be overcome but the cost of doing so, may be high and a different locality could avoid these initial costs. Clearly, services based on ocean sports, ski resorts and other outdoor health pursuits present severe geographical or environmental constraints on location.

9. **Regional regulations :** It is important to check at any early stage that the proposed location does not infringe any local regulations. A study must be made of the appropriate bye-laws and of any special regulations concerning the disposal of effluents, etc.
10. **Room for expansion :** It is unwise to build to the limit of any site unless the long-range forecast indicates very definitely that the initial building will never be required to increase in size. It is most unlikely circumstance, hence an adequate room for genuine expansion should be provided.
11. **Safety requirements :** Some production units may present, or may be believed to present potential dangers to the surrounding neighbourhood; for example, nuclear power stations, chemical and explosives factories are often considered dangerous. Location of such plants in remote areas may be desirable.
12. **Site cost :** As a first charge, the site cost is important, although it is necessary to prevent immediate benefit from jeopardizing long-term plans.
13. **Political, cultural and economic situation :** The political situation in potential locations should be considered. Even if other considerations demand a particular site, knowledge of the political, cultural and local prejudice (e.g., restriction of women or foreign workers) or economic difficulties can assist in taking decisions. For some service organisations, such as insurance companies, gambling casinos and private educational institutions, the 'business climate' of an area of city may be a major factor in site location.
14. **Special grants, regional taxes and import/export barriers :** Certain government and local authorities often offer special grants, low-interest loans, low rental or taxes and other inducements in the hope of attracting certain industries to particular locations. As these are often areas with large reservoirs of labour or natural resources, such offers can be most attractive. Location of facilities in foreign countries to avoid exportation difficulties is now well accepted and some Japanese companies have used this method successfully throughout the world.

Layout

Layout involves determining the space requirement for the facilities and arranging them in a manner to ensure steady flow of operations with minimum overall cost. In other words, a layout is a floor plan for arranging the desired facilities, machinery, equipment in an optimum locations so as to permit the quickest flow of materials and manpower at the lowest cost and with the least amount of in process handling from receipt of raw material to shipment of finished products.

Since, a layout once made cannot be changed /modified easily and without incurring considerable cost on one hand and disrupting the operations on the other hand, layout decisions are strategic decisions. Hence, layout has to be considered at the time of planning a new venture. A good layout should result in comfort, convenience, better appearance, safety, efficiency and profits. A poorly planned layout causes congestion, disruption in flow of man and/or materials, accidents, delays, rejections leading to frustration and inefficiency. In a production unit layout includes factory design, that is layout of workshop, raw material stock yards, finished goods stores, generator, compressor room etc. In hospitals it involves fixing the location of wards, operation theater, out-patient departments, canteen, doctors and nurses duty rooms etc. At another level layout planning involves layout of different machines, work stations etc., in the shop floor and patient's beds, drug store, doctors and nurses seats and other facilities in a hospital ward. Irrespective of the level at which the layout is being designed the following aspects are kept in view :

- Maximum use of the available space.
- Compatibility with the production technology and product mix.
- Minimum movement of materials as well as men.

- Provision of proper space for maintenance.
- Arrangement of proper in-transit storage and stacking space.
- Promotes effective supervision.
- Proper lighting and ventilation.
- Provision of maximum flexibility.
- Safety of operators and other staff.
- Minimum handling of materials.
- Provision for future expansion.
- Security against fire, theft, detoriation etc.
- Maximum flexibility to accomodate changes in production volume and product mix.
- Should meet the specific requirements of the production process viz. air conditioning, air cooling, dust control, humidity control as may be required.

Advantages of Proper Plant Layout

1. Increase in Productivity
2. Maximum Utilisation of Space
3. Effective Supervision and Control
4. Economy in Material
5. Improved Safety and Handling
6. Improved Working Environment and Morale
7. Better Quality Control.

Manufacturing Processes

Manufacturing or transformation process converts inputs into outputs and adds value to the product. Selection of the manufacturing process is also a strategic decision as changes in the same are costly. Therefore, the manufacturing process is selected at the stage of planning a business venture. The manufacturing process should meet the twin objective of (i) meeting the specifications of final product, and (ii) being cost effective.

Types of Manufacturing Processes

The manufacturing processes have been classified into four types :

1. Jobbing Production : Herein one or few units of the products are produced as per the requirement and specifications of the customer. Production is to meet the delivery schedule and costs as are fixed prior to the contract. When the job is complex and large it is called *project production.*

2. Batch Production : Herein limited quantities of each of the different types of products are manufactured on the same set of machines. Different products are produced separately one after the other.

3. Mass or Flow Production : Herein a production run is conducted on a set of machines arranged according to the sequence of operations. Several number of same products are manufactured at a time and are stocked for sale. Different product will require different manufacturing lines. Since one line can produce only one type of product. The process is also called *line flow.*

4. Process Production : Herein the production run is conducted for an indefinite period.

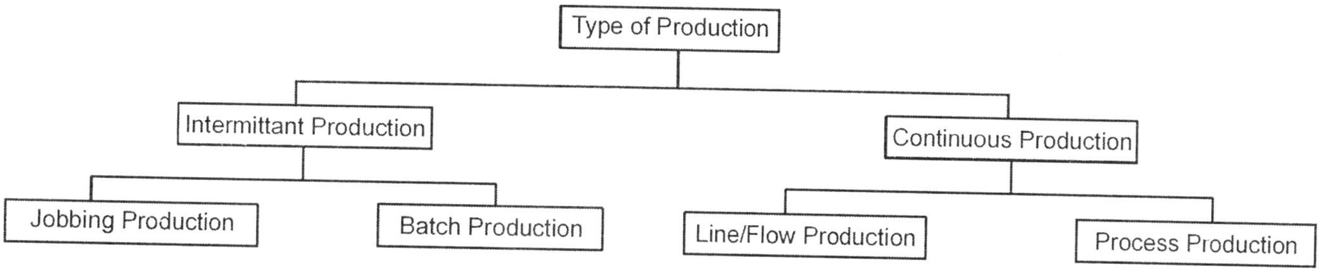

Fig. 12.1: Classification of Production Process

Manufacturing Process Choice Depends upon
- Volume
- Variety
- Plant Capacity
- Lead Time
- Flexibility
- Efficiency

Factors Influencing Choice of Manufacturing Process

The following factors effect the choice of the manufacturing process

(a) Effect of Volume/Variety. This is one of the major consideration in selection of manufacturing process. When the volume is low and variety is high, intermittent processes are suitable and with increase in volume and reduction of variety continuous processes become suitable. The following figure indicates the choice of process as a function of repetitiveness. Volume of goods produced divided by their variety represents the degree of repetitiveness in the production system.

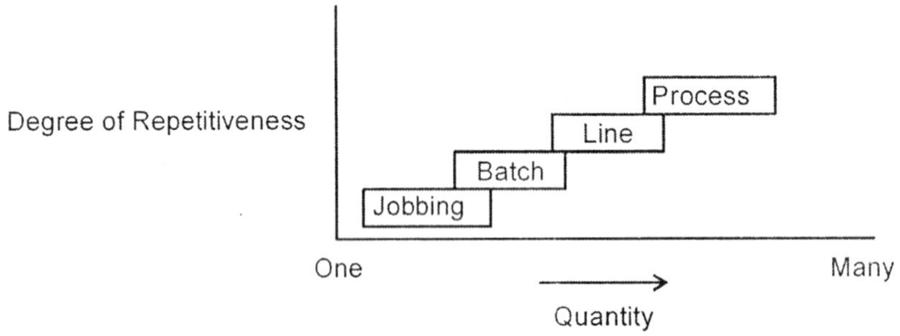

Fig. 12.2. Choice of Process and Repetitiveness

(b) Capacity of the Plant. Projected sales volume is the factor to choose between Batch and Line process. Fixed costs are high for line process and low for batch process. The converse is true for the variable costs which are low for line process and high for batch process. Thus, at low volume it would be cheaper to install and maintain a batch process and line process becomes economical at higher volumes.

(c) Lead Time. The continuous process normally yields faster deliveries as compared to batch process. Lead times and level of competition effect the choice of production process.

(d) Flexibility. Flexibility and product variety are inter related. If more variety is expected in future or future changes are contemplated, the manufacturing process needs to be flexible. Batch process is generally more flexible than line process.

(e) Efficiency. It means speed and cost of production. Efficiency is greater when products are mass produced.

Inventory Control

A business unit requires to keep inventories of raw materials, goods in progress (semi-finished goods), and finished goods, both in stock and in transit. It has many advantages : (1) Materials are readily available when required for production/use ; (2) Quantity discounts results in large orders ; (3) The finished goods inventory allows a firm to meet the requirements of the customers promptly ; (4) The demand may fluctuate over time and the finished goods inventory helps in reducing the impact of such fluctuations on the process of production.

However, "holding the inventory" has certain costs, called 'carrying costs'. Since, holding inventory has advantages and carrying costs, a balance has to be reached.

When to Order Inventory ?

In order to decide when to order an inventory, one has to decide :

(a) Order lead time: Average time that elapses between placing an order and receiving the goods;

(b) Usage rate : The average rate at which the inventory is drawn down over a period; and

(c) Reorder point : The level at which a new order must be placed so that the inventory is replenished before the stock reaches zero level (stock out).

A re-order point is estimated by using the formula

Reorder Point = Usage Rate × Lead Time.

Suppose a company uses 10 units of an item per day (usage rate), and the order lead time is 15 days, a new order must be placed when the inventory level reaches 150 units (reorder point 150 = usage rate 10 × lead time 15) so that the inventory is replenished before a stock out occurs.

How Much to Order ?

To determine how much to order, a concept called the *Economic Order Quantity* (EOQ) is used. Though maintaining large inventories involves carrying costs, the placing of an order also involves order-processing costs consisting of the cost of materials (stationery, stamps etc.) and purchase establishment expenses. If the ordered quantity is large, an order has to be placed less often. But as the order size increases, the inventory carrying costs also increases. Thus, the total order-processing cost increase when the size of individual order is reduced, but carrying cost increases when the order quantity is increased. The situation is depicted in the Fig. 12.3.

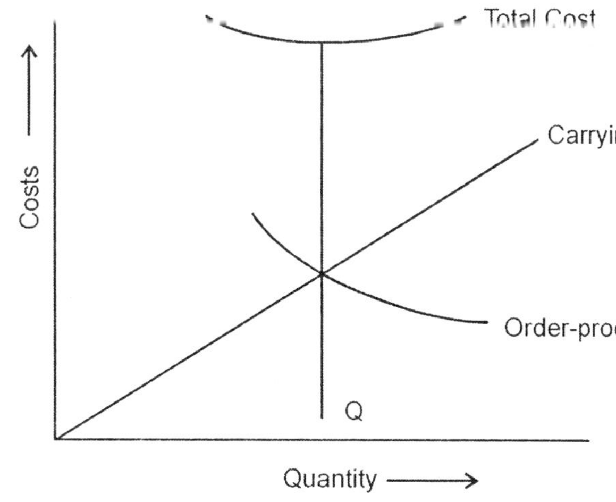

Fig. 12.3. Economic inventory Order Quantity

A balance between these two opposing costs - carrying costs and order-processing costs, can be achieved by computing the Economic Order Quantity Q*. with the help of the formula

$$Q^* = \sqrt{\frac{2CS}{1}}$$

where

C = the annual usage (or demand) of the item, in units

S = the cost to place one order

I = annual carrying cost per unit.

Suppose the annual usage of an item is 2000 units, ordering costs are Rs. 50 an order, and the carrying costs are Rs. 20 per unit per year then the Economic Order Quantity is

$$Q^* = \sqrt{\frac{2 \times 2000 \times 50}{2}} = 100 \text{ units}$$

The formula for EOQ is however based on the assumptions that

(a) ordering cost is constant, i.e., it does not vary with the size of the order;

(b) the cost of carrying an additional unit of inventory is constant;

(c) there are no quantity discounts available, and

(d) the usage or consumption is in a steady state and is known with certainty.

Which Items of the Inventory Claim Bulk of the Value ?

To know which items constitute the bulk of the value of total inventory, a technique commonly known as the **ABC analysis** is used.

It has been observed that out of a long list of inventory, a relatively small percentage, approximately 20 per cent lock up a major share (70-80 per cent) of capital, whereas relatively small cost (say 5 per cent of capital) is used to buy the bulk of the items in the inventory. These items, which occupy small volume (20 per cent) and account for major capital (70-80 per cent) are termed 'A' Category items.

Another 20 per cent of the items may account for 10-5 per cent of the total value and are termed 'B' Category items.

The remaining 60 per cent of the items which account for only about 10 per cent of total value are termed 'C' Category items.

Steps involved in ABC analysis

1. For each item calculate the total cost based on the number of pieces used.
2. Arrange these items progressively in decreasing order.
3. Calculate and write the cumulative total cost in third column.
4. Then compute the per cent of cumulative total to a) total cumulative, and b) total number of items and record a+b in column 4 and 5 respectively.

Tabulation

Item	*Total cost Rs.*	*Cumulative total cost Rs.*	*% of Rs. 20000*	*% of range of 200 items*
1	1000	1.000	5	5
2	900	1.900	9.5	1.0
3	850	2.750	13.75	1.5
20	300	12.000	60	10
40	100	16.000	80	20
100	20	18.000	90	50
198	5	19.992	99.96	99
199	5	19.997	99.98	99.5
200	3	20.000	100	100

Classification	*% of Items*	*% of Total Cost Amount*	*Cost per group of items*
A = item no 1-20	20	67	12,000
B = item no 21-60	20	22	4,000
C = all other items upto 200	60	11	4,000

Each item under category A is crucial to an organization in terms of inventory control, purchase efficiency, and working capital management.

ABC analysis is often supplemented by two other techniques, i.e., FSN and VED analysis.

FSN Analysis classifies goods into fast-moving, slow-moving and non-moving items and is similar to ABC analysis. It is based on usage rate or turnover of an item.

Inventory Turnover Ratio: Inventory is managed by using an accounting ratio i.e., *Inventory Turnover Ratio*

$$\text{Inventory Turnover Ratio} = \frac{\text{Cost of goods sold}}{\text{Average Inventory}}$$

A comparison of current year's inventory ratio with those of previous years is used in controlling the inventories. As per the usage rate or turn over ratio items are classified as under :

(i) Fast Moving Items : This is indicated by a high inventory turnover ratio. This also means that such items of inventory enjoy high demand. Sufficient stock of fast moving items is to be maintained for smooth and uninterrupted operation or else the production and sales is likely to be adversely effected.

(ii) Slow Moving Items : Low turnover ratio indicates slow turn over. Such items are maintained at the minimum level.

(iii) Dormant or Obsolete Items : These refer to items having no demand. An item not issued for 2-3 years can be completely weeded out. To curb further losses such items should be disposed of as early as possible.

VED Analysis : This is also similar in principle, the only difference is that it finds out materials and components that are valuable, which are essential and which are desirable. This classification helps in sizeable reduction of inventory.

Purchasing

It is estimated that, on the average, manufacturing company spends about half of its sales income on the purchase of materials and components. It is said that "a rupee saved is a rupee earned". An entrepreneur who fails to see the value of a rupee saved may soon be out of business.

Purchasing function is best performed by *buying materials of the right quality, in the right quantity, at the right time, at the right price, and from the right source.*

This is done by :

(a) Pursuing Open Document Policy ;

(b) Maintaining proper inventory records regarding stock at hand, detailed specifications, source of supply, reorder quantity, purchase price, usage rate etc. In case there are large number of items to be purchased, then ABC analysis may be required ;

(c) Developing good vendor relationships to ensure emergency supply, scope to modify an order, readiness to bear with delayed payments arising out of financial exigencies and finally to be sure about the quality of supply;

(d) Creating alternate sources of supply to minimise the chances of stock outs, dependency on single supplier who may start dictating terms and to avail benefit of cost reduction as per prevailing market price.

Quality Control

Quality refers to the intended use and the price of a product. A technically excellent product may be prohibitively costly, and there is no point in making a product that the customers cannot afford to buy. Quality, thus, is a relative term and must be viewed as such.

Concept of Quality

Even though we all talk of quality, it is not easily defined. One of the accepted definitions of *quality is fitness for use*. An equally good definition is *conformance to requirements*. Note that in both the definitions quality is defined relative to use, rather than as a general characteristic that may be intangible. By this simple, yet practical definition, if a product or service lives up to expectations, it is of high quality. On the other hand, extra fine finish or using materials that are far stronger than required does not add quality to an item unless it somehow causes the item to conform to its requirements better.

Cost of Quality

The term cost of quality is often a misnomer. Cost of quality is a measure of the cost to the firm for a lack of quality. It is very difficult to measure and often cannot be found in account books. One has to carefully calculate it, as most of the cost elements are hidden.

Quality costs are distributed throughout the organisation. Most organisations include only the cost of quality control departments whereas the cost of inspection, and measurement carried out in production departments are often ignored. More importantly the cost of bad workmanship, wastages, rework, etc., are often not included in quality costs. Careful examination of quality costs should account for Prevention, Assessment, Control Costs and also the costs due to lack of control.

"Quality is free, but it is not a gift". This statement sums up the opinion that effective, permanent quality improvement though difficult to achieve, yet it pays for itself in increased productivity.

When a company decides to manufacture goods or provide service of a particular quality level, it must ensure that this level of quality is maintained consistently. In technical terms, the variations in the quality of products/services must be kept within the specified tolerance limits.

Quality Management

Quality assessment is an investigation of the level of quality being achieved. Quality control on the other hand, begins with assessment, and includes action taken to eliminate unacceptable quality. The typical quality control programme is based on periodic inspection, followed by feedback of the results and changes or adjustments whenever necessary. It includes :

(i) Prevention of the occurrence of a fault,

(ii) Detection of it as soon as it occurs, and

(iii) Rectifying it at the earliest.

Quality assurance includes quality control, but it also refers to emphasis on quality in the design of products, processes and jobs and in personnel selection and training. Total quality control refers to the managerial commitment to quality so as to include the quality aspect in every functional area of work, production, marketing, finance and personnel. It also includs behavioural science based techniques like Quality Circles, Zero Defect Programmes. Naturally, the management of quality is an extensive area of study.

Quality assurance as an idea is quite old, but a systematic inclusion of quality assurance in organisations is a twentieth century phenomenon. Statistical methods of quality control were first proposed by Shewart in 1924, in the United States. Intensive training courses in statistical control popularised by the American and Japanese industry contributed to much of the success of quality control programme. Recently the concept of Quality Circles has been a runaway success in Japanese industries. A quality circle is a group of employees whose assignment is to identify problems, formulate solutions, and present their results to management with suggestions for implementation. It is getting increasingly popular with employees and management in India also.

Quality Control Steps

- Prepare specifications and quality standards
- Ensure quality of inputs — Raw material, tools, jigs and fixtures etc.
- Ensure quality during operations
- Pre shipment inspection
- Eliminate cause of rejection through methods study
- Apply statistical quality control
- Create quality consciousness in the enterprise

For attaining quality standard, there must be clearly stated standards with reference to raw materials, components, workmanship, packaging, performance and all other benefits that customers are expecting from the goods and services. Quality testing and measuring equipment, of the required specifications should be considered as essential components of the unit. Various methods like 100% inspection, spot checking, and inspecting as per a sampling plan are used for quality testing. Under sampling plan, only a portion of the incoming material is inspected. The number of items to be inspected, or the size of the sample, is determined statistically.

If the finished product is a high value item, 100 per cent inspection is usually carried out so that no substandard product reaches the customers. A stamp of quality approval is affixed on each item. In some cases even destructive tests like impact testing and test for resistance to fire are also carried out on a small fraction of the items. This should be considered as investment rather than wastage.

While the benefits, both tangible and intangible, of quality control are many, there are also costs involved in the process. As the quality control is made rigorous, the costs tend to increase. One has to strike a balance between the costs and the benefits arising out of quality control. This balance will depend upon the quality control needs of a particular organisation.

SUMMARY

Operation management is basically the management of the use of equipment and other resources of production which essentially include the element of planning organising and controlling of various components of production function.

Operation planning is the system for specifying the production procedure with a view to obtain the desired output in a given time at optimum cost in confirmity with specified standards of quality.

Plant layout is the disposition of the various facilities and services of the plant within the area of the site selected. The work of plant layout begins with the location of the work tables.

Quality is an important aspect of production system and it must ensure that services and products produces by the company conform to the declared quality standards at minimum cost. A total quality assurance system includes such aspects as setting standards of quality, inspection of purchased and sub contracted parts, control of quality during manufacturing and inspection of finished products including performance, testing etc.

REVIEW QUESTIONS

1. What factors decide the location of an industrial unit?
2. If you were to set up a unit, how would you go about selecting the location for the same.
3. What do you understand by plant layout ? What are the various considerations influencing the layout?
4. Discuss with example various manufacturing processes.
5. What factors effect the choice of manufacturing process?
6. Why is inventory management important for a business enterprise?
7. What do you understand by inventory carrying cost and ordering cost? How to fix the economic order quantity?
8. What is meant by ABC classification? Why is it necessary? Explain the use of ABC analysis in inventory control.
9. How would you go about ensuring quality of product or service?

❑❑

CHAPTER 13

FINANCIAL MANAGEMENT FOR NEW VENTURES

CHAPTER OUTLINE

FINANCIAL MANAGEMENT

Finance is regarded as the lifeblood of a business enterprise because finance is one of the basic foundations of all kinds of economic activities. It is that master key which provides access to all the sources for being employed in manufacturing and merchandising activities. The basic objective of any business venture is the earning of adequate profits through its survival and strong growth, though, there can be other objectives like social and national objectives. Proper financial management will assist in fulfilment of these objectives by analysing and forecasting needs, managing working capital, planning capital structure and the likewise. For the successful running of any business enterprise, the appreciation of financial management is as important as other areas like production and marketing.

FINANCIAL PLANNING

Financial planning is based on the financial appraisal of the projects proposed to be taken by the business entrepreneur. It deals with the ascertainment of total long-term and short-term financing requirements of the business and then deciding to choose amongst various sources, the ones which should cost the least as compared to the others. In order that the business enterprise gets the required funds at reasonable cost, it is also necessary that the funds are raised at the appropriate time. Thus, the financial planning helps an entrepreneur to develop the strategies, to set the goals in terms of volumes of profit and sales as well as acquisition of capital assets with a view to take care of future development and growth. While setting the goals, functional areas like production, marketing, personnel, inventory, taxation, etc., must be taken into account.

Financial planning would include the following steps to be taken by an entrepreneur :

(i) Determining the capital structure which should be based on along term plan of the business.

(ii) Forecasting the most probable course of events, which may include :

- (a) Quantum of finance, i.e., the amount needed for implementing the business plans;
- (b) Pattern of financing;
- (c) Policies to be pursued for implementing the proposed pattern of financing;
- (d) Time for floating various corporate securities.

During the course of financial planning, a financial forecast has to be made estimating the under mentioned elements:

(a) Fixed capital requirements.

(b) Working capital requirements.

(c) Credit policy to be followed.

(d) Debt-equity ratio.

(e) Other contingencies.

LONG-TERM AND SHORT-TERM FINANCE CREDIT FLOW

Credit is the prime input for sustained growth of any business venture and its availability continues to be a matter of concern. Credit provided for creation of fixed assets like land, building, plant and machinery is called long-term credit. Credit provided for running the enterprise for its day-to-day requirement for purchasing raw materials and other inputs like electricity and water etc., and for payment of wages and salaries is called short-term credit or working capital. Primary concern of an entrepreneur is to arrange financial resources to take care of all the operational requirements. Such financial resources could be long-term or short-term, which could come from internal or external sources.

The sources of long-term finance include :

(a) Owner's capital, i.e., equity.

(b) Term loans from financial institutions.

(c) Deposits or loans given by owners (partners/directors) to the firm.

(d) Hire-purchase or leasing facility from a NBFC or other organisations.

(e) Machinery purchase under Industrial Development Bank of India's Bill Rediscounting Scheme.

(f) Seed capital, venture capital, margin money, subsidy, soft loan from Government/Financial Institutions.

The source of short-term finance could be :

(a) Bank borrowing for working capital.

(b) Deposits/borrowing from friends, relative and others.

(c) Sundry creditors.

(d) Deposits received from customers.

The above are largely external sources for raising finance except owner's capital and loans/deposits from friends and relatives. Funds can be generated internally by the entrepreneur through personal loans on his assets like Provident Fund/Life Insurance Corporation/buildings/investments, etc. It could be through personal borrowings from friends and relatives. For a running enterprise, it could be through retention of profits or conversion of assets into funds.

Sound financial management implies that the entrepreneur should plough back a good part of earning into the business enterprise rather than withdrawing the same from the business as this ensures growth and stability. Such a policy will pay rich dividends in future and ensure easy access to borrowing from external sources in times of distress or when that enterprise is poised for expansion. To ensure sound health, it is essential that short-time funds are utilised by the unit for acquiring current assets like raw materials, stocks in process, finished goods, trade debts, investments, advance to suppliers, etc., i.e., items which are of a current nature and keep changing their form. They can normally be converted into cash within one year. Higher the current assets, better is the availability of working capital.

On the other hand, long-term finance should be utilised for acquiring fixed assets and partly for financing current assets to meet the margin on working capital.

While arranging funds, the entrepreneur should ensure their cost effectiveness. One must keep in mind the following factors :

(a) Volume of funds required on long-term and short-term basis.

(b) Period for which funds are required.

(c) Time required for obtaining such finance.

(d) Cost of borrowings.

(e) Repayment capacity keeping future profit generation pattern in view.

(f) Conditions stipulated by lenders of money.

The cardinal principle would be to have a mix of funds which works out to be the cheapest, is available most easily and involves minimum outside interference in day-to-day working. For Science and Technology entrepreneurs, and other specified categories special loan schemes have been formulated by financial institution and banks. These include soft loan and equity support. Since these are granted on liberal terms, efforts should be made to use them to the maximum.

From a practical point of view, at times, necessary co-operation and helpful attitudes may be missing when dealing with banks or financial institutions. One must not accept defeat or give up the project under such circumstances and should try another bank or another branch of the same bank after some time when the previous manager has changed. Such a strategy has been found to be very helpful in carrying out the project successfully. While dealing with bankers, it is important to bear in mind that exaggerated claims do not carry one very far. Bankers are moved to a favourable decision only based upon concrete plans and past performance. These are best presented through the financial statements.

STATEMENTS OF ACCOUNTS

Two statements of accounts are often used to describe the performance of an enterprise, i.e., (a) *balance sheet*, and (b) *operating statement* which is also referred to as profit and loss account. Besides indicators of performance, these statements are also viewed as legal requirements.

Statements of Accounts

Balance Sheet	**Operating Statement** (Profit and Loss Account)
• Shows what a firm owns and what it owes at a particular date in terms of assets and liabilities respectively	• Shows income, cost of sales, gross profit, expenses, tax and net profit during a period of time say year ending 31st March 2008.

BALANCE SHEET

A balance sheet is a statement of assets and liabilities. In simple words it is a statement depicting the uses of funds (assets) and the sources of funds (liabilities). It shows the financial position of a business enterprise as on a particular date. A simple format is presented in Exhibit 1. It may be observed from this exhibit that assets can be classified as :

(i) Fixed Assets

(ii) Current Assets

Fixed assets are items like land, building, plant and machinery etc. Current assets are items like stocks, sundry debtors, advance payments made to suppliers etc.

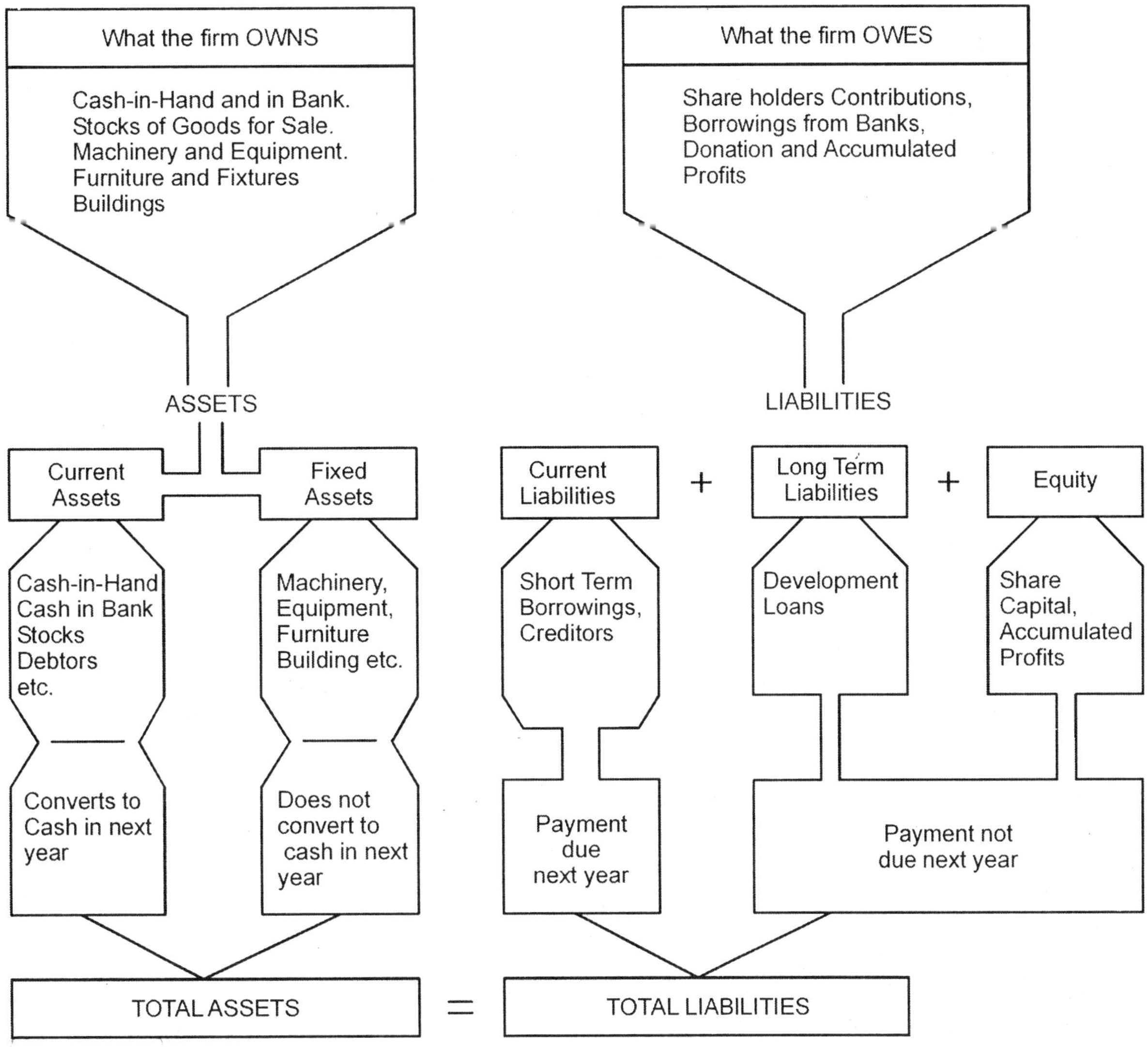

Fig. 13.1. Balance Sheet

The total assets always equal the total liabilities. In other words, they balance each other.

Similarly, liabilities can be classified as :

(i) Term liabilities

(ii) Current liabilities

Term liabilities include owner's equity, debentures, term loans, reserves etc. Current liabilities are items like sundry creditors, bank credits for working capital, provisions for expenses payable etc. Balance sheet is normally prepared at yearly intervals. At the beginning of the year one can think of preparing a projected balance sheet to plan out how funds will be obtained and how they would be utilised to improve the firm's financial position. At the end of the year a balance sheet that shall be prepared gives an idea of how funds were actually obtained and utilised. This will help in knowing why finances did not work out the way they were planned and assist in assessing sources which an entrepreneur was able to have easy access to.

Exhibit - 1

Balance Sheet of M/s. ABC Ltd.

as on 31.3.2008

In Rupees - '000s

Liabilities		Assets	
Current		**Current**	
Bank	4,800	Cash and Bank Investments (Marketable)	360
Sundry Creditors	1,020	**Stock**	
Tax and Other Statutory Liabilities	780	Raw Materials	3,360
		Stock-in-Process	450
		Finished Goods	960
Loans	600	Sundry Debtors	3,600
Other Liabilities (Specify)	900	Stores	300
Income Tax Payable	2,220	Others (including deposits and advances paid)	600
		Taxes Paid in Advance	2,220
	10,320		12,090
Deferred (Term Liabilities)		**Fixed**	
Friends & Relatives	750	Land & Building	900
Terms Loans from Bank	3,600	Plant & Machinery	6,300
		Furniture & Fixtures	1,200
	4,350		8,400
Capital and Surplus		**Miscellaneous**	
Capital	3,600	Long Term Advances	420
General Reserves	1,020	Preliming Exp.	240
Investment & Allowances	1,800		
Other Reserves & Surplus	60		
Total	6,480		660
	21,150		21,150

Operating Statement

The balance sheet gives the position as on a particular date. This is a snap shot picture of the financial position and does not indicate the financial condition. Given two balance sheets one can know the financial position on these two dates but what happens in between is connected by a *Profit and Loss Statement* known by various names like *Income Statement, Manufacturing, Trading and P/L A/c.*

The Profit and Loss statement summarises the transaction of the business enterprise for a given period of time (generally one year). The actual profit made or loss incurred is shown in the balance sheet as an increase or decrease in owner's equity. The formats of balancing sheet, profit and loss account vary with the form of organisation, that is, proprietorship, partnership, private limited or public limited company. A simple format of profit and loss statement is furnished in Exhibit-2.

An entrepreneur should know the major heads (accounts) of incomes and expenditure and exercise constant, personal control on them to improve profits. Analysis of this statement for last two or three years indicates the trend in each of the accounts and shall help in future planning.

Exhibit - 2

Profit & Loss Statement of M/s. ABC Ltd.
for the year ending 31.3.2008

In Rupees - '000

(i) Sales Realisation		28,980
(ii) Variable Expenses		
Raw Materials Consumed	19,314	
Wages	1,782	
Power & Electricity	60	
Consumables	600	
Repairs & Maintenance	264	
Interest on Working Capital Loan	600	
Selling Expenses	702	23,382
(iii) Contribution (i - ii)		5,598
(iv) Fixed Expenses		
Salaries	240	
Interest on Loan	618	
Depreciation	900	
Administrative Overheads	420	2,178
(v) Total Expenses (ii + iv)		25,560
(vi) Profit before tax (i – v)		3,360

Is profit of Rs. 50,000/- good or bad? Is a bank loan of Rs. 2 lakh high or low? These figures perse cannot help us in arriving at a judgement. They will require to be analysed and compared with other items before a fair judgement can be passed. Thus, a profit of Rs. 50,000 on a sales of Rs. 2,50,000 would be considered good but on a sales of Rs. 50 lakhs would be considered too meagre. This means that the financial condition is better understood by analysing the balance sheet and profit and loss statement by subjecting it to ratio analysis.

Analysis of Financial Statements

The Balance Sheet and Profit and Loss Statement are analysed :

(i) To enable understanding of the past/future performance ;

(ii) To provide inputs for financial decision making ; and

(iii) To help meet requirements of banks/financial institutions etc.

RATIO ANALYSIS

Over 100 financial ratios have been identified by financial analysts. Some of the most helpful ones are discusses below:

(i) Debt Equity Ratio

$$\text{Debt-Equity Ratio} = \frac{\text{Total Debts}}{\text{Owner's capital}}$$

Debt is the amount that an enterprise owes to others. This is taken as long-term debt (funded debt) by Financial Institutions and as total outside liabilities by commercial banks. The FIs generally like this ratio not to be exceed 2 : 1. No such norm is prescribed by commercial banks though a ratio above 4 : 1 would cause concern to them when they shall start exercising close control on day-to-day operations of the borrower.

If an entrepreneur keeps ploughing back a part of the profits generated the ratio will decrease progressively and this is construed as a healthy trend. A low ratio would indicate the capacity of the firm to borrow additionally, in case of need. In case of companies (Pvt. Ltd. or Public Ltd. Co.) owners capital = equity + reserves.

(ii) Current Ratio

$$\text{Current Ratio} = \frac{\text{Current Assets}}{\text{Current Liabilities}}$$

This ratio measures the liquidity of the firm and is of paramount importance in maintaining the health of the firm.

A good ratio is 2 and banks would not tolerate a ratio of less then 1.33. Liquidity of the firm is its ability to meet short-term debts. A ratio of 2 indicates that in case of need the firm can dispose of its current assets at half the book value and still meet its current liabilities.

Too high a ratio will lower the return on owner's capital and, therefore, most entrepreneurs do not favour it. Along with current ratio, an entrepreneur will endeavour to constantly increase net working capital.

Net Working Capital = Current Assets – Current Liabilities

(iii) Net Profitability

$$\text{Net Profitability} = \frac{\text{Net Profits}}{\text{Sales}} \times 100$$

It is difficult to state what is a good profitability ratio. This will depend upon past performance and on what similar units operating in the area obtain. A profitability of 10 per cent will be good if competitors achieve a lower percentage and will be deemed poor, if competitors report a higher percentage. An improved profitability over last year is a healthy trend.

(iv) Return on Equity (ROE)

$$\text{Return on Equity} = \frac{\text{Net Profits after tax}}{\text{Owner's capital}}$$

Between two projects which one to choose ? The answer is provided by this ratio. A project with higher return is preferable. Once in business, are the profits adequate ? Return on equity provides the answer. Mr. AB continues to obtain a return on equity of 14 per cent. Is it good? He may jolly well invest his capital in other forms of investment and earn easy 14 per cent return from interest income besides earning a salary by taking up a job ? Return on equity should always be higher than the return on other form of investment, then the business is good.

(v) Return on Investment (ROI)

$$\text{ROI} = \frac{\text{Net Profits before Interest and Taxes}}{\text{Investment}}$$

ROI should always be higher than the highest rate of interest paid on any debt. Under such circumstances borrowing more is worthwhile. If ROI is less than borrowing rate of funds, profits can be improved by reducing debts.

(vi) Debt Service Coverage Ratio (DSCR)

$$\text{DSCR} = \frac{\text{Net Profit after Tax + Depreciation + Interest on Term Barrowings}}{\text{Annual Instalment + Interest on Barrowings}}$$

It determines the firm's ability to service the debt, that is, pay interest and instalments on time. This ratio should preferably be 2 or more but not below 1.5 in any case.

While balance sheet is a static concept, an entrepreneur on the move would look forward to a dynamic concept to buttress the above analysis. This can be achieved through funds flow analysis.

FUNDS FLOW ANALYSIS

Funds flow statement indicates how business obtained its funds and having obtained them, how were these utilised during a given period of time. It indicates the ebb and flow of funds into and out of business. This statement helps financial management by providing answer to questions such as :

(i) When the unit was not earning sufficient profit or was incurring losses, how were dividends distributed / drawls made by the owners ?

(ii) How was debt repaid?

(iii) When net income was up, why did current assets go down or vice versa ?

(iv) How were additional fixed assets financed ?

(v) What happened to proceeds from sale of fixed assets ?

(vi) How was the increase in current assets financed ?

(vii) Were the funds utilised wisely ?

The advice rendered earlier may be recalled. Short-term funds should be utilised for current assets and long-term funds for fixed and current assets to ensure liquidity. Funds flow statement clearly depicts such situations.

To prepare a funds flow statement two balance sheets would be required, last year's and this year's or, this year's and next year's for preparing a projected funds flow statement. This statement is organised under two broad categories :

(a) Sources of funds ; and

(b) Application, disposition or uses of funds.

When the liabilities increase, funds are obtained and when they decrease funds are utilised. For example, bank loan increase is indicative of inflow of funds into the organisation. A decrease in assets is inflow of funds and an increase in assets is outflow of funds. When plant and machinery increases obviously money has been spent — outflow of funds — and, when the value of plant and machinery decreases, a part may have been sold. That is, funds flow in.

A comparative study of funds flow statements gives useful information on financial policies adopted in the past and provides critical clues for future planning.

Preparation

Exhibit 3, 4, and 5 provide the calculations involved in preparing a funds flow statement. How a few of the 'Current Year' figures in Exhibits are worked out and are explained. 'Depreciation' is Rs. 7,50,000 which figure is obtained from either Exhibit 3 or 4. The next item 'Net Profits before Tax' at Rs. 36,00,000 is taken from Exhibit 4. 'Increase in Unsecured Long-Term Loans' is obtained from Exhibit 3 (See 'Friends and Relatives' Rs. 10,50,000 – Rs. 750,000 = Rs. 3,00,000). Similarly, 'Increase in Fixed Asset's under 'Uses of Funds' is arrived at from Exhibit 3. An amount of Rs. 50,000 is added in 'Fixed Assets'.

"Decrease in Term Loan" of Rs. 900,000 is arrived at from Exhibit 3. Term Loan in previous year was Rs. 36,00,000 and in current year Rs. 27,00,000. Thus, based on the Exhibits 3 and 4 the Funds Flow Statement is prepared.

Having prepared, it would be more important to interpret it. Following conclusions can be derived.

(a) Sales rise expected is healthy and normal – 24.32 per cent during current year and 25 per cent during next year.

(b) Due to plough back of profits and decrease in term loan the debt equity ratio (total outside liabilities : net worth) improves from 2.15 : 1 in current year to 2.03 : 1 in the next year.

(c) Additional inventory and receivable amounting to Rs. 21.3 lakhs during next year shall be financed of the extent of Rs. 12.00 lakhs and Rs. 18.00 lakhs respectively by additional bank borrowings.

(d) Unsecured term loans go up by Rs. 300,000 to Rs. 10.50 lakhs during current year and are maintained at this level in the next year.

(e) Total surplus generated is showing a healthy trend, increasing from Rs. 43,50,000 in the current year to Rs. 51,72,000 during next year.

(f) Fixed assets are continuously added, Rs. 300,000 in current year and again in the next year.

(g) Closing cash balance is increasing from Rs. 510,000 to Rs. 612,000. This is desirable in view of increased operations.

One very important use to which funds flow statement should be deployed by all entrepreneurs is for analysing sources and uses of funds. Long–term funds should be used for long-term purposes, that is, fixed assets and, short-term funds for short-term purposes, that is current assets. Many entrepreneurs have been observed to use short-term funds for long-term purposes and in the process impairing liquidity, a major cause of industrial sickness. This can be avoided by making use of the funds flow statement.

Exhibit - 3

Projected Balance Sheet M/s. ABC Ltd.
as on 31st March

(In Rupees - '000)

Liabilities	*Previous Year (Actual)*	*Current Year (projected)*	*Next Year (projected)*	*Assets*	*Previous Year (Actual)*	*Current Year (Projected)*	*Next Year (Projected)*
Current				**Current**			
Bank	4,800	6,000	7,800	Cash & Bank	2,580	2,850	3,492
Sundry Creditors	1,020	1,320	1,560	Investments	240	240	240
Liabilities	780	780	780	Inventory	4,770	6,000	7,500
Losses	600	600	600	Sundry Debtors	3,600	4,500	5,640
Other Liabilities	900	1,050	1,050	Stores	300	300	300
Income Tax Payable	2,220	2,340	2,880	Others	600	900	1,050
	10,320	12,090	14,670		12,090	14,790	18,222
Deferred				**Fixed**			
Friends and Relatives	750	1,050	1,050	Balance	9,000	8,400	7,950
Term Loan	3,600	2,700	1,800	*Add*	300	300	300
	4,350	3,750	2,850		9,300	8,700	8,250
				Less : Depreciation	900	750	672
					8,400	7,950	7,578
Capital and Surplus							
Capital	3,600	3,600	3,600				
General Reserves	1,020	1,920	3,180				
Investment Allowance	1,800	1,800	1,800				
Other Reserves and Surplus	60	60	60	**Miscellaneous**			
				Long Term Advances	70	240	120
	6,480	7,380	8,640	Others	40	240	240
	------	-----	------		110	480	360
	21,150	23,220	26,160		21,150	23,220	26,160

Exhibit -4

Projected Profit & Loss A/c of M/s. ABC (P) Ltd.
for the years ended 31st March

(In Rupees - '000)

	Previous Year		*Current Year*		*Next Year*	
(i) Sales Realisation		28,980		36,000		45,000
(ii) Variable Expenses						
Raw Materials Consumed	19,314		24,600		31,500	
Wages	1,782		2,100		2,400	
Power and Electricity	120		150		180	
Consumables	600		720		900	
Repairs & Maintenance	264		300		360	
Interest on Working Capital	600		810		1,080	
Selling Expenses	702	23,382	900	29,580	1,140	37,560
(iii) Contribution (i-ii)		5,598		6,420		7,440
(iv) Fixed Expenses						
Salaries	240		300		360	
Interest on Loan	618		600		480	
Depreciation	900		750		692	
Administrative Overheads	420	2,178	1,170	2,820	1,428	2,980
(v) Total Expenses (ii + iv)		25,560		32,400		40,500
(vi) Profit before Tax (i-v)		3,420		3,600		4,500
(vii) Income Tax Payable		2,220		2,340		2,880
(viii) Profit after Tax (vi vii)		1,200		1,260		1,620
(ix) Dividend		360		360		360
(x) Amt. Transferred to General Reserves)		840		900		1,260

Exhibit - 5

M/s ABC (P) Ltd.

Funds Flow Statement

(In Rupees - '000)

	Funds Flow Statement for *Current Year*	*Next Year*
Sources of Funds		
Depreciation	750	672
Net Profit before Tax	3,600	4,500
Total Surplus Generated	4,350	5,172
Increase in Capital	–	–
Increase in Term Loan	–	–
Increase in Unsecured Loan	–	–
(Term Loans (Friends & Relatives)	300	–
Increase in Bank Borrowings	1,200	1,800
Increase in Sundry Creditors	300	240
Increase in Other Current Liabilities	150	–
Decrease in Long-Term Advances	180	120
Decrease in Other Assets	–	–
	6,480	7,332
Uses of Funds		
Increase in Fixed Assets	300	300
Decrease in Term Loan	900	900
Increase in Inventory	1,230	1,500
Increase in Receivables	900	1,140
Increase in Other Current Assets	300	150
Decrease in Other Current Liabilities	–	–
Taxation	2,340	2,880
Dividend	360	360
	6,330	7,230
Surplus (+) Deficit (-)	+150	+102
Opening Cash/Bank Balance	360	510
Closing Cash/Bank Balance	510	612

FINANCIAL FORECASTING

To plan financial requirements financial forecasting is required. Financial forecasting is systematic projection of expected actions of management in financial terms that is, financial statements, budgets and the like. It requires use of past data, funds flow behaviour, financial ratios and economic conditions expected in the industry and the unit. It is formulated for specified period by arranging future activities and serves as a working plan.

Financial forecasting enables optimum funds utilisation; helps in planning growth and setting goals; anticipates financial requirements and reduces adhocism in decision-making, particularly during emergencies; and serves as a sound basis for negotiating funds requirement with bank/financial institutions.

Projected Profit and Loss Statement

The purpose of this statement is to have a fair and reasonable estimate of expected revenue, costs, profits, taxes etc. The first and important step is to estimate the expected sales for the forecast period and the rest follows based on this.

Projected Balance Sheet

This is a forecast of expected sources and uses of funds. A typical projected balance sheet is furnished in Exhibit 3. How various items of assets and liabilities in a balance sheet are projected is explained below.

Assets

(i) **Cash :** The minimum amount of cash that is required to meet cash payments keeping in view size of operations. It is based on fair estimates relying on experience. One month's cash overhead expenses is a good thumb rule. It can also be a balancing figure to equalise assets and liabilities.

(ii) **Trade Debtors :** To forecast trade debtors, one has to study historical data about the industry as a whole and also of the unit, market conditions and nature of customers. Based on past performance/trend, credit policy, expected and the future pattern of customers, the number of days for which debtors/receivables are expected to be outstanding can be estimated and their rupee value worked out.

(iii) **Inventories :** Stock of raw materials, stock-in-process and finished goods that a unit will keep is a function of purchase policy, production plans and marketing management. Based on past operations and future potential rupee values of inventory levels are determined.

(iv) **Fixed Assets :** Outlays for land, building, plant and machinery, furniture, fixtures, vehicles, etc., are generally planned in advance. If additions are made in these or any of these old items is sold adjustments are made. Adequate provision for depreciation is also required to be made on year to year basis.

Liabilities

(i) **Trade Creditors :** By analysis the schedules of purchases and payments to be made during the period or with the help of creditors ratio the level of trade credits can be estimated.

(ii) **Loans and Advances :** The amount of loans or advance that the firm shall give can be determined through fair judgement.

(iii) **Accrued Liabilities :** Wages, taxes, interest amount and other expenses that will be incurred but shall not be paid are determined based on management policy.

(iv) **Provision for Taxes :** Closing balance of the provision is determined by adding new provision for taxes to the opening balance and deducting the actual payment of taxes.

CASH BUDGET

Cash budget is a schedule for a predetermined future period (say six months) to indicate cash inflows and outflows on a month wise basis during that period to locate the magnitude and timing of cash surplus and shortage. It helps the entrepreneur in inciating timely action for cash management and also determine his working capital requirements.

Cash budget can be prepared to forecast cash receipts and payments on day-to-day or month-to-month basis depending upon need.

Exhibit 6 illustrates a typical cash budget. From this it is observed that peak requirement of cash is Rs. 69,600 in August. Month in which cash will be in surplus or deficit are also highlighted enabling timely planning of investment of surplus cash and identifying sources for cash to meet cash deficits.

Any business entity grows by building a reputation of being able to meet its payments as and when due. Any supplier, financer, creditor or banker will be glad to supply materials or money to such firms enabling almost instant growth. The significance of cash budget is in its ability to help plan for maturing payments, that is, assist in the enterprise growth.

Exhibit - 6

ABC (P) Ltd.

Cash Budget

	July	*August*	*September*	*October*	*November*	*December*
Opening Cash Balance	1,27,200	5,640	(64,600)	(64,200)	(56,400)	15,120
Collection from Debtors	36,000	60,000	1,68,000	2,28,000	2,52,000	2,76,000
Total (A)	1,63,200	65,640	98,400	1,63,800	1,95,360	2,79,120
Payments						
Payments to Creditors	70,560	75,240	93,000	1,03,440	1,03,440	43,440
Wages	18,000	18,000	24,000	27,000	27,000	27,000
Direct Expenses	21,000	21,000	21,000	22,200	22,200	22,200

	July	August	September	October	November	December
Administrative Expenses	9,000	9,000	9,000	10,200	10,200	10,200
Selling Expenses	12,000	12,000	15,000	17,400	17,400	17,400
Machinery	–	–	–	13200	–	–
Taxes	27,000	–	–	27,000	–	–
Total (B)	1,57,560	1,35,240	1,62,600	2,20,440	1,80,240	1,20,240
Closing Cash Balance (A) – (B)	5,640	(69,600)	(64,200)	(56,640)	15,120	1,70,880

Note : *Figures in parenthesis indicate negative cash balances.*

WORKING CAPITAL MANAGEMENT

Working capital management is a significant part of financial management. It is important that the investment in current assets and the level of current liabilities will have to be geared quickly to changes in sales. It is also important that a portion of the working capital requirement is brought from long-term sources such as equity capital or long-term loans.

Part of the total capital employed in a business has to be deployed in financing current assets. Ignoring cash, the main current assets are : stock-in trade and trade debtors. On the other hand, the current liabilities of the business reduce the amount of the capital which the business has to provide to finance its operations. The main current liabilities are trade creditors and bank overdraft.

The excess of current assets over current liabilities is normally described as the working capital of the business. This is the share of the total capital of the business employed in financing current operations. An increase in current assets does not necessarily mean an increase in working capital. For example, if stock is bought on credit, both current assets and current liabilities increase by the same amount and the net balance of capital employed remain unchanged.

Broadly speaking the financial manager has two main objectives in relation to working capital.

(a) to manage the individual components (e.g., stock levels and the "age" of debtors and creditors) effectively; and

(b) to keep at a minimum (consistent, of course, with operational efficiency) the amount of capital employed in financing the working capital balance.

The Operating Cycle

The working cycle of any manufacturing organisation, as mentioned before, consists of five stages of conversion. These are :

(i) Raw materials to work-in-process.
(ii) Work- in- process to finished goods.
(iii) Finished goods to bills.
(iv) Bills to cash.
(v) Cash to raw materials.

These are shown in the following way :

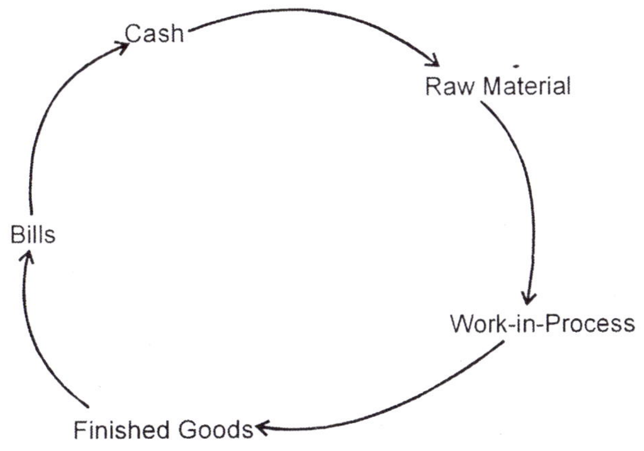

Fig. 13.2: Working Capital Cycle

The process of conversion of cash to cash through the working cycle cannot be done instantaneously. Depending on business conditions, delays are introduced in the cycle. For instance, where the raw material is scarce, more raw material is required to be held which implies blocking up of funds. The delay in work-in-process is again dependent on the nature of process. Thus, in a chemical processing unit, the entire process of conversion may be completed in less than a day while in an engineering unit it may be extended over a few months. Again, if manufacturing is carried out against specific orders then the finished product may be dispatched, as and when completed, thus avoiding the need for storing the finished goods. However, if the products are manufactured to stock for subsequent sales, the stock of finished goods is governed by market conditions. Delays in the last stage, namely conversion of bills to cash, depend on trade practices, economic factors, etc., Goods are sold on:

(i) Advance basis

(ii) Cash basis

(iii) Credit basis

To cite illustrations for purchasing goods like steel and refractory from manufacturers, one has to pay in advance, while goods like cotton *niwar*, slaked lime, etc., are sold on payment of cash. Most of the engineering goods are however sold on, credit basis. There are also goods which are sold both on cash basis and credit basis depending on to whom it is sold.

We thus see that depending on the environment, product and process, delays occur in the various stages of the working cycle, goods are held up between the different stages and these goods represent money value. The fund required to sustain the working cycle is called Working Capital.

The quantum of working capital requirements depends on two factors :

(i) level of activity

(ii) length of delay in the working cycle

For instance, if a unit producing 1000 units per month desires to produce 1300 units in the coming months then it requires larger working funds to cater to the increased requirement.

On the other hand, if for the same production level of 1000 units per month, the raw material procuring time changes from 10 days to 15 days, then more raw material is to be stored, which means more working funds. A similar situations might arise in respect of work-in-process, finished goods and bills.

Assessment of Working Capital

The components of working capital requirement are :

(i) Raw materials, consumables.

(ii) Work-in-process.

(iii) Finished goods.

(iv) Trade debtors (Accounts Receivable).

(v) Expenses.

The components which go to form current assets are :

(i) Raw Materials and Consumables : Funds requirements for holding raw materials depends on :

(a) Average consumption of raw material,

(b) Fluctuations in the raw material consumption (depends on whether the items are regularly consumed or bulk quantities are required at a time),

(c) Fluctuations in the raw material availability,

(d) Minimum quantities supplied by the market,

(e) Storage facility available.

(f) Critically of an item (i.e., how important an item is in order to maintain production).

This raw material requirements is generally expressed as 'so many months/days requirement'. To illustrate, if the raw material consumption in a year is Rs. 1,20,000 and depending on the various considerations listed above, if it is considered that 2 months raw materials will have to be kept in the unit all the time, then the requirement of working capital against raw materials is :

(Rs. 1,20,000 ÷ 12 months) × 2 month = Rs. 20,000

(ii) Work-in-Process : The funds blocked up in the work-in-process depend on the following factors :

(a) Time required for conversion of raw materials.

(b) Number of products handled at a time in process.

(c) Average quantities of each product processed at each time (batch quantity).

(d) The process, i.e., the manner in which raw material is added in the process.

To illustrate, the major raw materials in the case of a grey iron foundry are added in the initial stages while in an assembly unit, as in TV Industry, the major raw materials and components are added at the last stage of the process.

Hence, the funds requirement for work-in-process depend upon :

(a) Value of raw materials in semi-finished components products.

(b) Value added at each stage.

In case, where a number of components as involved, the general practice of valuation of work-in-process is given by raw materials + 1/2 (value added), i.e., it is assumed that the material have undergone half the processing where value added = selling price – profit – material cost.

(iii) Finished Goods : Goods may be manufactured against firm orders or against anticipated orders. In the former case the quantum of finished goods held depends on :-

(a) Delay due to inspection of the finished goods especially where an external agency is involved.

(b) Delay in preparation of dispatch documents.

(c) Delays in shipment.

(d) Delays due to non-availability of wagons.

(e) Minimum quantity that can be dispatched (e.g., full truck load).

In the case of goods manufactured to stock against anticipated orders, the quantity of finished goods held depends on:

(a) Average dispatch quantity of finished goods.

(b) Variation due to sudden requirement or slump in the market.

(c) Minimum quantities that can be dispatched.

(d) Delays due to non-availability of transport vehicles, trucks, wagons, etc.

The requirement of working funds against blocked up finished goods is expressed as 'so many days production'. The valuation of finished goods is at the full cost of production of the product.

(iv) Trade Debtors (Accounts Receivable) : If all sales were made for cash there would be no need to employ part of the capital of the business in financing debtors. Debtors arise as the result of sales made on credit. The amount of capital employed in financing debtors depends on the period for which credit is given and on the efficiency of the collection process at the end of this period. The main points to consider are :

(a) That appropriate terms are agreed in advance with customers and then enforced;

(b) That the necessary invoices, statements, reminders, etc., are prepared and dispatched promptly;

(c) That the following alternative possibilities of providing finance have been considered :

– offering discounts for prompt payment;

– using factoring services ;

– using credit collection agencies.

Discounts, factoring services and credit collection agencies are, however, expensive. Except in a tight liquidity situation the costs may outweigh the benefits.

It is, however, in the case of credit sales that working funds are required to meet delays in sales realisation. The quantum of working funds required depends on the period of credit given. The computation of the value of the working funds is based on the cost of production.

(v) Expenses : It is generally expected that about one month's requirement of cash expenses is required to be kept in the form of cash for meeting out contingencies like fluctuations in material prices, delays in sales realisation, etc. The quantum of such cash retention for meeting working capital requirements depends upon the process time. For activities having long processing time like ship-building, higher quantum of such cash balance has to be retained.

MANAGING VARIOUS ELEMENTS OF WORKING CAPITAL

It has been seen above that working capital has two distinct features — requirement of working capital and various sources to meet the requirement. Effective management of working capital primarily involves working with a lesser working capital to achieve a given quantum of sales. In other words, the unit should constantly strive to improve the sales to working capital ratio. In order to increase this ratio, each component of working capital needs to be managed efficiently.

(i) ***Raw Materials :*** For effective control of investment in raw materials, the enterprise should first devise a system of control and it should be seen that the system is followed properly. In adopting the system meticulously, however, the unit should keep a watch on the raw materials market, i.e., the system should be modified to take care of factors like price changes, governmental policies, scarcity of supply, etc. The enterprise in addition should also prepare a cash-budget in advance to ensure that material procurement will be carried out as per requirement.

(ii) ***Work-in-Process :*** The units should devise and adopt a suitable planning procedure so that production goes on uninterrupted. This will ensure the minimum blocking up of material in the process, and hence, minimum working capital requirement. Excessive build up of material, difficulty in identifying the right material, and excessive wastage should be avoided.

(iii) ***Finished Goods :*** Finished goods represent both material cost as well as conversion cost, hence, no delay in dispatch for want to packing material. Such a situation should be avoided totally.

(iv) ***Bills/Receivables :*** These represent the last stage of conversion to cash and receivables. Collection is an area where quite a few units have been found to have slackened. This may be due to the fact that entrepreneurs are able to raise finance from bankers for bills. Follow up bills for early recovery is as important an area as any other.

(v) ***Management of Cash :*** A reference to the working cycle shows that the surplus generated in each cycle is not withdrawn from the cycle. This surplus shows itself over a number of cycles as cash. The cash position of the unit however does not truly reflect the surplus position. Sometimes it shows itself as surplus, whereas, it is really meant for payment during subsequent months. This situation arises in cases where expenses are incurred on a specified date, e.g., Sales Tax, Bonus, Incomes Tax, etc. Hence, It is necessary to clearly identify the quantum of real surplus and those that are required to meet future expenditure. Diversion of short-term funds for long purposes due to short sightedness of the entrepreneurs has been noticed in a number of cases. This results in insufficient availability of working funds there-by crippling the activities. It is not hard to visualise a situation where for want of sufficient working funds, a business slowly grinds to a halt.

(vi) ***Management of Sources of Working Capital :*** We have already seen the different sources that provide funds for meeting the working capital needs. But these funds from different sources do not cost the same to the unit. Thus, short-term finance like advances do not cost the unit anything, while bank borrowings attract interest. Investment of one's own funds in the business also means the lost opportunity of investing the same elsewhere. Unhealthy raising of funds is likely in the long run to be costly and might result even in litigation and closure.

A judicious combination of the different sources of funds should be employed so that sufficient funds are raised at the cheapest cost.

Assessment of Working Capital Requirements

.	Anticipated monthly sales	Rs.
..	Cost of raw material per month	Rs.
...	Cost of production per month	Rs.

S.No.	Item	Stocking/ Payment Period	Working Capital Required Rs.	Margin Value %	Permissible Limit (Rs.)
1.	Imported raw materials	Months			
2.	Indigenous raw materials	Months			
3.	Work-in-progress	Weeks			
4.	Receivables	Months			
5.	Expenses	Months			
	Total				

Total working capital required (A)

Less :

(i) Advance payment received against orders (B)

(ii) Credit on purchases

Working capital required (A-B) (C)

Sources :

(i) Liquid surplus in balance sheet (D)

(ii) Limits from Bank

Net deficit (C–D)

How the deficit will be met?

Notes :

1. Sales to be computed at maximum level of anticipated production during the next twelve months.
2. Cost of production includes cost of raw materials plus all expenses.
3. State under "Working Capital Required" the value of receivable at cost, and under permissible limit, value thereof at sales value less margin.

   For items (3) and (4), the basis of calculation would be the cost of production. Deficit in balance sheet to be added to working capital requirement.

MANAGING CURRENT LIABILITIES

Current liabilities include trade creditors (accounts payable), bank overdrafts and deferred payments of tax, dividends, interest, salaries, wages, etc. Current liabilities are usually defined as all debts due for payment within a year. The aim is to ensure that current liabilities do not normally rise above the level of the liquid or near-liquid resources of the business which can be mobilised, as required, to meet the liabilities falling due for payment. These resources include the future earnings of the business; the so-called "quick" and "current" ratios, based on balance sheet information, are not reliable indicators for the entrepreneur (although they may be useful to the creditors or potential creditors).

Current Assets	Current Liabilities
Inventories	Bank Borrowings
Raw Materials and Components	Short-Term Loans
Work-in-Progress	Trade Advances
Finished Goods	Sundry Creditors
Others	Provisions etc.
Trade Debtors (Sundry Debtors)	
Loans and Advances	
Investments	
Other Current Assets (Cash etc.)	

CASH MANAGEMENT

Many business ventures which are profitable nevertheless go bankrupt because they run out of cash. Profits may increase but it does not necessarily follow that cash will do the same : indeed, in some instances the price of expansion may be a worsening of the cash position (i.e., the situation commonly known as "over-trading"). On the other hand, many enterprises hold excessive amounts of cash. This is a waste of resources. Cash itself yields a zero return. If held in an ordinary bank account it yields a very low rate of return. Even if surplus cash is "invested" in a readily-realizable form it normally yields less than the return expected on the assets employed in the firm's trading operations. This illustrates that cash is not in itself a desirable commodity for an enterprise to have.

COSTING

Costing is the calculation to determine how much each product or service costs to produce and sell.

Many small and even large businesses, more particularly technical entrepreneurs, get into trouble because they do not know their costs. Knowing the costs helps in setting prices, reducing costs and improving profits.

The information needed for costing comes from the book-keeping system from documents like pay rolls, time-sheets and invoices. That is why book-keeping must be in good order. But many technical entrepreneurs try to save on the cost of an accountant (who can even be employed on part-time basis) and book-keeper. The amount paid to an accountant for proper book-keeping gets paid over many times in business.

Types of Costs

In business, costs are of different types and can be classified either in terms of their identification with the product manufactured or in terms of the variability with the level of production. In terms of variability with level of production the costs are classified earlier as :

- Fixed Costs
- Variable Costs

In terms of identification, costs are of two types :

- Direct Costs
- Indirect Costs

Direct Costs are those that are readily identified with or are caused by the production of the product or the service. Example are costs incurred on raw materials, direct labour, power etc.

Indirect Costs (also called overhead costs) are those that are not readily identifiable with the products or services produced but are nevertheless essential for the smooth running of business. Examples are office rent, office stationery, postage, telephone repair and maintenance of machines, equipment and building, selling expenses, interest on loans, salaries to office staff like manager, accountant, watchman etc.

Example : A unit manufactures tables and employs 5 workers and one foreman on a monthly salary of Rs. 3500 and Rs. 6000 respectively. All workers are required to work for 40 hours a week and the unit remains closed for one week in a year and the employees get a paid leave for 4 weeks. The unit produces 1000 table per year. The direct material cost is as follow.

Material	Quantity	Cost (Rs.)
Plywood	10 sq. meter	25 per sq. meter
Steel pipe	6 meter	30 per meter
Paint	500 gms	100 per kg.

Indirect Costs

From last year's accounts the total overheads in the factory are as given below.

This year the costs are likely to increase by 20 per cent

Item	Rupees
Rent	30,000
Insurance	5,000

Power/Electricity	25,000
Telephone, Postage & Telegrams	8,500
Salaries to Office Staff	80,000
Selling expenses	32,000
Repair and Maintenance	15,000
Interest	3,500
Total Indirect Cost (Per Year)	1,99,000

Direct Cost

(i) Direct Material Cost (per table)

Sr. N.	Material	Quantity	Cost per unit (Rs.)	Cost Per table (Rs.)
1.	Plywood	10 sq. meter	25 per sq.m	250
2.	Steel Pipe	6 meter	30 per m	180
3.	Paint	500 gm	100 per kg	50
			Total Material Cost per table	480

(ii) Direct labour Cost

Annual Wage bill $= 12\ (5 \times 3500 + 1 \times 6000)$

$= 2{,}82{,}000$

No. of weeks worker work in a year $= (52 - 4 - 1)$

$= 47$

No. of man hrs per annum $= 47 \times 40 \times 5 = 9400$

Wage per man hour $= 2{,}82{,}000/9400$

= Rs. 30/Hr.

Time for Producing 1 table $= \dfrac{9400}{1{,}000} = 9.4$ hrs.

Direct labour Cost per table $= 9.4 \times 30$

= Rs. 282/-

Total Direct Cost per Table = Direct labour cost + Direct material cost

= Rs. 282 + Rs. 480 = Rs. 762

Indirect Cost

Total Indirect Cost of Previous year = 1,99,000

Add 20% Inflation = 39,800

Total Indirect Cost = 2,38,800

No. of tables produced = 1,000

Indirect Cost per table $= \dfrac{2{,}38{,}800}{1{,}000}$ = Rs. 239

Total Cost = Total Direct Cost + Total Indirect Cost

= Rs. 762 + Rs. 239 = Rs. 1,001.

Multi - Product Situations

Possibly the same firm can make chairs, almirahs, racks etc, besides tables. Different products consume different quantities of materials and labour. Material and direct labour costs can easily be calculated for each product if we know the amount of material used and labour hours required in manufacturing different items.

Computation of indirect costs poses a problem. Indirect cost for each item is calculated by charging a share of the indirect cost to various products manufactured on some reasonable basis. Normally, it is on the basis of time required to produce an item.

Example : The enterprise manufactures the tables and almirahs with the same labour force, that is 5 workers and the same indirect cost of Rs. 2,38,800. It requires 3 man days to make an almirah and need the following materials. Steel sheet worth Rs. 550, lock costing Rs. 150 and one kg of paint. Further a table needs six man hours of direct labour.

Total no. of man hours in a year

= 47 (weeks) × 40 (Hrs/week) × 5 (worker's) = 9400 hrs.

= 9400 hrs.

By dividing the total indirect cost by total no. of man hours in a year. Indirect cost per man hour is worked out:

$$\text{Indirect cost per Hr.} = \frac{\text{Total Indirect Cost}}{\text{Total Man Hours}}$$

$$= \frac{2,38,800}{9,400} = \text{Rs. } 25.40$$

No. of Man Hours per table	= 6
Indirect cost per table	= 25.40 × 6 = Rs. 152.40
No. of Man Hours per Almirah	= 3 × 8 = 24 Hrs.
Indirect cost per Almirah	= 24 × 25.40 = Rs. 609.60
Direct Material Cost per Table	= Rs. 480
(as calculated in previous example)	
Direct labour per table	
No. of Man Hrs required per table	= 6
Wage per man hour	= Rs. 30
Direct labour per table	= 6 × 30 = Rs. 180
Total direct cost per table	= Rs. 480 + Rs. 180
	= Rs. 660
Total cost per tables	= Direct Cost + Indirect Cost
	= Rs. 660 + Rs. 152.40
	= Rs. 712.40
Direct material cost of Almirah	
Steel	= Rs. 550
Lock	= Rs. 150
Paint	= Rs. 100
Direct material cost	= Rs. 800
Man Hrs per Almirah	= 24
Cost per man hour	= 30
Direct labour cost per Almirah	= 24 × 30
	= Rs. 720
Total direct cost per Almirah	= Direct Material + Direct Labour
	= 800 + 720
	= Rs. 1,520
Total cost per Almirah	= Direct Cost + Indirect Cost
	Rs. 1,520+ Rs. 609.60
	Rs. 2,129.60

If the entrepreneurs plans the finances, monitors the financial working, manages the working capital and initiates timely remedial action whenever actual working deviates from the plans, the business enterprise will not face financial problems. It will run successfully, generate adequate profits and shall remain adequately poised for growth.

SUMMARY

Financial planning is based on the financial appraisal of the projects proposed to be taken up by the business entrepreneur. Sound financial management implies that entrepreneur should plough back a good part of earning into the business enterprise rather than withdrawing the same from the business. This will ensure growth and stability. Such a policy will pay rich dividends in future and ensure easy access to borrowing from external sources in times of distress or when the unit is posed for expansion. To ensure sound health, it is essential that short-term funds are utilised by the unit for acquiring current assets like raw materials, stock-in-process, finished goods, trade debts, advances to suppliers, etc.

The basic objective of any business venture is the earning of adequate profits through its survival and strong growth, though, there can be other objectives like social and national objectives, proper financial management will assist in fulfilment of these objectives by analysing and forecasting needs, and proper management of working capital.

For the successful running of any business enterprise the appreciation of financial management is as important, as other areas like producing and marketing.

REVIEW QUESTIONS

1. Explain the importance of financial planning in setting up a new venture.
2. Explain the uses and sources of long term and short term funds.
3. What are the different financial statement and how are they useful for the entrepreneur?
4. How would you analyse the Balance Sheet and the Operating Statement?
5. What is a fund flow statement? Distinguish it from a balance sheet.
6. What are the limitations of a fund flow statement?
7. Give a Performa fund flow statement.
8. Explain the role and limitations of ratio analysis.
9. Describe how an entrepreneur can prepare financial projections.
10. What do you understand by working capital? What is the difference between the gross and net working capital?
11. Explain the concept of working capital? What are the major determinants of working capital requirements of an enterprise?
12. "The process of working capital begins with cash and ends with cash". In the light of this statement, delineate the operating cycle of working capital.
13. Distinguish between the fixed capital and working capital. What are the various sources of raising working capital?
14. Explain how the permissible bank finance for working capital is determined for a large as well as a small enterprise.
15. Explain Tandon committee and Nayak Committee norms for financing working capital.
16. What do you understand by a cash flow statement?
17. How can you prepare a cash budget?
18. Explain the concept of direct cost and indirect cost. How would an entrepreneur calculate indirect costs for different products?
19. Why is the knowledge of costing important for an entrepreneur?

Things to do

1. Collect the balance sheet of any company and prepare the fund flow statement from it.
2. Choose any industry, collect the balance sheets of at least two enterprises in that industry. Calculate different ratios of both the enterprise and analyse them.

CASE 13.1

ICE CREAM PARLOUR

Mrs. Shashi Pandey aged about 32 years holds a Master's Degree in Science with the specialisation on food products and also a Bachelor's degree in Education. She has set up a parlour for making and vending soft ice cream based on an Italian Machine imported from M/s Carpigiani S.R.L., Emilia, Italy. The multi-coloured ice cream is very attractive to customers particularly to younger ones. Ice cream in general and soft ice cream in particular are very popular among young generation. The demand for the product increases tremendously during summer months. This machine is capable of producing 20 kg/40 liters of ice cream per hour with 100 per cent of over run and each portion contains 125ml/ 80 gm of soft ice cream. Ice cream is served in a cone made of wafers. Mrs. Pandey had purchased the machine with all accessories for Rs. 4.60 lakhs and had spent Rs. 3,300 on miscellaneous assets i.e.,—an almirah for storage, stool for the operator etc. The venture had been financed by the State Bank of India under women entrepreneurship programme at an interest rate of 17.5 per cent and had sanctioned loan of Rs. 1.70 lakhs with a moratorium of one year. The first instalment is due at the end of second year. However, the interest is payable monthly.

She had set up the machine in a prestigious air-conditioned department store in a busy market. She had to give an interest free security of Rs. 50,000/-; pays Rs. 4500/- and Rs. 1500/- as monthly rent and fixed electricity charges to the departmental store. She had an agreement with M/s Zero Point (a famous ice cream of Italy) who are providing certain proprietary flavour and are charging a royalty of Rs. 0.40 per cup. She has hired two sales girls who are paid Rs. 2000/- per month and an incentive at the rate of 50 paisa per cup of ice cream sold. The ice creams are being sold at a rate of Rs. 8 per cup.

It is now end September and Mrs. Pandey is to review her contract with the departmental store. She has prepared her account for the first complete year as under :

Profit and Loss A/c of Ice Cream Parlour

A.	Sales Income		
	Sales of Ice cream	–	5,40,000
B.	Expenses		
	Raw material		
	1. Milk, Flavor and other ingredient	–	1,18,800
	2. Cones including wastages	–	27,216
	Total Materials	–	1,46,016
	Salary	–	48,000
	Sales commission	–	33,750
	Security	–	50,000
	Rent	–	54,000
	Royalty	–	27,000
	Electricity	–	18,000
	Maintenance	–	20,000
	Interest 17.5% of term loan	–	56,000
	Depreciation @ 15%	–	69,050
	Total Expenses	–	5,21,816
	Gross Profit	–	**92,640**

The profit and loss A/c of Ice Cream Parlour has some errors. Prepare the revised profit and loss A/c and update Mrs. Pandey of the actual profit/loss for the first year.

She intends to spend the earnings for private consumption. She would like to know her break-even point as number of ice cream cups per month. She is aware that during December—January the sales of her parlour will be very low and she expects to incur loss during these two months. She would like to know the minimum number of ice creams to be sold per month during these winter months so that she does not have to draw money form her savings.

CHAPTER

14

SOURCES OF FINANCE

CHAPTER OUTLINE

Long Term Financing
Concept of Leverage
Operating Leverage
Financial Leverage
Capital Structure
Factors Effecting Capital Structure
Features of Capital Structure
Instruments of Long Term Finance
Preference Share Capital
Short Term Financing
Financing of Working Capital Requirements
Project Appraisal
Project Appraisal Methodoloy
Submission of Loan Application
Scrutinising and Processing of Loan Application
Financial Institutions in india
Banks
All India Financial Institutions
SIDBI
State Financial Corporations
State Industrial Development Corporation (SIDCs)
The Venture Capital Spectrum
Start-up Finance
First Stage Finance
Second Stage Finance
Later Stage Financing
Replacement Capital/Money-Out Deal
Trun Around / Recovery Finance
Venture Capital Process
Factors Influencing Venture Capitalists Choice of Investment
Choosing a Right Venture Capitalist

LONG TERM FINANCING

The Need

While preparing the project report we had estimated the total funds required for setting up a project. The finances used for setting up an enterprise are tied up for a long time, for the whole life of the enterprise, till the enterprise is wound up.

As the enterprise grows, the finance needed for development and growth of the business outstrips the entrepreneurs ability to finance the same from internally generated funds. Hence, long term finance is not only needed while setting up a new enterprise but also for the growth of an existing enterprise.

The Sources

Broadly speaking, there are two main sources of finance, *equity* and *debt,* i.e., ownership capital and borrowed capital. *Equity* represents the owners interest. It is defined as financing source that has a residual claim on the cash flows and has an infinite life, does not have priority in liquidation whereas *debt* is defined as financing source that has a contractual claim on the cash flows of an enterprise, creates tax deductible expenses, has a fixed life and a priority in operating profits as well as in liquidation. Debt and equity have following differences:

- The main difference is debt has a prior claim on earnings and assets of the enterprise.
- Interest payable on debt is an allowable expense for tax purpose while the dividend paid on equity is not a tax deductible expense.
- Debt has a fixed maturity date when the repayment of debt becomes mandatory. As against this equity has infinite life.
- Interest on debt is a liability which is to be paid even in the absence of profit or surplus, whereas, equity holders may get the reward in the form of dividend only in case the income generated has a declarable surplus.

Table 14.1

Long Term Finance Equity Vs Debt		
	Debt	**Equity**
1. Claim on Profits and Assets	Priority and Fixed Claim	Residual Claim
2. Maturity	Predetermined and Fixed Maturity	Infinite Life
3. Repayment	High Priority	Lowest Priority
4. Tax Treatment	Tax Deductible	Not Tax Deductible.

It is important to have adequate risk capital in the initial phase of setting up a new venture. If the provision of risk capital is adequate it enables an enterprise to easily obtain loans or additional funds as and when the business passes through rough patches. If initially some plant and machinery or other facility is left out and additional funds are required for arranging the same, the inadequacy of the risk capital can be a hindrance in arranging additional funds from banks and financial institutions. Only a strong base of capital can provide the cushion for attracting financial support of debt funds when needed. This risk capital is to be provided by the entrepreneur starting the venture and forms the core of the equity often called as promoter's equity.

Concept of Leverage

Leverage refers to the relationship between two interrelated variables. It reflects responsiveness of one financial variable due to changes in some other financial variable. In leverage analysis, we aim at studying the relationship between the variables than the variables themselves. Leverage is defined as rate of change in one variable divided by the rate of change in some other variable.

$$\text{Leverage} = \frac{\text{Rate of change of dependent variable}}{\text{Rate of change of independent variable}}$$

The leverage analysis thus reflects the responsiveness of dependent variable to changes in the independent variables. There are two important relationships :

(i) Sales revenue and earnings before interest and tax (EBIT), called *operating leverage.*

(ii) Earnings before interest and tax (EBIT) and earnings per share, called *financial leverage.*

Operating Leverage

Operating leverage refers to the degree to which an enterprise has built in fixed costs. Some enterprises with automated or mechanised operations have high fixed cost and low variable cost. Their degree of operating leverage is often high with higher break-even point. In such cases, changes in the sales level leverage (increase) the profits.

When the sales change, the EBIT also increases or decreases. The operating leverage is the measure of relationship between sales revenue and EBIT. It measures the effect of change in sales revenue on the level of EBIT.

$$\text{Operating Leverage} = \frac{\text{Rate of change in EBTI}}{\text{Rate of change in sales}}$$

$$\text{DOL} = \frac{\Delta\text{EBIT/EBIT}}{\Delta\text{S/S}}$$

DOL = Degree of operating leverage

ΔEBIT = Change in Earning before Interest and Tax

EBIT = Earning before Interest and Tax

ΔS = Change in Sales Income

S = Sales Income

The direct relationship between sales revenue and earnings per share is the combined effect of operating and financial leverages and is called *combined leverage.*

When Degree of Operating Leverage (DOL) is more than 1, i.e., rate of change in EBIT is higher than the rate of change in sales revenue, the operating leverage exists. Operating leverage is due to the fixed cost. As a result of fixed cost, the net operating income, i.e., EBIT of an enterprise increase at a higher rate than increase in the sales volume. This level of fixed cost magnifies the EBIT. Thus, higher the fixed cost higher is the DOL. An enterprise with greater DOL will experience a magnified change in its EBIT for a smaller variation in sales. At the same time the operating profit (EBIT) will disappear or change to operating loss with decline in sales.

For safety an entrepreneur should avoid higher DOL. Higher DOL signifies a high business risk where a small change in sales causes a disproportionate effect on the profits.

Financial Leverage

Debt, that is, borrowed funds act as a lever in financing the acquisition of assets. Use of debt financing in a profitable and tax paying enterprise improves its return on equity. The effect of use of debt financing on the returns of an enterprise is known as financial leverage. In fact financial leverage refers to use of all fixed charge securities (i.e., term loan, debenture, preference shares) in the financing of an enterprise.

The amount of debt employed in an enterprise is expressed either in relation to the total assets or total equity. The two ratio's debt-asset ratio and debt-equity ratio can be computed from the balance sheet of an enterprise. Debt-asset ratio can rise at a constant rate from zero to one as assets are financed from equity alone (100% equity) to nil equity, i.e., 100 per cent debt. In these two extremes, debt-equity ratio increase exponentially to infinity. The two ratios are mathematically related:

$$\text{D/A Ratio} = \frac{\text{D/E Ratio}}{1 + \text{D/E Ratio}}$$

where D = debt

E = Equity

A = Assets

Financial Leverage FL measures the responsiveness of earning per share EPS to the changes in EBIT, i.e., earnings before interest and tax of an enterprise.

$$\text{Financial Leverage (FL)} = \frac{\text{Rate of change of EPS}}{\text{Rate of change of EBIT}}$$

$$\text{DFL} = \frac{\Delta\text{EPS/ EPS}}{\Delta\text{EBIT/EBIT}}$$

DFL is Degree of Financial Leverage

D indicates changes in....

Earnings per share is the total profit after interest and tax divided by the number of shares.

$$\text{EPS} = \frac{\text{PAT}}{\text{No. of shares}}$$

$$= \frac{(\text{EBIT} - \text{Interest})(1-t)}{\text{No. of shares}}$$

PAT = Profit after tax

t = tax rate

If the rate of increase in EBIT is lower then the increase in EPS it is due to the existence of fixed interest charge like loan and debenture. Let us assume that the cost of debts is 10 per cent and the benefit, that is, increase in return on assets or investment is 35 per cent. Herein, the surplus generated by employing debt is passed on to the shareholders, as a result the total earnings available to shareholders is magnified. The fixed interest charge is tax deductible and provides a tax shield. This tax shield provided by interest charge further increases the earnings available to the shareholders.

The effect of changes in EBIT (earnings before interest and tax) is magnified on the level of EPS. This magnification effect on EPS and its extent is determined by and is due to the existence of fixed charge financing. Higher the fixed financial (or interest) charge, greater is the financial leverage. Financial leverage may be defined as :

$$\text{FL} = \frac{\text{EBIT}}{\text{EBIT} - \text{Financial charge}}$$

As the proportion of debt increases, it not only magnifies the return but also increases their volatility. Increased volatility implies greater risk due to increasing interest burden which, if not met, may lead to bankruptcy.

Combined Leverage

The degree of operating leverage is combined with the degree of financial leverage. Since financial leverage measures the effect of changes in EBIT on earnings available to the entrepreneur, it can be calculated as follows:

$$\text{DFL} = \frac{\text{Rate of change of net income}}{\text{Rate of change in EBIT}}$$

High degree of leverage brings a higher magnification of equity earnings.

Degree of Combined Leverage (DCL) is the product of Degree of Operating Leverage (DOL) and Degree of Financial Leverage (DFL)

i.e., $\text{DCL} = \text{DOL} \times \text{DFL}$

i.e., $$= \frac{\text{Rate of change in EBIT}}{\text{Rate of change in sales}} \times \frac{\text{Rate of change in net income}}{\text{Rate of change in EBIT}}$$

$$= \frac{\text{Rate of change in net income}}{\text{Rate of change in sales}}$$

Thus, the combination of operating leverage and financial leverage measures the magnification in Net Income, Return on Equity (ROE) or Earning Per Share (EPS) due to increase in sales. Degree of Combined Leverage (DCL) indicates that small changes in sales produce wide fluctuations in Net Income or Earning Per Share. If the enterprise has a high degree of operating leverage the degree of financial leverage should be kept low so as to bring down the combined leverage.

CAPITAL STRUCTURE

The composition of equity and debt in overall capital of an enterprise is called "*Capital Structure*", Capital structure is the proportion of equity and debt and is expressed as debt-equity ratio, i.e., debt capital divided by the equity capital.

Capital structure of an enterprise is different from its financial structure. Financial structure of an enterprise represent the manner in which the firms total assets are financed. It includes both long-term and short-term finance. Capital structure refers to long term sources of funds that is long term debt and equity needed for financing the cost of the project, i.e., primarily fixed assets.

An enterprise is required to maintain a proper balance between debt and equity so that it can function efficiently and smoothly. The optimum capital structure is one which maximises the value of the enterprise and that of the entrepreneur's investment. The ideal capital structure is one where the cost of capital is minimum. There are benefits of debt, as a part of capital structure, as the interest payments are tax deductible expenses. This results in relatively higher profits for the entrepreneurs. As a normal practice debt equity ratio of 2:1 is considered most favourable by the banks and financial institutions. In order to promote entrepreneurship, Reserve Bank of India recommends a capital structure with debt equity ratio of 3:1 for small scale industries.

Factors Effecting Capital Structure

To determine the capital structure of an enterprise the important considerations are as follow :

Business Risk

The capital structure is directly influenced by the business risk faced by the enterprise. Business risk is the relationship between the earnings before interest and taxes and the sales revenue of an enterprise. It is a function of the operating leverage of the firm. It is directly effected by two more factors, that is, stability of cost and revenue. Cost stability means the inputs and their cost remain stable. If the input prices are unlikely to vary much, the business risk is lower. The firms sales revenue are stable if (i) there is a little variation in sales volume, that is, the product or service has a stable demand, (ii) the price of the product/service produced remain stable. The enterprise which have a unstable level of demand and/or product/service with unstable prices have a high business risk than those enterprises having stable demand and prices.

The enterprises, with higher business risk, have to be more careful in fixing their capital structure. Ventures with high business risk should use capital structure with law financial leverage and vice-a-versa.

Financial Risk

The financial structure of an enterprise directly effects the financial risk of the venture. Financial risk is the risk eminating from the financial leverage. The enterprises which have a higher proportion of fixed cost financing, i.e., debt, as a part of their capital structure carry a higher financial risk.

Size of the Enterprise

Size of the business venture is an important factor that effects the capital structure. As per banking norms prevalent in India, financial institutions and banks finance the smaller units with a higher debt equity ratio of 3:1 than larger enterprises which are provided term loans with a debt equity ratio of 2:1. However, the larger units have higher resources and can arrange debt from many other sources including public debt in the form of debentures and fixed deposits. Such options are beyond the scope of smaller enterprises.

Condition in the Capital Market

If the conditions in capital market are favourable and there is an excess liquidity in the market, especially with the financial institutions and banks, the enterprises find it is easy to get higher amount of debt than during the period of tight financial market when the capital structure with higher equity become more common.

Provision for Future

While fixing the present capital structure not only the present requirement of funds but also the future need for the growth and expansion of the enterprise are to be kept in mind. The capital structure should be such that in case of any urgent requirement additional funds can be managed easily. On one hand the entrepreneur should not put all his investable funds as equity, he should held back a part of it to be deployed latter to meet any contingent requirements. On the other hand, debt equity ratio be fixed in favour of equity so that the resultant capital structure has the necessary cushion for arranging further debt at short notice, without violating the norms fixed by lending agencies.

Features of a Good Capital Structure

The optimum capital structure, one that minimises the cost of funds and maximises the entrepreneurs wealth, is rather impossible in real life. However, if a capital structure has the following features, it is considered well suitable for the enterprise.

1. The capital structure should be such that the cost of funds is kept as low as possible.
2. It should be flexible enough with a built in cushion to meet future funds requirements with least hurdles.
3. The debt raised should be within the repaying capacity of the enterprise.
4. The capital structure should be such that it increases the profitability of the enterprise. If the rate of return on total assets is higher than the cost of debt, the financial leverage be enhansed to increase the entrepreneur's return.
5. The capital structure be so fixed that its keeps the total risk of the firm at a reasonable level. An enterprise with high business risk should aim at keeping the financial risk at a minimum level.

INSTRUMENTS OF LONG TERM FINANCE

Two main components for long term finance are equity and debt. Let us now discuss common instruments of equity and debt.

EQUITY

The equity capital of an enterprise is represented by two main instruments — *common stock* and *preferred stock*. As discussed earlier, both of these instrument form the risk capital of an enterprise. It is provided by the entrepreneurs, their friends and relatives. The promoters convince other investors to join and contribute to the equity capital. This is done by issue of the ordinary shares or common stock. Equity shares gives the following advantage to an enterprise :

1. Equity share is a permanent source of finance which provides the flexibility in use of funds.
2. The enterprise does not have an obligation to pay dividend to shareholders. The dividend can only be paid if there are sufficient profits to distribute.
3. No charge on any asset is created while raising equity capital.
4. There is no obligation to repay equity capital to the shareholders. Share capital is repayable only on the liquidation of the enterprise.
5. Equity acts as margin and provides the venture an opportunity to raise debt.

However, equity is to be used with caution. Firstly, excess equity may lead to over capitalisation and secondly, high level of equity in capital structure is likely to create inefficiency in the enterprise, as there may not be sufficient pressure to service or repay the equity funds.

Preference Share Capital

Equity is a risk capital. Ordinary investors are at times reluctant to take risk, especially for new projects or enterprises. The prospective investors are often required to be given certain preferences vis-a-vis the promoters. Some time, some of the promoters also agree to provide additional finances in lieu of preferential treatment. Hence, preference shares are issued. Preference shares occupy a position superior to the holders of ordinary shares in the distribution of income as well as assets, in the event of liquidation.

Preference share on one hand have a priority claim relative to equity shareholders in income and the firm's assets but on the other hand are subordinate to all debts in respect to earnings and assets. It is a hybrid kind of security having some attribute of equity and some of debt. It is part of an enterprises equity and the preferences dividend paid is not a tax deductible expense. Preference shares are fixed charge instrument as they carry a fixed dividend rate. Unlike ordinary shares, preference shares can be redeemed. Thus, they are redeemable equity.

Preference share capital legally represent the owners interest and is not a liability for the enterprise. An enterprise will not go in for liquidation in case of failure to pay preference dividend unlike interest on debt. In case of short fall of profits, or even otherwise payment of promised fixed rate preference dividend is not obligatory.

However, equity shareholders can not be paid dividend as long as preference dividends are in arrear, that is, remain unpaid.

The major advantage of preference share is that cost of capital of preference share is lower than that of ordinary equity. The popularity of preference capital keeps changing with changes in tax laws.

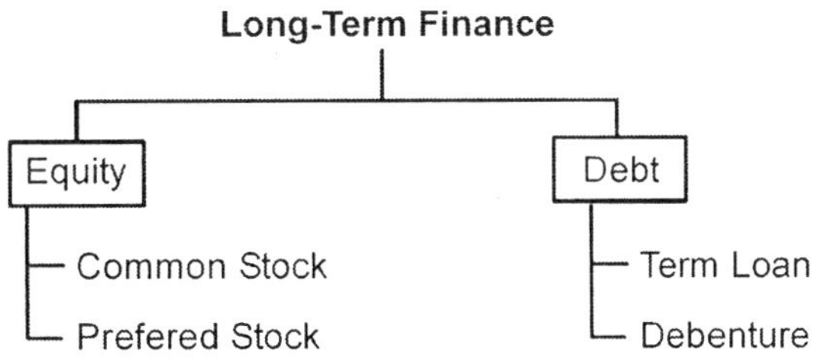

Fig. 14.1. Instruments of Long Term Finance

DEBT

Debt is borrowed fund and has an element of risk associated with it. It carries with it a commitment of not only ensuring timely payment of fixed interest but also repayment of the instalment as per a fixed schedule. Failure to service debt can lead a business to insolvency. Debt is normally a cheaper source of finance than retained earnings or new equity. The tax shield makes debt even cheaper.

The main instruments of debt financing are :

1. Term Loan 2. Debentures

Term Loan

It is also referred to as *term financing*. Financial institutions and banks provide term loan to business ventures for financing their fixed assets and permanent working capital. Long-term capital provided directly by a lender in the form of a negotiated contract according to all details of the agreement is called *term loan*. The main features of term loan are interest, schedule for repayment of principal, security and conditions of the lender. Term loan is normally provided for a period of 5 to 8 years and in certain cases upto the maturity of 10 years. The repayment start after a moritorium of 1 to 2 years. This time is provided to cover the gestation period till the new assets purchased start yielding returns.

TERM LOAN

Purpose	• For Purchase of Fixed Assets
Repayment Period	• 5 to 10 yrs
Moratorium	• 6 to 24 months
Charge	• All Fixed Assets of the Enterprise
Guarantee	Personal Guarantee of Promoters
Source	Financial Institutions and Banks.

The interest charged by the lending institutions depend upon the general level of interest rates, the financial position of the company, the risk perception of the lender, the security provided by the borrower besides the manner and period of repayment. Lending institution while considering term loan shift their emphasis from the status of the enterprise to the prospects of the business. Since the term loan is paid over along period the existing status of the enterprise can be misleading, lenders evaluate the future prospects of the venture and its potential cash flows. The term loan are sanctioned on a thorough appraisal of the investment proposal.

Debenture

It is in the form of a promissory note indicating the interest rate, maturity period as well as the amount. Debentures are securities under Indian Security Act and are listed at the stock exchange. When a company proposes to issue debentures it must keep investor's interest in mind. Normally investors' interest are protected by the trusteeship agreement. Herein, a merchant banker, a law firm or any eligible institution, registered with the Securities Exchange Board of India (SEBI) acts as a custodian of the debenture holders interest. Debentures are of two types secured and unsecured. Normally, debentures are issued for a period of 5 to 7 years. In India, SEBI norms require that all debentures issued for period of 18 months and above are to be secured debentures. Secured debentures are backed by the charge on certain assets of the company. Debentures are more secure as compared to company deposits in view of the protection it affords and also because no company can violate the debenture agreement on account of its serious consequences. Interest rates on debentures were controlled by the government and then the government decontrolled the interest payable on the debentures. Presently, depending upon the market forces, companies are free to offer any interest rate on their debentures. Further there is a practice, wherein the debentures are redeemed at a premium of 5 per cent on their face value at maturity, i.e., a debenture of Rs. 100 on maturity is redeemed at Rs. 105.

The debentures are of two types, convertible and non-convertible. The convertible debentures, are partly or fully converted into equity share at a predetermined rate and on a predetermined date. Non convertible debentures or non-convertible part of a convertible debenture and are redeemed on maturity. The convertible debentures are hybrid instruments that combine both debt and equity.

SHORT TERM FINANCING

As against long-term finance that is needed for a longer period, technically for more than a year, the short-term funds represent the money required for a shorter period that is less than a year. While long-term funds are needed for setting up a venture, the short-term finance is needed for its smooth operations. The working capital is the major component of short-term funds.

FINANCING OF WORKING CAPITAL REQUIREMENTS

Working capital needs of a unit are financed from various sources as follows :

(i) Own funds or equity

(ii) Sundry creditors

(iii) Other short-term finance

(iv) Short-term borrowings, and

(v) Bank borrowings.

(i) Own Funds : Regulations for financing of working capital needs by financial institutions stipulate a certain stake of the borrower to ensure proper management of funds. This stake of the owner, otherwise termed, 'Margin Money', is what comes out of the equity or own funds of the borrower. Thus, the owner's funds go partly to meet expenses towards acquisition of assets like land, building, etc., and partly as 'margin' towards working capital needs.

(ii) Sundry Creditors : Credits available against purchase of materials go to meet the working capital needs. To cite an illustration, a small scale unit is engaged in cloth printing on a job work basis where the customer himself gives the cloth to be printed. The unit gets about one month credit on purchase of dyes and chemicals for printing while many a time printing is completed in a week's time and the printing charges collected within 15 days.

(iii) Other Short-Term Finance : Industries in general also get credit for some of the expenses on a continuous basis. About 45 days credit is available on power bills, about 15 days in the case of wages paid monthly, etc. In addition, units also get advance for supplies.

(iv) Short-Term Borrowings : Working capital requirements fluctuate on a day-to-day basis depending on exigencies. Therefore, occasions do arise when the unit has to resort to short-term borrowing from friends, or other market sources. This happens because the various other sources are not adequate enough to meet the requirements.

(v) Bank Borrowings : Bank finance is a major external source of finance. Banks offer credit facilities against inventory, book debts and bills receivables. For inventory the facility of cash credit is most convenient, while book debts are also used for financing the stocks. For bills receivables and book debts, bill purchase and bill discount facilities are offered by the banks. Banks provide cash credit facility by way of hypothecation or pledge of goods. For example, pre-shipment and post shipment credits are provided by the banks for exports against pledge of goods.

When an enterprise purchases its supplies from a large and established firm banks provide an acceptance limit for this purpose. Facilities like letter of credits and guarantees are availed from banks to meet certain contingent situations.

The interest rate of bank borrowing is reasonable compared to other borrowings. Further the borrowing limit of banks are allowed depending upon the activity level. Banks normally have a flexible approach when lending to industrial units. However, when working capital requirement exceeds Rs. 40 lakhs banks normally follow the norms laid down by Tandon/Chore Committee.

Tandon/Chore Committee Norms for Working Capital Loan by Banks

With the liberalisation on banking sector, these norms are no more binding on the banks and they are allowed to provide working capital finance as per guideline laid down by their respective boards. However, in the absence of any other comprehensive norm banks still calculate the working capital requirements as per these norms. These norms represent the maximum level of holding, inventory and receivables in each industry. However, where circumstances justify, banks deviate from these norms.

According to the lending norms, a part of the current assets should be financed by trade credits and other current liabilities. The balance, i.e., net working capital is to be financed partly by the owner's fund or long-term borrowings and balance by short-term bank finance. Tandon committee, provides three methods for determining maximum permissible bank finance. Each successive method reduces the involvement of short-term bank credit.

First Method : Bank credit for working capital is maximum of 75 per cent of net working capital. The balance 25 per cent is to be arranged by the promoters through owner's funds and/or long-term finances. This method gives a minimum current ratio of 1:1. MPBF = 0.75 (CA – CL)

Second Method : This method stipulates the entrepreneur provides 25 per cent of the current assets that is the gross working capital need of the unit out of long-term funds. Total current liabilities inclusive of bank finance do not exceed 75 per cent of current asset. According to second method the minimum current ratio is 1.3:1. MPBF = 0.75 CA–CL

Third Method : This method considers core current assets, that is, the absolute minimum level of raw materials, stock in progress, finished goods and stocks in progress, to ensure continuity of production. This core current asset is reduced from the current assets for the purpose of bank finance. MPBF = 0.75 (CA – CCA) – CL. This is the most conservative method and is presently neither favoured by the entrepreneurs nor the bankers.

The three alternatives are illustrated by taking the following example of an enterprise's projected balance sheet for the next year.

Example:

Balance Sheet

Current Assets		Current Liabilities	
Raw Materials	300	Creditors for Purchases	150
Stock-in-Process	30	Other Current Assets	75
Finished Goods	135		225
Receivables	75	Bank Borrowings	300
Other Current Assets	15		
	555		525

Ist Method			
Current Assets (CA)			555
Current Liabilities (CL)*			225
Max Permissible bank finance MPBF	0.75 (CA–CL)		
	0.75 (525–225)	247.5	
Current ratio		1.17:1	
2nd Method			
Current Assets (CA)			555
Less : 25% of above from long term sources			<u>138.75</u>
			416.25
Current Liabilities (CL)*		225	
Max Permissible bank finance 0.75 CA – CL			
			191.25
Current ratio			1.33:1

* CL = Current liabilities extending bank finance for w.c.

Chore committee had recommended that borrowers enjoying aggregate working capital limits of Rs. 50 lakhs and above are compulsorily required to conform to the second method of lending prescribed above and would have a minimum current ratio of 1.33. The entrepreneur is required to submit to the bank a quarterly statement of funds and provide information of actual performance vis-a-vis the estimates.

Naik Committee

To promote entrepreneurship and provide adequate and timely financial assistance to small scale sector RBI had set up a committee called Nayak Committee who recommended that SSI sector should obtain 20 per cent of its annual projected turn over by way of working capital loan from banks. Reserve Bank of India has directed the banks to meet the working capital need of SSI by working out the normative requirement at the rate of 20 per cent of annual output subject to the limit of Rs. 2 crores. The promoters are required to bring in 5 per cent of the projected annual turnover as working capital margin.

PROJECT APPRAISAL

The objective of a project appraisal is take a decision to accept or reject an investment proposal. Many a times institutions also make recommendations on reformulating the project to ensure its better economic, technical, financial and commercial viability. Thus, project appraisal is an analysis of a proposed project to gauge its acceptability. The main objective of the appraisal is to ensure the efficiency of the use of resources. It requires the dynamic approach involving the projection of future trends of output, sales, estimates of costs, returns and flows of funds, and thus depend on the estimates of forecasts. Analysis of project involves use of highly competent skills in management, marketing, economies, engineering and other related areas. *Project appraisal has been defined as critical and careful second look at the project by a person not associated with the project preparation.*

Project Appraisal Methodoloy

Institutions follow the three progressive steps in appraising project for financial assistance

(i) Submission of an application form.

(ii) Scrutiny and processing of the application

(iii) Site inspection.

Submission of Loan Application

All financial institutions and banks have standardised application forms, that require a standard set of information and data to be submitted by the entrepreneur. The form is so designed that an analysis of the information supplied helps the lending institution to judge the viability of the project.

Scrutinising and Processing of Loan Application

The applications received are examined to ensure that sufficient information/data has been furnished against every item and also to check the correctness of the information furnished. It is checked against the following important criteria.

1. Promoters have a successful track record and good entrepreneurial capabilities.
2. Product /service proposed has a good market potential.
3. Project is based upon a well-proven technology.
4. Cost estimates are reasonable and compare suitably with similar projects.
5. Project falls under priority lending considerations or not.
6. Promoter's contribution and projected cash flows meet the norms set by the lenders.

Site Inspection

On receipt of favourable consideration from the scrutiny of application the appraisal team carries out an inspection of the proposed site for the project. The aim is to assess the suitability of site from various angles. Site inspection also verifies the suitability of the site from the angle of environmental protection.

Aspects of Project Appraisal

Financial institutions appraise an investment proposal from various aspects looking closely from managerial, marketing, technical and financial angles. The principal criteria are as follows:

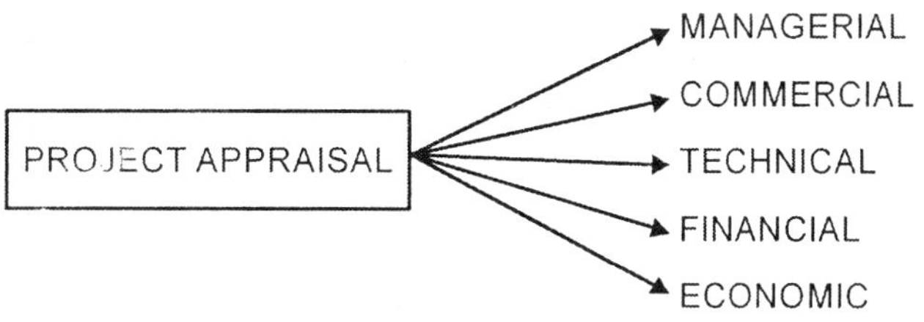

Aspect of Project Appraisal

Managerial Appraisal

It stresses on an efficient organisation and a responsible management suitable to handle the proposed new venture. If the management is incompetent the best of the ventures are likely to fail. If the project is weak it can be improved upon but in case the entrepreneur promoting a venture lacks in business accumen it is very difficult to reverse the situation.

Managerial review involves an assessment of the capabilities of the key technical and managerial persons of the enterprise, their training schedule and wage structure. Managerial appraisal attempts to find the managerial capability of the entrepreneur on three aspects.

ENTREPRENEUR APPRAISAL

1. Commitment
2. Project Understanding
3. Resourcefulness

Entrepreneur Appraisal

1. Commitment
2. Project Understanding
3. Resourcefulness

Commitment : The financial institutions measure the commitment of the entrepreneurs using various techniques. Zeal with which an entrepreneur works on his venture and the amount of resources, financial, managerial and other allocated to the venture indicate the level of his commitment.

Understanding : This is assessed in terms of the credibility of the project plan including the organisation structure, the estimated cost, the financing pattern. This includes the assessment of various inputs and marketing policy.

Resourcefulness : This is judged by the prior experience of entrepreneur relevant the venture, its technology, market etc. It indicates the ability of the entrepreneur to mobilise resources.

COMMERCIALAPPRAISAL
1. Demand Assessment
2. Marketing Infrastructure
3. Market Survey

Commercial Appraisal

In setting up any new ventures estimation of potential demand of the product/service proposed is the most important aspect of any appraisal. The three import components of market appraisal are:

Demand Assessment : The market survey report is critically examined to assess the reasonableness of the aggregate demand of the product or service. It should include the market share aimed at by the enterprise. The data is compared with the industry associations projections and independent market surveys wherever required.

Marketing Infrastructure : The proposed marketing set up is examined for the suitability of capturing the required market share, particularly taking the existing competition into account. Infrastructure in terms of promotional effort, distribution set up, logistics and stock levels is examined for the appropriateness and sufficiency of the financial provisions.

Market Strategy : The proposed market strategy is reviewed keeping in view the environmental factors, level of competition, product attributes, the stage of produced life cycle etc. The aim is to ensure that the implementation will result in meeting the sales target both in volume and price realisation.

Technical Appraisal

Technical appraisal by the lending institutions primarily concentrates of the following aspects of the venture.

— Processing of Manufacturing/Technology;
— Technical Collaboration/Engineering know how;
— Size/capacity of the plant and economy of scale;
— Suitability of the site and location;
— Plant, machinery and equipment and their suitability particularly for output— in quantity as well as quality;
— Plant layout and location of the facilities;
— Availability of right quality and quantity of raw materials, components and utilities.

The technical appraisal considers the background, reputation and capabilities of the suppliers of plant and machinery besides ensuring balancing of different items of plant and equipment. The emphasis is laid on size and capacity of the plant to ensure that the venture has the economy of scale similar to the other projects being set up. Mostly the institutions maintain their own list of minimum plant size for financing, e.g., presently minimum size of a mini cement plant to be financed is 100 tonnes per day or more.

Financial Appraisal

Financial appraisal by the lending institutions is particularly biased towords cash flows. **Institutions** are more concerned about solvency and debt recovery. However financial appraisal addresses the following aspects :

Cost Estimates of the Venture : While assessing the cost of the project, the reasonableness of the cost is to be verified. It is ensured that there is no padding of the costs, at the same time no cost component is under estimated. The costs are to be based on the actual quotations which have been properly negotiated. The inflation is to be accounted for by making appropriate provision of contingencies. In case of imported equipments the contingency should also make a provision of future currency conversion rates. Institutions verify the authenticity of the supplier's quotations and compare the same with similar projects financed by them.

Appropriateness of the Financial Structure : During appraisal, a special attention is paid to the means of financing the venture. It is ensured that debt equity ratio is as per the current norms of the lending institution or guidelines of Reserve Bank of India. Presently debt equity norm is 1.5:1 for large and medium projects and 3:1 for small scale industries.

Institutions normally insist that promoters contribute at least 20 to 25 per cent cost of the project cost. In case the enterprise plans to issue shares to public, the requirement of promoters contribution as laid down by SEBI norms as well as the listing requirements of the stock exchange are to be complied with.

The net worth of the entrepreneur and his sources of finance are studied in detail to check the entrepreneur's capacity to contribute a reasonable share of the project cost.

Adequacy of the Profits : It is important to ascertain the estimated profits from the venture are sufficient not only to meet the repayment liability of the enterprise but also the needs of the entrepreneur. The debt-service coverage ratio should not be less than 1.5 or 2.0 depending upon the needs of the enterprise and the entrepreneur. The net present value, internal rate of return and return on investment are calculated and compared with the similar units financed by the bank/institutions. To finance a project the IRR (internal rate of return) should be atleast 25 per cent higher than the proposed lending rate. However, lenders have flexible norms, which depend upon the risk perception of the venture and the status of the entrepreneurs and the securities offered.

Reasonableness of the Assumptions : All financial calculations are in fact financial projections about the future working of the enterprise. Future has uncertainty, so uncertainly is attached to all financial projections. The projections are based upon certain assumptions about the future working of an enterprise.

The major assumptions relate to :

1. Capacity utilisation of the plant.
2. Price of the product or service. Normally it is compared with the competitor's prices.
3. Input costs, raw material, labour, utilities etc. Normally their correctness is verified by checking the quotations.
4. The realistic estimates of demand.

FINANCIAL INSTITUTIONS IN INDIA

An entrepreneur needs two types of finances, i.e., short-term (for working capital) and long-term (for project finance). There are two distinct types of institutions to meet the two requirements that is Banks and Financial Institutions. Traditionally, banks have been a source of short-term finance and financial institutions had been specialising in long-term finances.

Banks

In India the schedule commercial banks are of three types, (i) nationalised banks, (ii) private banks, (iii) foreign banks. Initially, commercial banks provided assistance for working capital requirements and other short-term needs of the enterprises. Of late commercial banks have started term lending by participating in the consortium lending. RBI had been encouraging the commercial banks to provide term finance to small ventures, particularly small scale industries. For this RBI through its institutions namely IDBI and latter through SIDBI provided refinance facilities to banks for providing loan assistance to small ventures.

All commercial banks in India, including foreign bank branches in India, are required to earmark a specified part of their lending operation for priority sector. Lending to small scale sector is an integral part of the priority sector lending. Earlier the interest rate for the bank finance were governed by Reserve Bank of India. The lending rate's have now been freed (deregulated) and are fixed by the board of directors of the respective banks. Each bank declares prime lending rates for short-term as well as long-term finance. PLR is the lowest rate at which a bank provides finance to business enterprises. The actual interest rate can vary with the risk perception of the bank. The banks are allowed a maximum range of 4 per cent for this. For example, the long-term prime lending rate (on a particular date) is 13 per cent, the banks can provide term loan with interest ranging from 13 to 17 per cent depending upon their risk perception for different enterprises. The entrepreneurs can negotiate the interest rate. As per norms of Reserve Bank of India, the loans amounting up to Rs. 2 lakhs to small scale sector is provided at the prime lending rate.

Interest on term loan is levied quarterly. The repayment is also quarterly after a monetarism ranging from 6 to 18 months, this depends upon venture's ability to generate sufficient surplus.

In India, banks provide term finance for purchase of productive assets and long-term working capital. Banks do not provide loan for purchase of land and in specific case may provide finance for buildings. All fixed assets of the enterprise are mortgaged for providing the financial assistance.

All types of enterprises, small, medium, large or mega ventures, in any sector have to deal with banks primarily for their working capital and other short term financial needs. Banks are the major source of long-term finance to small and medium enterprises and a minor source for larger enterprises.

Financial Institutions

The set up of financial institutions in India consists of :

1. All India Financial Institutions
2. Investment Institutions
3. State Level Financial Institutions

All India Financial Institutions

They are also called development financial institutions. They have a developmental role in promoting industry and entrepreneurship and are thus contributing to the industrial development of the nation. Five major development financial institutions are :

(i) Industrial Development Bank of India Ltd. (IDBI)

(ii) IFCI Ltd. formaly (Industrial Finance Corporation of India Ltd.)

(iii) ICICI Ltd. formally Industrial Credit and Investment Corporation of India Ltd. (presently merged with ICICI Bank to form a universal bank)

(iv) Industrial Investment Bank of India (IIBI)

(v) Small Industries Development Bank of India (SIDBI)

Of these five institutions, the first four provide financial assistance to large enterprises. They normally consider projects costing Rs. 20 crore and above and avoid giving term loan below Rs. 10 crores. IDBI is the largest, IFCI is the oldest and ICICI was considered most efficient development bank. IIBI, was earlier called Industrial Reconstruction Bank of India, and was set up to assist in the redevelopment of large sick units. It has changed its mandate and name to Industrial Investment Bank of India. It is the smallest financial institute and its activities are concentrated primarily in eastern part of the country. Financial Institutions were primarily set up to provide long-term finance both in Rupee as well as foreign currency. Presently, they offer a wide range of product and services, especially tailored to the needs of the entrepreneurs.

They provide assistance to the entrepreneurs in the form of rupee and foreign currency loans, underwriting and direct subscription to issuance of shares and debentures, and guarantee to suppliers of equipment and foreign lenders.

Term loans are generally granted for a period ranging from five to seven years usually 60 per cent of project cost is financed by debt. That is institutions limit the debt equity ratio to maximum of 1.5:1. The promoter entrepreneurs are required to meet a minimum of 25 per cent of the expected project cost through their own sources. Herein term loans, in addition of funding the purchase of equipment and machinery may also finance the cost of land, construction facilities and related services, pre-operative and preliminary expenses including interest payment for the period of construction and installation, and margin money for working capital requirements. The interest rate is based on the prime term lending rate fixed from time to time. The actual rate with in the prevailing rate band depends upon the credit worthiness of the borrower and the risk perception. Also, there is an option of the floating rate of interest linked to LTPR and risk spread. Interest is now payable quarterly.

Foreign currency term loans are sanctioned for purchase of imported capital equipment, to finance services incidental to the cost of equipment, such as related technology and servicing fee, and to meet domestic expenditure related to the venture. Interest rate of foreign currency loan is a floating rate based on LIBOR depending upon the source of the currency plus a fixed spread according to the risk perception and maturity of the loan.

In addition, all financial institutions charge an amount equal to 1 per cent of the loan sanctioned as an up front fee. The first charge on movable and immovable fixed assets of the enterprise and personal guarantee of the promoter entrepreneurs is the prime security for the loan. In case of IDBI and ICICI the repayment is quarterly instalments and half yearly instalment are accepted by IFCI and IIBI. All FIs insist on the following undertakings :

1. Undertaking from promoters/entrepreneurs
   (a) To meet over run/shortfall in project cost or means of financing through their own sources.
   (b) Promoters will not dispose off their shares till repayment of the term loan.
2. Undertaking from Managing Director of the enterprise that he will not receive any commission, if the enterprise is in default on loan repayment.

All India Financial Institutions (except SIDBI) provide direct lending to larger enterprises, they helps the medium sector through the re-finance and equipment finance. Enterprises with a minimum net worth of 5 crore who are in operation for at least 5 years and continuously making profits for the last three years are provided loans for acquisition of equipments and machinery.

SIDBI

Small Industries Development Bank of India (SIDBI) was established in April 1990 as a wholly owned subsidiary of Industrial Development Bank of India to provide financial assistance to small scale sector. The SIDBI's financial assistance to the small scale sector is channelised through two routes.

(a) Indirect Assistance

(b) Direct Assistance.

Indirect Assistance

SIDBI's financial assistance to small scale sector is primarily channelised through the existing credit delivery system consisting of state level institutions, commercial and rural banks. SIDBI provides refinance to and rediscounts bills of Primarily Lending Institutions (PLI). In respect of some institutions, line of credit (LOC) is granted in lieu of refinance.

All forms of organisations in small scale sector (i.e., proprietary, partnership, company, co-operative society etc.) are eligible for refinance assistance. The assistance is available for setting up of new ventures, or expansion, modernisation, diversification of existing units for all activities. The promoters contribution varies from 12.5 to 25 per cent. The interest rate up to the loan amount of Rs. 2 lakhs is the Prime Lending Rate of SIDBI and for loan amounts higher than Rs. 2 lakhs the interest rate are determined by the PLI (prime lending institutions)

Direct Assistance

SIDBI also provides lending to new and existing small scale enterprises that are at least private limited companies through it own branches. The loans are available for new ventures, modernisation, technology upgraduation, diversification and expansion of existing well run small scale enterprises. Assistance is also available for service sector like marketing setups, hotels, hospitals, nursing homes etc. SIDBI's direct loans are available for business ventures costing not less than Rs. 150 lakhs and needing a term loan of at least Rs. 100 lakhs. Small scale sector is eligible for a maximum debt equity ratio of 2:1. Foreign currency loans for import of equipment are made available to export oriented small scale enterprises. It also finances export bills in foreign currencies and provides pre-shipment and post-shipment credit in Rupees to exporting SSI units.

SIDBI also provides venture capital assistance to entrepreneurs for their innovative ventures if they have a sound management team, long-term competitive advantage and a potential for above average profitability leading to attractive returns on investment. A special National Fund for Software and IT industry (NFSIT) has been set up.

Investment Institutions

Institutions like LIC and GIC and other insurence companies have lots of investable funds. They invest a part of these funds in Industrial Ventures. They subscribe to equity shares, debentures and bonds of Industrial Ventures during public issue as well as in private placements.

Most of the states in India have two state level institutions.

1. State Financial Corporations (SFCs)
2. State Industrial Development Corporation (SIDCs)

State Financial Corporations

SFCs have been set up in 18 states under State Financial Corporation Act, 1951. These institutions provide financial assistance to small and medium enterprises. SFCs have the same role in the state for small and medium industries, as IFCI had in whole of the country vis-a-vis large scale sector. SFCs were set up as a joint venture of state government and IDBI. All SFCs are headed by professionals appointed by the state governments with the concurrence of IDBI. They get refinance facilitates from IDBI and SIDBI for the assistance they render to medium and small industries respectively. All SIDBI' s schemes of indirect assistance to small scale sector are implemented through SFCs.

SFCs presently provide the following assistance to small a medium units :

1. Provide long-term finance to industrial units of proprietary, partnership, company and cooperative societies.
2. To subscribe to equity and debenture issues of industrial concern.
3. Provide financial assistance to small and medium enterprises engaged in transport, tourism, hotels, hospitals and nursing homes etc.
4. Provide seed capital assistance to technically qualified entrepreneurs.
5. SFCs now also provide working capital loans and meet various short-term needs of their clients.

Normally SFCs open their offices in different parts of the state and aim at providing the assistance at the entrepreneur's door steps.

State Industrial Development Corporation (SIDCs)

SIDSs were set up in different states as wholly owned companies incorporated under companies Act, 1956 for promoting industrial development in their respective state. Main functions of SIDCs are :

1. Provide term finance to all industrial enterprises (small, medium and large) being set up in the state.
2. Underwrite and directly subscribe to shares and debentures of industrial units being set up in the state.
3. Collaborate with private entrepreneurs to set up industrial ventures in joint and assisted sector.
4. Prepare feasibility studies, conduct market surveys and motivate private entrepreneurs to set up their industrial ventures in the state.
5. Many SIDCs also develop and provide infrastructural support in the form of developed industrial estates, or constructed industrial sheds.
6. IDBI's scheme of seed capital is implemented in the states through SIDCs.

In many smaller state like Manipur, Goa, Sikkim, SIDCs also discharge the function of the state financial corporations and implement SIDBI's refinance schemes. Most of the SIDCs have diversified and started equipment leasing and merchant banking activities. They also act as a refinance arm of IDBI for its assistance to medium scale sector.

VENTURE CAPITAL

Of late Indian economy has witnessed the arrival of a few venture capital institutions to cater to the need of industrial ventures involving higher risk on account of technology development and up gradation.

The concept of venture capital is nurturing under the dictum "no innovative concept shall meet death in its womb for genuine need for finance for venturism".

There is a constant need for such institutions which could mobilise the savings and channelise them into enterprises with innovative and untried business ideas that lack proven track record. Venture capital companies, a recent phenomenon, have arrived in India. The term "Venture Capital" comprises of two words'. "Venture and Capital". The venture means a course of proceeding, the outcome of which is uncertain but which is accompanied by the risk of danger of loss, 'capital' means resources to start the enterprises. Thus, *'venture capital' implies committing resources (capital) to enterprise that has risk and adventure,* i.e., funds made available for financing of new business ventures from scratch are called venture capital. The definition incorporates all high risk, high potential investments. Venture capital is to finance the early stage of a new company that wants to grow rapidly.

However, the term venture capital is used to describe a variety of investment vehicles. A much wider range of activities than purely start up situations are undertaken by the venture capital companies. It is the investment of long-term risk finance in new and untried enterprises that are 'lacking a stable record of growth'. It is the investment wherein the uncertainties have yet to be reduced to the risk which a normal financial institution is willing to take. Thus, venture capital has now become an important source of finance for new enterprises. Journal of Central Bank-U.K. defines venture capital as "*an equity by which an investor supports an entrepreneurial talent with finance and business skills to exploit market opportunities and thus obtain long-term market gains*".

Thus, venture capital besides providing funds also provides skills needed to set up the firm, design its marketing strategy, organise and manage it. Thus, it is a long term association with successive stages of the company's development under highly risky investment conditions, with distinctive type of financing, appropriate to each stage of development. Investors join the entrepreneurs as co-promoters and support the project with finance and business skills to exploit market opportunities. The primary return sought by the investors is an eventual capital gain, rather than a steady interest income or dividend yield. All this differentiates a venture capital company from a finance or a development finance institution.

The development finance aims at promotion of industry without any consideration for new technology or new entrepreneurial venture. In majority of cases, development finance is a loan with a very small proportion of equity, whereas venture capital is primarily for new entrepreneurial ventures often involving the use of new technologies and assistance provided is predominantly as equity. While the venture capitalist has an interest in the overall management of project and is involved in the project till the end, i.e., its entering production and providing an exist route for liquidation of the investment, the institution supplying the development loan have no say in the enterprise except safe guarding its interest as investor of funds with no right to interfere in management except ensuring flow of information and adherence to statutory requirement of effective management control.

Some financial institutions provide 'seed capital' as equity or semi-equity. It is very akin to venture capital but is normally provided to meet the gap in promoters contribution for normal project finance. Development finance and the seed capital is security-oriented and liquidity prone. The seed capital is given to deserving entrepreneurs with bankable projects and sufficient expertise to manage their projects but lacking the equity. This equity is normally an interest free loan, the entrepreneurs pays a service charge of 1 per cent and has to return the funds (equity provided as soft loan) after 5 to 7 years. The institution providing the seed capital looks for returns of the funds within 10-12 years. The general criteria for investment are : proven track record of the promoters, successful management, sufficient cash generation to provide for returns and so on. Mostly such assistance is provided to non innovative projects of smaller size with lowest risk.

The venture capital companies look for the commercial viability, select high risk projects wherein the expected returns, in case of success, are much higher, i.e., IRR at 30 per cent and above. Venture capitalist aims at higher returns by capital gains from high risk projects and finance up to 40 per cent of the project cost. The DFIs and nationalised banks have realised the ineffectiveness of seed capital as a vehicle to promote new ventures involving new technology, a new product and enterprise in innovative areas usually involving high technology and have also started venture capital financing.

The main characteristics of venture capital are :

(1) Investments are generally in equity instruments where investor's return is taxed as capital gains rather than ordinary income.

(2) Investments are mainly made in new enterprises using new technologies to produce new products in expectation of higher gains or specular returns.

(3) The investors are involved in management of the enterprises. However, venture capital investors can not interfere in day-to-day management of the enterprise but keep close contact with the promoter to protect and enhance the investment.

(4) The approach of the venture capitalist in different from that of a stock market investor as well as that of a banker.

(5) Venture capital investment, unlike a loan repayment schedule, is highly illiquid, i.e., not subject to repayment on demand. The investment is realised only on enlistment or sale of security or it is lost if the enterprise is liquidated for unsuccessful working.

IFCI and ICICI have set up specialised venture capital companies namely Risk Capital and Technology Finance Corporation Ltd. (RCTC) now renamed IFCI Risk Finance Ltd. and Technology Development and Information Company of India now renamed ICICI Ventures Ltd. IDBI, SBI and Canara Bank have set up specialised venture capital funds. The India Investment Fund is a Venture Capital Fund set up by ANZ Grindlays Bank, besides State Government of Gujarat and Tamil Nadu have set up venture capital companies to finance high technology, high risk innovative projects in their states. Presently 129 venture capital funds are registered with SEBI and are operating in India.

Stages of Funding/The Venture Capital Spectrum

Traditionally, venture capital financing has been thought of as the early stage financing of relatively small but rapidly growing companies. However, in reality the venture capital is far broader and more complicated. Venture capital finance different stages of an enterprises development. Each stage of corporate development in venture capital spectrum has distinot characteristics. Each venture capital fund/firm has distinct aptitudes and appetities for various stages of venture capital financing. The venture capital industry recognises these stages and plans its involvement on the basis of risk and timescale involved as shown in Table below.

Table 14.2

	Stages	*Risk*	*Time scale of investment (Years)*
I	**Early Stage Investment**		
1.	Seed finance	Extreme	7–10
2.	Start up finance	Very high	5–10
3	First stage finance	High	4–6
4	Second stage finance	High	3–7
II	**Later Stage Investment**		
1.	Development/expansion finance	Medium	1–3
2.	Replacement finance	Medium	2–4
3.	Turnaround recovery finance	Medium-High	3–5
4.	Buy-out/buy-in	Medium	1–3

Early Stage Financing

Seed Finance

Seed capital is defined as the financing of the initial product development or the capital provided to an entrepreneur to prove the feasibility of a project and qualify for start up capital. Objectives at this point in the enterprises life cycle include developing a comprehensive business plan, hiring a management team and proving that the concept is viable or that the prototype works or meets customer needs. Seed capital financing has the distinction of being the earliest and riskiest stage of venture capital investment.

Start-up Finance

The start-up is widely recognised as the essence of venture capital activity. Start-up finance is required for the product development, initial marketing and establishment of product facilities. Enterprises at this stage may be in the process of being organised or they may have been in business for a short time (one year or less). Risks are quite considerable in start-ups. The failure rate is in the order of one in three, but none the less it is a low price risk. Risk here can be controlled better as additional financing depends upon the right performance of the company. There has been reluctance on the part of traditional investors to fund the start-up stage but venture capitalists support such ventures.

First Stage Finance

First stage financing is provided to enterprises that have expanded their initial capital often in developing, test marketing a prototype and require funds to initiate full scale manufacturing and sales. More venture capital providers go for first stage financing as compared to earlier stages as it is the first where in the two fundamental aspects of a business are in place, a fully assembled management team and a marketable product. The number of risk factors like challenges from competitors, obsolescence risk and defection of key personnel remain.

Second Stage Finance

Second round financing attracts more venture capitalists then first stage financing. Second stage financing is additional injection of funds for the expansion of an enterprise that is producing and shipping and already has growing accounts of receivables and inventories. Although the company has made progress it may not be showing profits yet. The reasons could be due to internal or external factors. If the venture capitalist is fully aware of the genuine reasons for the loss, he should decide on second round of financing. At this stage original venture capital investor may reduce his holding and bring in others to spread the risk.

Later Stage Financing

Third Stage/Mezzanine Finance/Development or Expansion Finance

An enterprise having been established in a particular market, needs finance for capacity expansion and setting up proper distribution network so as to reach critical operating levels at which economies of scale can be made. It is easier to get this finances as it has lower risk associated with it. Venture capital funds seek to invest a small portion of their capital at this stage, as a hedge against having all of their investment in earlier stages.

Replacement Capital/Money-Out Deal

Replacement capital essentially means substituting one shareholder for another, rather than raising new capital. Need for this arise due to variety of reasons like one or more shareholders in need of cash may be forced to sell their shares; differences between shareholders, owners and management, etc. In these cases the entrepreneur instead of off loading their shares in the stock market sells the shares to an investing fund.

Trun Around / Recovery Finance

It is a rare form of later stage finance, in which few venture capitalists are prepared to invest because they have to accept a significantly higher degree of risk as most of the situations end up in failure despite hectic efforts. Turn around situations arise, when established company runs into trouble (even bankruptcy) and needs money to prepare for a major restructuring to revitalize profit growth.

In 1966, Ms Hema Hattangudi agreed to head a family run, business of energy saving components. The company's net with was completely eroded and Emercon was left with the daunting task of building the business all over again. Hema wanted Emercon to do every thing on its own-from manufacturing to marketing. The turnover of her company has grown from Rs. 1 Crore to Rs. 18 Crore and is one of the few non-IT companies to get funding from venture capitalists. VCs too, do not have much to complain since her company has been rewarding them consistently with dividends.

Management Buy-Out/Buy-In

This stage is defined in two ways, "Management buy-out" and `Management buy-in'. In management buy-out venture capitalist help the professional management of an enterprise to buy or take over the ownership of the business venture. This would help the management to restructure and reorganise the enterprise. In management buy-in, outsiders buys the existing business. Though such financings are less risky, the same are financed by the venture capital firms as a part of latter stage financing.

FINANCING INSTRUMENTS

Venture capital funds/firms have sufficient flexibility in providing financial assistance to the selected ventures. They use innovative financial instruments. However, the common instruments are as follow:

Equity

Venture capital funds/companies normally take a minority position in the equity of the assisted enterprise. While participating in the equity they reserve the right to appoint nominee (s) on the board of directors, authority to examine the books of accounts and conduct a concurrent audit. The timing of disinvestment is at the venture capital's option. Normally, they want the enterprise to list its shares on the stock exchange. However, on certain occasions venture capital firms go in for nonvoting shares or deferred ordinary shares or some similar innovative instrument.

VENTURE CAPITAL
Financing Instruments
1. Equity
2. Quasi Equity / Hybridised Debt
3. Normal Debt

Quasi Equity Instruments

The two types of quasi equity loans used are :

(i) A loan whose servicing is linked entirely to the enterprises performance. Venture capitalist participate totally in the downside and significantly in the upside in a manner agreed upon.

(ii) A loan having a minimum contracted obligation (e.g., payment of low level of interest or even repayment of only a part of principal) irrespective of performance and on upside a sharing component.

Quasi equity normally contain a charge on the assets, collaterals, a royalty on sales above certain levels or a share in profits. Protective convenants like appointing nominee directors or converting a part of loan into equity are often a part of the deal.

Normal Debt

It is the least preferred financial instrument both from the point of view of the entrepreneur as well as the venture capital fund/firm. Neither of the two is interested in regular cash flows. However, a small part of the capital structure of new venture consists of normal debt. Venture capital funds/firms normally provide debt to meet short/medium term requirements and to tide over temporary cash shortages. The common debt instruments used are: term loan, fully, partly or non-convertible debentures, deep discount bonds etc.

It is evident that in India, venture capital financing has come to stay. In Asian countries, 30 per cent of the investment in venture capital comes from corporate sector while in India, only 8 per cent of venture capital funds come from the corporate sector, and over 60 per cent is accounted by the All India Financial Institutions. Thus, the growth potential for this type of findings are tremendous.

It is seen that venture capitalists have adopted two distinct and different routes, i.e., venture capital funds and venture capital companies. Since the criteria of selection of projects for conventional and venture capital financing are widely different, a separate venture capital company does a better justice to venture capital financing and is normally better equipped to impart managerial skills, a very essential part of venture capital financing.

VENTURE CAPITAL PROCESS

Over the last few years Indian venture capital has evolved its own set of business process. This process is quite similar to the investment procedure followed by the venture capital world wide but is different from the way conventional financial institutions conduct their investment operations. It is important for an entrepreneur to understand, how venture capital choose their investments? This wall not only help him in knowing about the eligibility of his/her project for venture capital financing but also guide him/her in preparing for the same.

Factors Influencing Venture Capitalists Choice of Investment

The venture capitalists usually take into account the following factors while deciding on the investment :

1. **Track Record :** Track record of the promoters and the management team is the single most important factor. It is often said that three most important considerations in selecting the venture capital investment are "Management", "Management" and "Management". Venture capitalist look or a track record of success of the promoters in their previous vacations, what ever these might have been. They put their bets on successful people and avoid those who have tasted failures earlier.
2. **Relevant Experience :** The nature of the business and the promoters experience in the proposed or related business is an important consideration. Venture capitalists are the firm believer of the Corridor Principal that states that the probability of the venture's success when the business falls in the corridor of the entrepreneurs previous vocation or education.
3. **Risk Profile :** The business should meet the investment objectives of the venture capitalist in terms of risk profile, the return and the time horizon of the fund. In case of closed-ended funds, if the venture capital has earned a substantial return in the first round of investments, it is more open to investments with comparatively higher risk. In the initial stages of a fund the venture capitalist is normally willing to take a longer term exposure as compared the later period when the fund is nearing maturity. At this stage it goes in for balance investments.
4. **Industry Expertise :** The funds normal invest in selected industries where they have the knowledge and expertise. This helps them in providing value added services to the investee companies.
5. **Financial Indicators :** Project cost, scheme for financing and financial projection over next few years, including details of underlying assumptions are closely studied. The resultant internal rate of return (IRR) must meet the minimum fixed by the venture capitalist as the hurdle rate. The IRR is adjusted for any protection the venture might be enjoying in the form of subsidy or any other concession from any government or statutory body. This is to ensure the inherent earning potential of the investment in spite of policy changes by the government.
6. **Marketing Strategy :** Marketing strategy, including target market, market survey, marketing effort, market size and growths potential also effect the decision.
7. **Technology :** Technology and technology collaboration, if any, are looked at carefully.

8. **Others Factors :** Miscellaneous factors looked at include raw material availability, pollution clearances, government policy, rules and regulations - controlling the industry, location, water and electricity need etc.

Most of the venture capital firms for not want an introduction from any one. A **business proposal** that is well prepared is the best introduction that one can have. Most venture capital firms are interested in good investments and not in social contacts and introductions.

A detailed and well-organised business plan is the only way to gain a venture capitalist attention and obtain funding. The do not invest in two page summary. The summary is needed as a start but not as a substitute for a sound plan. A well-prepared business plan serves two functions. Firstly, it informs the venture capitalists about the entrepreneur's ideas, secondly it shows that the entrepreneur has thought about the intended business, and knows the industry and has thought through all the potential problems. Venture Capital's plan should be an integral part of the business proposal/summary.

Choosing a Right Venture Capitalist

It is important to chose the right venture Capitalist because he will sit on the Board of Director, often for the duration of their investment and will assist in getting second round of financing. When choosing a VC, it is imperative to consider their qualifications in the following areas :

1. **Security Research :** It is important to research the Venture capitalist to understand his background, its mission statement, it's investment criteria and the people running it if Angel happens to be an organisation. Security research is also conducted to ensure there are not any SEBI sanctions associated with the organizations or its officers or other problems with the companies financed by them.
2. **Track Record :** It is to be verified if the Venture Capitalist has a portfolio of successful investment and understand the reasons for their failures. Does it has a successful track record for preparing companies for "second round" financing within the agreed time frame.
3. **Size and Focus :** Ensure that the angel is capable of handling the size of entrepreneur's need. Venture capitalist must have successfully invested in the enterprises of similar size, it should not be making that small or that large investment for the first time. Also enure that the angel has experts in the proposed industry sector.
4. **Value Added Management :** Since most of the venture capitalists will become a Member of the Board of Directors, it is important that the venture capitalist helps in completing the gaps in the management team. It is better if the venture capitalist belongs to a functional area where the management team is weak.
5. **Relationship with Investment Bankers :** Does the venture capitalist has an investment banker that could be used as a source of "second round" financing The venture capitalist's inks with other established venture capital firms, private investors or banking channels are important consideration in choosing a venture capitalist.

SUMMARY

There are two main sources of finance: equity and debt. Equity represents the owners interest. Debt has a fixed maturity date when the repayment of debt becomes mandatory. The composition of equity and debt in overall capital of an enterprise is called "Capital Structure" Capital structure is the proportion of equity and debt and is expressed as debt-equity ratio.

Capital structure of an enterprise is different from its financial structure. Financial structures of an enterprise represent the manner in which the firms total assets are financed. It includes both long-term and short-term finance.

The concept of venture capital is nurturing under the dictum "no innovative concept shall meet death in its womb for genuine need for finance for venturism". The venture capital besides providing funds is also an inputs of the skills needed to set up the firm, design its marketing strategy, organise and manage it.

REVIEW QUESTIONS

1. What are the major sources of long-term finance?
2. What do you understand by leverage?
3. Distinguish between operating and financial leverage.
4. Define capital structure. What is an optimal capital structure?
5. What factor determine the capital structure?
6. Describe the features of an appropriate capital structure.
7. Derive the relationship between leverage and risk.
8. What are different sources for raising term loan for a new venture? Discuss.
9. What are the considerations in fixing the debt equity ratio of a business venture? Also explain the characteristics of debt and equity.
10. Explain the importance of project appraisal.
11. What does a banker look for while appraising a project for sanction of term loan?
12. State the features of term loan and contrast the same with debentures.
13. Explain the different sources of financing a new venture, their merits and demerits.
14. Explain various stages of financing through venture capital.
15. Explain the instruments of venture capital financing.
16. How would you go about selecting a venture captialist of finance your project?

CASE 14.1

Bio-Technology Pharmaceutical Company

Introduction

M/s Jayaprada Clonetech (P) Ltd., a new company has proposed to set up a unit for manufacturing bio-technology pharmaceutical products, i.e., Monoclonal antibody (Mab) based Diagnostic Kits for Thyroid and pituitary hormones and insulin at Uppal Village, Ranga Reddy District, Andhra Pradesh with an installed capacity of 8000 kits per annum. The project was originally appraised by Industrial Development Bank of India-Technology Fund (IDBI-TF) under its Venture Capital Fund (VCF) scheme in September, 1990. The project cost was estimated as Rs. 77.00 lakhs and IDBI sanctioned a VCF term loan on Rs. 65.00 lakhs and APIDC sanctioned an equity assistance of Rs. 1.80 lakhs. During the implementation IDBI felt that though the project progress is satisfactory and is expected to be completed earlier than the originally envisaged time frame, there is expected to be some overrun in the cost of the project. Subsequently in December 1991 IDBI-TF re-appraised the project and re-estimated the project cost as Rs. 147.00 lakhs resulting in a cost overrun of Rs. 70 lakhs. IDBI sanctioned an additional VCF term loan of Rs. 37.90 lakhs totaling its assistance to Rs. 102.90 lakhs.

IDBI increased the promoters (Jayaprada and Associates) contribution from Rs. 12.00 lakhs in the original proposal (15.6% of the project cost) to 44.10 lakhs in the revised proposal (30% of the project cost). APIDC recently sanctioned an additional equity assistance of Rs. 4.80 lakhs to the company. The Promoters are technologically well qualified and first generation entrepreneurs with limited means and therefore approached APIDC-VCL to bridge the gap in equity in view of the sharp increase in project cost for reasons beyond their control.

Background

The Company M/s Jayaprada (P) Ltd., has been incorporated as Private Limited Company under Companies Act, 1956 in September 1990 with its registered office in Hyderabad. The authorised share capital of the company is Rs. 10.00 lakhs. It is promoted by team of four technocrats under Dr. (Mrs.) A. Jayaprada (aged 62) an accomplished bio-technologist. She is also its managing direction and assisted by six technical personnel for developmental work. The company has already succeeded in developing the following MAbs, using certain facilities available with research institutions such as University of Hyderabad and JNTU.

Item	*Quantity (mgs)*	*ELISA Plates (nos.) (32 wells)*
T3	15	4500
T4	20	6000
TSH	20	6000
Insulin	10	3000

Dr. Jayaprada, also indicated that the research team has achieved a near breakthrough in developing diagnostic kits for ascertaining pregnancy at a very early stage.

Project Proposal

The company will manufacture diagnostic kits for T3, T4, TSH, LH, Prolactin and Insulin hormones with an installed capacity of 8000 kits per annum.

T3 and T4 hormones are secreted by thyroid gland and their secretion, is controlled by thyroid stimulating hormone (TSH) secreted by pituitary gland. Any change in their concentration in body results in disorders related to overall metabolism of body and heart. Again follicle stimulating hormone (FSH), Leutenising hormone (LH) and prolactin are secreted by pituitary gland and control various functions of reproductive system of the body. Insulin is secreted by specific cells of pancreas gland and controls sugar levels in blood. Hence, measurement of these hormone levels in body would help both in diagnosis as well as monitoring the treatment of disorders related to these hormones.

RIA method involves radioisotopes and needs special facilities as well as greater care in handling and desposing EIA, using monoclonal antibodies, is more specific and sensitive than ETA with polyclonal antibodies.

The company has developed EIA kit based on monoclonal antibodies for FSH, got it tested by some diagnostic centres in Hyderabad and has found it satisfactory. Technology for other hormone kits (which is akin to FSH), i.e., T3, T4, TSH LH, Prolactin and Insulin is also developed. The kits have been tested at the Med vin Endocrine Diagonistic Centre in Hyderabad. The Diagonistic Centre informed that the trial kits are quite comparable with the imported STG Imuno Assay Kits.

Costs

Estimated cost of the project is Rs. 147.00 lakhs, as per details below (Table 1):

Table 1 : Project Costs and Financial Means *(Rs. in lakhs)*

	IDBI's Revised Estimate	***Expenditure incurred***
Land and Site Development	4.56	4.56
Building and Civil Works	27.54	31.89
Plant and Machinery (Imported)	37.19	
Plant and Machinery (Indigenous)	17.48	36.35
Erection and Commissioning	0.20	—
Miscellaneous Fixed Assets	14.65	9.33
Operating Expenses (incl. advances)	14.00	17.48
Prelim and Pre-op Expenses	7.00	3.37
Marketing Expenses	4.00	0.18
Contingencies	2.00	—
Interest during Development Period	8.24	3.12
Margin Money for Working Capital	10.00	—•
Total	146.86	116.52
Say Rs.	147.00	
Finance	Revised Proposal	Money raised
Equity		
Promoters	30.20	28.39
APIDC	6.60	4.80
APIDC-VCL (Proposed)	7.30	—
Equity	44.10	33.19
Loans		
IDBI-VCF Term Loan	102.90	83.00
Total	102.90	83.00

• Cash and bank balance and bank guarantees provided include Rs. 5.24 lakhs.

Reasons for Overrun

There is an overrun of Rs. 70 lakhs in the project cost (91% of the original project cost). The major reasons for overrun as given by IDBI are as follows :

(i) Land (+ Rs. 2.06 lakhs) and (ii) Civil Construction (+ Rs. 14.24 lakhs): It was originally envisaged that the factory would have a covered area of 5400 sq. ft. @ Rs. 246/sq.ft. Due to general increase in cost of building materials, the cost of civil construction has gone up to Rs. 278/sq.ft. (by about Rs. 2 lakhs). (iii) The variation in the cost of major items of plant and machinery resulted in an additional burden of Rs. 26.47 lakhs and (iv) miscellaneous fixed asset like elec. generators caused additional Rs. 4.45 lakhs and (v) Operating expenses (+ Rs. 6.4 lakhs) and Preliminary and Preoperative expenses (+ Rs. 4.10 lakhs): Based on the expenses incurred upto end-October, 1991, reasonable estimates have been made to cover the expenditure likely to be incurred upto December, 1992 — the tentative period for competition of the venture.

Market Scenario

IDBI has estimated the demand for T3, T4, TSH, LH, Prolactin and Insulin hormones kits is about 5000 kits each per year. All the immuno diagnostic kits are being imported as there are no indigenous producers. The traditional methods for diagnostic of diseases have certain disadvantages like low specificity requirement and costly and sophisticated equipment, etc., on the other monoclonal antibody diagnostic kits developed by the company have the advantageous of high specificity, long shelf life, high sensitivity, simplicity in operation, reproduceable result and cost effectiveness. The cost of the imported kits is around Rs. 6000 per kit as against the selling price of Rs. 4500 per kit of the company. The substantial difference in the cost of the kit in addition to the hefty margins offered to the dealers and may push the product in the market without much difficulty. Imported financial indicators are given in Table 2 and expected returns on the investment are given in Table 3.

In Table 3 disinvestment is assumed in the 7th year of APIDC-VCL. Buy back disinvestment prices are calculated based on Book value in the year of disinvestment.

Table 2 : Important Financial Indicators

Parameters	*1994*	*1995*	*1996*	*1997*
Installed Capacity (Kits/Annum)	8000	8000	8000	8000
Capacity Utilisation (%)	50	60	75	75
Production (Kits/Annum)	4000	4800	6000	6000
Total Income (Rs. Lakhs)	180	216	270	270
Raw Materials/Income (%)	25	25	25	25
Interest/Income (%)	15.89	11.48	8.74	7.70
Net Profit/Income (%)	–2.06	3.94	7.04	6.74
Operating BEP (%)		53.00		
Project IRR (%)		33.00		
EPS (RS)	–0.84	1.88	4.31	4.13
Return on APIDC-VCL Equity (%)		18.80		

Table 3 : Expected Returns to APIDC-VCL

Year of Operation	*Year*	*% Dividend*	*Amount*	*Book*	*Disinvest-ment*	*Total*
I	1993-94	0	0	9.16	–	–
II	1994-95	0	0	11.04	–	–
III	1995-96	0	0	15.35	–	–
IV	1996-97	19	1.387	27.57	–	1.387
V	1997-98	19	1.387	19.57	–	1.387
VI	1998-99	19	1.387	21.27	–	1.387
VII	1999-2000	19	0	22.63	16.52	16.520
			4.161		16.52	23.661

The expected returns to APIDC-VCL in such a case is 18.80 per cent.

The actual disinvestment by APIDC-VCL would be made based on a fair price calculated at the time of disinvestment and the first option of buying back the shares would be given to the Promoters.

It can be seen that the expected returns to APIDC-VCL is quite low. This is mainly because the company has to service VCF term loan of Rs. 102.90 lakhs by way of interest @ 18.5 per cent after the commercial production and royalty on sales 5 per cent giving them an over all return of around 33 per cent.

Schedule of Implementation

Civil construction is completed in March 1992 and the majority of the machinery are received and installed. The company has completed the developmental work of the kits in December 1991 and the kits are trial tested till April 1992 and the commercial release of the kits into the market is expected by the end of June 1992.

Conclusions and Recommendations

The project of the company has been originally appraised by IDBI Technology Fund (TF) under its Venture Capital Fund scheme in September 1990. With a project cost estimated as Rs. 77.00 lakhs and IDBI sanctioned and VCF term loan of Rs. 65.00 lakhs and APIDC sanctioned an equity assistance of Rs. 1.80 lakhs. During the implementation IDBI felt that through the project progress is satisfactory and is expected to be completed earlier than the originally envisaged time frame, there is expected to be some overrun in the cost of the project. Subsequently in December 1991 IDBI-TF reappraised the project cost as Rs. 147.00 lakhs totalling its assistance to Rs. 102.90 lakhs. IDBI increased the promoters contribution from Rs. 12.00 lakhs in the original proposal (15.6% of the project cost) to 44.1 lakhs in the revised proposal (30% of the project cost). APIDC recently sanctioned an additional equity assistance of Rs. 4.80 lakhs to the company.

The demand for the product is quite good and the indigenous requirement is being met by imports. The project is ready for commercialisation. The expected returns to APIDC-VCL are around 18.80 per cent which are quite low.

In view of the foregoing, the company's request for Venture Capital assistance of Rs. 7.30 lakhs in the form of direct subscription to equity of the company subject to the standard terms and conditions given in Annexure 1 is paced before the investment Committee for guidance and sanction.

Discussion : In the light of the facts mentioned and information provided, the following issues merit further discussion :

(1) Do M/s Jayaprada Clonetech (P) Ltd. qualify for inclusion in the Venture Capital portfolio? Comment on the nature of Terms of Reference laid down by APIDC for extending equity support to APIDC-VCL.

(2) To what extent is the company's management structure professional?

(3) Is the existing pattern of project appraisal by APIDC-VCL and IDBI appropriate? Should there be multiple evaluations of the same project by the Venture Capital Funds?

(4) Is the process of project appraisal suitable to examine the Venture Capital proposals?

(5) Is the rate of return estimated for M/s Jayaprada Clonetech (P) Ltd., adequate for it to be accepted by APIDC-VCL and IDBI?

(6) Are time and cost overruns in the case of M/s Jayaprada Clonetech (P) Ltd., justified in the existing frame of situation?

(7) Is there a need to privatise M/s Jayaprada Clonetech (P) Ltd.? If yes, then work out the modalities for privatisation.

Prof. B.K. Mishra, Dean Institute of Public Enterprise, Osmania University, Hyderabad.

Adapted from Productivity. Vol. 40, No. 3, October-December, 1999.

Annexure 1

TERMS AND CONDITIONS FOR EQUITY PARTICIPATION

1. The company shall carry out such alterations to its Memorandum and the Articles of Association in consultation with and to the satisfaction of APIDC-VCL so as to safeguard the interest of APIDC-VCL arising out of is assistance granted to the company.
2. The company/promoters shall enter into a suitable investment agreement with APIDC-VCL to the satisfaction of APIDC-VCL.
3. The company shall produce permission/clearance from the appropriate government agency to setting up the unit.
4. The company shall raise its authorised capital upto Rs. 50.00 lakhs.
5. The subscribed share capital of the company shall be Rs. 44.10 lakhs.
6. The contribution of the private promoters shall not be less than Rs. 30.20 lakhs in the equity share capital of the company. The contribution by the APIDC-VCL shall be made on pro-rata basis with that of the contribution of the promoters and their associates in the equity share capital of the company after obtaining necessary clearance from financial institutions and other government agencies. APIDC-VCL shall release its share of contribution only after the shares subscribed and paid up to the extent of 100 per cent of its promoters' contribution towards equity of the company.

7a. The promoter directors shall give an undertaking to the APIDC-VCL in such form as may be prescribed by the APIDC-VCL that they shall procure for the company such additional finances as may be required to meet the shortfall, if any, in financing the project and/or for working capital. The funds brought in shall not be withdrawn without the prior approval of APIDC-VCL.

7b. The company/promoter directors shall make necessary arrangements to the satisfaction of APIDC-VCL for raising a term loan to the extent of Rs. 102.90 lakhs required for financing the project from Banks/other financial institutions.

8. The company/promoter directors shall not raise any further term loans/deposits other than the amount of Rs. 102.90 lakhs as mentioned above except with specific written approval of the APIDC-VCL.
9. It shall be the responsibility of the company to raise short-term borrowings from scheduled bank for working capital requirements of the company.
10. The actual expenditure incurred by the promoters for the project shall be subject to the scrutiny and approval of the APIDC-VCL.
11. The company shall not without the proper consent and written approval of the APIDC-VCL pay any commission to its promoter directors or concerns in which directors are interested and for furnishing guarantees for any financial assistance obtained by the company for the purpose of its project.
12. The company shall broad base the Board and finalise the composition of its Board of Directors to the satisfaction of the APIDC-VCL.

13a. APIDC-VCL shall have the right to appoint and remove from time to time directors(s), on the Board of Directors of the company: such director(s) is (are) hereinafter referred to as 'Nominee Director(s)', so long as the APIDC-VCL holds shares in the equity, as a result of direct subscription.

13b. The number of directors to represent APIDC-VCL on the company Board shall be in proportion to the APIDC-VCL's share-holding in the company with minimum of one director and the APIDC-VCL's nominees shall not be required to hold any qualification shares.

13c. At least one of the nominees of the APIDC-VCL shall be non-rotational director. The articles of association of the company shall contain suitable provisions in this behalf.

If at any time, the Nominee Director is not able to attend a meeting of the Board of Directors or any of its Committees of which he is a member, APIDC-VCL may depute an Observer to attend the meeting. The expenses incurred by APIDC-VCL in this connection shall be borne by the company.

14. Provided however, APIDC-VCL shall have the liberty and discretion to appoint such directors immediately after the acceptance of the letter of intent by the company, but such appointment shall not be construed as any commitment on the part of the APIDC-VCL to disburse the financial assistance unless the APIDC-VCL is fully satisfied that the company has complied with all the stipulated terms and conditions precedent to such disbursement.
15. The Managing Director of the company shall be the nominee of the promoter of the company who shall be appointed to the satisfaction of the APIDC-VCL.
16. The APIDC-VCL reserves to itself the right to inspect the factory, properties and assets, documents and records, books and accounts etc., of the company during the period the APIDC-VCL holds shares in the company.
17. The company shall keep the APIDC-VCL informed in such manner and in such form as may be prescribed by the APIDC-VCL from time to time of the progress made in the implementation of the project and of the working of the same and also of any expenditure/diversification thereof, as long as the APIDC-VCL holds any shares in the company. The company shall furnish to the APIDC-VCL all additional information, data, documents, and explanations as may be called by the APIDC-VCL in relation to the working and affairs.
18. The company shall furnish to the APIDC-VCL all notices in respect of the Board Meetings, shareholders meetings of the company together with notes and minutes of thereof in addition to the circulation of the same to the nominees of the APIDC-VCL on the Board of the company.
19. The Management of the company vest in the Boards of Directors and the day-to-day affairs shall be entrusted to the Managing Director/Committee of Directors.
20. The Promoter directors shall not transfer dispose off or pledge or in any way encumber their shareholdings in the company without the prior consent and written approval of the APIDC-VCL and the company shall not recognise or register any such transfer of shares without the consent of the APIDC-VCL.
21. The company shall issue the share certificates to the APIDC-VCL in marketable lots for the subscription made by it towards the equity share capital of the company.
22. All the matters relating to the affairs of the company and the project such as capital expenditure raising loans awarding contracts, placement of orders for goods and services etc., shall be decided by the company in consultation with the representatives of the APIDC-VCL on the Board of Directors of the company or a Committee of Directors consisting of the APIDC-VCL's nominee(s) and the Managing Director of the company and any other directors of the company.
23. Any change in the management of the company and its project shall only be made with the prior consent and written approval of the APIDC-VCL so long as the APIDC-VCL holds any shares.
24. The company shall not embark upon or undertake any new project expansion/diversification programme without the prior approval in writing of the APIDC-VCL, so long as the APIDC-VCL holds any shares.
25. So long as the APIDC-VCL holds equity shares in the company, the company shall not, without the prior written approval of the APIDC-VCL.

25a. Make any inter-corporate investments and/or advance/deposit money in any other corporate bodies; and

25b. Repay the deposits/loans that may be obtained from directors, their relatives and friends etc., for the project.

26. The company shall arrange in consultation with and to the satisfaction of the APIDC-VCL for appointment of suitable technical and managerial personnel and for provision of the necessary training facilities to them and that in matters of recruitment of personnel required to man the project, the company shall give preference to local personnel.
27. APIDC-VCL reserves to itself the right to alter, modify or change all or any of the above terms and conditions and in addition, the APIDC-VCL may impose at its discretion such further conditions as it may deem fit.

Annexure 2

M/s Jayaprada Clonetech Private Ltd., Cost of Production and Profitability Statement (Year Ending June 30)

(Rs. in Lakhs)

	1994	*1995*	*1996*	*1997*	*1998*	*1999*	*2000*
Installed Capacity (No. of Kits/Yr.)	8000	8000	8000	8000	8000	8000	8000
Capacity Utilisation (%)	40	50	60	70	70	70	70
Production (Kits)	3200	4000	4800	5600	5600	5600	5600
Sales (value)	64.0	80.0	96.0	112.0	112.0	112.0	112.0
Cost of Production							
Raw Material	8.0	10.0	12.0	14.0	14.0	14.0	14.0
Utilities	1.0	1.2	1.4	1.7	1.7	1.7	1.7
Salaries	9.2	10.1	11.1	12.2	13.5	14.8	16.3
Repairs and Maintenance	0.9	1.0	1.1	1.2	1.3	1.4	1.6
Admn. Expenses	1.0	1.1	1.2	1.3	1.4	1.5	1.6
Selling Expenses	19.2	24.0	28.8	33.6	33.6	33.6	33.6
Total	**39.3**	**47.4**	**55.6**	**64.0**	**66.5**	**67.0**	**68.8**
Profit/Loss	24.7	32.6	40.4	48.0	46.5	45.0	43.2
Interest-VCF-Bank	9.8	9.0	7.5	6.0	4.5	3.0	1.5
Depreciation	7.0	7.0	7.0	7.0	7.0	7.0	7.0
Royalty	3.2	4.0	4.8	5.6	5.6	5.6	5.6
Profit Before Tax	1.3	8.9	16.9	25.2	25.2	25.2	25.2
Net Profit	1.3	5.3	10.1	15.1	15.1	15.1	15.1
Tax	0.0	3.6	6.8	10.1	10.1	10.1	10.1
Dividend (@ 18%)	–	–	2.2	2.2	2.2	2.2	2.2
Cash accruals	8.3	12.3	14.9	19.9	19.9	19.9	19.7

CHAPTER 15

HUMAN RESOURCES MANAGEMENT FOR NEW VENTURES

CHAPTER OUTLINE

— Personnel Function
— Legal Aspects for New Venture Creation
— The Workmen's Compensation Act, 1923
— The Employee State Insurance Act, 1948
— The Industrial Employment (Standing Orders) Act, 1946
— The Indian Trade Union Act, 1926
— The Payment of Wages Act, 1936
— Industrial Disputes Act, 1947
— Objectives of the Act
— Important Definitions
— The Payment of Gratuity Act, 1972
— Role of HRD For New Ventures

PERSONNEL FUNCTION

Human resource planning is mainly concerned with demand and sources of manpower and is very important for any business, small or otherwise. But looking at the changed times and conditions of the present industrial scene, there is a necessity of trained and specialised human resources for business enterprises and that success or failure of a new venture is mainly dependent upon its human resources which constitute one of its most important aspects. Hence, proper attention has to be given to human resource planning, recruitment, selection and training by an entrepreneur.

The need for this function whether in small or large organization cannot be underestimated. Wherever there are human beings, this function is required. It is however a different matter, who carries out this function — an executive solely incharge of this function or another executive who has been asked to look after this function in addition to his own function. The importance of this function is due to the importance of manpower in an organisation. It is the manpower which adds value to the product or the service being provided by an enterprise. If this manpower is not looked after well, you cannot expect proper value addition in the enterprise. Therefore, it is required of any enterprise to give due importance to this function.

Thus, we could define personnel management as the process of planning, organizing and co-ordinating, procurement, development, compensation, maintenance and incurvation of the human resource required for an enterprise.

The above functions need to be performed irrespective of the size of the enterprise. However, certain functions assume greater importance for smaller enterprises than the larger enterprise. The functions which need to be looked more carefully are motivational and maintenance functions. These functions are important as motivation enables management to increase productivity of the workers, while the maintenance function helps to maintain peace in the organisation by keeping the work force satisfied. Moreover, the maintenance function highlights the need to comply with the required legal framework so that it does not attract any penalties. The important labour laws are :

* Industrial Disputes Act.
* Factories Act.
* Provident Fund and Miscellaneous Provisions Act.
* Employees State Insurance Act.
* Payment of Wages Act.
* Minimum Wages Act.
* The Payment of Gratuity Act.

This does not mean that the recruitment functions are less important, infact they assume great importance in the present day changing environment of technology and global competitions. With the need to meet global standards, entrepreneurs are becoming keen on improving the quality of their products. For this purpose training of the work force has assumed importance. The workers are being trained to acquire more than one skill so that the work force becomes more flexible and can adjust to changing requirements.

Compensation management is changing the old system and giving way to new system, where the annual increments are now based on percentage of the salary. The concept of commitment to organisations and to the management is changing to commitment to the profession.

Therefore, the role of the personnel has acquired much importance and those organisations which are not paying proper attention to this function will be the losers in the long run.

The following personnel functions are considered important for new ventures.

1. **Manpower Planning Function :** Every organisation that hires people to carry out its work, whether it be a small business, medium size business, an institute or hospital, needs a personnel plan in which various phases of personnel work are tied together into an integrated programme.

   The manpower planning must incorporate the information on the following subjects :

   (*i*) Functions to be prerformed by employees.

   (*ii*) Personnels objectives.

   (*iii*) Personnel policies.

   (*iv*) Assignment of duties and responsibilities.

The above mentioned functions are planning functions. It helps in the selection of a future course by action from various alternatives. It is meant to decide in advance what to do, how to do, when to do, and the person who would do it. Thus, all other functions of an entrepreneur depend upon his manpower planning.

2. **Recruitment, Selection and Development Function :** Recruitment is concerned with attracting and ensuring a supply of needed manpower, and selecting requisite manpower in number and quality as found most appropriate and suitable. A study of an industrial area showed that kinship (relation) and friendship played a significant role in the process of recruitment in new ventures. The entrepreneur generally use the methods of direct and indirect recruitment. It includes the following activities which are undertaken by an entrepreneur :
   (*i*) Sources of supply of manpower for different jobs.
   (*ii*) Interview of applicants by entrepreneur himself or by a trained interviewer.
   (*iii*) To assign employees to jobs for which they appear best qualified on the basis of the selection techniques.
   (*iv*) To develop pre-job and service training programmes for manpower.

3. **Performance Appraisal : Training and Development Functions :**
   (*i*) To develop appraisal system for all personnel.
   (*ii*) To design appropriate appraisal forms for each class of employees.
   (*iii*) To develop a promotion policy based on periodic reviews of manpower records.
   (*iv*) Determining training needs.
   (*v*) Selection of training methods.

   Performance appraisal is one of the oldest and most universal practices of management. In new small ventures, it is not much used because an entrepreneur personally knows all the employees. Training is the process, whereby, people learn the skills, attitudes and behaviour needed in order to perform their job effectively.

4. **Wage and Salary (Employee Compensation) Functions :** The oldest and most common system of paying employees in on basis of time, i.e., rate per hour, per day, weak, per month or per year. But it is not considered the best method or a good compensation plan. The following functions are important in employee compensation :
   (*i*) To grade jobs in relationship to other jobs.
   (*ii*) To formulate wage scales for each job classification.
   (*iii*) To consider effective means of stimulating and rewarding employees.
   (*iv*) To provide for stability of employment

5. **Motivation :** A motivated employ does not need outside stimulation again and again. An entrepreneur's approach to motivation is largely determined by his assumptions about the fundamental nature of his men.

6. **Communication :** Communication is very important for proper functioning and survival of the organisation. Communication is the best means by which people are linked together in an organisation to achieve a common objective or purpose. Communication is the sharing (exchange) of messages, facts, opinions, ideas or attitudes and emotions between a sender and receiver or between two or more people.

   Management is getting things done through others. Hence, all entrepreneurial acts must pass through the bottleneck of communication. Entrepreneurial ideas, plans and decision are put into effect through communication. An entrepreneur may have the best business plans, but until they can be communicated, they are worthless. The process of communication explains how information, meaning and understanding can be transmitted from person to person. The entrepreneur can adopt the following components of communication ;
   (*i*) Source (communicator or sender of the message)
   (*ii*) Encoder (enclosed message)
   (*iii*) Message
   (*iv*) Channel
   (*iv*) Receiver

(*vi*) Decoder
(*vii*) Meaning
(*viii*) Feedback
(*ix*) Noise

Legal Aspects For New Venture Creation

The Workmen's Compensation Act, 1923

With the installation of machinery operated by motive power, the number of accidents in factories have increased considerably. Many times workers have lost their limbs, sometimes their hands and feet and in some cases even their lives while working on machines in the factories. This meant loss of earnings for those who were involved in accidents and in cases, where a worker died, his dependents were left to starve. From a purely humanitarian point of view, it would be natural to expect that the employers would give some compensation to the victims or their dependents. Some enlightened employers did pay compensation to their employees when they suffered accidents, but large majority was not willing to accept this responsibility. The workers, however, could not claim compensation as their right. Whenever an amount was paid, difference of opinion existed between an employer and an employee as regarding the fairness of the amount paid. In order to provide some basis for a statutory claim for compensation to be paid to the disabled factory worker, Workmen's Compensation Act has been passed in almost all the countries. The following provisions of the Indian Workmen's Compensation Act are :

Employer's Liability for Compensation : If an unary is caused to a worker by an accident arising out of and in the cause of his employment, his employer shall be liable to pay compensation in accordance with the provisions of this Act.

When Employer is not Liable : The employer, however shall not be liable if (a) the injury results in a partial or total disablement of the worker for less than three days, (b) if the injury can be directly attributed to the worker having been under the influence of drink or drugs, or (c) if the injury can be directly attributed to the willful disobedience be the worker of an order expressly given, or (d) to the willful removal of or disregard by the worker of any safety guard or other devices known to have been provided for the purpose of ensuring his safety.

Occupational Diseases : If a worker is engaged in any employment which involves the handling of wool, hair bristles or animal carcasses loading and unloading of such merchandise, or in the process carried on in compressed air, or in the process which involves the use of lead or tetrayetthyle or in process involving exposure to nitrous fumes, contracts diseases like anthrax, compressed air illness, lead poisoning or poisoning by nitrous fumes respectively; or when engaged continuously for not less than six months in any employment specified in part B of schedule III, contracts any disease specified in this schedule as an occupational disease, the contracting of such disease shall be regarded as an injury by accident and shall be demand arisen out of and in the employment.

Types of Injuries : Injuries for the purposes of this Act have been classified into the following categories (a) death, (b) permanent total disablement, (c) permanent partial disablement, (d) temporary disablement, partial or total.

Amount of Compensation : The act provides for compensation for these categories of injuries in Schedules I to IV.

Medical Examination : A worker who has given notice of an accident shall submit himself to a qualified medical practitioner and get himself examined free of charge. Similarly, a worker who is in receipt of half-monthly payments under this Act shall submit himself to such medical examination from time to time. If a worker refuses to submit himself to such a medical examination without sufficient cause, his right to compensation shall be suspended.

The Employee State Insurance Act, 1948

Experience in the working of the Workmen's compensation Act of 1923 revealed the benefits conferred by it upon factory workers in many cases did not reach them. This was due to various reasons. Firstly, a claim of compensation for injury has to be filed in an ordinary court of law and the lack of finance often make it impossible for a worker to file such a suit and fight it out. Secondly, with the kind of expert legal advise available, it was often possible for an employer to prove that the accident either did not arise out of and incourse of employment or that it was due to the worker concerned being under the influence of drink or drug at the time of accident or that it was due to negligence or his disobedience of safety rules. In such conditions, workers preferred to accept whatever compensation employers choose to pay out of a sense of pity or charity. The Employee's State Insurance Act of 1948 was framed to prevent such victimisation of worker by the employer.

The main provisions of ESI act are as follows :

- The ESI Scheme has been implemented under Section 1 (3) of the ESI Act, and if 10 or more persons are presently employed or were employed for wages on any day of the preceding 12 months in a factory where power is used in the manufacturing process.
- 20 or more persons are presently employed or were employed for wages on any day of the preceding 12 months in a factory where manufacturing process is carried on without the aid of power.
- The scheme stand extended to the following classes of establishments under Section 1(5) of the ESI act or deemed to have been extended by virtue of enforcement provided in this section to such areas where it has not been extended earlier and the employer has on any day of the preceding 12 months employed 20 or more persons for wages.

(*a*) Road Motor Transport Undertaking / Agencies.

(*b*) Hotel and Restaurants (10 persons or more where power is used in manufacturing process and 20 persons or more where power is not used in the manufacturing process).

(*c*) Cinema including preview theaters.

(*d*) Newspaper establishments.

(*e*) Shops.

(*f*) Beedi manufacturing establishment employing 10 or more persons.

The principal employer, is responsible to register his factory or establishment and cover all such employees coverable under ESI Scheme and to comply with all the provisions of the ESI Law. The entrepreneur should :

(*a*) Get his factory or establishment registered if at any point of time the enterprise is coverable under the Act.

(*b*) Fill up declaration forms in respect of all covered employees and submit the same to appropriate ESI office.

(*c*) Pay the contributions within 21 days of last day of the calender month in which the contribution falls due.

(*d*) Submit the return of contribution (in quadruplicate) in revised form No. 6 (6 (a)) in case of advance payment system) along with receipted copy of the challan for the contribution period ending March 31, in regional office. In any case non-submission of return of contribution in time is an offense under the ESI Act, 1948.

(*e*) Maintain the requisite records/registers.

Contributions : Every person, who is employed for wages in or in connection with the work of a factory or establishment to which this act applies, shall be insured. All the insured workers, except those who earn wages for less than one rupee per day shall pay their contribution to the employee's state insurance corporation at the rate specified in 1st Schedule of the Act. The employers shall also pay their contributions at the rates specified in the above schedule.

Distribution of benefits under the Act :

- Sickness benefits—duly certified.
- Maternity benefits—periodical payment
- Disablement benefits—insured person sustained injury.
- Dependents benefits—who dies as a result of an injury.
- Medical benefits—for and attendance of an insured person.

Penalties : If a person makes a false statement for than purpose of causing any increase in payment or benefit or for the purpose of causing any unauthorised payment, he or she shall be punishable with imprisonment for a term of three months or with fine upto Rs. 500 or both.

Penalty is imposed on person who fails to pay any contribution, or deducts employees wages for the contribution etc.

THE INDUSTRIAL EMPLOYMENT (STANDING ORDERS) ACT, 1946

The absence of standing orders clearly defining the rights and obligations of the employer and the workers in respect of recruitment, discharge, disciplinary action, holidays, leave etc. was one of the most frequent causes of friction between management and workers. One the recommendations of the tripartite labour conferences held in 1943, 1944, 1945 the Government of India passed the Industrial Employment (Standing Orders) Act in 1946. This act provides for the framing of standing orders in all establishments employing 100 or more persons. It requires employers to submit within six months of the enactment of the law standing orders governing the classification of workmen (permanent temporary etc.) the manner of intimating to them their hours of work, holidays, pay days and wage rates, the procedure to be followed while applying for leave and holidays, the termination of employment or notice of discharge and for disciplinary action. In pursuance of this Act, the central government published the central rules in 1946 which were applicable to commissioner's provinces and to the undertaking under the central government. Its lead was promptly followed by all state governments. In Maharashtra, it has been made applicable to establishment in which fifty or more persons are employed.

The Indian Trade Union Act, 1926

The experience of the working of the system of free enterprise in the industrial field revealed that though theoretically both the employers and workers were free to enter into a contract and to agree upon the wages to be paid and received. The fact is that, for various reasons, this freedom did not benefit the workers in an way. Firstly, the commodity that a worker has to sell is higly perishable in the sense that if he refuses to work on a particular day because the wages offered are low, he cannot store up his labour of that day to be used the next day. This compels him to accept work even if the wages offered are unsatisfactory. Secondly. Secondly, as his income is very low, he is hot able to accumulate any savings on which he can fall back when he refuses to work. The only alternative to refusal to work because of low wages is, therefore, starvation. These two factors compel a worker to accept low wages, hence the theoretical freedom of contract is not of much use to him. Lastly, the fact is that a worker is a small-scale seller and the employer is a large-scale buyer. This reduces his bargaining power to a very great extent. It is possible for the employer to engage somebody else who is willing to work on a lower wage. It is, however relatively difficult for a worker to find an alternative employer who would pay him the wage he demands. Worker's weak bargaining position, thus, compiles him to accept whatever wages are of freed to him. This Act unites the workers and increases their bargaining power.

The Payment of Wages Act, 1936

The payment of wages to factory workemen in particular form and at regular intervals without any unauthourised deduction is the objective of this act.

Scope of the Act : The provisions of this Act are applicable to workers engaged in factories as defined by the Factories Act of 1948, and to persons employed on any railway by contractor or subcontractor. The state government may after giving three months notice of its intention by a notification in the official gazette extend the provisions of this Act to any class of persons employed in any industrial establishment.

The Date of Payment of Wages : The wages of every person employed in a factory or industrial establishment or a railway, where less than 1,000 persons are employed shall be paid before the expiry of the 7th day after completion of wage period, generally a month: the wages for a month for example shall be paid before the 7th day of the next month. In the factories in which more than 1,000 persons are employed the wages shall be paid before the expiry of the 10th day of the next month. The wages of a person whose services have been terminated shall be paid on the next working day after such termination The payment of wages shall be made on a working day.

Authorised Deduction : The act authorises an employer to make deductions from wages for the following purposes only :

- Fines.

- Absence from duty.
- Damage to or loss of goods or money where such damage or loss is due to the negligence or default on the part of the employee.
- Housing accommodation supplied by the employer.
- Amenities and services as authorised by the state government and provided by the employee.
- Fines shall not be imposed on any employee unless he has been given an opportunity to show cause why the fine should not be imposed.
- No fine shall be imposed on persons below the age of fifteen.
- A fine imposed on any employee in any wage period shall not exceed specified percentage wages payable to him for a period.
- The fine so imposed shall be recovered in installments or after the expiry to 60 days from the day on which it was imposed.
- The fine and the actual amount recovered shall be recorded in a separate register in the prescribed form and all amounts of fines realised shall be utilised only for such purposes as are beneficial to the employees and as are approved by the prescribed authority. Applications for the recovery of fines or of deduction not authorised under the Act, for delay in payment of wages shall be presented within six month of the date on which such fines were imposed or deduction were made or wages were due.

Industrial Disputes Act, 1947

Prior to the year 1947, The Trade Disputes Act, 1929 used to settle industrial disputes. Experience of the working of the Act, 1929 revealed various defects which needed to be overcome by a fresh letgislation.

The Statement of Objects and Reasons appended to the Industrial Disputes Bill, 1946, which was published in The Gazette of India, 1946 reads thus

"Experience of the working to the Dispute Act, 1929 has revealed that its main defect is that while restraints have been imposed on the rights of strike and lock-out in public utility services no provision has been made to render the proceedings unstatutable under the Act for the settlement of an industrial dispute, either by reference to a Board of Conciliation or to a Court of Inquiry, conclusive and binding on the parties to the dispute. This defect was overcome during the war by empowering under Rule 81 A of the Defence of India Rules, the Central Government to refer industrial disputes to adjudicator and to enforce their awards. Rule 81 A, which was to lapse on the 1st October, 1946 was kept in force by the Emergency Powers (Continuance) Ordinance, 1946, for a further period of six month; and checking industrial unrest with this rule was self evident. This Bill embodies the essential principles of rule 81A, which have proved generally acceptable to both employers and workmen. The two new institutions for the prevention and settlement of industrial disputes provided for in the Bill were the Works Committees consisting of representatives of employers and workmen, Industrial Tribunal consisting of one or more members possessing qualifications ordinarily required for appointment as Judge of High Court. Power has been given to appropriate Government to require Works Committees to be constituted in every industrial establishment employing 100 workemen, or more and their duties will be to remove cause of fraction between the employer and workemen in the day-to-day working of the establishment and to promote measures for securing amity founded on voluntary settlement and it is hoped that work committies will render recourse to the remaining mechinery provided for in the bill for the settlement of disputes infrequent. A reference to an Industrial Tribunal will lie where both the parties to an Industrial Dispute apply for such reference, and also where the appropriate Government considers it expedient to do so. An award of a Tripunal may be enforced either wholly or in part by the appropriate Government for a period not exceeding one year. The power to refer disputes to Industrial Tribunals and enforce their awards is an essential corollary to the obligation that lies on the Government to secure conclusive determination of the disputes with a view to redressing legitimate grievances of the parties thereto, such obligation arising from the imposition of restraints on the right of strike and lock-out, which must remain inviolate, except where considerations of public interest overside such rights.

The Bill also seeked to re-orient the administration of the conciliation machinery. Conciliation is compulsory in all disputes in public utility services and optional in the case of other industrial establishment. With a view to expedite conciliation proceedings time limits have been prescribed for conclusion thereof 14 day in the case of Conciliation Officers and two months in the case of Board of Conciliation from the date of notice of strike. A settlement arrived at in the course of conciliation proceedings will be binding for such period as may be agreed on by the parties and where no period has been agreed upon, for a period of one year, and will continue to be binding until revoked by a 3 month's notice by either party to the dispute.

Another important feature of the Bill relates to the prohibition of strikes and lockouts during the pendency of conciliation and adjudication proceedings of settlement reached in the course of conciliation proceedings and of an award of Industrial Tribunals declared binding by the appropriate government. The underlying argument is that where a dispute has been referred to conciliation for adjudication a strike or lock-out, in furtherance thereof, is both unnecessary and inexpedient. Where, on the data of reference to conciliation or adjudication a strike or lock-out is already in existence, power is given to the appropriate Government to prohibit its continuance least the chances of settlement or speedy determination of the dispute should be jeopardized.

Objective and Scope of the Act : The Act makes provisions for the investigation and settlement of industrial disputes and for certain other purposes. It ensures progress of industry by bringing about harmony and cordial relationship between the employers and the employees.

Objectives of the Act

(*i*) Promotion of measures of securing and preserving amity and good relations between the employer and workmen.

(*ii*) Investigation and settlement of industrial disputes between employers and employers, employers and workmen or workmen and workmen with a right of representation by registered trade union or federation of trade unions or an association of employers.

(*iii*) Prevention of illegal strikes and lock-outs.

(*iv*) Relief to workmen in matter of lay-off and retrenchnment.

(*v*) Promotion of collective bargaining.

The act extends to whole of India.

Important Definitions

1. **Industry :** Industry means any business, trade, undertaking, manufacture or calling of employers and includes any calling, service, employment, handicraft or industrial occupation or a vocation of workmen.
2. **Industrial Disputes :** Industrial disputes means any dispute or difference between employers and employers, or between employers and workmen or between workmen and workmen, which is connected with the employment or non-employment or the terms of employment or with the conditions of labour of any person.
3. **Workman :** Workman means any person (including an apprentice) employed in any industry to do any manual, unskilled, skilled, technical, operational, clerical or supervisory work for hire or rewards, whether the terms of employment be expressed or implied and for the purposes of any proceeding under this Act in relation to an industrial dispute, includes :

   (*a*) Any such person who has been dismissed, discharged or retrenched in connection with, or as a consequence of that dispute, or

   (*b*) Any person whose dismissal, discharge or retrenchment has led to the dispute.
4. **Strike :** Strikes means a cessation of work by a body of persons employed in any industry acting in combination or a concerted refusal, or a refusal under common understanding of any number of persons who are or have been so employed to continue to work or to accept employment.
5. **Lock-out :** Lock-out means the temporary closing of a place of employment, or the suspension of work, or the refusal by an employer to continue to employ any number of persons employed by him.

   Lock-out is an antitheses to strike. Just as strike is a weapon available to the employees for enforcing their industrial demands, a lock-out is a weapon which forces the employees to see the employer's point of view to accept his demands.

6. **Lay-Off :** Lay-off means the failure, refusal or inability of an employer to give employment due to certain reasons, to a workman whose name appears on the master rolls of his industrial establishment and who has not been retrenched.

The important provisions of the Industrial Disputed Act of 1947 are :

(*i*) If any industrial dispute exists or is apprehended, the appropriate government may, by order in writing, (a) refer the dispute to a board for promoting a settlement thereof; or (b) refer any matter appearing to be connected with or relevant to the dispute to a court of inquiry, or (c) refer the dispute to a tribunal for arbitration.

(*ii*) If either of the parties to a dispute or both of them apply to the government to refer the dispute to the board, court or a tribunal, the appropriate government is satisfied that the person applying represents majority of each part, shall make the reference accordingly.

(*iii*) If a dispute has been referred to a board or a tribunal, the government may prohibit the continuance of any strike or lock-out in connection with such dispute.

(iv) A settlement arrived at in the course of conciliation proceeding under the Act, or an award which is declared by the government is binding on all the parties to the dispute for at least six months.

(*v*) An award declared by a government shall come into operations on such date as may be specified by the government and shall remain in operation for a period of one year, or a shorter period, if so fixed by the government.

(*vi*) Workers employed in public utility industries shall not go on a strike and the employers in such industries shall not resort to lock-outs.

(*a*) During the pendency of conciliation proceeding; or

(*b*) During the pendency of proceeding before a lobour court, tribunal or national tribunal; or

(*c*) During a period in which a settlement or award is in operation.

A strike or a lockout in contraventions of any of these provisions shall be illegal.

The Payment of Gratuity Act, 1972

"Gratuity" imports an idea a "gift" or a "present" in return for flavour of services generally, but the Payment of Gratuity Act reverses this norm. The Payment of Gratuity Act, 1972, a social security enactment, provides a schemes for the payment of gratuity to employees engaged in factories, mines, oilfields, plantations, ports, railway companies, shops or other establishments and for matters connected therewith or incidental thereto. To fulfil a long-felt need of the statute as a measure of social security to workmen, the Parliament has enacted to provide for the claim for payment of gratuity to employees engaged in the aforesaid concerns. It fulfilled the universally recognised need of compensation for loss of income due to unemployment arising either out of incapacity to work due to invalidity, old age, etc. or otherwise.

The Act has been made applicable to every factory, mine, oilfield, plantation, port and railway company, every shop or establishment within the meaning of any law for the time being in force in relation to shops and establishments in a State, in which ten or more persons are employed or were employed on any day of the preceding twelve months, and such other establishments or class of establishments in which ten or more employees are employed or were employed on any day of the preceding twelve months, as the Central Government may, by notification, specify in that behalf. The Act was amended in 1984 for making its provisions more effective and beneficial. Persons employed in administrative or managerial capacity were made eligible for gratuity. The employees of seasonal establishments have been brought on par with similar employees of non-seasonal establishments and shall be entitled to gratuity at the rate of seven days's wages for each season.

The Income Tax Act, 1961, lays down that any gratuity received by an employee on his retirement or on his becoming incapacitated prior to such retirement or on termination of his employment, or any gratuity received by his widow, children or dependents on his death, to the extent it does not in either case, exceed one-half month's salary for each year of completed service, calculated on the basis of the average salary for the ten month immediately preceding the month in which any such event occurs, subject to such limit as the Central Government may, by notification in the Official Gazette, specify in this behalf having regard to the limit applicable in this behalf to the employees of that government, provided that where any gratuities referred to in this clause are revived by a employee from more than one employer in the same previous year, the aggregate amount exempt from income tax under this clause shall not exceed the limit so specified; Provided further that where any such gratuity or gratuities was or were receive in any one or more earlier previous years also and the whole or any part of the amount of such gratuity or gratuities was not included in the total income of the assessee of such previous year or years, the amount exempt from income tax under this clause shall not exceed the limit so specified as reduced by the amount or, as the case may be, the aggregate amount not included in the total income of any such previous year or years.

Section 4(3) of the Principle Act has been recently amended by the Payment of Gratuity (Amendment) Act, 1998 enhancing the ceiling of gratuity payable from Rs. 2.5 lakh to 3.5 lakh.

Welfare measures such as pension, provident fund, gratuity, etc., are in comformity with the direcitve principles of State Policy as adumbrated in Part IV of the Constitution of India.

Protection against loss of income due to invalidity or incapacity to work, old age, etc., is a generally accepted social norm. Gratuity is social benefaction statutorily generated independently. The significance of the Payment of Gratuity Act, is as a compulsory statutory retrial benefit.

ROLE OF HRD FOR NEW VENTURES

The Role of HRD has always been challenging although there has been variation in the same with the passage of time. The Government policy of 90's was of liberalisation instead of licensing. The concern for promotion of export and import substitution has been shown at the highest level of Government. Industries are shifting their operation from labour intensive to a capital intensive units using high technology, rationalising their operations and modernising the same to keep pace with their competitors. Impact of the above changes on HRD is going to be tremendous as there is a shift from organisational career to independent career and more dependence on the middle management. HRD in charge has to have commercial skills of marketing, finance and production in order to be effective in his job.

Another fertile area for innovation in HRD is in the training and development processes. American industry spends an incredible sum on training its employees. This has become the need for all present day entreprenuers.

SUMMARY

The role of Human Resource Management today and in future, needs to be perceived bearing in mind the changing profile of the enterprises. This discipline has over the last fifty years, constantly evolved and responded to changes in the economic and social scene.

The rapidly changing environmental conditions are continuously creating new challenges for the Indian enterprises. In the wake of the ever increasing competition, many of the established organisations are craving for survival. Due to the rising cost and falling productivity, more and more organisations have started giving serious look into the HR policies. It is, therefore, essential to see the problem in its totality. A planned approach is needed for optimising the Human Resources. Enterprises having excess and poorly utilised manpower can not think of growth and, due to lack of resources will not be able to generate more employment through expansion and diversification.

Further wwith employees becoming more educated, knowledgable and concious of their rights. It is important for an entrepreneur to remain on the right side of the labour laws.

REVIEW QUESTIONS

1. What are the functions of HRD?
2. Explain the role of HRD for a new entrepreneur.
3. Suggest suitable measures for developing human resource in new enterprise.
4. Discuss the causes of slow growth of HRD in India.
5. Give an account of the efforts made by government to stimulate HRD in India.
6. Explain various labour laws enacted for welfare of workers.
7. What was the need of Industrial Dispute Act, 1947? Explain its main feature.
8. Do you see a linkage between Workmen Compensation Act, 1923 and Employees State Insurance Act, 1948. Explain.
9, Enumerate the salient features of ESI Act.

CHAPTER

16

INTELLECTUAL PROPERTY RIGHS

CHAPTER OUTLINE

— Introduction
— Intellectual Property—Types
— Copyright
— Patents
— Patents—A Route to Profit Making
— Why Patent Protection Rights?
— Trade mark
— Trademark Protection
— Collective Marks
— Well-Known Marks
— Geographic Indication
— Industrial Designs
— Licencing IPR -A Business Strategy
— Developing IP Strategy

INTRODUCTION

The intellectual property is the creation human intellect, thus designated as 'Intellectual Property'. The long chain of small or big innovation — be it changes in designs or improvements that make the product look or perform the way it does today. In the global economy, particularly when the world has become boundryless and access to information is at the touch of the key it has become emperitive to protect the intellectual property from piracy, copy or gray market. The intellectual property includes copy right, patent and industrial designs. It also includes trade marks, service marks and appellations.

Think for a moment about the financial investments in the name and trade mark of Coca Cola since 1886 when it was first developed. Imagine the corporate and financial loss if Coca Cola looses the exclusive rights to its trade mark. In other sense, the corporate organisation keep the continuous watch on their intellectual property assets so that there is no infringement of these. The corporate have created permanent cell with brand cop lawyers who spend whole of their time in tracking the offenders and do web surfing to ensure nobody misuses the logo and brand name of the corporation. The trade research department of the corporations continuously monitors and investigates the cases which are related to trade mark violations.

INTELLECTUAL PROPERTY—TYPES

The types of intellectual property are described below :

Copyright

Copyright is more extensive than trade mark. It give the copyright holder exclusive right to reproduces, perform or display "original work of authorship". For example in the field of advertising, this may included photos, TV commercials, video illustrations sound recordings, advertisements, brochures, displays and literary work. Ideas, facts slogans and symbols cannot be copyrighted. Copyrights should always be registered in order to receive the full protection under the Copyright Act.

Copyright relates to rights of creators of literacy, scientific and artistic works. For example, the field of advertising is field of creativity and advertisers are concerned about the protection of their creativity for two reasons.

1. Firstly, to maintain ownership over their property which is the original work that they have written, photographed, or recorded
2. Secondly, with the copyright the advertiser is given protection and the right to sue if the material is subsequently used without permission.

There are still some areas, where it is very difficult to keep a check and till date these are remain unresolved to a considerable extent, e.g., Internet. Once you place your material up on the internet and it is publically available to everyone, it is unclear hoe its copyright can be protected.

For any work to enjoy copyright protection, it must be original work. Copyright owners have the reproduction rights, performing rights, recording rights, motion picture rights translation and adoption rights, and broadcasting rights. Copyrights provide protection upto 50 years after the death of the creater, i.e., copyright holder.

Why protect copyright? Copy rights and its related rights are essential to human creativity. It gives the creators incentives in the form of recognition and fair economic rewards. Under the system of rights creators are assured that their works can be disseminated without fear of unauthorized piracy. This helps to increase access to and enhance the enjoyment of culture, knowledge and entertainment all over the world.

Patents

Patent rights are exclusive rights given to inventors. Any invention is patented in the name of the inventor who subsequently may give the rights for commercial exploitation. Inventions, industrial designs or original aesthetic creation determining the appearance of industrial products. The nights are available for a limited duration.

Patents provide property right for inventions. The essential criteria for registering a patent are :

* It must be new
* Involves an inventive step and be capable of industrial application.

The following products or the processes are allowed to be excluded from being patented.

1. Diagnostic, Therapeutic and Surgical methods for the treatment of humans or animals.
2. Plants and animals other than micro organisms.
3. Essentially biological processes for the production of plants and animals other than non-biological and micro biological processes.

Patents—A Route to Profit Making

Successful business is the consequence of innovativeness and creative ideas. Ideas by themselves, however, have little value. The need to be developed, turned into innovative products or services and commertialised successfully, so as to enable organisations to reap the benefits of innovation and creativity. Intellectual Property (IP), patents in particular, can be crucial for turning innovative ideas and inventions into competitive products that significantly increase profit margins.

You may use patents to earn royalty revenue by licensing such patented inventions to other firms that have the capacity to commercialise them. This may not only save you money, but also provide you with a stream of income from your invention or the inventions of your employees without the need to invest in their commercialisation.

Why Patent?

The patents help an entrepreneur in following ways :

- **Exclusive rights :** Patents provide the exclusive rights which allow the enterprises to use and exploit the invention for a specified period from the data of filing of the patent application.
- **Strong market position :** Through these exclusive rights, an enterprise can become a market leader and reduce competition.
- **Higher returns on investments :** Under her umbrella of the exclusive right the patent holder can capitalise the market and earn higher returns on the investment.
- **Opportunity to license or sell the invention :** If you chose to exploit the patent yourself, you may sell it or license the rights to commercialise it to another enterprise which will be a source of income for your organisation.
- **Increase in negotiating power :** If you entreprise is in the process of acquiring the rights to use the patents of another enterprise, through a licensing contract, your patent portfolio will enhance your bargaining power. That is to say, your patents may prove to be of considerable interest to the enterprise with whom you are negotiating and you could enter into a cross licensing arrangement where, simply put, the patent rights could be exchange between your enterprise and the other.
- **Positive image for your enterprise :** Business partners, investors and shareholders may preserve patent portfolios as a demonstration of the high level of expertise.

Why Patent Protection Rights?

- **Somebody else might patent them :** In most countries the first person or enterprise to apply for a patent for an invention will have the right to the patent. This may in fact mean that if you do not patent your inventions or inventions of the employees of your entreprise, somebody else—who may have developed the same or an equivalent invention later—may do so and legitimately exclude your enterprise from the market, limit its activities to the continuation of prior use, where the patent legislation provides for such exception, ask your enterprise to pay a licensing fee for using the invention.
- **Competitors will take advantage of your invention :** If the product is successful, many other competitor firms will be tempted to make the same product by using your invention but without having to pay for such use. Larger enterprises may take advantage of scale of economies to produce the product more cheaply and compete at a more favourable market price. This

may considerably reduce your company's market share for that product. Even small competing enterprises can produce the same product and often sell it at lower price as they do not have to recoup research and development costs incurred your enterprise.

- **Possibilities to license, sell or transfer technology will be severely hindered :** Without IP right, transfers of technology would be difficult if not impossible. Transfer of technology presupposes ownership of a technology which can only be effectively obtained through appropriate IP protection Moreover, wherever negotiations do take place for transferring a given technological development without IP protection over the technology in question, parties are suspicious of disclosing their inventions.

TRADE MARK

A trade mark is defined as any work, name, symbol or device that is adopted and used by manufacturer or merchant to identity his goods and distinguish them from those manufactured by others. The trade-mark may consist of one or more distinctive words, letters, slogans, names, numerals, figurative elements, geometrical shapes and combination of colours. Such a sign may combine any of the above mentioned elements. As the basic purpose of a trademark is to distinguish the laws of most countries provide that any product to be marked should be distinctive.

For any organisation, brands are among thee most valuable assets. When a product is manufactured and a brand is created—it must be distinctive from the competition and must be protected. There are several types of company and product identifications. The trade-mark, also called a brand name, is the name by which people can speak of the product. Very often a trademark will include some pictorial or design element. If it does, the combination is called a **logotype** for simply **a logo**).

Trademarks can also be termed service marks when used to identify a service. In general, a trademark for goods appears on the product or its packaging, and a service mark is used in advertising to identify the services.

The logo design is an extremely important element in the successful marketing of a product. It is difficult to sell a product until a reasonable level of name recognition is achieved among consumers. In fact, the creation of a logo is so important that a number of firms have been established whose primary function is design of logos, packages, and corporate identity. Most designers attempt to forge a compatible relationship among the package design, logo, and advertising for the product. A strong logo on the package and in product advertising creates an environment of recognition.

Trademark Protection

Because a trademark is so valuable, companies go to great lengths to protect their brand names. In recent years, there have been a number of court cases involving allegations that one company has infringed on the trademark of another.

In deciding where trademark infringement has taken place, several factors are considered by the courts :

1. The distinctiveness of the complainant's mark
2. The similarity of the marks
3. The proximity of the parties products
4. The likelihood of the complainant's bridging the gap between non-competing produucts.
5. The similarity of the parties trade channels and advertising methods
6. The quality of the alleged infringer's products
7. The sophistication of the particular customers

Beware if your trademark is based on a common word. It will be considered legally weal, and difficult to protect. Police unpermitted use of trademark vigorously, and don't let any competitor use your mark even briefly. And, if you want to start a trademark infringement suit, don't do it unless you keep detailed records and can document lost profits accurately.

There are different kinds of marks than can be legally registered for protection. A trade mark identifies who makes a given product where as a service mark does the same for the service provider. A certification mark is usually given by a trade association or other kind of governing body and affirms that product meets its set of standards. Organisations can themselves register a collective mark which identifies them as a group that works co-operatively together. Trade marks are usually followed by a word ® which means that mark has been registered and can not be copied or used by any one else without permission.

Fig. 16.1. Sample of Trade Mark

Companies are usually very protective of their trade mark and will sue to maintain that exclusivity. A company such as McDonald's which spends billions of dollars each year to promote a certain image and unique brand quality, does not want its name to be associated with unfavorable products or services. When someone tried to register the name McDonald's for a Web site on the Internet, McDonald responded immediately to prevent that from happening. In return for the individual giving the rights back to the company, McDonald gave a donation to his high school.

Collective Marks

Fig 16.2. Samples of Collective Mark

The collective marks are being used extensively for providing protection and is one of the key marketing strategies. The use of collective mark (by a cooperative or an association of enterprises), e.g., Agmark or ISI mark allows the member to benefit from a reputation acquired on the basis of the common origin or other common characteristics of the goods produces or services rendered by different enterprises. This is, particularly, the case where the origin or other common characteristics are the main contributing factor indeterminate the quality or good taste of a product or service. The use of a collective mark may foster an alliance or facilitate cooperation with other organisation so as to take full advantage of common resources.

Fig. 16.3. Agmark

While the definition may vary from one country to the other, collective marks are usually defined as signs which distinguish the geographical origin, material, mode of manufacture, quality or other common characteristics of goods or services of different enterprises using the collective mark. The owner may be either an association of which those enterprises are members or any other entity, including a public institution or a cooperative. Most countries require that an application for a collective mark be accompanied by a copy of the regulations which govern the use of the collective mark and of not allow for the licensing of a collective mark. Like trade/service marks, collective marks are also maintained upon payment of renewal fees.

WELL-KNOWN MARKS

Well-known trade and service marks enjoy in most countries protection against signs which are considered a reproduction, imitation or translation of that mark provided that they are likely to cause confusion in the relevant sector of the public. Well-known marks are usually protected, irrespective of whether they are registered or not, in respect of goods and services which are identical with, or similar to, those for which they have gained their reputation. In many countries, they are also, under certain conditions protected for dissimilar goods and services. It should be noted that, while there is no commonly agreed detailed definition of what constitutes a "well-known mark, contries may take advantage of the WIPO Joint Recommendations on The Protection of Well-Known Marks.

Protection of Well-Known Marks

Many countries protect unregistered will-known marks in accordance with their international obligations under the Paris Convention for the Protection of Industrial Property and the Agreement on Trade-Related Aspects of Intellectual Property Rights (the TRIPS Agreement). Conseqently, not only big companies but also SMEs may have a good chance of establishing enough goodwill with customers so that their marks may be recognized as well-known marks and acquire protection without registration. It is nevertheless advisable to seek registration, taking into account that many countries provide for an extended protection of registered well-known marks against dilution (Art. 16.3 TRIPS), i.e., the reputation of the mark being weakened by the unauthorized use of that mark by others.

You should be aware of the fact that a number of trademark laws merely implement obligations under Article 16.3 of the TRIPS Agreement and protect well-know registered trademarks only under the following conditions :

- that the goods and services for which the other mark is used or is seeking protection are not Tidentical with or similar to the goods for which the well-known mark acquired its reputation,
- that the use of the other mark would indicate a connection between these goods and the owner of the well-known mark, and
- that his interests are likely to be damaged by such use.

GEOGRAPHIC INDICATION

The aim of geographic indications is to inform the consumer that a good has the quality reputation or other characteristics which is essentially attributable to its geographical origin. According the TRIPS agreement the countries shall not permit registration of trademarks containing a misleading indication of geographic origin of goods.

For Example

"Champagne" is a term associated with wine produced in certain region of France. In principle it is not permissibnle to call wine produced elsewhere as 'chanmpagne' even though the wine may be regard in the producing countries as comparable to French Champagne.

The potentiating of Indian Basmati Rice had been patented by Rice—tech an American company and given its name Texmati. India was rightful in taking up a case against patenting of Texmati in US patent office as Indian Basmati has exclusive marketing rights being a geographic Himalayan Tarai Region and possess qualities or a reputation that are due to that place of origin. Most commonly, a geographical indication consists of the name of the place of origin of the goods. Agricultural products typically have qualities that derive from their place of production and are influenced by specific local factors, such as climate and soil. Whether a sigh functions as a geographical indication is a matter of national law and consumer perception. Geographical indications may be used for a wide variety of agricultural products.

Industrial Designs

Human being has a weakness to get attracted to attractive things. The marketers exploit this emotional attribute by creating visually attractive designs which may be able to captivate a demanding and extremely diversified clientele. Through creative designs, you could reach out to and appeal to diverse group of customers from different age groups, regions, cultures, etc. Having design rights on an attractive shape or style of a product may give an enterprise the much needed edge over the competition.

Industrial designs cover the ornamental features of the products including shapes, lines, motives and colours or any 3-dimensional forms which give special appearance to a product or handicraft. Industrial designs are protected mainly in consumer articles of which textiles, leather and leather products and motor cars are a few examples.

The designs thus need to be either novel or original to qualify for protection. The owner of the protected designs has exclusive rights to its use and can even prevent third parties who have not obtained his or her consent from making, selling or importing articles bearing or embodying a design which is a copy or substantially a copy of the protected design. They protect the ornamental or aesthetic aspects of a useful article which usually appears to the sense of sight or touch and can be reproduced in significant quantities.

Protecting Industrial Designs

In most countries,, protection of industrial designs can only be acquired through registration. In a number of these countries, no search is made and no examination as to subteens is carried out prior to registration of the industrial design. Some countries provide for a search and examination in the event that the industrial design application has been published and a third party has objected to its registration by giving notice of opposition. In very few countries, protection may also be available for unregistered industrial designs.

As a general rule. to qualify for protection through registration, the design must be "new" or "original". The duration of protection differs from country to country. While the usual term of protection is 15 years (an initial periods of five years with the possibility of renewal for two further periods of five years each), some countries including India provide protection for only 10 years, while others allow even 25. Renewal of protection is usually subject to the payment of a renewal fee. However, unlike marks, protection of industrial designs, once granted, is not subject to cancellation if they are not actively used.

Intellectual Properly	Life of Protection
Patent	20 years
Trademark	10 years
Industrial Design	10 years
Copy Right	50 years after the death of the copyright holder.

Table 16.1

Licencing IPR -A Business Strategy

You may be interested in starting a new business, expanding an existing business (extending your territory or the nature of business) or improving the quality of the goods or services of your enterprise and thereby its market position. In many situations, licensing of intellectual property rights is an effective tool for achieving these business goals.

A licensing agreement is a partnership between an intellectual property right's owner (licensor) and another who is authorized to use such rights (licensee) in exchange for an agreed payment (fee or royalty). A variety of such licensing agreements are available, which may be broadly categorized as follows :

- Technology License Agreement
- Trademark Licensing and Franchising Agreement
- Copyright License Agreement

In practice, all or some of these agreements often form part of one single contract since in transfers of this nature many rights are involved and not simply one type of intellectual property right. You may also come across licensing agreements in other circumstances, such as, during a merge or acquisition, or in the course of negotiating a joint venture.

All of these mechanisms either on heir own or in combination will provide your an enterprise, as a licensor or licensee, a wide variety of possibilities in conduction business in your own country or elsewhere. As an intellectual property owner and a licensor, the enterprise can expand its business to the frontiers of your partners business and ensure a steady stream of additional income. As a licensee, your entreprise can manufacture, sell, import, export, distribute and market various goods or services which it may be prevented from doing otherwise.

In the international context, a formal licensing agreement is possible only if the intellectual property right you wish to license is also protected in the other country or countries of interest to you. If your intellectual property is not protected in such other country or countries then you would not only not be able to license it, but also you would have no legal right to put any restriction on its use by anyone else.

DEVELOPING IP STRATEGY

- Check trademark databases to avoid using an exiting trademark and protect trademarks before launching a new product or service with a new brand name. It is important to consider export markets when doing so and avoid using brand names that may have an undesirable meaning in a foreign language.
- Identify patentable subject matter and make sure it is patented early enough to avoid losing the invention to competitors.
- Make sure that patentable inventions are not shared with others or published before filing a patent application. In order to meet the patentability criteria inventions must be considered "new". Each disclosure of an invention (e.g., through publication) will compromise the chances of the invention being considered new, and therefore patentable.
- Make sure that trade secrets are kept within the enterprise and prepare, where appropriate, confidentiality agreements when negotiating and sharing information with business partners in order to protect trade secrets.
- For export-oriented firms, make sure IP is protected in all potential export markets. In the case of patents, it is important to bear inn mind that an enterprise generally has 12 month from the date of filing of a national application to file the same patent application in other countries.
- Use your IP portfolio as leverage when seeking sources to finance your business (e.g. include IP assets, particularly patents,, utility models and industrial designs, in your business plan as it may help to convince investors of the market opportunities open to your enterprise).
- Use patent information available in patent databases to develop your business strategies.
- When conducting joint research with other enterprises or research institutes, make sure that there is sufficient clarity on who will own potential IP generated from the research project.
- Monitor the market and make sure that your IP assets are not being infringed. If violation of your IP rights is detected it may be advisable to contact a lawyer.
- If you are unsure about how to best protect your company's intangible assets, conducting an IP audit may be a good first step in order to identify all your company's valuable information and to develop an IP strategy. On occasions, companies are unaware of the wealth of assets they possess in the form of information, creative ideas and know-how and may, therefor, not take adequate steps to protect them.

SUMMARY

Intellectual property allows entrepreneurs to own their creativity and innovation in the same way that they can own physical property. The entrepreneur owning intellectual property can control and be rewarded for its use. Intellectual property rights are the rights granted by society to individuals and enterprises principally over their creative works, inventions, literary and artistic works, and symbols, names, image and designs used in commerce. The creator gets the right to prevent others from making unauthorised use of their property for a limited period.

These laws encompass four separate and distinct types of intangible property, namely-patents, trademarks, copy rights and trade secrets. Intellectual property is an asset, that can be bought, sold, licensed, exchanged or gratuitously given away like any other property.

Intellectual property rights are divided into two main areas : Copyrights and Industrial property. Copy right protects the rights or the authors of literary and artistic works for a period of 50 years after the death of the author.It includes, books and other writings, musical compositions, paintings, sculpture, computer programs and films. The industrial property is further divided within main areas. Protection of distinctive signs that is trademarks, geographical indication and patents, industrial design, trade secrets etc., which need protection to stimulate innovation and creation of technology.

Trade marks provide exclusive rights for 10 years to use distinctive sings, such as, brand name, colour, letters, shapes or names to identify the producers os a product to protect its associated reputation. Trade mark aims at protecting the customers from being misled or deceived. Where the origin to common characteristics are the main contributing factors in determining the quality of a factor, the same are protected by what is commonly called collective marks.

Geographic indication are to identify the specific geographical origin of a product and the associated qualities, reputation or other characteristics.

Patent is an exclusive right awarded to an inventor to prevent others from making, selling or distributing products/processes without license or authorisation for a period of 20 years. In return the society requires the patent applicant to disclose the invention in a manner that enables others to put it into practice.

Patenting an innovation provides the entrepreneur the exclusive rights to its exploitation, a strong market position, higher return on its investment, an opportunity to license or sell the invention, and increases its negotiating power. It also improves the image of your enterprise Industrial designs protect the aesthetic aspects like shape, texture, pattern, colour of an object rather than its distinguishing features for a period of ten years.

Any enterprise, traditional or modern regularly uses intellectual property to prevent others from encroaching on its due rewards or taking advantage of its goodwill in market place. Every entrepreneur has to tale steps to identify,. Protect and manage its intellectual property assets and develop an intellectual property strategy so as to get best possible gain from these assets.

Any IP management strategy should include a policy on IP acquisition, exploitation, monitoring and enforcement. In many situations licensing of Intellectual property rights is an effective level for achieving business goals.

REVIEW QUESTIONS

1. Define intellectual property. Why it is necessary to protect it?
2. What are the various intellectual properties. Explain them in brief?
3. Explain how intellectual property right give an advantage to the holder over the competitors.
4. Explain the trade mark. How it can be protected?
5. Explain the steps to be considered for developing an intellectual property strategy.
6. Write short notes on :
   (*a*) Collective marks
   (*b*) Industrial designs
   (*c*) Copy right
   (*d*) Patent

CHAPTER

17

PROBLEMS OF NEW VENTURES

CHAPTER OUTLINE

— Basic Concept of New Entreprise's Problems
— Problems of Small Industries In India
— Financial Problems
— Administrative Problems
— Marketing Problems
— Production Problems
— Technology up-gradation Problems
— Technology up-gradation by Indian Small Industry
— Problems in Business through Internet
— Changing Scenario
— Understanding World Trade Organisation (WTO)
— About WTO
— Challenges

BASIC CONCEPT OF NEW ENTREPRISE'S PROBLEMS

The grim reality facing India today is the twin problems of poverty and unemployment. Both these issues are intimately inter-linked. In addition to backlog of unemployment of about 100 million people, about 15-20 million people are joining the labour force every year, a large number of them are educated youth. Besides, there is also a sizeable level of disguised unemployment. In the absence of well-developed infrastructure of power, transport, roads, ports, railways, tele-communications, etc., big enterprises cannot be set up on a large scale. The employment potential of big projects is extremely limited. At the same time the need for creating large scale employment opportunities can neither be over-emphasised nor delayed any more because of its social implications. The rising aspirations and expectations of the modern youth hold the potential for a violent upheaval. A viable option left to the policy makers and others concerned, therefore, is to focus attention on promoting new ventures. In addition, new ventures serve a number of economic and social objectives. They require relatively low level of capital investment per unit of output and employment, use local skills of artisans and other technically trained and educated people, meet local demand for a large variety of products and services. These can be set up in a dispersed manner, thus sub-serving the national objectives of industrial dispersal, development of backward and remote region and reducing urban congestion, slums and social tensions. Therefore, in the new millennium, India desperately needs a conscious and well thought out policy, strategy and a detailed programme of institutional and other assistance for promoting and facilitating the development of new ventures in the emerging scenario of globalisation and liberalisation of world economies. It is pertinent to mention here that new ventures play a significant role in the economies of all countries — developed, developing or under-developed.

In the new millennium, globalisation has thrown open vast opportunities. India and Indians can ill afford to stand aloof. All our leaders, irrespective of their political affiliations are committed to economic growth and reforms and impliedly a regime of liberalised economic policies.

It has now become imperative to be internationally competitive even to survive in the domestic markets. In the given scenario, the Indian new ventures also have no choice but to go global because international competition has already arrived at our door steps. Although the winds of change have been blowing for almost a decade now, it appears that given the Indian psyche, majority of the new ventures are either unaware about the impending situation or are deliberately ignoring it; for some of the more discerning units, however, there is a 'creeping concern' about the future. In any case, ignoring globalisation may not only hurt industry in the immediate future but may prove extremely harmful not only for individual ventures but also for the national economy, in the long run. Therefore, at the moment the question uppermost in the mind of the policy makers, administrators, industrialists, experts and non-government organisations and others concerned is whether the new ventures will be able to take up the challenges of emerging competitive environment? If yes, how best new ventures should take advantage of the enormous opportunities for expansion and growth that have been thrown open.

PROBLEMS OF SMALL INDUSTRIES IN INDIA

Entrepreneurs across the country feel that fund, talent and support infrastructure are the biggest hurdles for start-ups in the manufacturing space. Venture capitalists and private equity investors ignore them, while the government takes them for granted. While bank loans to SMEs have gone up in the recent years, the trend has still a long way to go. Infrastructure and timely availability of finance are the biggest problems an entrepreneur has to face.

The going is tough for small guy in the manufacturing sector. Funds are probably the biggest problem for the manufacturing industry. The cost of funds without collateral is too high. In fact, most banks even public sector banks, do not consider giving loans without collateral. High capital requirements and a long gestation period keeps VCs away from hard-core manufacturing activity. Private equity funds is a matter of knowing the right people at the right time.

Entrepreneurs complaint that most VC funds invest in start-ups, but only in the technology or service segments. Moreover, some of the prominent VC funds try to replicate models, which exist in US or other developed markets. Manufacturing is not seen as an exciting area by venture funds. The capital required for a manufacturing sector is sometimes too large for VC funds. They have traditionally not looked at manufacturing, and it seems like an area where private equity funds may be more interested.

Private equity funds do not consider manufacturing unless an entrepreneur can convince them about its competitive edge and hence arise their interest in a particular proposal. It is also very difficult for small entrepreneurs to get funds for expansion. These days even the duties and taxes are not proprietor friendly. The hassles for running a manufacturing venture are more as compared to a service venture. The general business environment is tougher for small and medium manufacturing units. There is too much government involvement, checks and balances and most of it is illogical. Setting up and managing a factory is much more difficult task in the current scenario.

It seems as if no one wants small scale industries. Most states are wooing players in services, IT, and retail sectors. All these factors make it difficult to attract the best talent to this sector. There is a lack of skilled workforce for the manufacturing sector. Due to service boom talent is shifting, creating a shortage for SSIs. Moreover, poor infrastructure means that need to spend themselves, thus initially operate at sub-optimal levels. Most manufacturing units are located in the remote areas and companies need to setup infrastructure like schools, medical facilities, which is otherwise the job of the state government. Supply chain infrastructure in the country is also poor and underdeveloped. This tends to lengthen the lead time for manufacturing as sourcing raw material and intermediate products remain scattered.

FINANCIAL PROBLEMS

Finance is as crucial to an enterprise as is blood to the human body. Almost everywhere in the world, the requirement of finance is inevitable for setting up a new enterprise. However, funds for setting up new enterprise has been made available more liberally to the entrepreneurs in the western world then in a developing one. Setting up of Development Financial Institutions was meant to support new enterprises, but slowly they have started equating themselves with commercial banks in terms of stringency and rate of interest.

Easy availability of credit, both in terms of need and cost, is a pre-requisite of all enterprises. In India despite the government having taken several measures to expand availability of credit to small and medium enterprises through commercial banks for working capital and through term lending institutions (SIDBI, SFC etc.), for project finance, expansion modernisation, etc., the problems of SMEs are far from over. There is a general feeling that Small scale sector is underserved or even avoided by banks. It is true that most Indian banks do not have a consistent strategy towards the SME segment. Entrepreneurs have two needs – credit needs and transaction needs. Serving their credit needs can be very profitable for banks but is risky. SME segment has a higher mortality rate than large corporate segment. Thus banks must evaluate and price their SME risk properly. But SMEs are seldom rated by a rating agency and the information available through their financial records is of poor quality. Banks need to develop customised models for evaluating risks supported by very effective monitoring structures.

To serve their transaction needs well banks are not only required to have a product that serves needs of small business but the same are to be supported by a good distribution. Small entrepreneurs value distribution and service quality perhaps more than the price. They require relationship managers who understand them and their needs. They value continuity in the relationship managers who serve them. It is important for the regulatory framework to keep these needs in mind while it considers any regulation for this sector.

Large companies that source inputs from small and tiny enterprises are now required to pay within 45 days of procurement, irrespective of any written agreement between them. With parliament passing the Micro, Small and Medium Enterprises Development (MSMED) Bill, large scale enterprises will have to pay an interest rate of 19 percent on delayed payments.

This apart, a new set of rules and regulations will now govern the small-scale sector, Small-scale and medium enterprises have been freed from the hassle of registering their units and have been given the option to shut shops if the business is not profitable. Sick units in this sector had not been allowed to exit easily as they required clearance on labour standards, sales tax registration and partnership related issues. As the bill has already become an act, SSIs do not require any registration. A memorandum with the government is optional, in case the unit wants to apply for concessions. As far as medium enterprises are concerned manufacturing units will need to sign a memorandum with the government while those operating in the services sector need not do so.

The Act also provides for setting up of a facilitation council for settling disputes regarding delayed payments by medium and large enterprises to SSIs. However, the Act stipulates that no appeal against the order of the council will be entertained by any court without the deposit of 75 percent of the decreed amount. This has been done to protect small and tiny enterprises that often turn sick due to huge dues.

Many a times the projects are delayed. In such cases, the interest burden can really take a toll on the entrepreneur. In such circumstances, the last option is to take the banker into confidence and present a fair picture to them. Better communication with banks and financial institutions helps. Once the institution is aware of its money being used for constructive purpose its level of confidence in the project rises. If required one should go for a rescheduling of the loan.

Despite of all these facilities, the new enterprises have been facing major problems relating to :

1. Credit
2 Working capital.
3 Long term capital.
4 Recovery.
5 Taxation.
6 Inadequate finance.

ADMINISTRATIVE PROBLEMS

In this environment of competitiveness, it is essential that all the resources are put to optimal use. In this context, the Human Resources are assuming importance as optimal usage of other resources would largely depend on them.

Some of the European countries have excellent vocational training and apprenticeship programmes. Despite that, SMEs there have experienced both quantitative and qualitative skill shortages. Similarly, in the developing countries, skilled manpower continues to be short in supply. Lack of resources also hinder development of training programme for human resource. Most of the small enterprises in India are "one man show". There is hardly any scientific management in most of small enterprises. However, awareness both at the enterprise and government levels is increasing and a number of programmers are being drawn up.

There is need to evolve an integrated plan of action for upgrading the skills of the workers, supervisors and office staff of SMEs to enhance their productivity and to equip them for global competition.

Also the industry associations will have to work in close collaboration and liaison with the vocational training institutions including ITIs to ensure that job-oriented training skills are imparted to the youth. It will not only ensure availability of right type of skills but also employability of trained manpower for the new and modernising enterprises. As regards rural industries, it should be kept in mind that keeping in view the present situation, while a uniform education policy for imparting the knowledge is ensured for all, planning for their employment in rural industries may be taken up early in their lives. By the time the rural youth reaches the middle school level, depending upon their aptitude, their vocational training in terms of familiarisation and working of the tools of the craft or trade should be complete. Further, specialisation and training will depend upon the attitude of the worker for hard work and desire to progress. The following are the major problems in administrative area:

1. Lack of proper planning.
2. Poor project implementation.
3. Poor management.
4. Labour problems.
5. Inadequate capacity utilisation.
6. Low level of technical skills.
7. Lack of strategies.
8. Problems of inadequate infrastructure (location, power, water, communication).
9. Lack of scientific and industrial research.
10. Bureaucratic red tape and regulations.

Another important factor is the partner you choose for your project. The partner can be any provider of funds as a co-promoter or a bank/financial instution. It pays to choose a practical, mature and nimble partner. The partner should have faith in the entrepreneur and should be willing to take risk. He should not be a person known to be encumbered by set regulations or guidelines that are impractical. Such a partner can wreck a project.

MARKETING PROBLEMS

As regards marketing, this stands out to be the crux for the ultimate success of an enterprise. Goods produced must be sold fast because the new and small entrepreneur scan hardly afford inventory build up.

Most business ventures fail in understanding the market correctly. Many entrepreneurs enter an industry too late. That is when market is over heated and hence cannot sustain any new entrant. For example, at one time many people felt that induction furnaces were making a lot of money and the process was fairly easy. Hence they thought of it as an ideal venture opportunity. But at the time of starting their venture they did not see or study the fate of rolling mills, which is the main buyer of their finished product. As and when the rolling mills started winding up, the induction furnaces also became sick.

It is essential to recognise that sub-contracting is widely practiced in Japan and it is a major source of strength for competitiveness of Japanese industries against the American and European counterparts. About two-thirds of enterprises in Japan have been involved in sub-contracting. As opposed to this, only about 25 per cent of industries in India are involved in some kind of ancillary work, sub-contracting or job work. Despite the recognition of gainful role of sub-contracting, its commercial application is not widespread in our country.

Ancillary development in India did gain considerable ground with the Indian government setting up of the first ancillary industrial estate in the country during 1970s at Bangalore through collaborative efforts of HMT as a parent company. While NSIC provided machines and equipments, the State Government was responsible for developing infrastructure and sheds. The parent-child relationship between company and the ancillary units had a good impact during 60's and 70's. But it has undergone a considerable change over the time into a natural business relationship between the main firm and its sub-contracting component manufacturers. Smaller enterprises have grown, by and large, independently of large industrial undertakings in India but at the same time subcontracting relationships have been getting stronger wherever they are existing.

Sub-contracting is expected to emerge as a major mechanism of strategic alliance between large and small firms to make them globally competitive. This would also be a major area of opportunity for the smaller enterprises as sub-contracting will offer smaller enterprises access to improved technology and manufacturing processes as well as markets. Small enterprises invariably seem to have better and efficient organisational features like quick decision-making, focused product development, lower production costs etc., and hence are cost effective. Therefore, strategic alliances of large and small industries are mutually beneficial.

Studies have shown that the scope for sub-contracting is huge, particularly in the automobiles, electronics and several other sectors including software.

In India, it has been noted that small enterprises supplying manufactured products in the open market as well as to large scale units as ancillaries continue to remain at the receiving end due to irregular payments. This seriously affects the production cycle and is one of the main reason for closure of many small enterprises. Even legislation in this matter has been of little help as the small entrepreneurs neither have time nor grit and financial capacity to wait long for payment in respect of goods supplied. Although sub-contracting by large firms to small units is most beneficial for both, appropriate procedures, norms and code of behaviour have to be devised to make sub-contracting arrangements successful. It has been found that where sub-contracting relationship between large and small enterprises is based on mutual benefit (such as Maruti, Hero Honda, Bajaj, etc.) and smaller enterprises are progressing very well. However, despite all these facilities provided by the government, smaller enterprises are facing the following marketing problems:

1. Lack of knowledge about the markets.
2. Competition from large industries/imports.
3. Branding problems.
4. Poor after sales services.
5. Distribution problems.

6. Inadequate advertising and sales promotion.
7. Poor bargaining power.
8. Unfamiliarity with export procedures and markets.

The worlds over transactions are shifting from shops to cyber-space. Consumers are surfing the internet to compare prices across states, even across countries, and then paying online by credit cards. The cost of delivering goods to consumer's homes is less than the cost of displaying and selling goods in shops. E-business cuts distribution costs for producers and prices for consumers. Middleman like retail shops and agents are being squeezed out. The volume of e-trade is still a small percentage of total sales, but is growing exponentially. Companies the world over are rushing to sell through internet.

PRODUCTION PROBLEMS

Technology and modernisation of the industry particularly of the smaller enterprises is going to play a very important role. So far as the smaller enterprises are concerned till few years ago the thrust of technology policy has been on indigenisation and improved technologies through indigenous effort. But this approach is undergoing a change. The technology environment is changing very rapidly and astonishing technological changes are taking place in almost all the fields.

(i) ***Technology Revolution:*** Industrial revolution ushered in the last century propelled the growth of industries backed by the inventions with far reaching consequences. The world is undergoing a technology revolution touching every human being in all walks of life. Changes are indeed so fast that a generation can see them by itself. First generation computers filled the entire big sized room and it took 35 years to fit the machine on the desk. However, Desk Top to Lap Top came in less than a decade. Similarly, fax, voice mail, electronic mail and now Internet have all come into a wide spread use in less than a decade. According to John Naisbitt (Global Paradox), telecommunications encompassing telephones, televisions, computers and consumer electronics will be the driving force and simultaneously create huge global economy and make its parts smaller and more powerful. The predictable scenario is emerging in the 21st century, whereby all the telecommunication capabilities could possibly fit on our desk, in our car, or even in the palm of our hand (e.g., Cellular phone). Obviously, information technology will drive changes just as surely as manufacturing brought changes in the industrial era. Further, the global industrial scene in the next decade is expected to undergo wide spread changes. New ventures have a formidable challenge before them to move with the changing technologies, imbibe them and make their operations efficient and globally competitive.

(ii) ***Indian Technology Scenario:*** Coming to Indian new ventures, the thrust of technology policy has been on indigenisation and development of improved technologies through indigenous R & D centres. Presently more than 8,000 products from industrial goods, consumer items, components, intermediates to many sophisticated products, both for domestic use and for export, are being produced by the smaller enterprises. Out of this, 836 items are reserved for exclusive production by the SSI sector now only 21 items are on the reserved list. This is so because of technological changes requiring higher investment for quality products. These policies were framed on the assumption that the small scale industries apply labour intensive technologies and would manufacture economically a large volume of goods.

Despite all these facilities, the problems in production area are :

1. Shortage of raw material.
2. Under utilised capacity.
3. Poor quality control.
4. Inadequate utility services.
5. Problems of outdated technology.
6. Low scale of production.
7. Lack of standardisation.

Technology Up-gradation Problems

Technology provides the cutting edge of success in a world striving to improve the quality of life through better products and services while protecting environment. The Indian small industry, which already accounts for 40 per cent of industrial output and 35 per cent of the total exports of the country, can play a far more active role in the country's economy by focussing on technology up-gradation. The need of the hour for the smaller enterprises, therefore, is to be technology sensitive and follow a technology plan in their vision for a globally competitive enterprise. This will result in making the 'Made in India' brand a reality.

Problems in technology acquisition and up-gradation

— Lack of information on availability of relevant technologies,
— Need for a better investment climate in India,
— Non availability of venture finance for ventures based on new technology,
— Need to strengthen indigenous technological infrastructure including R&D and enterprise linkages, industrial engineering design, consultancy services, etc.
— Compliance with environmental norms.

Technology Up-gradation by Indian Small Industry

In order to fully exploit the potential and capabilities of the Indian small industry and to integrate them with world economies, there is a need for evolving integrated policies and programmes revolving around technological acquisition and modernisation. A four-pronged strategy for technological up-gradation of small industry is outlined below:

1. **Standards and Testing:** In order to make the small enterprise competitive and to put a pressure on its output quality, it is important that certain minimum standards are developed and adhered to. This is better achieved through self-certification. Another aspect of this is to facilitate raw material testing for small enterprises. Often the quality of raw material is an important factor determining the final product quality. Big industries can join hand and establish a common testing facility for their vendors (like automobile manufacturers association for auto components). In agro and healthcare sector more innovative ways need to be found. Strong user groups, medical professionals and industry may set-up testing facilities for these sectors which directly affect the health of public at large. Some portion of the National labs can be converted into standardisation and testing facilities laboratories, e.g., National Physical Laboratory (NPL) is doing good work in material testing. Such facilities in laboratories may not be under their direct administration but can be managed by user groups or NGOs.
2. **Development of Ancillarisation**
    - Large scale units should have an ancillary/vendor development department which can functions as a single window for smaller enterprises — for information, for orders, for payments, for assistance and also for raw material selection.
    - New ventures may require loan of necessary tooling in initial production years. Manufacturing engineering items requires special tools like dies, jigs, inspection fixtures, etc., which can be provided by the mother units.
    - Technical assistance is often sought by small units and for this they prefer to work with the development/engineering department of their sourcing companies. This is important and large companies should extend this support for the overall technology/quality enhancement of the final product.
    - Demand for products manufactured by the large company may fluctuate. There are products with seasonal demand, wherein it is advisable to fix the inventory norms so that the small vendors and mother units each holds a pre-determined level of stock.
    - The big companies can facilitate their vendors in product testing and quality assurance.

SMEs and large companies have a symbolic relationship and both are dependent on each other. Auto components sector is a reasonably good example in this field. The focus should now be made to strengthen ancillarisation in sectors like capital goods, bio-medical, advanced composites and white goods.

3. **Environment Protection**

Increasingly companies are failing for non-compliance of environmental norms. For example, when European union decided to make HAPCC (hazard analysis critical control point) for sea food companies many went out of business. In today's time, it is not only important to operate the business but also see into the future. In such an exercise, the internet is a good help, and informs you about the global standards.

PROBLEMS IN BUSINESS THROUGH INTERNET

The Internet is driving down costs for transactions and distribution and reshaping the relationships of companies with their customers. The NET produces more competition among vendors and greater access to vendors by potential customers.

In pre-internet days, the only way the consumers could get goods, from most manufacturers, was through distributors and resellers. Today, they can deal directly with manufacturers eager to offer their product through the Internet. Now-a-days any manufacturer provide an equivalent of their factory outlet on internet.

Gathering the required information for financial products, travel options and other consumer products requires a lot of time and effort. A multitude of service companies make their money by collecting and organising thus kind of information for customers. Today, despite imperfect search tools, consumers themselves can go to the Internet and find out a great lot of the information they need. Now, without having to set up branches at different places but using Internet technology, an entrepreneur can dispense valuable information to its clients including prospective clients.

The term friction-free capitalism is used to describe how the Internet is helping to create Adam Smith's ideal marketplace, in which buyers and sellers can easily find one another without loosing much time or spending much money and effort.

In most markets finding the other interested party is the first problem. The second is understanding the nature and quality of the goods and services being offered. **The Internet makes it easy for a buyer to get back ground information about a product — and it's rating by the consumer organisations.**

Business Lessons for Small Enterprises

— The Internet will help achieve 'friction-free capitalism' by putting buyer and seller in direct contact and providing more information about each other.

— As the Internet drives down the cost of transactions, the middlemen will disappear or evolve a new value addition.

— Only few business will succeed by having the lowest price, so the majority will need a strategy to include customer services.

— Enterprises taking a service approach will, arm their workers with digital information tools to connect them with customers and manage relationships.

An E-revolution has set the ball rolling in India. From shopping and chatting to trading and banking, every service and product is a mouse click away, and the Internet is transforming our lives.

E-commerce is no longer a luxury, but a reality staring at our face. While Delhi housewives log on to cyberspace for placing an order for vegetables, 'paans' are made available in Mumbai on the Net. And imagine farmers from Madhya Pradesh logging on to update themselves on the wholesale prices of vegetables and commodities in the region before deciding on the price for the day. The initial signs of the E-revolution are already there.

Whether it is e-banking, e-shopping or e-searching for a service, you can do it sitting at home or in the office and it's all part of e-commerce. It is all about business transactions executed electronically between parties such as companies (business-to-business or B2B), companies and consumers (business-to-consumer or B2C) and consumers to consumers (C2C).

For starters, e-commerce offers enormous opportunities in every sphere of business. It allows low cost trading worldwide and offers enterprises a chance to enter the global market at the right time.

Changing Scenario

E-commerce props up the latest buzz — "the consumer is king". He gets the choice and the best service. Consumers can drive hard bargains on the NET, as the sellers can cut on showroom costs and related supply chain expenses. Besides, the consumer can get a whole range of goods to choose from, available through the computer screen. Companies are wiring up with stockists and transportation agents so that the rush for goods on the NET can be met.

UNDERSTANDING WORLD TRADE ORGANISATION (WTO)

About WTO

The World Trade Organisation (WTO) is an international body dealing with international trade rules. It aims at facilitating trade among countries by creating conditions of competition that are fair and equitable. Towards this end, it encourages countries to enter into negotiations for the reduction of tariffs and the removal of other barriers to trade and requires them to apply a common set of rules to goods and service produced, imported or exported.

These rules are contained in the following legal instruments:

- General Agreement on Tariffs and Trade (GATT), whose rules apply to trade in goods;
- Other Agreements on Goods;
- General Agreement on Trade in Services (GATS), whose rules apply to trade in services; and
- Agreement on Trade-Related Aspects of Intellectual Property Rights (TRIPS).

Fundamental changes are taking place in the international trading system. The WTO is the focal point of these changes. Indian industry must keep itself abreast of these changes and must take a pro-active and long term approach to the emerging issues.

Challenges

The basic implication of the WTO agreements is that competition has intensified in both our domestic market as well as the international markets. The nature and character of this competition is markedly different from what the Indian Industry has been used to in the past.

As far as the domestic market is concerned, competition intensifies from:

(a) Imported goods coming into the domestic market at lower tariffs, and

(b) Foreign companies, especially MNC's establishing subsidiaries, and acquiring domestic firms in India, primarily for accessing the Indian market.

Their strength will emanate not only from their financial and staying power, but also from their well known trademarks, proprietary technology and international networking.

As far as the export markets are concerned, Indian industry faces stringent competition, for the kind of goods pre-dominating our export basket, from other developing countries, especially those from South East and East Asia including China.

The main threat to our exports to other industrial country markets is from non-tariff barriers especially in the form of environmental, health and safety standards. Other factors such as, labour standards (including child labour) and intellectual property protection also effect our exports.

BRANDED FURNITURE IS GIVING UNORGANISED SECTOR A RUN FOR ITS MONEY

In these times, the average Indian consumer is as consider about brands as they come. Even the furniture segment, so far the exclusive domain of the good ol' carpenters, hasn't been spared. The global names are entering this segment too, much to the glee of desi style gurus. We look at the issues which guide the dynamics in the furniture segment.

They say Indian furniture is a statement on the diversity of the country's culture. However, there are few organised players and it's tough to estimate the size of the market. The organised segment accounts for only five per cent of market.

The players in the organised office furniture sector include Godrej and Blowplast. In home furniture, Gautier India, a joint venture between the Birlas and French furniture major Gautier, is a leading player.

The furniture business has gradually become value-driven, following the entry of foreign players in the last 3-4 years. Italian and French brands have become especially popular, grabbing a lion's share of the premium segment. The foreign brands adopt local styles and use material to suit the climate. For instance, the entire range of Camel, the Italian furniture brand which entered India recently, is designed to suit the tropical climate and the lifestyle.

Gautier score on marketing. The brand gives utmost importance to display and its actively pursuing tie-ups with prominent showrooms. It is also planning to add 23 more distribution centres to its existing 47 in India. With their savvy skills, the brands have been luring the discerning Indian buyer.

So where does that leave the desi companies. Since Gautier's entry, there has been a lot of activity in the domestic market. However, the activity is more in terms of trading rather than manufacturing. Retailers have set up chains, like Concept in Mumbai and Modfurn in Chennai, and are selling readymade furniture in a big *way.* In addition, there are several regional players. For example, there's Jayabaratham Furniture & Appliances in Chennai, which is trying to go the professional way.

However, Indian furniture makers still shy away from marketing their products under a brand name. Not sure of being accepted as a desi brand companies dealing in plywood, hardwood or furniture prefer to promote the brands which they import.

The domestic market's shift to branded furniture is due to many reasons. Quality, perhaps, is the most important factor. In case of a branded, readymade item, customers can actually see what they intend to buy. In the indigenous sector, quality and the outcome of the final product is often suspect. Then there's warranty and after-sales service. For example, Gautier gives a written one-year warranty to the customers.

However, the trends do not imply that the unorganised segment is being swept away in this tide of branded goodies.

India has peculiar demand patterns. In the West, most people go in for the readymade items which are mass produced. It doesn't matter whether similar goods are owned by others. In India, consumers demand variety even at low price points. Thus, the major brands, which come at a price, won't really affect the indigenous sector.

While the organised sector is growing at over 25 per cent, the un-organised sector, too, is growing at 20-25 per cent.

It's too early to gauge the impact of these organised entities on the SMEs. However, its' clear that the consumers are ready to pay for quality and the brands are giving the local players a run for their money.

To conclude, entrepreneurs are heroic in overcoming all the hurdles posed by laws, institutions, policies, markets but still new ones keep on crapping. Perhaps that is why the game is so interesting and the charm of entrepreneurship so enticing.

It is time for the entrepreneurs to shrug off the chains – perceived or otherwise. While a large number of infrastructural problems need to be solved, the entrepreneurs need to do a lot more themselves. Thinking global is not just setting up business in other countries. It is about having the passion, the zeal and the confidence to beat anybody and everybody whether at home or in new markets world wide.

SUMMARY

In the post-independence period, the government at the centre and in the states have established a number of specialised institutions to cater to the varied needs of new ventures. These promotional institutions assist in setting up new ventures but they do not ensure the provision of adequate working capital, raw materials, power supply, nor do they help in developing marketing outlets for the sale of their products.

The entrepreneur needs to re-orient his attitude and develop special leadership qualities necessary for taking decisions based on wider implications rather than narrow path. The problems of new entrepreneurs are multidimensional. These can be solved by the coordinated efforts of entrepreneurs, co-ordinated functioning of promotional agencies, and governmental assistance without red tape or bureaucratic delays. The entrepreneur has to be educated and he should have a proper training in acquiring the necessary skills in running an enterprise.

REVIEW QUESTIONS

1. Explain the various problems faced by new ventures.

2. Ancillarisation can be developed as an extensive tool to face the various problems of new venture. Do you agree? How?
3. The fast changing technology is causing problems to conventional ventures. Please comment.
4. Discuss the causes of slow growth of new entrepreneurship in India.
5. What are the obstacles to new entrepreneurial growth in India ?
6. What suggestions would you give to overcome the problems faced by new enterprises in their growth in India?
7. Will Internet and E-commerce help solving the problems of new ventures? If yes, explain how?

CASE 17.1

BIG BOYS OF SOFT TOYS

WHILE STILL in college, Rajarshi Chakroborty and Tapas Bagchi, had decided that working for others was not their cup of tea. They had to set up shop on their own. Which they did after passing out from Jadavpur University in 1977 with BE (Electronics). They began to make power sources for the Department of Telecommunications (DOT), naming their company Shockley Hall Electronics (P) Ltd in memory of William Shockley and Graham Hall, the American inventors of the transistor and known as the fathers of modern electronics engineering.

Soon Shockley Hall had become DOT's biggest supplier of power sources and remainded so till 1988 when the entry of multinationals such as French major Alcatel and the German giant Siemens queered its pitch. Rajarshi and Tapas realised they could not compete anymore with the technology that these biggies had to offer. They had to change tack and picked toys as their business of choice.

A trip to South Korea in 1988-98 saw them come back with a technical tie-up with one of Korea's top toy makers — Newko Toys. Today, besides running other businesses, Rajarshi and Tapas have helped make Shockley Hall one of the very few toy exporters from India.

"We dominated the domestic market till 1997-98 with our Nick Nack brand of soft toys and electronic toys as the demand for our products far outstripped supply," says Rajarshi.

Meanwhile, other bigger branded players began to enter the market. Funskool of the Chennai-based MRF Group tied-up with global major Hasbro while Mattel followed suite soon. In the global toy market. Hasbro and Mattel are like what Coke and Pepsi are in the soft drinks market. Shockley Hall then found that it had become more profitable to tap the $ 70 billion global market and in the process became one of the first Indian companies to export toys.

"We realised if we had to concentrate on the domestic market we would have to compromise on quality and operate at the lower end of the market. Instead, we chose to export and began to get orders from Germany, UK, Switzerland and Austria. Recently we have also been able to penetrate the US market which is extremely price sensitive. But then, over the years, we have learnt how to compete with the Chinese and offer similar prices for better products," Rajarshi claims. This is done through design innovations which help to bring down material costs while maintaining quality.

In 1997, the enterprising duo floated another company Electromed Toys Pvt Ltd, a joint venture with Ei-Tech GmBh of Germany for producing construction sets and other educational toys. Presently, work is going on for further expansion of business in partnership with another German toy major. "If everything goes according to plan, Kolkata can soon become a major destination for toy makers," Rajarshi claims.

Due to Rajarshi's determined lobbying, the West Bengal government has now decided to set up a toy park in Kolkata.

Being a private limited company, Shockley Hall is wary of disclosures and its claimed turnover of Rs. 3 crore seems rather understated. But with three factories in Kolkata working to full capacity and two more coming up soon, Shockley Hall is surely going places.

One can only wish Rajarshi and Tapas all the best because of their efforts bear fruit Kolkata may soon emerge as a major destination on the world's toy industry map.

CHAPTER

18

INSTITUTIONAL SUPPORT FOR NEW VENTURES

CHAPTER OUTLINE

- Support System
- Incentives and Facilities
- Credit Policies
- Rajiv Gandhi Udyami Mitra Yojana
- Small Industries Development Organisation (SIDO)
- National Institute for Entrepreneurship and Small Business Development
- Entrepreneurship Development Institute of India (EDI), Ahmedabad
- Technical Consultancy Organisations (TCOS)
- State Level Institutions
- Khadi and Village Industries Development Scheme
- Small Industrial Development Bank of India (S.I.D.B.I.)
- The National Science and Technology Entrepreneurship Development Board (NSTEDB)

SUPPORT SYSTEM

In order to support entrepreneurship, government of India come up with Micro, Small and Medium Entreprises Development (MSMED) Act, 2006. The definition of Micro, Small and Medium Industry as per this act is given in Box I.

The enterprises covering a wide spectrum of industries in medium and small, including tiny sector occupy an important position in planned development of Indian economy and has grown to be the most vital sector of our nation .The liberalised policy of the government has thrown open this industrial sector to the large and giant multinational companies offering challenges as well as opportunities to the small scale sector. As on March 2008, there are 13.4 million micro and small enterprises in the country, these industries were providing employment to around 32.3 million people producing goods worth Rs. 140 billion at current prices. This sector accounts for exports of Rs. 33 billion, i.e., 33% of total exports. Because of the credit-able contribution of the SME sector towards economic progress of the country, the Government of India is committed to promotion and deyelopment of this sector and besides providing various incentives it also co-ordinates the functioning of all the institutions engaged in similar activities.

DEFINITIONS OF MICRO, SMALL AND MEDIUM ENTERPRISES

In accordance with the provision of Micro, Small and Medium Enterprises Development (MSMED) Act, 2006 the Micro, Small and Medium Enterprises (MSME) are classified in two classes.

(*a*) Manufacturing Enterprises : The enterprises engaged in the manufacture or production of goods pertaining to any industry specified in the first schedule to the industries (Development and regulation) Act. 1951). The Manufacturing Enterprise are defined in terms of investment in Plant and Machinery.

(*b*) Service Enterprises : The enterprises engaged in providing or rendering of services and are defined in terms of investment in equipment.

The limit for investment in plant and machinery / equipment for manufacturing/service enterprises, as notified, vide S. O. 1642 (E) dtd. 29-09-2006 are as under.

Manufacturing Sector

Enterprises	Investment in plant and machinery
Micro Enterprises	Does not exceed twenty five lakh rupees
Small Enterprises	More than twenty five lakh rupees but does not exceed five crore rupees
Medium Enterprises	More than five crore rupees but does not exceed five crore rupees

Service Sector

Enterprises	Investment in plant and machinery
Micro Enterprises	Does not exceed ten lakh rupees
Small Enterprises	More than ten lakh rupees but does not exceed two crore rupees
Medium Enterprises	More than two crore rupees but does not exceed five crore rupees

INCENTIVES AND FACILITIES

Fiscal Incentives : Excise concession is available for both registered and unregistered units on turnover upto Rs. one crore. While SSIs with a turnover of Rs. 50 lakh are entitled to full exemption of excise duty, concessional rate of excise duty has been fixed for units with a turnover between Rs. 50 lakh and Rs. 100 lakh. Normal rate of duty is applicable for any unit thereafter.

Reservation: Reservation of a 21 products for exclusive manufacture in SSI sector.

Preference: Price and purchase preference to products manufactured in SME sector in government purchase programmes are as indicated in Box II.

Infrastructure: Infrastuctural support to Entrepreneurship Development Institutes is provided to augment their training capacities.

Entrepreneurship Development: Entrepreneurship Development Institutes have been set up at national and state level.

Collaborative Programmes: A number of joint programmes with the State Bank of India and Small Industries Development Bank of India has been launched by the government for modernisation and technology upgradation of specific industry clusters.

NGOs: Assistance is provided to industrial associations and voluntary agencies to set up testing centres and other facilities to assist local entrepreneurs.

Special Programmes: Special programmes on vendor development, quality awareness and pollution control are also organised at different level for the benefit of entrepreneurs.

Quality Certification: Quality Certification Scheme has been launched to improve SSI product quality. Financial support is provided to small enterprises to acquire ISO-9000 certification.

TDTF: A scheme for creation of Technology Development Trust Funds in the states has been launched with the involvement of respective state governments and industry associations.

Government's Price and purchase Preference Policy for Marketing MSME Products

The marketing assistance to the small scale units through preferential purchase by the Central and State Purchase Organisations was emphasised in the comprehensive programme for the development of MSME sector drawn in early 50's in pursuance of industrial Policy Resolution of 1984. The emphasis was reiterated in the Government Policy in 1991.

I. Purchase Preference Policy

The policy of reservation of items for exclusive purchase has been in vogue since late 60's as a measure of market support to the MSME sector. The Stores Purchase Policy of the Government prior to 1989 was in the form of categorisation of items in six major groups as detailed below :

Group-I Items which are of no interest to small scale units and can be solely procured only from large scale units (128 items).

Group-II Items which can be purchased solely from large sale units but where it is possible for the large scale units to job contract accessories and components to MSME units (159 items).

Group-II Items which can be purchased both from small scale and large scale industrial units.

Group-IV Items which are reserved for exclusive purchase from small scale units (409 items).

Group-V Items which are to be procured exclusively from the MSME units to the extent of 50% of the requirement (13 items).

Group-VI Items which are to be procured exclusively from the MSME units to the extent of 50% of the requirement (28 items).

However, with effect from july 28, 1989, the Purchase Policy of the Government was modified in a major way and the categorisation of the items was reduced to the following two major group viz.

(*i*) Items of stores reserved for exclusive purchase from KVIC/Women's Development Corporations/Small Scale units and

(*ii*) Others not so reserved.

The first group comprised of 409 items earlier reserved for exclusive purchase from the small scale sector. The list of 409 items reserved for purchase from the MSME sector was reviewed and after deleting items having common nomenclature and making the entries more generic as well as addition of new items, a revised list of 358 items was approved by the Committee (set up to consider the question of inclusion of additional items) which also includes 8 handicraft items reserved for purchase from the Handicraft Sector.

II. Price Preference Policy

Assistance under Government Store Purchases Programme in the form of reservation of products for exclusive purchase from small scale sector and price preferring is one of the major instruments for providing marketing support to the small scale industries. The Director General of Supplies and Disposals, the Central Purchasing Organisation of Government of India provide a number of facilities to small scale industries under its Government Stores Purchase Programmes. These include reservation of certain products for exclusive purchase from the small scale sector and price preference upto 15% in case of selected items which are produced in both large scale as well as small scale units. The Single Point Registration Scheme of NSIC was launched as a market support measure for the MSME Sector. Under the Scheme, the following benefits are given to MSME units which get themselves

Registered with the NSIC

(*i*) Availability of Tender Sets free of cost;

(*ii*) Exemption from payment of Earnest Money Deposit;

(*iii*) Exemption from payment of Security Deposit;

(*iv*) Price preference upto 15% over the lowest quotation of the large scale units (on merits).

The NSIC while registering a unit under this scheme is required to undertake capacity assessment of the applicant through the institutional set up of the SISI in the country. They are also required to obtain confidential report from the bankers of the manufacturers about the credit worthiness/financial standing of the same. The units registered with NSIC under this scheme are given a registration certificate indicating items for which registered and monetary limit upto which registered. The Policy of the Price Preference of 15% is a critical benefit available to the MSME sector. The benefit is available to compensate them on account of non-availability of economies of scale, poor resource base, poor access to raw-material etc. As compared to the large scale sector. The policy of the Price Preference of 15% is an independent policy and is no way linked with the price preference of 10% to the PSUs and other purchasers.

Credit Policies

- Lending to SSIs is considered a priority sector lending by banks 10% of priority sector lending is earmarked for SME sector.
- During 2006-07 SME sector received credit of Rs. 45,000 crores from bank and Rs. 12,000 crores from other sources like Venture Capital, Private Equal external co.............. barrowing etc.
- Concessional/Fixed rates of interest are charged for loans upto Rs 2 lakh to SSI units.
- SMEs get a leberal treatment for sanction of working capital loan by the banks.
- Working capital limits are computed on the basis of minimum 20 per cent of projected annual turnover with fund based working capital requirement up to Rs. 100 lakh.
- Government has launched Credit Guarante Fund scheme to provide collateral-free credit to Micro and Small Enterprises. The scheme enables the small entrepreneurs to get credit upto Rs. 50 lakh without providing any collaterial security or third party gurantee.

Due to insufficient investment and lack of awareness of both the quality standards and access to modern technologies, a large percentage of SSI units continue with outdated technology and plant and machinery. With increasing competition due to liberalisation of the economy, the survival and growth of the SSI units are critically dependent on their modernisation and technological upgradation. Upgradation of both the process of manufacture and corresponding plant and machinery is necessary for the small enterprises to reduce the cost of production and remain price competitive at a time when cheaper products are easily available in the global market.

The Scheme aims at facilitating technology upgradation by providing upfront capital subsidy to MSME units, on institutional finance (credit) availed of by them for modernisation of their production equipment (plant and machinery) and techniques. The Scheme provides for 15 per cent capital subsidy to MSME units, on institutional finance availed of by them for induction of well established and improved technology in selected sub-sectors/products approved under the Scheme. The eligible amount of subsidy is based on the actual loan amount not exceeding Rs. 1 crore.

To provide mentoring and hand-holding services to new generation entrepreneurs the Government of India has launched a Udyami Mitra Yojana.

RAJIV GANDHI UDYAMI MITRA YOJANA

In order to accelerate the process of setting up the units and making them operational by the first generation entrepreneurs and the others, the Ministry of Micro, Small and Medium Enterprises lanched the Rajiv Gandhi Udyami Mitra Yojana (a Scheme for promotion and hand-holding of Micro and Small Enterprises).

The objective of the Scheme is to help and facilitate the potential first generation entrepreneurs in completion of various formalities and tasks necessary for setting up and operationalisation of their enterprises. It aims at assisting potential firsi-generation entrepreneurs, who have undergone entrepreneurship/skill development training of atleast two weeks' duration, or have undergone vocational training from ITIs.

The Scheme is being implemented through various lead agencies, i.e., *Udyami Mitras,* viz; Entreprenourship Development Institutions (EDIs), Central/State Govemment Public Sector Enterprises (PSEs) involved in promotion and development of MSEs, Entrepreneurship Development Centres (EDCs).

The udyami Mitras would be networking and coordinating with various Government deparments/ agencies, regulatory/support agencies, for channelising the benefits available under various Schemes to the first generation entrepreneurs with a view to assist them in setting up their enterprises. They would provide assistance to the potential entrepreneurs in preparation of project report, arranagement of finance, establishment of work-shed, sanction of power load/connection, selection of technology, installation of plant and machinery/office equipment, obtaining various registrations/licenses/clearances/no objection certificates (NOCs), putting into place arrangements for supply of raw materials as well as marketing of products/services, linkage for mentorning support, etc.

Scope of **National Equity Fund Scheme** providing equity type assistance at 1 per cent service charge enhanced to cover whole country except metropolitan areas to support expansion, modernisation and technology upgradation. Ceiling of soft loan assistance enhanced to 25 percent of the project cost subject to a maximum of Rs. 2.5 lakh. Projects upto Rs. 10 lakh are eligible for assistance under this scheme. This scheme is being operated through SIDBI.

Technology Development and Modernisation Fund Scheme launched for modernisation and for improved and updated technology to export oriented units. This scheme is operated through SIDBI. Refinance assistance under this scheme has been extended through State Financial Corporations, State Industrial Development Corporations and scheduled commercial and cooperative banks.

SUPPORT ORGANISATION

Given below are the important organisations providing institutional support and offering various schemes for the development of the new ventures.

1. SIDO 2. NIESBUD 3. EDI 4. TCO's 5. STATE LEVEL INSTITUTIONS
6. KVIC 7. SIDBI 8. NSTEDB

SMALL INDUSTRIES DEVELOPMENT ORGANISATION (SIDO)

Support Services

Small-scale sector is one of the success stories of the modern India. Its success is written large over the face of the country and is equally visible all around. This is a sector that has emerged victorious in the face of rising competition from large sectors inside and from multi-nationals abroad. Despite its several shortcomings, innumerable handicaps and severe limitations, this sector is widely acclaimed for its indisputable role in employment generation, production, exports etc.

Currently, SSI sector accounts for 95 per cent of industrial units, 40 per cent of the industrial production, and 35 percent of the country's total exports. The contribution of this unorganised industrial sector is next only to agriculture. The question arises: Why small scale sector? Why should it be developed?

Is it the self evolved or a developed growth? These are the questions which, though prima facie easy, are difficult to answer in the changed scenario.

Small-scale industries are defined in terms of their investment in plant and machinery. Presently, small-scale industries are defined as units with investment in plant and equipment upto Rs. 1 crore. Tiny Enterprises and Small Scale Service and Business Enterprises under SSI Sector have the investment limit of Rs. 25 lakh regardless of their location. However, a small unit cannot be owned, controlled by or be a subsidiary to another industrial undertaking. The large enterprises and NRIs can hold upto 24 per cent equity in SSI units. However, the investment in Plant and Machinery can go upto Rs. 5 crore if 50 per cent of the production is exported.

Significantly, small scale sector is known for wide range of items covering about 7,500 products. In fact the range is so wide that there is hardly any product around us in our day to day life which has either not been produced or sourced directly or indirectly from or sub assembled in an SSI unit. While on one hand there are mass consumption products like leather, plastics, rubber, readymade garments and hosiery, the SSI sector also produces such sophisticated products as colour TV sets, computer assembly, electronic calculators, and digital measuring instruments. Looking back during the last four decades we find that the small scale units existed in one form or the other even when no formal definition of small scale industry was in force. Small scale industries developed as it were on their own inherent strength and their innate capability. However, their planned and systematic development took place with the onset of planning era when Village and Small Industries sector was recognised as an important tool for employment generation.

Accordingly, the plan outlays also rose for this sector and has been continuously rising phenomenally over the years.

Pioneering the institutional structure for the development of small-scale industries at the central level is the Delhi based Small Industries Development Organisation (SIDO) in New Delhi with a large number of field outfits and subordinate formations that provide a wide range of techno-economic consultancy and support services.

SIDO is also known as the office of Development Commissioner (SSI), under the Minstry of Micro, Small and Medium Enterprises. Ministry of Industry, Government of India, New Delhi and acts as the nodal agency for the development of this sector. It has a large number of field agencies for this purpose. Important ones are:

1. **Small Industries Service Institutes (28) and Branch Institutes (30).**

   They provide

   Economic consultancy/information/EDP consultancy.

   Trade and market information.

   Project profiles.

   State Industrial Potential Survey.

   District Industrial Potential Survey.

   Modernisation and in plant studies.

   Workshop facilities.

   Training in various trades/activities.

2. **Regional Testing Centres (4) and Field Testing Stations**

   Their activities include :

   Testing facilities.

   Training programmes.

   Consultancy services.

3. **Tool Rooms /Tool Design Institutes (10)**

   The specialise in

   Assistance in tool design.

   Manufacture of tools, jigs, fixtures, moulds, etc.

   Training facilities to tool makers.

   Common service facilities.

   Consultancy.

4. Process-cum-Product Development Centres (6)

These were set up to :

Serve as R&D institution in various dense industry clusters.

Product design and innovation.

Product and process improvement.

Development of improved packaging techniques.

Common facility centre.

Manpower development.

This network is further supported by other associated specialised institutions like NSIC, New Delhi (provides machinery on hire-purchase basis, marketing support, technology assistance, equipment leasing, development and training). SIDBI, Lucknow (providing refinance to SFCs and banks and direct financing of SSI projects), NIESBUD, New Delhi (Institute of entrepreneurship development), and N1SIET, Hyderabad (training) etc. Co-ordination between the Central and State/UT Governments is effected by the Small Scale Industries Board. In addition, these are supported by a large number of institutions and organisations in the States/UTs to provide other various specialised inputs and services. These are:

1. Commissioners and Directors of Industries.
2. District Industries Centres.
3. State Industrial Development Corporations.
4. State Small Scale Industries Development/Export Corporations.

There are many advantages of small scale sector. While the SSIs easily adapt new technology in new environs they are also bestowed with operational resilience unique to their character. Economies of scale in production is another contributory factor. However, due credit is also deserved and rightfully so by the trait of entrepreneurship which blossomed during the post independence period ironically because there wasn't any institute of entrepreneurship then. However, lack of formal training or education did not retard the growth of entrepreneurship, rather it was more than supplemented by the entrepreneurs own urge, their grit, and determination to succeed against all conceivable odds.

As a result rags to riches stories are a plenty, success profiles are abundant and the entrepreneurial canvas is radiant with first generation entrepreneurs. But the role and importance of well planned policy directions, institutional support and organisational assistance need not be belittled. At the micro level small and medium sector has succeeded in diffusing entrepreneurship and played a critical role in equitable distribution of national wealth by utilising and tapping the locally available human, physical and material resources and converting them into productive assets.

As this sector does not enjoy economies of scale in operations and has to face many hurdles and handicaps, a number of promotional policy measures have been stated so as to provide a level playing field. Notable among these measures are: priority sector lending by banks/financial institutions, excise exemption scheme, reservation of items for exclusive production and purchase and price preference. These measures are in addition to a host of other institutional services, fiscal incentives and financial assistance being provided by other Central Departments and State/UT Governments.

Entrepreneurship Development

(i) Various types of EDP programmes are run by the SISIs/Branch SISIs. Management inputs are provided to beginners and specialised courses are organised for targeted groups of entrepreneurs. This is followed by escort services/practical help to entrepreneurs to set up their units. These courses are conducted by the technical personnel available with the SISIs/Branch SISIs.

(ii) State Governments provide assistance for the promotion of small and medium enterprises by way of:

- Infrastructural facilities such as developed industrial plots/sheds.
- Capital subsidy in backward areas.
- Power subsidy.
- Sale tax loan/deferment.

The nature of assistance varies from one state to another.

(iii) National Institute for Entrepreneurship and Small Business Development (NIESBUD), New Delhi.

It was set up in 1983 to provide training to EDP trainers and generate a variety of training aids and materials for use by regular trainers and extention officers.

(iv) National Institute for Small Industry and Extension and Training (NISIET), Hyderabad.

It provides training to entrepreneurs, managers and various developmental functionaries of state governments, financial institutions and other agencies. It also undertakes research and consultancy for the development of small industry and also acts as an important resource and information centre for the same.

(v) Integrated Training Centre, Nilokheri

A part of SIDO organisation it provides technical training to artisans and workers sponsored by the state government. It also organises training of Extension Officers engaged in various developmental organisations.

(vi) Skill Development

Training in development of technical skills is given to technicians and workers in various workshops attached to the SISIs and institutions such as Testing Centres and Tool Rooms. Central Footware Training Institutes (CFTI's) provide training to the workers in footwear trade.

(vii) Assistance to Entrepreneurship Development Institutes (EDIs)

A new scheme has been formulated to assist the state governments by way of capital and revenue grants not exceeding Rs. 50 lakh per state for strengthening and setting up EDIs in the states.

(viii) Institute for Entrepreneurship in North-Eastern Region

Indian Institute of Entrepreneurship has been set up at Guwahati to promote entrepreneurship in predominantly tribal areas of North-East.

Pollution Control

In order to educate and train the small-scale units in the matter of pollution abatement, awareness and motivational programmes are organised by SIDO/DC(SSI) with the active/financial support of the Ministry of Environment and Forests. Specific programmes on waste minimisation and cleaner production in some of the highly polluting sectors like electroplating, textile dyeing and bleaching, foundries, glass/ ceramic, potteries, leather tanning, asbestos, paints and chemicals and food processing industries are being conducted by Small Industries Service Institutes at various clusters for the benefit of smaller units. The response from the small units has been found encouraging as a result the following waste minimisation circles have been established:

1.	Pulp and Paper	Muzzafarnagar (UP)
2.	Electroplating	Ludhiana (Punjab)
3.	Cotton & Dyeing	Ludhiana (Punjab)
4.	Hosiery	Kanpur (UP)
5.	Textile Hosiery	Tirupura (Tamil Nadu)
6.	Textile Weaving	Erode (Tamil Nadu)
7.	Manmade Textiles	Surat (Gujarat)
8.	Metal Finishing	Chennai (Tamil Nadu)
9.	Metal Finishing	Mumbai (Maharashtra)
10.	Tannery	Chennai (Tamil Nadu)
11.	Tannery	Vaniyambadi (Tamil Nadu)

Energy Conservation Programme

Keeping in view the high cost of energy and higher levels of energy consumption in some of the specific industrial sectors namely floundry, forging, re-rolling, glass, ceramic, porcelain industries, plywood industries etc. Small Industries Development Organisation (SIDO)/DCSSI conducts Energy Conservation

Programmes through its field offices at various places in the country for the benefit of small units. Some of the identified energy-intensive clusters are:

1. Re-rolling mills at Mandi Gobindgarh (Punjab).
2. Refractories in Durgapur, Dhanbad and Ranchi.
3. Foundry units in Agra, Coimbatore, Batala and Howrah.
4. Glass industries at Firozabad.
5. Plywood industries at Muzaffarpur.
6. Forging units at Ghaziabad, Kanpur.

In addition to educational workshops by SISIs, Small Industries Service Institute, Kolkata is also extending the service of Energy Audit Studies to the SSI units in the eastern region.

Technology Upgradation and Quality Improvement

Under this scheme, techology upgradation studies and quality improvement trainings are organised by SISIs for the benefit of SSI units.

Awareness and educational programmes on various aspects on Total Quality Management and ISO-9000 certification are organised by SISIs and RTCs at various places in the country for encouraging quality management among SSI units.

In addition to the above mentioned training programmes, SSI units are given financial support by way of reimbursement of 75 per cent of their expenses subject to a maximum of Rs 75,000/- for obtaining ISO-9000 certification.

NATIONAL INSTITUTE FOR ENTREPRENEURSHIP AND SMALL BUSINESS DEVELOPMENT

The National Institute for Entrepreneurship and Small Business Development, registered as a Society under the Societies Registration Act, XXI of I860, was set up on July 6th, 1983 by the Ministry of Industry, Government of India as an apex body for coordinating and overseeing the activities of various institutions/agencies engaged in entrepreneur ship development, particularly in the area of small industry and small business.

The major activities of the Institute include evolving model syllabi for training various target groups, providing effective training strategies, methodology, manuals and tools, facilitating and supporting Central/State Governments and other agencies in executing programmes of entrepreneurship and small business development, maximising benefit and accelerating the process of entrepreneurship development, conducting programmes for motivators, trainers and entrepreneurs which are commonly not undertaken by other agencies and organising such activities that help in developing entrepreneurial culture in the society.

Entrepreneurship and self-employment development being a promotional and industrial extension activity, programmes of the Institute are largely organised by the government fund. The Institute's training activities are focused on areas of stimulating, supporting and sustaining entrepreneurship. NIESBUD plays a supportive and catalytic role by helping organisations which are directly or indirectly engaged in developing and promoting entrepreneurship and self employment in the country. Programmes initiated/sponsored by NIESBUD are constantly evaluated and revised enabling it to adapt to the changing needs of entrepreneurship and small business development. The Institute is engaged in creating a climate conducive to emergence of entrepreneurship and in developing favourable attitude amongst general public in support of those who opt for entrepreneurial career by removing the prevalent misconceptions.

The announcement of various employment generation schemes by the government designed to provide employment opportunities to unemployed youth both in rural and in urban areas, through setting up micro level enterprises like Prime Minister's Rojgar Yojana etc., has thrown new challenges to the Institute to demonstrate its crucial role in propagating mass self employment by bringing out model syllabi, manuals for beneficiaries and instructors, preparing innovative training aids like Video films and also organising training for the trainers.

The Institute's faculty comprises of senior and experienced professionals with specialisation in the areas of entrepreneurial competency and motivation, project identification and formulation, finance and credit, small enterprise management, women entrepreneurship and entrepreneurial education.

The Institute is presently functioning from NSIC-PDTC campus, Okhla Industrial Estate, New Delhi.

Training Programmes and Their Impact

The Institute being an apex body in the area of promotion of entrepreneurship and development of small businesses offers innovative training packages for different target groups-entrepreneurs, trainers, promoters, development functionaries etc. In order to maintain their effectiveness, the training programmes are so designed as to meet the specific training requirements of each target group. The course content of the programmes are continuously revised to keep them in tune with the changing entrepreneurial environment. Besides its regular training activities, the Institute also conducts tailor-made training programmes as per the requests received from various organisations/agencies designed to cater to their specific training requirements.

The Institute organises training programmes for different target groups. In accordance with its objective of strengthening the trained work force available for imparting entrepreneurial teaching in the country, regular programmes are conducted for trainers. Keeping its emphasis on promotion of entrepreneurial behaviour among women and weaker sections of the society, the Institute organises training programmes for these sections of the society. Entrepreneurship orientation programmes are specially conducted for the Community Leaders and Women Group leaders for example, DEEPALAYA — an NGO working for the upliftment of slum dwellers of the city. The other training programmes conducted are under the women empowerment through enterprise development project of the Ministry of Industry, Government of India wherein its officials are being provided training to develop and deliver women friendly training and support strategies for enterprise development.

The Institute organises a three-day workshop on entrepreneurship development 'Living On Your Own' with the basic objective of creating an awareness about the entrepreneurial spirit among the student participants and making them appreciate the role and functions of an entrepreneur. The short term programmes organised included Excellence in Enterprise Performance Through Managerial Effectiveness and Creative Selling and Effective Advertising for Entrepreneurs and Small Business Owners. The international training programmes conducted include a one-week group study of participants sponsored by the International Labour Organisation (I.L.O.) on women issues and an orientation programme for a delegation of the different foreign Government on policies and programmes for income generation activities.

A brief description of the training programmes organised by the Institute during the year, is presented below:

I. Tranning of Trainers/Promoters

(a) Trainers' Training

The necessity of having adequate number of trained trainers in country for not only motivating the people at large to take up entrepreneurial and income generating activities but also equipping the existing/ prospective entrepreneurs with requisite skills for sustaining their enterprises cannot be over emphasised. The existing man power base in the country in the form of trained trainers for imparting entrepreneurial teaching, has come under great pressure in recent years due to the launch of a number of employment generation schemes by the government. These schemes are designed to provide employment opportunities to unemployed youth both in rural as well as urban areas through setting up micro enterprises. Recognising the need for training of the beneficiaries of these schemes and ensuring successful launch of their economic enterprises and also their subsequent effective operation, most of these schemes have incorporated compulsory training inputs as a pre requisite for grant of numerous benefits under them. The requisite task of providing EDP training to a large number of prospective beneficiaries cannot be accomplished in the absence of the required number of trained trainers for the purpose. The task of providing continuous training to the trainers/promoters also assumes significance in view of the sweeping changes taking place in SME sector due to liberalised economic environment.

The Institute has been contributing towards strengthening the available man-power base through conducting different types of trainers' training programmes which can be broadly classified into two categories — (a) exclusively for trainers, and (b) for trainers/ promoters.

The programmes thus conducted included Accreditation Programme for Entrepreneurial Motivation Trainers (First Phase and Final Phase), Project Identification, Formulation and Appraisal, Industrial/

Business Project Appraisal Techniques, Trainers Programme for Self Employment under Prime Minister's Rojgar Yojana (PMRY) and Promotion of Income Generation Activities.

(b) Small Business Promoters Programme

The introduction of various liberalised economic measures in the economy has necessitated structural changes in the policy framework and the environment in which SMEs operate. This is essential for providing sustenance to this vital sector and enabling it to discharge its crucial role in the new competitive environment. Accordingly, a number of measures including raising of investment ceilings for SSI sector, encouraging imports of latest technology/machinery, easing out various controls, restriction etc., improved sources of finance, facilities for marketing of the products, dereservation of certain items earlier exclusively reserved for SSI sector etc., have been taken/announced. The role of this crucial sector of the economy in creating direct and indirect employment both in rural and urban areas and also in removal of regional imbalances, poverty alleviation and herald of an egalitarian society cannot be over emphasised. As of today, the sector has provided employment to about 165 lakh persons. The task of promotion/providing sustenance to SME sector cannot be handled by the government alone in the face of the obvious constraints. The burden in this *regard* has to be equally shared by large number of NGOs/Voluntary Organisations. In order to enable the officials/functionaries of these organisations to discharge their functions effectively and efficiently, NIESBUD has been conducting different types of training programmes for equipping them adequately in their endeavour. MESBUD has also been concentrating on promotion of entrepreneurial behaviour among women and weaker sections of the society.

II. Small Enterprise Continuing Education for Sustaining Entrepreneurship (SECEP)

The SME sector has proved its mettle even in the changed competitive liberalised economic environment. Its contribution to both Gross Domestic Product (GDP) and exports from the country have been continuously increasing. The liberalised economic environment has not only thrown challenges to small enterprises in the form of increased competition both from big economic players and other SMEs in the area but has also proved a blessing in disguise for such enterprises by making newer avenues available to them for attaining the high levels of growth and development. In this competitive era of today, the need of the hour is to suitably strengthen SMEs by equipping them with latest technology upgradations, managerial techniques, methods of production and effective marketing strategies so that the units in this vital sector could operate profitably.

For providing sustenance to small-scale enterprises and to make such units a viable entity, the Institute has been conducting training programmes for practicing entrepreneurs through its Small Enterprise Continuing Education Programme (SECEP). Under this scheme short duration courses are offered which helps entrepreneur build in-depth knowledge and acquire working skills in critical functional areas of management of the enterprises. These programmes cover areas of working capital assessment and management, excellence in enterprise performance through managerial effectiveness, effective marketing techniques, project identification and selection, exports marketing, financial forecasting for fast growing business entrepreneurs and creative selling and effective advertising for entrepreneurs and small business owners. The programmes on export marketing for small entrepreneurs and effective marketing techniques for small business received enthusiastic and warm response from the participants. The entrepreneur has to keep abreast of the latest developments/trends in various functional areas of the management and government policies, schemes etc. The reason for this being that these changes in management systems, production techniques, management approaches, government rules, regulations, schemes etc., affect an entrepreneur in one way or the other. In order to suitably equip the entrepreneurs with these changes, NIESBUD has been conducting training programmes on the new emerging thrust areas in management.

III. Efforts for Orienting Heads of Departments (HOD) and Senior Executives

NIESBUD has been endeavoring to provide orientation in various functional and operational areas pertaining to decision making, implementation of the various schemes/projects, sharing experiences in developing enterpreneurship and discussing the various problem areas in the field with the Head of Departments and senior executives of various governmental/ non-governmental sectors.

So the Institute organises such programmes providing participation to senior officers.

IV. National Seminars/Workshops

In order to bring the policy planners, government officials, functionaries of NGOs, professionals and consultants, experts engaged in the promotion of entreprenurship together for evolving the emerging techniques, discussing thrust areas and formulating appropriate policies in the area, the Institute has been conducting workshops, seminars, symposia etc., on different aspects of entrepreneurship.

NIESBUD organises workshops on entrepreneurship development in association with various National and International Associations. The broad areas of discussion relate to entrepreneurship as career alternative, understanding and developing entrepreneurial competencies, formalities/steps in setting up an enterprise, opportunity sensing and interface with entrepreneurs to understand the functioning of enterprises.

V. International Training Programmes, Workshops, Seminars, etc.

The Institute has been conducting different kinds of training programmes meant for trainers/ promoters, officials concerned with development of entrepreneurship/small business, from different Afro-Asian countries. These programmes provide a platform for sharing the rich and varied Indian experience in development of entrepreneurial culture and promotion of small business among different streta of the society. This also provides an opportunity to the Institute to examine and learn from the different approaches being adopted in other countries for sustaining the numerous income generating activities. These 8-week training programmes are aimed at equipping the participants with the necessary techniques and methodologies etc., to enable them to perform their duties of training/promotion of small business effectively in their respective countries.

Besides its announced international programmes, the Institute also conducts tailor-made training programmes on requests received from different international organisations/agencies and sovereign governments.

Some of the International training programmes/ study visits organised by MESBUD are as follows :

(a) **Small Business Creation and Development for Women Entrepreneurs (SBCD-WE)**

Eight week training programmes are designed to help the participants be become effective trainers/promoters/counsellors in the area of developing women entrepreneurs.

(b) **Group Study on Women Issues (I.L.O.)**

The one-week study visit of a group of participants from different countries is sponsored by the International Labour Organisation. It is designed to promote exchange and enhance knowledge and information especially in the areas of gender equality, women working rights, freedom of association, social protection and international labour standards, health and safety, labour inspection etc., and women participation in trade unions.

(c) **Business Advisors' Training (BAT) Programme**

A regular training programme on Business Advisors' Training (BAT) is organised by the Institute with participants from developing countries of Asia and Africa. The programme is conducted with the basic objective of developing skills and knowledge in identifying business opportunities, business appraisal techniques, basics and application of business finance, business management skills etc., and providing insights into policies and programmes for entrepreneurship development in developing countries.

(d) **Small Business Planning and Promotion (SBPP)**

The training programme on Small Business Planning arid Promotion is another regular feature. The course content is divided into seven major modules, small business creation, small business planning, appraising small business opportunity, entrepreneurial qualities for small business entrepreneurs, small business management skills, small business promoters' role and functions and field studies to various small business enterprises and support organisations.

(e) **Orientation Programme for Foreign Delegations on Policies and Programmes for Income-Generation Activities**

The one-week orientation prograinme-cum-study visit for delegations of different foreign

Government are specially organised at the request of the Ministry of Foreign Affairs. The programmes for the delegation are designed with the basic objective of familiarising the participants with different approaches, policy framework and incentives and support systems being adopted for entrepreneurship training and spread of entrepreneurial culture and development of small business.

(f) **Entrepreneurship Development and Promotion of Income Generation Activities (ED-PIGA)**

A regular training programme on Entrepreneurship Development and Pro-motion of Income Generation Activities (ED-PIGA) is organised annually for participants from Asia and Africa. The programme is conducted with the basic objective of developing insights into the process of entreprenurship development for income generation and imparting knowledge and skills for designing/planning techniques for identifying, creating, developing and running the micro enterprises.

(g) **Entrepreneurship for Small Business Trainers/Promoters (ESB-TP)**

Another regular training programme is Entrepreneurship for Small Business Trainers/Promoters (ESB-TP). The programme is designed to enable trainers and promoters from developing countries to acquire an understanding of the entrepreneurship development process, team designing and conducting Entrepreneurship Motivation Training (EMT) workshop for prospective entrepreneurs, acquire skills in identification of potential entrepreneurs and use appropriate selection techniques/ tools for locating them, understand the dynamics of enterprise launching covering the ability of scanning opportunity, project formulation, appraisal and mobilising resources, gain capability of guiding the beneficiaries in managing their enterprises successfully and develop insights into planning and extending support to them in setting up their enterprises.

VI. Testing EDPs

The Institute specially designs and field tests new formats of EDPs for different target groups like women entrepreneurs, S & T entrepreneurs, ex-servicemen, school dropouts, SCs/STs, rural youth etc. This is necessitated on account of need to bring about desired modifications in the policies being pursued for the promotion of entrepreneurship among different target groups of the society owing to changed liberalised, competitive economic scene in the country.

Training-cum-Incubation Centre : Garment Manufacturing

The Training-cum-Incubation Centre : Garment Manufacturing is operational at the Institute's campus in NOIDA. The Centre earlier set up with the financial assistance from the Ministry of Micro, Small and Medium Enterprises (MSME), has been engaged in organizing training programmes in Apparel Sector and is expected to provide the required support to the first generation entrepreneurs during the start-up period after which the entrepreneurs are expected to be on their own.

The Centre fully equipped with ultra modern machines and other apparatus and manned by the qualified, experienced and motivated and motivated small work-force has so for organized 48 training activities with 931 beneficiaries since August 2007. The training programmes organized were in the areas of Sewing Machine Operations Machine Embroidery and Tracing Cutting and Tailoring and Artificial Gems and Jewellery. In order to ensure greater participation and on account of convenience to the participants, majority of the training programmes have been organized at different locations like Dadri, Khurja, Sardhana and Harra (Meerut), Haridwar, Dehradun, Ghaziabad, Modinagar and Ambala.

The major achievements of the Centre include assisting 118 participants in getting employment immediately after the training including absorption of 20 participants as Sewing Machine Operators in AMS Fashions, a subsidiary of ITC Ltd., handling brand names like John Players etc., initiation of 11 participants into the micro enterprise building process through execution of small orders for stitching of the clothes in their neighbourhood and facilitating 75 participants in forming Self-Help Groups in the Meerut which were also addressed by the high ranking officials from the Oriental Bank of Commerce and support organizations for improving the market linkages of Groups.

It is heartening to note that the Centre has evolved into a self-generating Centre.

Publication and Training Aid Material

Various audio visual equipment and training aid materials are being increasingly used in the teaching of entrepreneurship. The use of these aids not only facilitates the work of trainers but also leaves an impregnable impression on the trainees. This also makes the instructions effective and meaningful for them. In view of the changing economic environment, there is a constant need of revising and updating the existing literature available on entrepreneurship and related topics and also of improving different training aids being deployed for entrepreneurial learning. NIESBUD has been making concerted efforts in this direction. The efforts of the Institute are also directed towards supplementing the publications available on the subject and developing various audio-visual and training aid materials to make teaching as well as learning purposeful.

(a) Publications

The Institute has been bringing out publications in the form of manuals, text books, ready recknors, case studies, model syllabi etc. The prominent ones are: Model Syllabi For Entrepreneurship Development Training Programmes, Women in SSI Sector in India, Udyamita, Trainers' Manual on Developing Entrepreneurial Motivation, Cases on Entrepreneurship etc. A few of the publications are also available in Hindi.

(b) Video Films

In order to make the task of imparting instructions convenient, meaningful and effective, NIESBUD has brought out 12 video films covering a wide range of topics related to entreprenurship. The films especially on *How to Launch Your Own Enterprise Sensing Opportunity, A Path of Your Own, A Path for Women Too and Formulation of a Project Report* are popular among users.

(c) Entrepreneurial Motivation Training (EMT) Kits

The Entrepreneurial Moti· ation Training Kit assembled by the Institute is a unique collection of six games and exercises. It is a very useful aid for developing entrepreneurial behaviour and motivation.

ENTREPRENEURSHIP DEVELOPMENT INSTITUTE OF INDIA (EDI), AHMEDABAD

The Entrepreneurship Development Institute of India (EDI), was set up in 1983 as an autonomous institution sponsored by the Industrial Development Bank of India (IDB1), Industrial Finance Corporation of India (IFCI), Industrial Credit and Investment Corporation of India (ICICI), and State Bank of India (SBI), with the active support of the Government of Gujarat. The institute situated near village Bhat, Chandkheda, Ahmedabad, is a resource centre and is committed to education, research and training. It has earned a great deal of national and international recognition.

The institute has trained a large number of trainers and helped the entrepreneurs in preparing the feasibility study during entrepreneurship development programmes conducted by this institute. It has prepared a manual on "How to prepare a project report?" for preparation of industrial feasibility studies and to assist the professionals and entrepreneurs in preparing the feasibility reports.

EDI has also developed a software called "FAME" in 'clipper' language. It is a menu driven comprehensive package for feasibility studies and can be easily operated by consultants, appraisal officers, students of management schools, trainer, motivators, bankers and project people.

Mission of the Institute

The EDI believes that entrepreneurs are not necessarily born they can be developed through well conceived and well directed activities. The mission of the EDI is :

- To augment the supply of industrial entrepreneurs through education and training;
- To produce multiplier effect on opportunities for self-employment; To improve the managerial capabilities of small-scale enterprises;
- To contribute to the dipersal of business ownership and thus to expand the social base of Indian entrepreneurial class ;

- To contribute to the creation and dissemination of new knowledge and in-sight in entrepreneurial theory and practice through research;
- To augment the supply of trainer-motivators for entrepreneurship development;
- To participate in institution building efforts; and
- To collaborate with similar organisations in India and other developing countries to accomplish the above objectives.

The Target Groups

Consistent with its mission and objectives, the EDI has launched a series of activity and programmes targeted to developing new entrepreneurs from a variety of groups, viz;

- Technical Employees: turners, fitters, machine operators, repairmen, fore-men, supervisors.
- Other Employees : supervisors, managers, accountants, stores and purchase staff, salesmen, teachers, civil servants.
- Young Engineers : degree/diploma holding freshers. Artisans/Craftsmen : rural artisans, skilled traditional craftsmen, cottage industry owners.
- Traders : small traders, employees of merchants/shops. Undertaking programmes to improve performance of existing enterprises. Mounting innovative programmes for family business, inheritance , successors (prospective leaders) with a view to sustaining the entrepreneurial vision.

Activities of EDI

The principle activities of EDI are as follow :

1. Conducting and organised Entrepreneurship Development Programmes (EDPs) for potential Entrepreneurs throughout the country.
2. Generation and Dissemination of New Knowledge.
3. Trainer's Training Programmes for Entrepreneur Trainer — Motivators/Small Enterprise Counsellors/Self Employment Promoters.
4. Conducting Seminars and Workshops on various themes and different aspects of entrepreneurship development activities.
5. Extension Motivation Programmes for Officers of Support Agencies/Institutions/Organisations involved in Entrepreneurship Development.
6. Awareness Programmes for Officers of financial institutions/banks on new assessment technique (Focussed Behavioural Event Interview).
7. Performance improvement programmes for existing entrepreneurs.
8. EDP Appreciation/Awareness programmes for Officers of support agencies/Institutions/ Organisations.
9. Orientation Programmes for NABARD officers on Rural Entrepreneurship and for students of technical institutions.
10. Growth Programmes for Existing Entrepreneurs for Creating Strategic Awareness.
11. Institution Building.
12. Competent Management Assistants Programnme for umemployed non-technical graduates.
13. Succession Planning for Entrepreneurial Continuity for sons/daughters of existing entrepreneurs.
14. Professional support extended to Technical Consultancy Organisations (TCOs). Educational and Training Organisations, Voluntary Agencies, Banking Institutions, Management Schools, Small Industry Promotion Organisations and State Industries Departments.
15. Conducting research studies on First Generation Women Entrepreneurs, Evaluation of EDPs. Growth of Small Scale Manufacturing Units etc.

As a national resource organisation, the EDI has developed teaching materials, counselling packages and ready guides for entrepreneurs, as well as, Trainer—Motivator — Facilitators and Teachers of Entrepreneurship. The following are some of the important publications of EDI;

1. SELF-MADE *IMPACT MAKING* ENTREPRENEURS.
2. ENTREPRENEURSHIP DEVELOPMENT PROGRAMME IN INDIA and ITS RELEVANCE TO DEVELOPING COUNTRIES.
3. DEVELOPING NEW ENTREPRENEURS.
4. IN SEARCH OF IDENTITY—The Women Entrepreneurs of India.
5. PERFORMANCE IMPROVEMENT SERIES FOR EXISTING ENTREPRENEURS OF *SSIs*.

TECHNICAL CONSULTANCY ORGANISATIONS (TCOS)

Provision of appropriate and inexpensive consultancy services to small and new entrepreneurs is a pre-requisite for achieving wider geographical dispersal of small and medium enterprises all over the country. For this purpose, technical consultancy organisations (TCOs), were set up in the early 1970s and early 80s. IDB1, IFCI and ICICI in collaboration with state level financial/development institutions and commercial banks established a net work of TCO's. There are 18 TCOs in the country, some of them covering more than one state. TCO's have been set up to provide a package of total consultancy services to state governmets, state-level development financing institutions and banks. The major thrust of TCO's operations is in the area of preparation of project reports and feasibility studies. Having gained experience over the years, TCOs have diversified into the fields of identification of potential entrepreneurs and their training, project implementation, rehabilitation, management consultancy, detailed design engineering and turn-key services besides energy audit and conservation.

STATE LEVEL INSTITUTIONS

There are three important development agencies constituted at state level which provide financial assistance for setting up of industrial projects under small and medium scale sector. These institutions also participate in modernisation, expansion and diversification programmes of existing industrial units. The area of operation of these state level institutions is limited to their respective states.

Small Industries Corporations

All state government have set up small industries corporation with the aim of providing assistance to and facilitating the entrepreneur in setting up small scale industrial venture in the state. In their earlier days, their role was limited to providing scarce raw materials to SSI sector. Presently, they extend marketing support to SSI's sector in the state. Some of the progressive SIC's have their export wing to promote exports of SSI sector.

State Financial Corporations (SFCs)

State Financial Corporations have been established under the State Financial Corporation Act, 1951. At present there are 18 SFCs operating in various states as per list given in Appendix II. State Financial Corporations generally provide long term finance for setting up of the smaller projects within their region.

State Industrial Development Corporations (SIDCs)

State Industrial Development Corporation operate at slightly higher level than SFCs. Though these institutions are also primarily working as development banks promoting industrial projects in small and medium scale is their major objective. As a representative of the state, they participate in ventures of private individuals in setting up industrial ventures in joint and assisted sector. A joint sector has minimum of 26 per cent equity by the SIDC or some other state organisation. In case of assisted sector joint equity participation by various Govt. agencies is below 25 per cent. A list of SIDCs is given in Appendix III.

KHADI AND VILLAGE INDUSTRIES DEVELOPMENT SCHEME

The Khadi and Village Industries provide important opportunities of non-farming employment to the rural people. In the budget for 1995-96 a proposal was made for beginning a new scheme under which the Khadi and Village Industries Commission (KVIC) was provided Rs. 1000 crore on a consortium basis through banking system. KVIC grants loans to Khadi and Gramodyog units directly or through state level Khadi and Village Industries Boards (KVIB). Centre and the State governments provide guarantees on loans given by commercial banks to Khadi and Village Industries Board.

SMALL INDUSTRIAL DEVELOPMENT BANK OF INDIA (S.I.D.B.I.)

In response to the long standing demand of the small scale sector in India, Small Industries Development Bank of India (SIDBI) was set up by an Act of Parliament as an apex institution for promoting, financing and development of industries in the small scale sector and for co-ordinating the functions of other institutions engaged in similar activities. SIDBI is a wholly owned subsidiary of Industrial Development Bank of India (IDBI). It commenced its operations on April 2, 1990 by taking over the outstanding portfolio and activities of IDBI pertaining to the small scale sector. SIDBI operates through its head office at Lucknow and a network of 5 regional offices and 33 branch offices in all the states.

SIDBI under the charter has, inter alia, been assigned the task of being the main provider of term finance to the small-scale sector in the country. Small scale industrial units, artisans, village and cottage industrial units in the tiny sector and small road transport operators are extended financial assistance mainly by way of refinance through Primary Lending Institutions (PLIs) viz., State Financial Corporations (SFCs), State Industrial Development Corporations (SIDCs), and banks which have a wide network of branches. Term loans extended by eligible PLIs to small scale industrial projects irrespective of the location and form of organisation of the units are eligible for refinance assistance.

With a view to encourage bills culture and helping the SSI units realise their sale proceeds of capital goods/equipment and components/sub-assemblies/intermediates, SIDBI directly discounts bills arising out of these transactions and also rediscounts those bills that are discounted by the banks. In addition, SIDBI has also introduced direct finance schemes for specialised marketing agencies, sub-contracting/ ancillary units and infrastructure development agencies so as to fill in the gaps in these areas in the existing credit delivery mechanism. SIDBI has been providing assistance to well run companies on a selective basis for acquiring machinery/equipment both indigenous and imported for modernisation/ expansion/diversification/balancing scheme etc., under its Equipment Finance Scheme (EPS). Project loans are also considered on a selective basis. It also provides assistance for working capital, credit rating, quality certification and vendor development. Besides, SIDBI operates a venture capital fund for support to ventures in the small scale sector which have special features in terms of techonology, market prospects, return on investment or entrepreneurial profile.

All projects in the small-scale sector are normally eligible for assistance. The minimum promoter's contribution prescribed under the schemes generally varies between 10 per cent and 25 per cent. The debt equity ratio up to 3:1 is normally applicable under all refinance schemes in respect of loan amount up to Rs 10 lakh and up to 2:1 above Rs 10 lakh. Interest rate for most activities is related to size of Joan under various schemes of assistance. Repayment period for the term Joan is fixed after taking into account the profitability and debt servicing capacity of the project.

Micro-Credit

In India, Micro-credit programmes are run primarily by NABARD in the field of agriculture and SIDBI in the field of Industry, Service and Business (ISB). The success of Micro-credit programme lies in diversification of services. Micro Finance Scheme of SIDBI is under operation since January, 1999 with a corpus of Rs. 100 crore and a network of about 190 capacity assessed rated MFIs/NGOs. The Government of India provides funds for Micro-Finance Programme to SIDBI which is called 'Portfolio Risk Fund' (PRF). This fund is used for security deposit requirement of the loan amount from the MFIs/ NGOs and to meet the cost of interest loss. At present, SIDBI takes fixed deposit equal to 10% of the loan amount. The share of MFIs/NGOs is 2.5% of the loan amount (i.e., 25% of security deposit) and balance 7.5% (i.e., 75% of security deposit) is adjusted from the funds provided by the Government of India. The MFIs/NGOs may avail the loan from the SIDBI for further on lending on the support of the security deposit.

Details of individual schemes and procedure for availing assistance may be obtained from the offices of SIDBI/PLIs.

THE NATIONAL SCIENCE AND TECHNOLOGY ENTREPRENEURSHIP DEVELOPMENT BOARD (NSTEDB)

Constituted by the Department of Science and Technology, it operates entrepreneurship development programmes and has recently launched a pilot project called 'open learning in entrepreneurship development training programme' in order to develop the spirit of entrepreneurship among engineering graduates and the youth.

NSTEDB has started this project in the 3 states of Karnataka, Gujarat and Maharashtra To start *with,* they have trained 200 persons in operating and administering the programme, which is similar to the distance education/correspondence course pattern with the stress on giving suitable inputs to the unemployed diploma holders and graduates in engineering, through the local languages, to make the trainees develop the requisite skills. The duration of the training is 11 months.

The NSTEDB has also planned to provide data including profiles of the industrial potential of different regions and export possibilities for the engineering products.

SUMMARY

Entrepreneurship Development is a human resource development task, a process which deals with human motivation, skills, competencies, social and economic risks and investment of technical and physical resources of the individual and the state. The importance of promoting and developing first generation entrepreneur is increasing day-by-day in all developing countries. It has been realised by planners in these countries that the massive problem of growing unemployment can be tackled by establishment of hew ventures which can generate employment opportunities.

Government of India at an early stage realised the importance of promoting new ventures particularly small-scale industries as a means of employment generation. Small Industries Development Organisation was set up at the apex level to provide technical inputs and guidance to small industries. Khadhi and Village Industries Commission was established to promote village industries. The need for providing financial assistance was felt at an early stage and state financial institutions were set up to provide term loans for small-scale units. State Industrial Development Corporations were set up to promote entrepreneurship and assist in setting up of new ventures in their respective scales by providing infrastructure as well as finance.

In 1984 Government of India set up NIESBUD an apex organisation for promotion of entrepreneurship and small business. At the same time, financial institutions, under the leadership of IDBI establish Entrepreneurship Development Institute of India (EDI) with the same objectives. NIESBUD and EDI have been conducting research in entrepreneurship development and training of trainers and extension workers in the field of entrepreneurship development. These institutes did a pioneering work in selection and training of entrepreneurship and brought a number of publications.

Technology plays an important rate in setting up and growth of enterprises. All India Finance Institutions took a lead to provide technical consultancy to entrepreneurs in setting up their new ventures and established 16 Technical Consultancy Organisations which catter to different parts of the country.

REVIEW QUESTIONS

1. Name two entrepreneurship development institutions and describe their activities.
2. What are the problems that are encountered in developing entrepreneurship in a developing country like India?
3. What is SIDO ? Describe its role in new venture creation in India.
4. Explain the various schemes and facilities available for setting up a new unit.
5. How can the educated unemployed youth be motivated to set up new units in backward areas of the country?

Appendix 1

Addresses of Small Industries Service Institute (SISIs)

1. SISI Narsapur Cross Road, Bala Nagar, Hyderabad - 500 037.
2. SISI Industrial Estate, Bamuni Maidan, Guwahati - 781 021.
3. SISI Patliputra Industrial Estate, Patna - 800 013.
4. SISI Opp. Okhla Industrial Estate, New Delhi -110 020.
5. SISI Audhi Mapari Building P.B.No. 334, Margao - 4503 061.
6. SISI Harsiddh Chambers, 4th Floor, Ashram Road, Ahmedabad - 380 014.
7. SISI Janak Kuti, Chambaghat, Solan -178 213.
8. SISI Sector -13 SFC 137-38, Urban Estate, Karnal -132 001.
9. SISI 36, B/C Gandhi Nagar, Jammu Tawi -180 004.
10. SISI Industrial Estate, Rajaji Nagar, Bangalore - 560 044.
11. SISI Krishna Jagar, Kanjany Road, P.O. Ayyanthole, Thrissur - 680 003.
12. SISI 10, Industrial Estate, Pologround, Indore - 425 003.
13. SISI Kurla- Andheri Road, Saki Naka, Murnbai - 400 072.
14. SISI Shed No. C-17-18, Bit No. 23, Ind. Estate, Takyelpat, Imphal -1.
15. SISI Vikas Sadan, College Square, Cuttack - 753 003.
16. SISI Industrial Area 'B' Ludhiana -141 003.
17. SISI 22 Godown, Industrial Estate, Jaipur - 302 006.
18. SISI Tadong Housing Colony, P.O. Tdong, Gangtok, Sikkim - 737 102.
19. SISI 65/1, G.S.T. Road, Gunidy, Chennai - 600 032.
20. SISI Industrial Estate, Kalpi Road, Fazalganj, Kanpur - 208 012.
21. SISI 111-112, B.T. Road, Kolkata - 700 035.
22. SISI A-208, Kamla Nagar, Agra - 282 005.
23. SISI E-17/18, Industrial Estate, Naini, Allahabad - 211 009.
24. SISI Bela Industrial Estate, P.O.R.K. Ashram, Muzaffarpur, Bihar -16.
25. SISI Industrial Estate, Kokar, Ranchi - 834 001.
26. SISI Industrial Estate, Gokul Road, Hubli - 580 030.
27. SISI C.G.O. Complex, Seminary Hills, Nagpur - 425 007.
28. SISI 21, Harish Thakur Road, Agartala (Tripura) - 799 001.

Appendix 2

List of State Financial Corporations

1. Andhra Pradesh State Financial Corporation, 5-9194, Chirag Ali Lane, P.B.No. 165, Banglore-560001.
2. Assam Financial Corporation, G.S. Road, Ganeshguri Chanali, Guwahati -781 005.
3. Bihar State Financial Corporation, Frazer Road, Patna - 800 001.
4. Delhi Financial Corporation, Saraswati Bhawan, 'E' Block Connaught Place, New Delhi-110 001.
5. Haryana Financial Corporation, Nos. 17, 18 and 19, Sector 17A, (Opp. LIC Building) Chandigarh - 160 017.
6. Gujarat State Financial Corporation, Jaldarshan Building, Navrangpura, Ahmedabad - 380 009.
7. Himachal Pardesh Financial Corporation, Kishore Bhawan, The Mall Simla - 171 001,
8. Jammu & Kashmir State Financial Corporation, (June-Novemaber): Gulam Mohi-ud-Din, Trust Building, Sherwani Road (Opp. bank of Baroda), Srinagar-191 001, (December-May): Augaf Building, New Uttam Talkies, Virmarg, Jammu - 180001.
9. Karnataka State Financial Corporation, Sankaranarayana Building (5lh Floor), 25, Mahatma Gandhi Road, Banglore.
10. Kerala Financial Corporation, Vellayambalam, Trivandrum - 695 001.
11. Madhya Pradesh Financial Corporation, Financial House, Bombay-Agra Road, Indore-452001.
12. Maharashtra State Financial Corporation, New Exercelsior Building (7-8 and 9th Floor), Amrit Keshav Nayak Marg, Mumbai - 400 001.
13. Orissa State Financial Corporation, OMP Square, Cuttack - 753 003.
14. Punjab Financial Corporation, No 772/3, Sector 17B, 1" floor, Ashram Road, Bank Square, Chandigarh -160 017.
15. Rajasthan Financial Corporation, Surya Niwas, C-18, Bhagwandas Road, P.B.No. 63, Jaipur - 302 001.
16. Tamil Nadu Industrial Investment Corporation Ltd., Arun Malai, 26, Whites Road, P.B.No. 410, Chennai - 600 004.
17. Uttar Pradesh Financial Corporation, 14/88, Civil Lines, Kanpur - 208 001.
18. West Bengal Financial Corporation, 4, Kiran Sankar Roy Road, Kolkata -700 100.

Appendix 3

List of State Industrial Development Corporations

1. Andhra Pradesh Industrial Development Corporation Ltd., Parishrama Bhawan, 59-587 B, Fateh Maidan Road, Hyderabad - 500 029.
2. Arunachal Pradesh Industrial Development Corporation Ltd., Itanagar.
3. Assam Industrial Development Corporation Ltd., Zoo Road, Guvvahati - 781 003.
4. Bihar State Credit and Investment Corporation Ltd., Jeewan Jyoti Bhawan, S.P. Verma Road, Patna - 800 001.
5. Economic Development Corporation of Goa Daman and Diu Ltd., Shree Saraswati Mandir Building, 2nd Floor, 18th June Road, P.B.No. 316, Panaji - 403 009.
6. Gujarat Industrial Investment Development Corporation Ltd., Chunibhai Chambers, Ashram Road, Ahmedabad - 380 009.
7. Haryana State Industrial Development Corporation Ltd., S.C.O. 40-41 Sec-tor 17A, Chandigarh - 160 017.
8. Himachal Pradesh Mineral and Industrial Development Corporation Ltd., Himrus, Circular Road, Simla - 171 001.
9. Industrial Promotion and Investment Corporation of Orissa Ltd., 3A, Satya Nagar, Bhubaneshawar - 751 007.
10. Jammu and Kashmir State Industrial Development Corporation Ltd., Haft Chinar, Srinagar - 190 001.
11. Karnatka State Industrial Investment Development Corporation Ltd., Hari Niwas, 36, Cunningham Road, Banglore - 560 052.
12. Kerala State Industrial Development Corporation Ltd., TC10/402-1, Keston Road, Kawadiar, Trivandrum - 695 003.
13. Madhya Pradesh Audyogik Vikas Nigam Ltd., 2nd floor,, Panchaman Bhawan, Malviya Nagar, Bhopal - 402 003.
14. Meghalaya Industrial Corporation Ltd., Meghalaya Additional Secretariat Building, Third floor, Room No. 413, P.B.No. 9, Shilong.
15. Mizoram Small Industries Development Corporation Ltd., Aizawl.
16. Nagaland Industrial Development Corporation Ltd., P.B.No. 5, Dimapur -797119.
17. Pondicherry Industrial Promotion Development and Investment Corpora-tion Ltd., 38, Romain Rolland Street, Pondicherry - 605 001.
18. Punjab State Industrial Development Corporation Ltd., S.C.O. 54-56, Sector 17A, Chandigarh - 160 017.
19. Prodeshiya Industrial and Investment Corporation Ltd., 100, Jawaharlal Nehru Marg, Jaipur - 302 001.
20. Rajasthan State Industrial and Mineral Development Corporation Ltd., 100, Jawahar Bhawan, Ashok Marg, Lucknow - 226 001.
21. Sikkim Industrial Development and Investment Corporation Ltd., Gangtok, Sikkim.
22. State Industrial and Investment Corporation of Maharashtra Ltd., Nirmal, Nariman Point, Mumbai - 400 021.
23. State Industrial Promotion Corporation of Tamil Nadu Ltd., 51 /52, Greams Road, Chennai - 600 006.
24. Tripura Industrial Corporation Ltd., Agartala.
25. West Bengal Industrial Development Corporation ltd., 23A, Netaji Subhas Road, Kolkata - 700 001.

Appendix 4

List of Items Reserved For Exclusive Manufacture By Micro and Small Enterprise Sector
(As on 10 October, 2008)

	S.No (As per Gazette Notification)	*Product Code*	*Name of the Product*
	20-21	Food and Allied Industries	
1.	3	202501	Pickles and Chutneys
2.	7	205101	Bread
3.	11	21100102	Mustard Oil (except solvent extracted)
4.	13	21100104	Groud nut oil (except solvent extracted)
		27	Wood and Wood Products
5.	47	276001	Wooden furniture and fixtures
		28	Paper Products
6.	79	285002	Exercise books and registers
			Injection Moulding Thermo-Plastic Product
7.	147	30391201	PVC Pipes including conduits-Upto-110 mm dia
		30393501	Fittings for PVC pipes including conduits upto 110 mm dia.
			Other Chemicals and Chemical Products
8.	253	305301	Wax candles
9.	308	314201	Laundry soap
10.	313	317001	Safety matches
11.	314	318401	Fire works
12.	319	319902	Agarbatties
			Glass and ceramics
13.	335	321701	Glass bangles
		33-35	Mechanical Engg. Excluding Transport Equipment
14.	364	340101	Steel almirah
15.	394	341004	Rolling shutters
16.	402	34200602	Steel chairs-All types
17.	404	34200702	Steel tables-All other types
18.	409	342099	Steel furniture-All other types
19	428	343302	Padlocks
20	447 A	345207	Stainless steel utensils
21.	474	345202	Domestic utensils-Aluminium

Integrated Case Study–1

PRATHISTA – A SUCCESS STORY

Mr. Chander Mohan, Associate Editor, Science Tech Entrepreneur, interviewed Mr. KVSS Sairam a first generation techno entrepreneur and Managing Director of Prathista.

EARLY DAYS

Mr. Sairam says, we hail from District East Godawari, Andhra Pradesh. I was born in Amalapuram located in the coconut belt. We are three brothers, my eldest brother is a Chartered Accountant and my second brother is Mechanical Engineer with MBA presently working with TATA group. I am the youngest and I have also one sister. Our parents, despite being simple peasants, gave us complete freedom to evolve and grow and never interfered in our lives.

I completed my chemical engineering from Osmania University in 1987 and PG Diploma in Project Management from IGNOU. This was through correspondence as I did not want to stop studying just after graduation. In fact, I have also done a course in Export-Import Management from AP Productivity Council and even now I am persuing, PG degree in Environmental Engineering from Indian Institute of Environment and Ecology, New Delhi.

FIRST JOB

During my campus interview itself I got selected by Ion Exchange India Ltd., and for two years I worked as a Trainee Engineer. The company specialises in water treatment. Afterwards I switched over to Unicorn Organics. I feel that is when my career really took off. The company was manufacturing starch and its derivatives like sorbitol, dextrose, etc., using maize and tapioca starch.

EXPERIENCE IN A LARGE GROUP

In 1990 I got a major breakthrough in my career when I was selected by Bharat Starch Ltd., a unit of the Thapar Group, which at that time was amongst the top five groups in the country. Initially, I joined as a Senior Engineer (Process) in their Unit at Yamunanagar. After that I was given additional responsibility of research. I was very dedicated and after seeing my ability and capacity I was asked to look after project implementation also. I worked in Bharat Starch for four years. The Thapar Group allows its employee to explore and realise his potential and turns him into a true professional. They have their own Thapar Corporate Research and Development Centre (TCRDC) at Patiala in Punjab and I was given an additional responsibility of coordinating with their research station in their Yamunanagar Plant in Haryana. The TCRDC is basically meant for in-house R&D only and their activities are directed towards captive consumption only. They don't usually sell technologies, products and processes developed by them to outsiders. There 1 was involved in the development of various bio-fertilisers particularly based on corn gluten which is a waste from the maize processing unit. It was developed at the lab scale and then upscaled to a 200 litre bench scale.

MAJOR BREAKTHROUGH IN CAREER

In August 1993,1 got married and was given a transfer, to a Modified Starch Plant based on tapioca at Pondicherry. I was at Pondicherry for three months but after 3 months due to various reasons I switched to Starchem Industries, Hyderabad where I realised my entrepreneurial capabilities for the first time. Whatever, I had learnt during my stint with Thapars, I was able to implement the same. The project was in technical collaboration with Lurgi of Germany and I joined at the grassroots level. This Rs. 27 crore project was financed by IDBI and I coordinated it as Implementation Manager. I worked for two years and six months there right from Concept to Commissioning. I was promoted as Works Manager, as the project was implemented before schedule. Another unit of the company for manufacturing Sorbitol however, was commissioned later.

We did not invite our collaborator for commissioning assistance and we did it on our own, though I was trained by Lurgi in Thailand in 1994. I got opportunity to prove my capability which was appreciated by Lurgi as the very first batch of the product was approved by US Govternment. Because of the international quality of its products, the company is surviving today.

ON MY OWN

However, to get the best out of a person in the private sector some of the promoters make tall promises and ultimately they don't fulfill them. Same thing happened with me but I considered that as a blessing in disguise. I decided to work for myself. While working for others I had sacrificed my family life despite being recently married, virtually giving my blood for the organisation and I realised that I had the potential and requisite expertise to conceive a project and implement it fully. So I started my hunt for the right project based on my background and experience.

THE VENTURE

During my tenure at Thapar I had developed bio-fertiliser and cattle feed. During my survey, I realise that these products were going to become popular in due course of time because of the abundant knowledge now available with public about the hazards associated with synthetic fertilisers. Also, both the State and Central Government were promoting use of bio-fertilisers. I was quite confident about the feasibility. So I prepared the project report and went to Thapars. They refused to help in the beginning on the grounds that their technologies were not meant for outsiders. Somehow I convinced them that I would not mis-utilise the technology. Then I finalised my project report and like any other first generation entrepreneur started moving from one agency to the other.

ENABLING ATTITUDE OF BANKERS

I approached State Bank of India (SBI) and they were able to see my latent entre-preneurial skills and they started appraising the project in the right earnest. I must admit that I was fortunate to meet some very positive thinking officials of SBI. A person who helped me a lot was Mr. S.S.Sharma, Chief Manager, SBI Consultancy Cell. He was truly a catalyst in the project. When I told him that I had the necessary knowledge and expertise for implementing such a project, he insisted that backup of a well known name was required to establish the product in the market as this was a relatively new concept. He was convinced about my technical knowledge and capability as an employee but felt that entrepreneurship was a different ball game altogether. He visited TCRDC and then made the necessary corrections in the project. Other financial institutions insisted on equity participation by Thapar while SBI did not make an issue out of this and just asked me to acquire the technology. SBI also advised us to first prove our work by starting a small project and later take the quantum leap. They appraised the project very quickly after getting convinced about the entrepreneurial abilities of promoters particularly my partners Mr. J.Srinivasa Rao, Executive Director, and Mr. D.L.N.Shastry.

SBI then sanctioned Rs. 225 lakhs out of total project cost of Rs. 402 lakhs while we brought Rs. 107 lakhs. Our friends and family members gave us their whole hearted support. We then stopped all our other activities including quitting the job as I was till then working as General Manager, India Vitamins Ltd. after helping them in tying up for the technology for which they had offered me a post on the Board.

MALADIES AND REMEDIES

Rs. 70 lakhs were left to be taken from some financial institution as venture capital. That is where we faced some serious difficulties. All the venture capital companies that I approached neither appreciated the new concept nor our capabilities, but were only concerned with commercial aspects. Then we came to know of Technology Development Board (TDB), Department of Science & Technology (DST) and their schemes of assistance for entrepreneurs through an advertisement in the newspaper. Initially, my reaction was that of skepticism—this must be another governmental agency with its associated red tape and they would kill the project even before it was born. However, as there was no other opening available, I decided to meet Mr. S.B. Krishnan, Secretary, TDB and that meeting changed my life. Right in the beginning he clarified that TDB could give us soft loan and was not interested in equity participation.

He asked us to immediately submit the proposal and to our pleasant surprise it was cleared within 8 weeks. The project was appraised by well known experts like Dr. C.R.Bhatia, Dr. Karan Singh and Mr. Mohan Kumar. They were fully convinced about the concept and the promoter's capabilities and also the viability of the product getting acceptance in the market. After clearing all doubts. TDB gave us the first instalment in the third week of March 1998. We didn't waste a single day.

ABOUT PRATHISTA

Prathista was registered as a limited Company in December 1996 though I continued working elsewhere till the TDB sanction came in. We performed the Bhoomi Puja in 1998 and within a record time of four months we were able to start trial run by September 1998. To prove our capabilities and our sincerity to the project both to our promoters and financers we commissioned a pilot plant on 3rd May, 1998. In fact we are now working on our second project Prathista Bio-tech Ltd. for which we have signed another MOU with TDB on 10th February, 1999. Prathista means Prestige I am confident Prathista will bring prestige for promoters and supporters and also the society and the country.

MARKETING

Our product "Suryamine" is now sold all over the country though we are obviously stronger in the South due to locational advantage. The product, a plant growth tonic, increases the production and quality of variety of plants and crops. It is an import substitute. We have also introduced a low cost high protein cattle feed which has been very well accepted by the market. Though Prathista had entered into an agreement with an Andhra based Distribution Company to market its products, we now sell directly also all over India. Further, we have exported small quantities to Germany and plan to sell globally. In the first three months of operations, our turnover crossed Rs. 1 crore mark.

My work force in the factory is only 40 people, while I have more than 100 persons working in the marketing department.

PRODUCT REPORT

Our concept is re-circulation of proteins back to the soil. According to the findings of Central Research Institute for Dry - Land Agriculture, use of Suryamine on Castor crop has led to vigorous growth of plants with self strength and also led to an in-crease in the yield by 130 kgs/ hectare. Similarly, the yield of cotton, sunflower and chillies crop also increased substantially.

We want to reduce overheads at the factory level and increase promotional level activity at the farmer level and educate them in the use of bio-fertilisers. Our product quality has been rated as "Excellent" by the end user. Spurred by the success of this product, we have introduced new formulations of Suryamine for wheat, paddy, sunflower and maize crops. We have got excellent reports from all over Andhra Pradesh and parts of Tamil Nadu, Karnataka and Punjab. We have recently had a tie up with the Delhi based company for marketing and distribution of our products in this part of the country. We have such a tie up with Thapars that if any development that takes place in this filed will be given to us. In fact there is a lock in period of 7 years during which Thapars will not give this technology to anybody else.

COMPETITION

Basically, agricultural community is such that fly-by-night operators in this field are cheating the farmers by making large claims about their products. They even pass on any chemical which they can lay their hands on cheaply as the bio-fertiliser which later creats lot of problems for established players like us. However, they can sell the product only for one crop or one season and as the product does not deliver the expected yield the farmers become wary of such products. Otherwise, there is not much Competion as such, as number of genuine manufacturers are very few. Fortunately this menace is being now checked by both State as well Central Government and the farmer is being educated by them. In fact once we also were brought in the net by State Government but we were able to prove our worth and now our product is approved by the State Government. Otherwise, we could have crossed Rs. 2 crore turnover by now.

RESEARCH AND DEVELOMENT

Since the product is accepted at the grassroots level, we have also put up our own R&D unit, as advised by Mr. Krishnan, with the intention of creating better products for the farmer. Prof. V.S.Ramamurthy, Secretary, DST, advised us to use our own fertiliser in the 30 acre plot of land we have and virtually convert our backyard into field testing laboratory. We bought some cattle to experiment with our cattle feed and see the results. We now have a full fledged R&D lab which is an independent entity of the Prathista Group. We have installed state-of-the-art equipment and a dedicated team of scientists working in this 3000 sq. ft. unit. We have applied for recognition of our R&D Centre by Department of Scientific and Industrial Research. We have been able to develop a liquid cattle feed which has been sent to Germany for analysis and whose field trials by the farmers have shown excellent results.

FUTURE PLANS

All of us, who have promoted the Prathista Group, are technically very strong in the field of starch and its derivatives, particularly from corn and tapioca and our focus in on expansion in the related fields. As I have mentioned earlier, we have already promoted our second venture in biotechnology and we are very confident that we will again complete the project before schedule. We have selected new generation derivatives for making lactic acid and also maltoseanc malto-dextrin from starch. No friends circle but only thorough professionals like Mr. K.G. Murthy, its Managing Director are in-volved in the group. We have over a decade long association and understand our strengths.

TEAM WORK

I strongly believe that my group's success largely depends on the excellent team working with the group. All the Directors are professionals with clear cut responsibility for various functions. I look after Marketing and Finance while Mr. Srinivasa Rao looks after Operations. None of us is related to each other. Even if any of us is not there, the company can run on its own. This is all due to the total commitment of the team and that is why we are probably the very first company who will get soft loan from TDB for its second project also.

FAMILY

I must admit that my main strength is my wife Pranita. Ours was a love marriage and we got married after five years of courtship. We have a very good understanding. I strongly believe that behind every successful man there is an understanding and devoted wife. Without support of the family members it is not possible to do much. I have two children—a son and a daughter and bringing them up is Pranita's major occupation though she is also a Director in the company. I am not able to devote much time to them but still we are a very cohesive unit. I am able to play with my son in the morning and with my daughter late at night. Of late my wife has sometimes complained that I am not devoting much time to the family but that is just a temporary phase. She knows that this is just the beginning of my entrepreneurial career. If I don't work at this stage of my life, I will not beable to fulfil my dreams and aspirations.

STRENGTHS

As mentioned earlier our major strengths are technical expertise and perseverance of the promoters, choice of the product, commitment of the entire team, support from family and friends, enabling attitude of Bankers, TDB and State Government, agencies and above all Faith. Though I belong to an orthodox peasant family I believe that God helps those who help themselves.

Questions

1. Explain how the concept of window and corrider contributed to Mr. KVSS Sairam becoming an entrepreneur.
2. Mr. Sairam had a very successful carrier as an engineer and a manager. Discuss the motives that prompted him to become an entrepreneur.
3. Discuss the role of Financial Institution in promoting new ventures. How did SBI and Technology Development Board help in the creation of "PRATHISTA"?
4. Discuss the factors that contributed to the success of PRATHISHTA.

Source: Science Tech Entrepreneur, March-April, 1999.

Integrated Case Study–2

SUMEET'S INNOVATIVE SUCCESS

In the beginning, middle-aged housewife Madhuri Mathur clucked in annoyance as her Barun mixer coughed to a halt. "Motor is burnt" diagnosed husband Satya Prakash, a mechanical engineer at Siemens. "Damn these imported mixies", he said.

This dismay gave way to a dream. Was it possible to design a mixer that would stand heavier grinding loads? Mathur dashed of a few designs. He designed a mixer with a 400 watts motor with 30 minutes rating, that was better than any imported mixer. As he painstakingly poured over them checking for flaws, he could feel the excitement. The dream grew into an obsession.

In 1963, Shri Satya Prakash Mathur and his wife Madhuri stared Power Control and Appliances Pvt. Ltd. In those days there were a lot of restrictions on imports, and imported mixers were available only as smuggled item. No Indian manufacturer could even meet the standards of these smuggled mixers, yet PCA instead of competing with other indegeneous manufacturers decided not to compromise on quality. Their aim was to develop a machine that woud help a Indian housewife and working women.

With Rs. 40,000 raised by selling his car and borrowings from friends Mathur acquired a 600 sq. feet shed at Mulund, a Mumbai suburb. Here they started manufacturing the mixers. The first batch of "Sumeet" mixers consisted of 250 machines which were bought mainly by friends and relatives. Shri S.C.Mathur, Satya Prakash's cousin, an engineer with Brown Boveri in Germany left his lucrative job and joined Mathurs.

The feedback provided by there customers was crucial. Mrs Mathur acted as a customer for the company. For a long time her testing and approval were a must before any item was shipped out.

In five years time, the Sumeet mixers had secured a place in middle class Indian households. The demand exceeded the production. The company attributes two reasons for the same, (i) quality and versatility of their mixers, (ii) import restrictions on consumer durables. Since, the production of domestic kitchen machines was reserved for small scale sector, there were restriction on the expansions. Mathurs set up eight separate ventures. Sumeet Research and Holdings Private Limited become the owner of the trademark 'Sumeet'.

At a time when many other companies were scurrying to the west for colaboration, Sumeet decided to do it alone. Nor does it plan to depart from this track in the near future says Ajay Mathur, Satya Parkash's elder son, who now heads Sumeet Machines Private Ltd. "Collaboration in India is a rip off".

How did Sumeet made good on its own stream? Answer : It found the right mix *of* marketing strategy and product development that the mixer market needed. This gave it an immediate edge over the imported mixers that were around in the sixties. It sustained this approach through the seventies, when sales spiralled. By the times others work up to the possibilities, Sumeet was already deeply entranched with a solid brand image. Even in eighties, the 40 and odd competing brands—among them, many regional ones such as Rico in the west, Meenu mix in the south or Gopi in the north—have been unable to budge Sumeet from its dominant position. In ninties Sumeet had 55 to 60% market share.

Mathur says : "We know, no one will believe our product was better than the imported ones unless we demonstrated it. We had to convince them that our machine was especially designed for Indian cooking which needed ingredients to be ground to a fine powder. Indian housewife needs a tough grinding machine. European working, in contrast, is based on blending and liquidising — which are totally different concepts". Sumeet tried to incorporate these differences into the very design of the mixers. "We had to design a high powered motor which could run at a high speed" says Mathur.

But desgining a suitable product was not enough. Consumers, essentially housewives also had to be shown that the mixers actually worked better. It had to be proved that practical utility of a "tough work horse" like Sumeet out weight the prestige of owning an imported brand. This was the challenge Sumeet faced.

Mathur says, "we selected 18-20 young people in different regions. These were clerks who needed part time jobs and so on. We asked them to hold demonstrations in their regions. People would bring their in gredients for idlis or dosas (in the south) or chatni, and we would grind it for them".

This technique worked. It enabled Sumeet to reach countless kitchens without the hassle of setting up an enormous sales organisation. As sales grew, so did the incomes of Sumeet's representatives. Over a period, 18-20 representative emerged as authorised service dealers. Service network is the back-bone of Sumeet. It has 36 main service centres in the country presently. It provides two years guarantee and all its products confirm to BIS specifications. Ajay Mathur says : "At Sumeet consumer has always been the king".

The representative and service centre network provided Sumeet with another vital resource : feed backs. Most common problems went back to Mathur and his group of engineers, who tried to solve them by improving upon the original design. The original glass jar was abandoned for an aluminium jar in 1967, and stainless steel jar in 1975. A team of dedicated engineers constantly worked to meet the growing consumer demands through product innovation. Through the feed back system they realised that grinding masala for the dosa was a tougher job and different from the dry grinding. The R & D team innovated and developed a wet grinding blade that pulverised the batter for dosa to the satisfaction of a South Indian housewife. Now Sumeet mixer comes with a set of four replacable blades. Latter a food processor and juicer attachments were added. "If we could add any new feature, we would. Developing new attachments and product upgradation have always been important elements of our marketing strategy."

These constant efforts at redesigning the mixers enabled Sumeet to evolve a product that responded to the consumer needs. Price on the other hand, was kept low. Any concessions on exercise or sales tax were passed on to the customer. Thus, while sales climbed steadily, price rose slowly.

Meanwhile, the market place was changing, increasingly, at least in the cities, fewer families were *'sick'* (single income, couple of kids) and a rising number of *'dink'* (double income no kids). While the disposable income of 'dinks' grew, less time was becoming available for cooking. Both these factors helped Sumeet increase its sales exponentially.

Mounting sales forced Sumeet to confront another thorny problem of servicing. The volumes were no longer manageable by dealers alone. The company hit upon a unique solution of mobile vans in every town and the 40 service centres all over the country. Mathur says, "Each van houses a service centre. They go from dealer to dealer once a week. We have to keep every machine working".

Sumeet's dealers claim that this servicing technique gives them an edge over competition. A dealer says, "If we get any complaints, we ask the customers to bring their machine to our shop on any Friday. This way they can get is repaired in a week or two". The competing brands do not offer this advantage.

Through constant innovation Sumeet launched SP–16. The electronic food processor. "This has been a major break through," claims Mathur. "It is totally a new concept. There is no comfortable product either here or abroad." SP–16 became increasingly popular abroad. In two years time it added Rs. 8 crore to Sumeet's turnover as against 30 crore from other domestic machines. SP–16 was another instance based upon Sumeet's own R&D.

"We did not had a very high R & D budget," says Mathur. What we have is plenty of enthusiasm and desire to learn. When we make a product, we spend a lot of time perfecting it. Building an appliance is very emotional experience. A lot of feeling goes into what we do. This is our approach towards R & D. As a result, the SP–16 can perform many jobs which the mechanical Sumeet could not. Mathur claims, it has a bigger motor, a jar with greater capacity and an electronic control. " Electronics had made Sumeet so much better", says Mathur. "It still looks similar, but engineering is much advanced ".

In 1990, a food processing attachment that could provide the user the functions of kneading, chopping, shredding, grating, slicing etc., was added. The food processor also does the functions of the old mixer and is thus a complete kitchen machine.

What keeps Sumeet going ahead, more than anything else, is the combination of professionalism with family feeling. S.P. Mathur's eldest son Ajay, an MBA from USA joined as marketing director and the second son Vivak, a qualified electronics engineer has joined as director incharge of R & D. "We all tend to get involved as a family", observes Mathur. "Our products go to other families, and we have a family commitment towards them".

It was family feeling which gave SP–16 its name. "It was a gift I gave my father", smiles Mathur. "The initial represents his name, Satya Prakash, and his birthday is on 16th". He hopes that some day, "my son will do what I have done. I would like to give him the same support my family gave me. This family commitment binds one generation to another".

All the allied companies of Sumeet pay better salaries than other simmilar units. Get-togethers are regularly organised for the workers by the management. Three-fourth of the workers are women and their approach to the labour is personalised. Most women work on with Sumeet even after their marriage.

But it has not been roses all the way for Sumeet. Like other companies, it has its share of set backs. It launched a hair styling product — Dry & Style's. The product bombed as they realised that people who used hair styles preferred imported stylers. The product was soon withdrawn. Sumeet's success lies in the fact that over 2.5 million house holds are happy using this machine.

Questions

1. How did Mathur's family contributed to success of their enterprise?
2. Describe the corridor principle and how it seemed to propell Mr. Mathur in setting up Sumeet.
3. Identify the main success factors of Sumeet.
4. Discuss the role of innovation in an entrepreneur's success. How did it help Mathur's?

Integrated Case Study–3

Mr. RAMAN

Mr. Raman sat puffing a cigaratte fidgeting with his spectacles, wondering which way the smoke will below. Mr. Raman, 35 architectural consultant was under pressure. He was wondering as to how to arrange Rs. 10 lakh within 10 days' time to grab the Rs. 45 lakh project from M/s Nova Continental Corporation Ltd.

In 1975 as a fresh graduate in Architecture, Mr. Raman had discovered that it was not easy to get a lucrative job (say for Rs. 1800/- per month). He had taken competitive examinations, had tried some foreign assignments, but all in vain.

Mr. Raman's elder brothers aged 28 and 25 were technically qualified and employed with big corporations. They were earning more than Rs. 3,000/- per month. His father had five more years to retire from government service.

Mr. Raghu, a friend of Mr. Raman used to visit Mr. Raman now and then. Mr. Raman used to share some of his problems and anxieties with Mr. Raghu. In one such meeting, Mr. Raman said to Mr. Raghu, "My family is basically a service base one. I also tried first to get a job. However, my efforts to get a job came to an end in September 1975. I was partially successful in the sense that I got a part-time job with an architectural firm that did not offer a lucrative salary. I accepted the offer. Later on, however, I found that to do justice to my job, it required my full time attention. It was then that I made up my mind to go for my own architectural firm. Though I had made up my mind to set-up my own architectual firm, yet for three months I was in a dilemma as to whether actually do so or try for another job elsewhere".

Mr. Raman set up his own architectural consultancy firm at Oklha, Phase I in September 1976 called M/s Raman & Company. As a specialist in interior designing he could get some small jobs from local factories and offices for designing the interiors of their premises. The units annual turnover was in the range of Rs. 1.75 lakhs to 2.25 lakhs.

After two years Mr. Raman won a hotel contract for architectural designing. The three star Hotel Triveni was a Rs. 3 crore project for which Mr. Raman had won the contract against competing with other reputed architectural firms. He charged Rs. 2.5 lakh as consultancy fee for this project. He had quoted the lowest amount which an architect would never quote for such a big job. According to him, other consultants had quoted a consultancy fee of Rs. 4.5 lakh to Rs. 6 lakh for the same job. He said to Mr. Raghu, "Though I has quoted the lowest fee for the work, I felt proud of handling it successfully. However, that big job with a great deal of involvement but proportionately less income affected my unit's local functioning at Delhi. I had often thought of expanding my team to handle big projects but I was not sure of getting big projects on a continuous basis. I came to realise that taking up a big project with the existing staff was not a profitable proposition".

Meanwhile, Mr. Raman's father who had by now (1981) retired from government service, advised him to stop worrying about his own consultancy firm and take up a salaried job-elsewhere. His elder brothers also held the same opinion, mainly due to his physical strain involved in carrying out time-bound jobs. His father and brothers persisted with their suggestions. Mr. Raman said to them, "I am not ready for a salaried job anywhere. I will run any own firm any how".

Mr. Raman got a project from M/s Blue Diamond Co. for interior designing of their office building and the house of the proprietor. Mr. Raman took keen interest in accomplishing the task in time and submitted the final designs and plans to M/s Blue Diamond Co. However, the proprietor of M/s Blue

The case is prepared by NIESBUD, New Delhi.

Diamond Co, Ltd., Mr. B.R. Kapoor entrusted the task of executing the plans to Mr. Raman himself, something that no one had asked him before.

Mr. Raman's estimate for the interior designing of the factory and house was Rs. 55,000/- under various heads such as flooring, ceiling, furniture, curtains, carpets, electrical fittings, window panel, paints etc. With the task of implementing the plans in hand, Mr. Raman began to have doubts about the accuracy of his estimates. He had neither done such a job before nor did he have any feedback on his plans. However, Mr. Raman decided to take up the implementation part of the plans too. M/s Blue Diamond Co. Ltd. approved of Mr. Raman's estimates. They had laid the condition that no further price escalation would be acceptable. They also agreed to pay to Mr. Raman a 10% commission on the total estimates.

Mr. Raman said to Mr. Raghu, "Even though I had some doubts about my own estimates. Yet I decided to implement the job to test these estimates". He went on to add, "during execution, the furniture part made me mad. It was not easy to get the furniture items as per my specification and rates. There was no other go as I was already half-way through with the project. The expense on furntire items not only escalated but quality was not as expected and took most of my time". After five weeks Mr. Raman was able to execute the plans and got his commission. The proprietor of M/s Blue Diamond Co. Ltd., said to Mr. Raman, "Well done Mr. Raman I like your taste. You have really done an excellent job".

But Mr. Raman had spent five weeks time on this alone. Meanwhile, his unit was unable to complete other assignments in time. The proprietor of M/s. Blue Diamond Co. Ltd. invited Mr. Raman for his 'Grahapravesh' (House warming) ceremony. There Mr. Raman was introduced to the industrialist circle, who were all special invites of M/s Blue Diamond Co. Ltd. Mr. Raman said to Mr. Raghu, "At the function, though I was smiling and mingling with the guests, I was feeling bad about having taken a risk as well as the additional role of execution".

After two weeks of the ceremony, Mr. Raman started getting similar types of assignments for interior designing and execution. Mr. Raman recalled to Mr. Raghu that he was not able to jump happily at the assignments, as the furniture items were a headache and would swallow both time and profit. At the same time, Mr. Raman found that his consultancy alone (without taking execution of jobs) was not providing a comfortable margin. To support the firm, he had to take up work involving implementation and execution. Mr. Raman had three such assignments, each with a different budget.

It was a major decision to take up the execution part of all the three jobs at the same time. In the process, he said, he had to consider going in for a furniture unit of his own. He shared with Mr. Raghu that he was bothered about how to manage the initial investment on furniture item? How much money was needed to invest on such a furniture firm? He felt sure of one thing that unless he manufactured the furniture items he was not going to make money out of the jobs involving execution. Moreover, he said to Mr. Raghu, "It was not just the money or profit I was bothered about but also the quality of the furniture supplied to the clients. I used to receive complaints on furniture supplied (through other dealers), for which I had to depend on the supplier for service or repairing. This was also one of the reason why I decided to go for the furniture venture too. At that time, however, I had only Rs. 2000/- with me. I still decided to carry out the jobs".

Mr. Raman took up all the three jobs at the same time and asked the parties to pay him an advance of 50% of the estimated amount. The parties paid him some advance. The total amount that he received as advance was barely enough to start his furniture unit.

The decision to start a furniture unit was questioned by members of Mr. Raman's family, and also his previous professor. His professor asked him as to why did he have to manufacture furniture; designing would be an appropriate job (to handle) for an architect. An architect was not meant to go for furniture-mart. Mr. Raman told his professor that he had no complex about taking up a furniture unit and thought that it was quite all right to do so. His family members told him that going for a furniture unit was not a dignified job for an architect.

Mr. Raman also told them that in order to get job satisfaction he would not only like to design furniture, but would also enjoy the risk and involvement needed for a furniture venture, and derive pleasure out of giving the best possible furniture to his clients.

The wood was expensive. After making a thorough survey, Mr. Raman fixed a dealer for supply of necessary wood for his new unit. However, Mr. Raman had to give the wood dealer an advance of 50% of the value of the wood ordered. Mr. Raman was not happy to spend so much on wood alone without having enough order, and also his unit's establishment expenses were pressing. Mr. Raman's previous employment experience with an architectural firm came in handy to enable him to locate wood suppliers, dealers, carpenters etc.

His next step was to complete atleast the committed assignments. This time, he worked out a systematic plan by charting out the various functions involved, Mr. Raman's chart of functions from the procurement stage to implementation stages are given in Appendix I. He executed the three jobs in time keeping within the estimated budget and earned a profit. Mr. Raman said to Mr. Raghu that he felt encouraged and now wanted to take up big projects in interior designing and execution.

One such project came from M/s Nova Continental Corporation (NCC). He was surprised to learn that he had won the contract despite severe competition. The project was worth Rs. 45 lakhs and 20% of the total cost, *i.e.,* Rs. 9 lakhs as advance he got from NCC Ltd. Even after taking Rs. 9 lakh as advance Mr. Raman needed an additional Rs. 10 lakhs to carry out the order. Mr. Raman knew that carrying out the order without sufficient capital was not feasible. He also knew that his involvement in this project would divert his units activities from his local clients.

Mr. Raman had to state his willingness to take up the work within 15 days time, *i.e.,* after taking up the order and the execution time was 90 days from the date of acceptance; else NCC Ltd., would withdraw their offer and give the assignment to the firm that was ranked second to Mr. Raman'sfirm. Mr. Raman said, "This involvement would definitely put my unit to go for full time furniture job and architectural unit will take a secondary role". Mr. Raman was worrying what to do and how to go about it.

QUESTIONS

1. Discuss different barriers faced by Raman in his persuit for self-employment and what factors motivated him to setup his own enterprise.
2. The growth of Raman's enterprise was not smooth. If you were in his position how would you react? What traits in Raman helped him pull on?
3. Put yourselves in Roman's position and how would you solve the dilemma?

APPENDIX I

Execution Chart

Owners Name ....

Address ....

Telephone No........ Date of Giving Estimate................

		Labour Charges					Material Cost				
S. No.	Description of Item	Carpentry	Polish	Weaving of Upholstery	Carving or Inlay	Laith or Curve	Wood or Ply Board	Glass & Sunmica	Dori & Upholstery	Cloth & Leather	Polish or Hardware

Total

Note :— 1. Upholstery Buyer .... Terms & Conditions
2. Quantity of Cloth ....
3. Date of Requirement .... 1. Cartage
4. Design & Shade ....
5. Approx Cost ....

S. No.

Date of Order .... Date of Delivery .... Job No...................

Valuation			Remarks			Carpentry Schedule			Polishing	
Total L+M	Overheads 45%	Total Cost	Profit 15%	Sale Price	Carpanters Name	Start Date	Complete Date	Polishers Name	Start Date	Complete Date

Details of Advances

Date	Amount	Cheque No.	Bank

Estimated Cost ....

Actual Cost ....

Less Advance...................

Balance Due ....

Integrated Case Study–4

RATNA ENTERPRISE

Ratna thought that problems had become a part of her life. She had learnt to live with them; she had also learnt to find ways of solving them. It is like a game of balance "the more one practices the more adept one becomes, but with a danger of falling". She said thoughtfully to Latika.

Latika was an entrepreneurship development trainer. She had known Ratna for a long time and used to visit Ratna now and then. Latika had developed a close friendship with her. Ratna too used to find Latika a good friend with whom she could talk about herself and what was happening to her.

She shared aloud with Latika that even though her efforts had been well rewarded, yet she has been confronting her problems at the cost of her physical health. Ratna, was married to Sunil Bhargava in 1982. She was the eldest of her two sibilings. Her father was a Senior Government Official. She had done her Post Graduation from Jawaharlal Nehru University (JNU) at Delhi. Subsequently, she had also done a Diploma in Pustho-Afghani. She had earned an assignment in Afghanistan but had given that up on account of her marriage.

Sunil Bhargava, her husband was running a printing press called 'Skylark' with his younger brother Anil. The youngest brother Kapil was independently engaged in Liaison work. Sunil's father, Vikram Bhargava, in his late sixties had retired from his job with the railways. Mrs. Padma, Sunil's mother was a housewife.

Soon after stepping into the Bhargava's household. Her mother-in-law told Ratna that her expectation from her was that she would do the household, chores. Ratna observed that women in Bhargava's family confined themselves to the home. She being the eldest daughter-in-law took it upon herself to shoulder the responsibility of the household jobs.

After about six months, Ratna began to feel stiffed within confines of the four walls. A job of Rs. 1500 /- per month with a Public Undertaking materialised at that time. This was a job that she had applied for before her marriage. She wanted to take that up. But Sunil, Anil and her father-in-law said, "It is not worth a job of Rs. 1500/- per month," Ratna fell discouraged. "But 1 did not give up", she commented Latika.

Ratna thought of convincing Sunil, "An educated women's place was not only at home. I could contribute elsewhere too". She said to him. She thought that Sunil was convinced as he said "I understand you Ratna, but how can I speak to my father on this issue?" Ratna throught that Sunil wouldn't be of much help.

Skylark was started by Sunil and Anil in 1979. The press was earning a gross profit of 10 to 15 per cent on the investment, Anil thought that this was not good enough. Sunil discussed this with Ratna. She thought that Sunil and Anil lacked proper planning and pointed this out to them. In a joint discussion, Anil commented, "Ratna Bhabi, business is not your cup of tea. You better concentrate more on the family. Ratna felt hurt. "I suppressed my feelings but decided that I'll show them that I too can manage a business. I took it as a challenge." She told Latika, "Sunil in the meantime, thought that some of her suggestion regarding their funds flow, overhead expenses and execution of orders were helpful. He thought of looking into these points. Following her suggestions he was able to control his overhead expenses and manage his orders better "I feel proud of you Ratna", he said to her.

Ratna too felt a deep sense of satisfaction and encouragement. She shared her idea wth her family. Except Sunil nobody either encouraged (or discouraged) her, she felt determined to go head.

The case is prepared by NIESBUD, New Delhi.

After almost two years of marrige, in December 1983, Ratna attended an Entrepreneurship Development Training Programme for Women at the National Institute for Entrepreneurship and Small Business Development (NIESBUD) at Delhi. This was where she had first met Latika. "This was a turning point for me. I got a sense of direction and impetus towards what I wanted to do", she said to Latika.

During the training, Ratna decided Sunil could have been of some help in that, but more because that she would take up specialised printing work. She thought of printing because she wanted to show her-in-laws that she could do the same job in a better way.

After the training, the National Small Industries Corporation (NSIC) at Delhi provided her a loan of Rs. 1,53,902 for buying two machines, a printing machine (Mercedse) and a machine for Dye cutting and Punching. This was under the hire purchase scheme, where the loan repayment had to be made in 13 instalments by the end of the seventh year.

Reflecting upon that period she said to Latika, "this was a trying time for me. The Government officials thought that I only wanted to help my husband. I had to prove my genuineness to them on the one hand and the other I also had to prove my competence".

After a period of 11 months "Ratna Enterprises" was born adjacent to Skylark. Since the beginning, she did not take my any help from the Bhargava family, she said to Latika that she only needed Sunil's moral support, which she got. Ratna began with a working capital of Rs. 1,83,902/-. She took Rs. 20,000/- from friends of Sunil and she contributed Rs. 10,000/- of her own money.

With Sunil's assistance she hired two skilled workers. She decided to aim at earning - credibility in the market with her specialised job and also to plan her actions. Ratna enterprises took the job of printing for medical and pharmaceutical packaging. Ratna got her first order of Rs. 20,000 from Global Pharmaceutical Laboratory (GPL.). Mr. Harish the Managing Director to GPL was known to Sunil. Ratna worked nearly 12 hours a day to get her first orders ready in time. She spent time in learning the technical know how and attending to quality inspection. Her first order proved to be the beginning of a boom. By the end of the first year her order position rose from Rs, 20,000 to Rs. 1.05 lakhs.

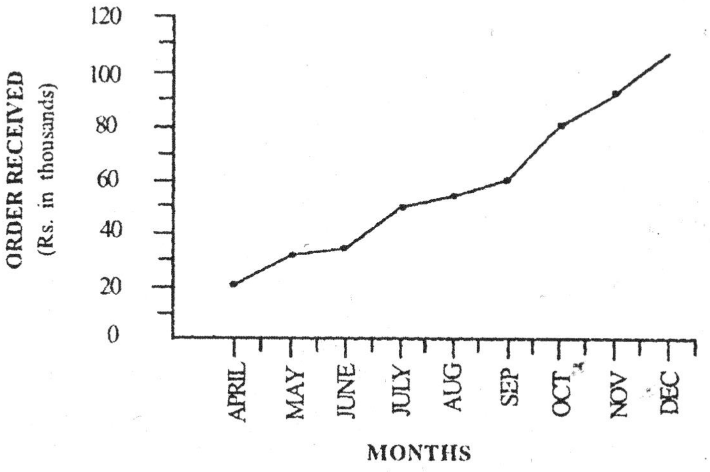

She used to pay her suppliers either immediately or at the most within a week. Through GPL Ratna got some contacts around Delhi and also at Patna.

Ratna told Latika that she expected that this would give her recognition in the Bhargava family. Her father-in-law told her to wait and watch. While Anil and Kapil did not say anything. On the other hand Padma Bhargava said that she was neglecting her house and her household responsibilities. Sunil intervented and said "how can she do the house job when she is in the factory for so long". Padma felt that her son was taking his wife's side. She stopped speaking to Ratna. Sunil felt tensed.

Ratna felt guilty and wanted to restore the family peace at any cost." I did not keep any time for any relaxation. I used to get up at five in the morning, serve tea and breakfast to everyone and prepare lunch before going to the factory. She said to Latika that she wanted to show her in-laws that she could be a good housekeeper too.

With the increase of workload, both at home and at the unit, she employed two salesmen.

Sunil said that he would like to help her but she told him that she would seek his help when she needed it. She did not want to disturb him.

The network of Ratna Enterprises started expanding, 70 per cent of her clients belonged to Patna,

GPL had helped her in establishing contacts at Patna. Reflecting with a smile in her eyes she said to Latika, "Now I can spread my wings and fly".

With the increase in business in 1987 the liquidity become lean. Payments were taking longer than expected. "There has always been a problem". Ratna however maintained her payment policy towards her suppliers and clients. But gradually she thought that the situation was going beyond her control. "Although I wanted to be a very good paymaster, my hands are tied. I was afraid that I would lose my credibility in the market". She said helplessely to Latika.

Ratna Enterprises despite having orders was stuck due to lack of funds. She did not want to disturb her fixed cost and moreover the loan repayment of Rs. 3,500 per month had to be made. She thought of sharing her problems with Sunil whom she knew was concerned about her. But Anil and Kapil were watching the fun and speculating as to what would happen next. By then Rs. 1,80,000 was due from the market. Ratna personally launched a drive to collect the money. She managed to collect Rs. 30,000. The GPL owed the maximum amount of Rs. 1,00,000/- although initially she hesitated, but finally she approached Mr. Harish. He asked her to contact Mr. Singh who was a partner and was looking after the marketing office at Patna. She thought that Mr. Harish had handled the situation very diplomatically.

Ratna went to Patna for a day. She wanted to face the situation alone. She met Mr. Singh and said, "I need my payment which is overdue for 10 months. Till I get it. I will not leave this office. Mr. Singh said, "I appreciate your problem but I am unable to pay more than Rs. *25,00(11-* to you at the moment. 1 am helpless". However, Mr. Singh went on to add casually, "Why don't you take our new Maruti Van instead of Rs. 85,000/-. "Ratna took on the spot decision and agreed to the proposal. "I felt great", she exclaimed to Latika.

When she came back to Delhi, Anil commented, "What a Luxury!". Her father-in-law told Sunil that, he should have accompanied Ratna. This was not a good decision he thought.

But the van proved to be an asset. Ratna's transport expenses come down to Rs. 500/ - from Rs. 1500 /- per month. Her sales shot up as she was more mobile now, her in laws began to use the van whenever they needed. Sunil's parents appreciated her for the first time. She felt good about it.

Anil got married in mid 1986. Within two months of his marriage, he expressed his inability to contribute to the family expenditure. Ratna's in-laws were silent. They did not say anything to their son. Ratna thought that, she should take responsibility. Sunil felt that it would be too much of a burden on her. "I got a chance to prove my worth" Ratna shared with Latika with a sparkle in her eyes.

Her financial contribution to the family rose from 60 percent to 80 per cent. The family members and some close relatives even commented that Ratna had proved to be a son rather that a daughter-in-law. Padma said to Latika, "Ratna brought peace in my house".

Ratna thought that peace had came and her respect had been restored in the family never mind even if it had been at her own cost. She told Latika, "My health started deteriorating. 1 lost about 4kg of weight. I was under constant pressure to please everyone I had no time for myself I was tense all time". Thoughtfully she added to Latika, was all this worth it. How long can I go on like this?

QUESTIONS

1. What made Ratna to start her own business?
2. What factors inhibited Ratna's Entrepreneurial drive?
3. Do you agree that Ratna is competent to become an entrepreneur?

Appendix

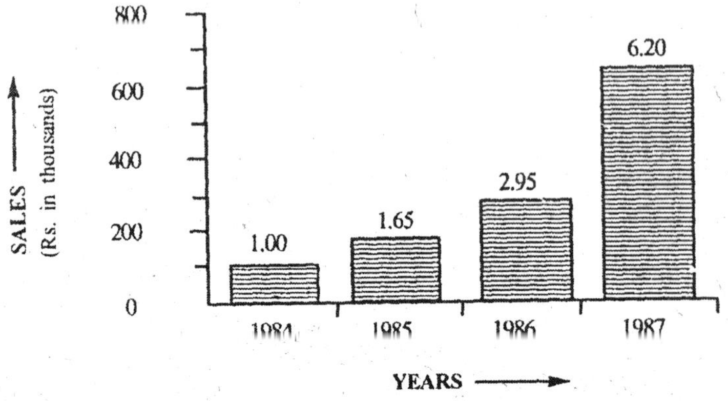

Integrated Case Study–5

Supreme Garage and Work Shop

Anil Adwani, an ITI diploma holder had been working with M/s Supreme Garage and workshop for the last ten years. He had joined as a technician. He was recognised as the best mechanic of Supreme Garage. A good number of clients preferred to get their cars repaired by Anil. In three years time he was promoted as a supervisor. Anil then joined distance education programme of IGNOU and completed his graduation. He studdied accounts and would assist the owner Mr. Ramachandran in maintaining the accounts. Mr. Ramachandran liked him very much and two years back Anil was promoted as the manager of Supreme Garage and Workshop.

Mr. Ramachandran had set up this business about 18 years back when he was retired from Indian Army due to a leg injury. Due to good customer relations and quality service, Supreme Garage had earned a very good reputation and was known as best motor garage in the district. A large number of clients from the neighbouring district would bring in their vehicles to Supreme Garage. The workshop was known for engine overhauling. It had an electrical section for auto electricals and an agency for Exide batteries. Supreme Garage specialised in denting and painting and maintained good relations with insurance companies. It maintained its own two truck and did good business on accidents and break-downs. A large number of clients from the nearby districts were using the services of Supreme Garage. It presently employed ten full time mechanics, one supervisor besides Anil and Ramachandran who were manager and owner respectively. During the rush season the workers worked overtime and additional casual labour was also employed to meet delivery schedules.

For the last one year, Mrs Ramachandran was not keeping well. Six months ago, she had a minor heart attack. Mrs. and Mr. Ramachandran had decided to shift to USA and join their daughter who was a heart specialist at Los Angles, USA. Since, Ramachandran had no family to succeed him, he had decided to sell off the business. He wanted the buyer to run the business on similar lines and maintain its reputation.

He called Anil and made him an offer to sell his business. The initial offer was for Rs. 57.50 lakhs. He also proposed to assist Anil in financing the purchase.

Ramachandran provided him with the information on past earnings with projections for five years. He also provided him with the Balance Sheet and Profit & Loss Accounts of Supreme Garage and Workshop as on 31 March, 2000. He informed Anil that based upon the business flow, he had valued the goodwill as Rs. 15 lakhs.

Anil was excited about the offer. He knew that the business was very profitable and its profits had been increasing by years. It had never been a loss. He consulted a friend who was a banker and also a Chartered Accountant. He had advised him differently. He knew there was a scope of negotiation over the price of the business. Anil now needs assistance.

Sales and Profits of Previous Years

Year	1998	1998
Net sales	81,95,000	90,34,000
PBT	7,37,500	7,56,600
PAT	5,25,000	6,23,200

Summary of Projected Sales and Earnings

Year	2001	2002	2003	2004	2005
Net sales	110,00,000	120,00,000	125,00,000	130,00,000	135,00,000
PBT	8,65,000	9,50,000	10,50,000	12,00,000	12,50,000
PAT	7,00,000	7,80,000	8,60,000	9,30,000	9,75,000

PBT. Profit before tax, PAT Profit after tax.

QUESTIONS

1. Evaluate the value of Supreme Garage and Workshop using discounted cash flow and multiple earning method (Assume 20% required rate of return).
2. How do you think the banker will value this business? Discuss the method and calculate the value.
3. If you were the banker, will you finance?
4. How would you evaluate the goodwill of Supreme Garage and Workshop.
5. As a consultant would you advice Mr. Anil to buy Supreme Garage and Workshop or not. Explain with reasons.

ANNEXURE 1

SUPREME GARAGE and WORKSHOP
Balance Sheet (As on 31.03.2000)

	Rupees
Liabilities	
Capital	16,00,000
Retained Profits	18,10,880
Building Loan	26,99,200
Term loan	12,16,000
Current Liabilities	8,14,400
Total Liabilities	81,40,480
Assets	
Gross Block	66,56,000
Depreciation	14,22,720
Net Block (at the end)	52,33,280
Current Assets	
Stocks	6,65,600
Receivables	13,31,200
Cash in Hand	9,10,400
Total Current Assets	29,07,200
Total Assets	81,40,440

DEPRECIATION SCHEDULE

Rupees

Asset	Gross Block	Depreciation	Net Block
Land & Building	38,40,000	6,16,000	32,24,000
Plant & Eqpt	26,24,000	7,34,720	18,89,280
Other Assets	1,92,000	72,000	1,20,000
Total	66,56,000	14,22,726	55,33,280

SUPREME GARAGE AND WORKSHOP PROFIT & LOSS ACCOUNT
(for Year Ending 31.03.2000)

	Rupees
Net Sales	99,64,800
Cost of Sales	
Direct Wage	30,78,400
Contract Materials	18,83,200
Supplies	2,36,800
Mix Costs	4,24,000
Cost of Sales	56,22,400
Gross Profit from Operations	43,42,400
Operating Expenses	26,35,200
Total Depreciation for the Year	3,76,272
Net Income Before Interest & Taxes	13,30,928
Interest	4,97,440
Profit Before Tax	8,33,488
Income Tax	1,58,240
Net Profit After Tax	6,75,248

SUCCESS STORIES OF ENTREPRENEURS

INTRODUCTION

There are plenty of stories of entrepreneur successes in India. In the following success stories we have selected, a mixture of Rags to Riches cases. The successes mentioned is a mixture of knowledge creativity and innovation with tonnes of individual labour put in by them to take India on the path of global success.

The global economy is changing into a knowledge based economy and it is anticipated that India would be a great business power with further growth of software entrepreneurs as mentioned herein. On this background we have laid stress on the present trends of knowledge based successes which have become role models for generations to follow.

The following examples clearly depicts as one of the business magazines mentions *Democratisation of Indian Business*. Earlier Indian business was run by four clans, they were the Marwaris, Gujrati, Parsis and Chettiars. But many of these families barring few have gone to oblivion because not understanding the need to change and complacency have given way to people with new ideas, creative talent, with risk taking ability and keeping up with new trends.

The success stories of entrepreneurs is recognised as an important source that inspires new entrepreneurs. These stories can be used not only to inspire and motivate the new generation entrepreneurs but as a reservoir of tools and techniques used by the early adapter entrepreneurs to overcome various barriers faced by them.

I. McDQNALD'S

McDonald's is one of the world's premier entrepreneurial success stories. In 1954, 52 years old milk shake machine salesman, Ray Kroc saw a hamburger stand in San Bernardino, California and envisioned a massive new industry- FAST FOOD.

In 1922, Kroc worked as a salesman for the Lily Tulip Cup Co. In the course of selling paper cups he encountered Earl Prince, who had invented a five-spindle multimixer and was buying Lily cups by the truckload. Fascinated by .the speed and efficiency of the machine, Kroc obtained exclusive marketing rights from Prince. Indefatigable, for the next 17 years he crisscrossed the country peddling the mixer.

On his travels he picked up the beat of a remarkable restaurant in San Bernardino, California, owned by two brothers, Dick and Maurice McDonald, who had ordered eight mixers and had them churning away all day. Kroc was entranced by the effectiveness of the operation. It was a hamburger restaurant, though not of the drive-in variety popular at the time. People had to get out of their cars to be served. The brothers had produced a very limited menu, concentrating on just a few items. For less than 50 cents, one could get a cheeseburger, French fries and a shake.

It was Ray Kroc in whose hands the fortune of McDonald's took a hairpin turn. He proceeded to build the company into a global powerhouse. Kroc, ever the instigator, started thinking about building McDonald's stores all over the U.S. & even persuaded the brothers to open up several restaurants. Kroc was so much driven away by the idea of the business that he eventually cajoled them into selling out to him in 1961 for a paltry $2.7 million. Post 1961, Ray Kroc began recruiting franchisees at a feverish pace. The revenues that the company received from the franchisees made it easier for Kroc to raise capital in the financial markets. By 1963 more than 1 billion hamburgers had been sold, a statistic that was displayed on a neon sign in front of each restaurant.

Throughout the company's spectacular growth, Kroc maintained a delicate balancing act, imposing rigorous system-wide standards while encouraging an entrepreneurial spirit that

welcomed ideas from all levels. He revolutionized the American restaurant industry by imposing discipline on the production of hamburgers, French fries & milk shake. By developing a sophisticated operating & delivery system, Kroc ensured that French fries customers bought in Miami would be the same as the one's purchased in San Francisco. Such consistency made McDonald's the brand name that defined American fast food.

Once the domestic market was saturated with McDonald's franchisees, Ray Kroc turned his attention overseas. McDonald's rapidly expanded & improved over the years to become a giant fast food corporation of more than 30,000 stores in about 117 different countries serving about 50 million customers each day.

ENTREPRENEURIAL MILESTONES

- ***Identifying the right opportunity:*** Kroc sensed that America was a nation of people who ate out, as opposed to the Old World tradition of eating at home. Yet he also knew that people here wanted something different. Instead of a structured, ritualistic restaurant with codes and routine, he gave them a simple, casual and identifiable restaurant with friendly service, low prices, no waiting and no reservations. The system eulogized the sandwich — no tableware to wash. One goes to McDonald's to eat, not to dine.
- ***A strong drive to achieve:*** At the age of 52 Kroc had diabetes and incipient arthritis. He had even lost his gall bladder and thyroid gland in earlier campaigns, but still he was convinced that the best was ahead.
- ***An instinct & fetish for hygiene & cleanliness:*** Kroc was a demon for cleanliness. From the overall appearance, to the parking lot, to the kitchen floor, to the uniforms, cleanliness was foremost and essential. "If you have time to lean, you have time to clean," was one of his favorite axioms. He was even quoted saying, "The first impression you get from a restaurant through the eyes and nose is often what determines whether you'll go back."
- ***Innovative firsts:*** Ray Kroc was the first businessman to apply the principles of mass production in a service industry. Though he was a school drop out but a master of creating an everlasting brand. McDonal.ds has taught many corporations how to run their business.
- ***Constant innovation:*** In 1963, 500th McDonald's restaurant opened and the famous clown & mascot, Ronald McDonald, made his debut. Children throughout the country soon knew him, and kids were critical in determining where the family ate. According to John Mariani in his remarkable book *America Eats Out,* "Within six years of airing his first national TV ad in 1965, the Ronald McDonald clown character was familiar to 96% of American children, far more than they knew the name of the President of the United States."
- ***Tailor-made services:*** McDonald's tailor-made its offerings depending on the in-country in which it was operating. In order to make the chain's name more easily pronounceable for Japanese consumers, it was changed to *Makudonaldo.* In India and in the Middle East, pork is not served. In Ireland the promotions proclaimed, "Our name may be American, but we're all Irish."

"The definition of salesmanship is the gentle art of letting the customer have it your way. "

-Ray Kroc

2. NIKE

He might never have played pro sports or owned a sports team, but Philip Knight has been dubbed as the "most powerful person in sports" by Sports Illustrated. Knight turned an idea he first penned in a college essay into the largest sportswear supplier in the world. Philip Knight was a track runner at the University of Oregon. Knight's track coach at the University was Bill Bowerman who had been experimenting with new shoe designs using his wife's waffle iron. In those days running shoes were low quality by today's comparison, with many being made by tire companies and costing as little as $5. Knight, not being the best on the team, often found himself experimenting with Bowerman's latest shoes. Bowerman and Knight worked together to continue to develop the ideas that would become Nike shoes.

Right after graduation Knight enlisted in the Army for a year, and then enrolled at Stanford Graduate School of Business. There was one course in particular that struck his fancy & that was Frank Shallenberger's Small Business class. Shallenberger had given his students an assignment in which they had to invent a new business, describe its purpose, and create a marketing plan. Knight's paper was called, "Can Japanese Sports Shoes Do to German Sports Shoes What Japanese Cameras Did to German Cameras?" In it, Knight developed a blueprint for superior athletic shoes, which could be produced cheaply in Japan "That class was an 'aha!' moment" ...& Knight said to himself: "This is really what I would like to do."

After getting a job with a Portland-based accounting firm, Knight decided to make a trip to Japan to refine his ideas, and help quench his high interest in all things Asian. It was here that he visited an Onitsuka plant, which was making Adidas running shoe knock-offs. So impressed with quality and low cost, he decided to cut a distribution deal in the U.S. with them before leaving.

Together, Knight & Bowerman, each invested $500 and used it to purchase the Tiger shoes from Japan. They founded Blue Ribbon Sports Inc. and set about selling their products. During the day, Knight still worked as an accountant. That is, until 1971, when business had been so successful that he was convinced he should be focusing on his shoe

business full-time. In its first year, Blue Ribbon Sports sold $364 worth of Japanese athletic shoes. However, by the end of the decade, sales had skyrocketed to over one million dollars. In 1972, Knight decided his company needed a makeover in the form of a new name and logo. Knight liked the name "Dimension Six," but his 45 employees didn't. Then, one of the company's salesmen, Jeff Johnson, suggested something that would stick-Nike-after the Greek winged goddess of victory. It had come to Johnson in a dream, and it would prove to be a dream decision for the company. Knight paid $35 to commission a new logo - the 'swoosh' that today has become so famous the world over - and debuted the new design at the 1972 Olympic trials in Eugene, Oregon.

That year, Nike sales reached $3.2 million. The company's profits would double over each of the next ten years. True to Knighf's vision, Nike surpassed Adidas as the industry leader in the U.S.

Entrepreneurial Milestones:

- ***Marketing:*** Few companies have been as successful as Nike in creating powerful and lasting messages to promote its products. From its internationally recognized "Just Do It" slogan to its 'Swoosh' logo to the athletes that stand behind it, Nike has become a relentless marketing machine. Knight pushed the boundaries of sports marketing, taking it to new heights that many questioned the very legitimacy of.
- ***Risk:*** He signed Michael Jordan before he became the international superstar 'Air Jordan' and he signed Freddy Adu before he had even had his 15th birthday. Time after time, Knight has demonstrated his willingness to take the risks he needed to take his company to the next level. With no guarantee that any of his moves would make the mark, Knight took the gambles that in the end would take him to the top.
- ***Focus:*** Knight and all of his Nike employees are adamant about the fact that they don't work for a fashion company. Nike is about athletics and producing shoes that will create high-quality athletic performances. They didn't get sidetracked and simply focused on their end goal. Once this focus was clearly defined, there was no stopping the company from climbing to the top of its game. ***Competition:*** Knight has created a company that is fiercely competitive; willing to do whatever it takes to distinguish itself from its main competitors. It was by instilling a war mentality throughout his company that Knight was able to constantly stay ahead of the pack.
- **Conviction:** Rarely has there been a time when Knight was not at the centre of some controversy or another. From being accused of upholding poor labor standards to signing deal endorsements with such controversial athletes as Dennis Rodman, Nike has been a lightening rod for public criticism. But, Knight has taken it all in stride, standing strong in his belief that what he was doing was right and necessary, and refusing to baek down in the face of public controversy.

1

N.R. NARAYAN MURTHY

Vision of Putting India on the Global Software Map

Leveraging Indian brainpower and sweat equity 53 year old N.R. Narayan Murthy built a world-class software company from scratch.

As founder chairman and CEO of Rs. 513 crore Infbsys Technologies, he heads the country's most successful Silicon-Valley-style start-up, one that is right at the forefront of India's charge on the global software market. With 4,800 employees, 11 software development centres in India and 13 overseas offices, Infosys is a world class act, deriving 97 percent of its revenues from exports.

In the past five years Infosys has grown at breathtaking speed : sales grew at a compounded annual rate of 74 per cent and profits by 78 per cent, a performance that puts Infosys way ahead of its peers.

Last March this software player, a pygmy by world standards, declared its ambition to enter the global big league. It created history by becoming the first Indian registered company to list on an American stock exchange-Nasdaq-with an issue of two million American Depository Shares that raised $ 70 million. Infosys' pioneering step has paved the way for other Indian IT companies.

BREAKING AWAY

Breaking from conventional wisdom is an art that the independent-minded Murthy honed early in life. Growing up in a lower middle class family in Mysore, he felt the weight of his father's expectations, who was keen that his youngest son join the civil services. But Murthy harboured a different dream: to be a junior engineer working at hydroelectric power plants.

After topping his school exams, the small-town teenager was all bright-eyed and charged up. His dream of studying engineering at the most elite institution in the land was at hand. Not only had he passed the Indian Institute of Technology (IIT) entrance test but he had also managed to secure a scholarship. But destiny had something else on cards for him as his father N.Rama Rao pointed out that the scholarship would be disbursed only at the end of the academic year and on his modest school–teacher's salary of Rs. 250 a month, he could ill-afford setting aside Rs. 100 for his son's monthly tuition and expenses. Swallowing his disappointment, the youngster enrolled at the local engineering college at Mysore. Four years later, as a top-ranking graduate in electrical engineering, he got another scholarship–to do his M. Tech at IIT, Kanpur.

The faculty at IIT Kanpur, was full of young, American-educated professors brimming with energy, providing a heady, intellectural cocktail for the earnest student. Thanks to IIT links with eight American universities, the institute was at the receiving end of their largesse. Thus, when IIT got its IBM 7094 computer, an IBM 7044 was shipped out to Kanpur. Introduced to this "wonder machine', Murthy was hooked.

Trained in computer sciences, a new frontier then, Murthy naturally had the pick of jobs as a post graduate. Turning down better paying offers from giants like Air India, HMT, ECIL and Telco, he made a curious choice: to join as a chief systems programmer at the Indian Institute of Management, Ahmedabad – earning Rs. 800 a month.

IIM was in the process of installing a HP minicomputer and would be the second business school after Standford to have a time-sharing operating system. It would mean working almost 20 hrs. a day, warned J.G.Krishnayya, IIM professor of Information Systems but it provided a great learning opportunity to Murthy. It was a laborious phase working 20 hrs, a day, returning to his apartment at 3 a.m. very often but then there was chance to do cutting-edge work like designing and implementing the country's first BASIC interpreter (for ECIL). From Krishnayya, whom Murthy regards as his mentor, he learnt to aspire for ever higher targets.

Krishnayya recommended Murthy's name to Sesa, a French software company that was looking to hire programmers for a special project – building up an operating system for handling air cargo at Charles de Gaulle airport in Paris. Murthy, who didn't know French worked like a dervish, taking upon himseld to master French as quickly as possible. The two years in Paris influenced his thinking deeply and changed his political outlook.

At the end of the project, he came back to Pune and teamed up with his mentor Krishnayya, who was setting up SRI. But it was in Pune only, that Murthy met his wife Sudha Kulkarni, also an electrical engineer, who was then working with Telco. After three-year courtship period, they married in 1978, by which time Murthy had left SRI and joined Patni Computer Systems (PCS), a Mumbai - based company. Joining PCS as head of software, he recruited those six professionals who were to eventually partner him in his first experiment of "creating wealth' namely Nilekani, S.Gopalkrishnan, Ashok Arora, N.S.Raghavan, K. Dinesh and S. Shibulal.

When he mooted the idea of creating a software supplier leveraging Indian skills and aimed at overseas markets, they readily bought into the concept.

Infosys Consultants was formed in July 1981 with the pooled savings of the seven partners of Rs. 10,000/-, mostly borrowed from their wives. Murthy's HDFC-financed Shivajinagar apartment in Pune was the first registered office.

SUCCESS JOURNEY

It was a struggle every step of the way. Though the concept of offshore development was unknown then, the Infy men were clear right from day one that they wanted to add value from India eventually. But getting a license to import a computer in that restrictive age took about 12 to 24 months and funds was another major problem, with ANZ Grindlays rejecting their project application. A chance encounter on a plane with K.S.N. Murthy of KSIIDC brought Murthy to Bangalore and within a fortnight Infosys had the money — Rs. 52 lakh — to buy its first computer.

According to Murthy, the big breakthrough for Infosys came with economic liberalisation after 1991. The company's turnover, a mere Rs. 5 crore, then, grew 100 folds since.

Infosys has very systematically moved up the software value chain from an on-site to an offshore software developer, then to product develolpment and finally towards providing complete solutions. Having grown organically, Infosys is now scanning the universe for potential acquisitions for its next phase of growth.

Source: Business India, Nov. 15, 1999 and Business World, Jan. 7, 2000.

2

Mrs. SHAMPA SIDDIQUI

Elegant and Gutsy. These two words describe Shampa Siddiqui quite nicely. From studying English literature to manufacturing and exporting repro-furniture, it has been a long and eventful journey for Shampa. "I've never been afraid to take risks," she declares. "And there can be no success without meaningful risks".

In 1977, Shampa came to New Delhi from Calcutta (where she had graduated in English) to join her parents. Her father was posted in the capital as the director general in the Ministry of Surface Transport. It was then she met Shamsher Siddiqui at a party. They married soon after.

Hailing from Moradabad in Uttar Pradesh, Siddiqui's family was in cloth business. In Delhi, however, the Siddiqui couple set up a company called Evergreen Fabrics by investing their savings along with a loan from SIDBI. The Siddiqui's started supplying furnishings to embassies in the capital. Slowly, the business started expanding because of the efforts of the two entrepreneurs.

In 1982, when the fabric business showed signs of falling, both Shampa and Shamsher discovered that Indian repro-furniture was a great draw with foreigners and they set up Evergreen International with an additional initial investment of Rs. One lakh. They employed craftsmen from Bihar and Uttar Pradesh and put a small unit in the backyard of their house.

During the early phase, Evergreen International made and exported furniture to west Asia mainly through its contacts in the embassies. The Gulf war stopped all that. "It wiped out six years of our business," says Shampa.

To survive, the Siddiquis then started dabbling in diverse fields such as leather garments and home furnishings along with furniture. They used to manufacture according to the demand. A decade later for the first time, Evergreen International participated in a trade fair overseas. The company went for the International Trade Fair in Berlin and exhibited leather garments, cotton furnishings and silk carpets. Unfortunately, however it didn't work. "It was a disaster", Shampa recollects. "We didn't get a single order". Not to be cowed down, the Siddiquis kept going and prepared more samples and participated again the next year." There was some encouragement this time, but the most important outcome of this was that we learnt a lot", says Shampa. "We learnt that the international market is far removed from the domestic set up". They got lot of contacts, but very few orders. What they had however was more information and based on this they made their fresh set of samples and restarted the whole thing.

"In the beginning we got some contacts through the embassies, but our financial position was not very sound", Shampa remembers. Economising became the watchword. "We used to spend many nights travelling in trains, to get the samples in time and not waste time". The hard work paid off. Suddenly a contact in Belgium invited them to go and meet a customer who was available only for a brief period.

Shampa returned a week later, with an order for leather garments. The business picked up from then on, when it got too big to handle, the Siddiquis decided to split the divisions. Shampa got furnishings and whatever was left of the furniture business. In 1996 came the most important breakthrough, through a business contact for leather garments, they came to know of a furniture supplier in Indonesia who introduced them to a very large buyer in Holland. "He wanted us to supply Indian style furniture. We had no infrastructure, no land, no factory, but we had the order. It was for two container loads or Rs. 12 lakhs", says Shampa. This was the breakthrough for Evergreen International's furniture business which today brings in Rs. 12 crore out of Rs. 50 crore turnover of the entire company (including leather and furnishings).

Shampa sources furniture styles from all over the country, gets samples and then leaves it to the customer to choose, decide and sometimes, suggest variances. Shampa's marketing strategy is simple: charm your buyers. She visits Europe every year, to ascertain the latest trends and preferences. The samples and offers are made accordingly. The main customer that Evergreen caters to, in Holland has a large business ready for them and buys up nearly 20-40 feet container loads every month.

The craftsmen hail mostly from Bihar and Uttar Pradesh. The wood comes from Bihar and is treated chemically for termites, then seasoned to prevent warping or bending. It is then fashioned into the required piece. Finally polished with imported wax and lacquer to finish the piece. Packing is usually done in cartons, as most of the items are shipped in semi knocked down condition.

Being a woman and running such a business did have its initial problems but today that has given way to grudging respect. "I have employed more women here, in all positions. Supervisory positions are dominated by them", she says. It took the men a while to get used to the idea of taking orders from a woman. "They would discuss every issue with Shamsher, then slowly they started realising that I could also solve problems. Now they are all with me", she says. "I work on the floor with them, that is why they respect me".

At present there is a recession in the market for furnishings but Evergreen is still on a growing path. When not planning strategic moves, Shampa spends time with her children. Thanks to her joint family, her children have never missed close bondage, even though their mother was working extremely hard when they were growing up. On the contrary, it has set up an example for them that hard work, dedication towards one's work leads to fruitful results.

Source : Global, June 1999.

3

KARSHANBHAI PATEL

Circa 1976. A young chemist working with Municipal Corporation of Ahmedabad responded to an advertisement in the local daily. The Indian Petrochemical Corporation Ltd. (1PCL) was inviting entrepreneurs to set up a small-scale business. All they had to do was mix linear alkaline benzene with soda ash to make detergents. Almost 40 people attended the workshop conducted by IPCL.

One of the students who set to work immediately was Karsanbhai Patel. Converting his backyard into a mini-factory, he soon began pedalling a detergent packed in polythene bags. Riding his bicycle, he personally went and sold it in the local markets. Branding it after his favourite daughter, he created a new pattern in distribution. Using migratory labour, Nirma was made available in most of the soft-water areas of west, south and north India.

He gave the Rs. 6 a pack on credit. Soon, Nirma, the cheapest detergent in the market, was the rage in Gujarat.

Nirma's success became part of marketing folklore, propelling Karsanbhai as the quin-tessential case study in corporate India. With one stroke, Karsanbhai was hailed as the David who single-handedly humbled the mighty Anglo-Dutch conglomerate Hindustan Lever, which under the 'license raj' had no cheap product in its marketing arsenal. He also wiped off more than 2,000 small-scale soap units in the state at that price.

"More than this, we believe his greatest contribution was the way he changed washing habits", says a manager at Hindustan Lever. Consumers renounced the ubiquitous bar of soap for the detergent. Since then, Karsanbhai has stretched his famous brand every way. From bath soaps to salt to toothpaste: his latest dream being packaged foods.

Like many entrepreneurs, Patel is still obsessed with being hands on the job. "It is better to keep in touch with thing directly. That way you don't have to depend on reports. You can also take decisions on the spot", he says. He is a man who likes working and creating with his hands. His abundant and restless energy does not allow him to take things easy and he tirelessly keeps at his job.

Despite his dream run, Karsanbhai remains an unassuming man. Executives at Lever House say that Karsanbhai of ten visits the place to meet HLL Chairman Keki Dadiseth.

A man of few words, he keeps in touch with all his contemporaries. And recently, when Patel had a wedding in the family, corporate India was represented in full force.

Today, his dream is to make Nirma synonymous with quality. He has said, "Nirma is not merely a brand or a product, it is a dynamic phenomenon, a revolution, a philosophy. To measure Nirma's success by yardsticks of physical achievements is a fallacy".

4

KALANITHI MARAN

Six years ago, when he was only 27, Kalanithi Maran became the first and the youngest private entrepreneur in the country to launch a satellite television service in a regional language. Sun TV, the first international Tamil satellite TV service, changed the cable network concept in his home state of Tamil Nadu and created a revolution in the media world.

Right from the outset, the channel was successful, generating revenues from its first day of operations. The reason for its success was not far to seek. The channeel came as a boom to the entertainment-starved Tamil speaking population across Asia. They immediately took a fancy to its rich and quality programming and went on increasing its patronage and viewership.

The thumping success of Sun TV inspired Maran to launch more ventures in south Indian languages. Udaya TV is the first Kannada satellite channel. Germini TV became the first international Telugu satellite channel. More recently, Surya TV was introduced as the first digital Malayalam satellite channel. All the ventures have met with immediate success. The various channels now fall under a common umbrella called the Sun Network.

The Sun Network, which is the satellite television leader over south India and the only diversified television network in the country, has added the latest feather to its cap—becoming the first private satellite television broadcaster to uplink its entire network transmission from Indian soil at Chennai.

Not content with making his mark in Chennai, Maran has always looked beyond Indian shores and globalization has always been on top of his agenda. He has been telecast-ing his channels across Asia through satellite transponders with footprints covering entire Asia. Other steps which he has taken towards globalization of his network have included a tie-up with Singapore Cable Vision to telecast his channel terrestrially across Singapore; a tie-up with Maharaja Television Network of Sri Lanka to telecast his channel terrestrially across Sri Lanka; a tie-up with TV Asia of the UK to telecast his channel across Europe and launch of Sun World TV in the USA to telecast his channels across USA and Canada.

The man behind it all is a music buff who loves watching Discovery Channel and surfing the Internet. He plays tennis, squash and cricket as leisure activities. Maran also pens a column in the Tamil weekly magazine Kungumam. After completing his schooling from Chennai's premier school, he had done his graduation from Loyola Autonomous College, Chennai, with a first class in 1985. Two years later, he completed his post graduation in management from the University of Scranton, Pennsylvania, USA.

He returned to India immediately thereafter to join his family's publication business (Kungumam Publication). In 1990, Maran pioneered the frist vernacular video newsmagazine (Poomalai) which was a runaway success before launching the satellite channels and making a name for himself in the satellite TV world.

While making forays into an entirely unexplored world, Maran took with him a team of young, aggressive, talented, inexperienced staff whom he eventually converted to hardcore professionals. In the process, he also created many employment opportunities at Sun Network and provided a luxurious working environment.

His management style is noteworthy. He brings in core professionalism into his operations by personal intervention at all levels without breaking the official hierarchy. His passion for accuracy, paced operations and updating the technology requirements of his company have made him a round-the-clock worker towards ushering in a new era. Maran is an idol for his staff, a guiding force and an example setting Managing Director.

Maran did not rest on his laurels by being the pioneer in vernacular satellite TV. Knowing well that competitors would soon be snapping at his heels if he stood at one place, he has constantly been innovating, trying out various schemes and techniques at his channels so that the viewer is always refreshed with something new. With his urge to try new ideas and his boldness to face the result, Maran brought in breathtaking novelty to involve the viewers to the channel and make them participate in its operations. Unique concepts in programming, wide variety of software and living up to the expectations of the viewer have been his forte.

Some of his interesting innovations :

- A live phone-in interaction between the viewers.
- Stage shows and their telecast, thus, connecting the viewers and the channel.
- Revolutionary gifts and on screen as well as off screen contests. This facilitates instant participation of the viewers.
- Making viewers convert their dreams into reality. A special train was organised from Kanyakumari to Chennai carrying selected viewers to watch a world cup match and telecast.
- Similarly, a train carrying selected viewers from Kanyakumari to Chennai brought viewers to watch their favourite movie stars.
- Special flights were booked from all the main cities in Tamil Nadu and Bangalore to watch an Indo-Pak cricket match in Chennai.

A socially aware and responsible citizen, Maran has often committed himself to uplifting the downtrodden. His donations towards relief funds and his media support to fight against the social evils have earned him a distinguished place in society. Maran has often associated his media to fight against AIDS, eradicating polio and upliftment of orphaned children.

All those who have come in contact with Maran have appreciated his interpersonal and communication skills. He is a very good public relations officer of his company who is in himself a friendly and warm human being. With his politeness, straight forwardness, truthfulness and good manners, he has attracted many admirers. His clear and committed communication, his neutral and mutually beneficial approach and his hardcore professionalism have created goodwill of his own. Maran has been a perfect ambassador of his country in all the major international media meets that he has participated in.

Source: Business Today.

5

SHIV NADAR

Shiv Nadar has been the only entrepreneur in the last decade, apart from Azim Premji of Wipro, to successfully manage hardware business and software ventures. Infact the 53-year-old Nadar has successfully straddled the entire spectrum of information technology: from hardware, software, and services, to training.

The HCL empire, which spawns from Japan in the east to US in the west, was conceived in a garage in Noida near New Delhi when Nadar quit his job with DCM and, armed with Rs. 1.5 lakh, started making and selling calculators in 1976. His big break came when he ventured into the hardware business.

Armed with a degree to Electrical Engineering from PSG College of Technology Coimbatore in 1967, he started work as a systems analyst at Cooper Engineering and within a year moved out to DCM as a senior management trainee. The next seven years of his life were spent uneventfully as he climbed up the ladder and started Data Products Division. He was heading it until he quit in 1975 and laid the foundation of HCL group from an attic in Noida.

PREDICTED THE COMPUTER BOOM

People laughed at him when he predicted the future for Information Technology in the country and the scope it provided to HCL. His understanding was that sooner or later, when the time came, HCL could cash in on the computer boon in the country. He proved them wrong and had the last laugh, as within a short span of three years HCL was able to develop India's first micro-processor based commercial computer, the HCL-8c.

By this time the HCL team was able to gather in-house expertise for developing the hardware, controllers, languages, systems software, utilities and even application software for its computers. Finally with the technology jump in the next four years 8c became a museum piece, HCL was able to step in with an advanced version, also developed in-house. This symbolised the galloping pace of changes in the international market and HCL's nascent efforts to move along.

Under Shiv Nader's stewardship HCL has grown from strength to strength. Nadar's contemporaries say that his greatest attributes include ability to execute a business strategy ruthlessly and ambition to became the number one in the business he enters into. These traits are complemented by his hands-off management style: he adopts an idea and then gives his employees a free hand to execute it, and build the business.

"In many respect he has been way ahead of times. He is a visionary who thinks beyond his time and his greatest gift from god is the ability to find the right people for the right job, give them the right freedom to operate and reap the benefits", says a former associate. Another feels that the main reason for his success has been his ability to be a venture capitalist and entrepreneur at the same time.

That is what happens in his case. While most other prefer a hands-on approach, he is the man who does the least himself, apart from strategic thinking or prioritising and leaves it to his team to find the best path to capture the objective. But isn't that leadership is all about.

The most famous example in this regard is of Rajendra Pawar (then an HCL manager and Managing director of NUT) who Nadar felt, had a great idea in 1981: a training institute to tap the massive potential in computer education. By bankrolling Pawar and giving him the freedom to run the business Nadar has created a software training and services giant second to none in India, with a market capitalisation of Rs. 8,390 crore.

Nadar also picked Vineet Nayar, a regional manager with HCL, to work with him on new businesses and made him CEO of HCL Comnet, one of the country's largest V-Sat providers.

Since 1993, he has stopped running companies and confines himself to once-a-quarter meeting with CEOs. He now heads the group apex body of HCL Corporation, whose charter is to set standards and create policies in areas such as new business opportunities, financial and accounting practices, HRD and corporate communications.

While he is quick to reward performers, Nadar is known to be ruthless when performance is not quite up to his exacting standards. This has created some troubles with his partners. Arjun Malhotra, one of the co-founders of HCL, quit the group after Nadar bought over his stake.

The ruthless attitude, in the final analysis, is the reason for his success. According to a former HCL group executive, Nadar is clinical while evaluating new business proposals. He demands clear answers broken into bottomline numbers. The questioning and discussion are so incisive and frank that the story goes that if Nadar is convinced, the business will succeed.

Source: Sun Magazine Oct., 1999 and other sources.

6

SABEER BHATIA

Sabeer Bhatia arrived at Los Angeles International Airport at 6 pm on September 23, 1988. His flights from Bangalore had taken 22 hours, and he was starving. The California Institute of Technology, which had offered him a scholarship, had sent him directions that said merely, "Take a shuttle to campus." But Bhatia didn't know what a "shuttle" (coach) was. He was 19. In his pocket he had $400. He didn't know a single person in America.

Bhatia intended to get his engineering degrees and then go home to work. His mother, was a bank manager, and his father, chief administrative officer at Defence Research Organization. Bhatia grew up, like most Indian kids, presuming that starting a company is impossible unless you are a superhuman.

As a graduate student at Stanford University, Bhatia was drawn to meetings where he heard entrepreneurs like Sun Microsystem's Scott. McNealy and Apple's Steve Wozniak. Bhatia's impression was that they really were fairly ordinary intelligent guys.

When he graduated, he took a job as a hardware engineer at Apple Computer. Soon he started attending cocktail parties of a group of Indian-born entrepreneurs in Silicon Valley, where he met many successful older Indian men. And again they seemed like such ordinary guys!

"Jack!" He'd say to his friend, "What are we doing here, wasting our lives?" "Jack, given the enormous opportunities here, if we can't make it, then we are complete failures." They agreed: Bhatia would be the business manager; Smith the technology architect of their as-yet-to-be-created venture.

Bhatia and Smith brainstormed ideas. They wanted to e-mail each other, but were afraid their bosses might glean their e-mail. Jack Smith was driving home one day in December 1995 when it occurred to him: Free e-mail accounts that could be accessed anonymously, over the Web.

When Smith called Bhatia, their minds melded as they talked, completely in sync, leaping from one ramification to the next. Bhatia stayed up all night, writing the business plan. The next morning he looked so haggard that his boss said, "You've got to cut out the partying, Sabeer."

Bhatia needed $300,000 to create a working version of the e-mail program. He shopped around his business plan and another for a Net-based personal database to 19 venture capitalists–with no success. Then he met Steve Jurvetson of Draper Fisher Jurvetson, who was interested but skeptical of Bhatia's revenue estimates and dismissed the projections outright, but Bhatia insisted, "You don't believe we're going to do that?" For their $300,000 upfront, the firm wanted a 30 percent stake. Bhatia offered 15 percent. Negotiations seemed to be going nowhere. The next day Draper Fisher Jurvetson accepted 15 percent.

Bhatia and Smith quit their jobs at Apple Computer and opened a tiny office in Fremont, California. By June, Bhatia and Smith were running out of money, but the product would be ready to launch in a month. Another venture capitalist, Dough Carlisle, was interested in investing, but Bhatia knew that if he and Smith launched the service first, they would keep more control of the company they created. He convinced a bank to loan them $100,000.

On July 4,1996–Bhatia and Smith launched their company, called Hotmail. The morning of the launch, Bhatia and Smith wore hip beepers, programmed to flash every hour with the number of new subscribers. The first users found Hotmail all by themselves, then e-mailed their friends: a hundred users in the first hour, 200 the next hour, 250 in the third.

By the time Sabeer went back to Doug Carlisle to say in effect okay. Hotmail had 100,000 subscribers and a valuation of $18 million.

Hotmail began to deliver news and other Internet content into the e-mail boxes of its subscribers. This was nothing new, but the way the money flowed was. The sites supplying the content took the position. "Hey, if you want our news for free, then you'd better pay us." But Bhatia wanted the sites to pay Hotmail for the privilege of having its content run. Surprisingly, the businesses agreed to these terms, and soon Hotmail was growing so fast that some content providers couldn't handle the traffic that came in from Hotmail.

Every morning, he scoured the Internet for signs of competition. It was six months before the first-appeared.

He'd always been concerned that Hotmail could be copied. "What to keep Microsoft from copying the concept and eating him for lunch?" It was like riding a tricycle in the head lights of a lorry."

Microsoft came bidding to buy Hotmail in the autumn of 1997. Six company executives flew down and offered Bhatia a figure that would have put tens of millions of dollars in his pocket. He rejected it, a week later they were back, and every week thereafter for two months.

They asked Bhatia to go over and talk to Microsoft founder Bill Gates. In the interview, Gates began to ask questions. "The same things I had been asked by investors all along. And it suddenly occurred to me that Bill Gates is not superhuman either. He's flesh and blood, same as me." With this understanding, Bhatia relaxed, his confidence restored.

Bhatia took a straw poll among his investors to see what price they might anticipate. Doug Carlisle's figure, $200 million, was the lowest. Privately, Bhatia had half-jokingly been saying he wanted a billion dollars. So he challenged Carlisle's figure: "You don't think we can get more than that?"

Bhatia went back to Microsoft with the price of half a billion. "You're crazy," the negotiators shouted. Tensions were rising as Microsoft piled cash on the table: $200 million, $250 million, $300 million.

Bhatia, stood firm: no sale. When the negotiation team offered around $350 million, most of Hotmail's management team was in favour of accepting.

"Saying no to that offer was the scariest thing I ever did," Bhatia says. "Everybody had told me, "This is on your head if you screw it up."

On New Year's Eve 1997, a deal was announced. Hotmail had been exchanged for 2,769,148 shares of Microsoft, at that time worth a walloping $400 million.

Bhatia remained his company's top executive after it became a subdivision of Microsoft's Web Essentials. By then, Hotmail had 144 employees.

Only eight months after the New Year's Eve, announcement, Microsoft's $400 million price tag looked to be a bargain, particularly considering that Hotmail's user base had more than doubled in size since the company was purchased. With 22 million active e-mail accounts, the company was signing up new users at a rate of 125,000 a day. Bhatia had built Hotmail's user base faster than any media company's in history.

"In retrospect," says Steve Jurvetson, "I'm not sure that a billion dollars wasn't the right figure.

So, is Bhatia lucky or is he great? He refuses to give the credit to anything other than the culture of the Valley itself: Where two 27 year guys get $300,000 from men they had just met. Two 27-year-old guys who had no experience with consumer products, never started a company, never managed anybody, no experience even in software. All we had has the idea."

In March 1999, Sabeer Bhatia quietly left Microsoft to begin a new venture called Arzoo.com, a web site that brings information-technology experts and corporations together to solve technology-related problems on the Internet. His goal is to "create the world's largest network of human intellectual capital on the web."

1

Feasibility Report Solar Lighting Systems

India is facing a major energy crisis, with a huge demand and supply gap. The per capita electrical energy consumption is as low as 16 percent of the global average. The central and state governments with 96 percent of the total capacity have monopolised Indian energy production.

Indian energy sector is dominated by conventional energy. Thermal power alone has a share of 72 percent.

Breakup by Type of Plant	Share in Total Energy Production
Thermal	7.21%
Hydel	25.1%
Nuclear	2.6%
Unconventional	0.2%

Source : CRISIL-Energy report (1999-2000).

India is a country of villages with a vast geographical area and dominance of conventional energy that has led to huge gap in the demand and supply of energy. A major factor in this gap is transmission and distribution (T & D) loss. Delhi alone experiences T & D loss of 50 percent. This mean that half the power supplied to Delhi is wasted due to negligence of electricity board authorities.

With the depleting stock of conventional fuel non-conventional energy is the right, choice of the hour. India today has the world's largest programmes for renewable energy. There has been an increase in the use of renewable energy sources as a sustainable energy base only since the early 1970s. And, in the last 30 years, there has been a significant effort in terms of the development and dissemination of various renewable energy technologies (RETS) for use in different sectors. The renewable energy programme of the Ministry of Non-Conventional Energy Sources (MNES) has covered all major sources such as biogas, biomass, solar energy, wind energy, small hydro power and certain other emerging technologies. Also resources assessment, R & D, technology development and demonstration programmes are undertaken in each of these areas. Today, several renewable energy systems and products are not only commercially available but are also economically viable in comparison to fossil fuels, particularly when the environmental costs of fossil fuels are taken into account. But despite of all these efforts, renewal energy has been able to contribute only 0.2 percent of total production of energy.

Renewal energy is gaining popularity in all parts of the country because of its low initial investment, almost zero running cost and easy to use. As India has abundance sun light, the solar energy can become a major source of power in both urban and rural areas.

INSIGHT TO SOLAR ENERGY

Solar energy is one of the better options of renewable energy. It is a radiant energy produced in the sun as a result of nuclear fusion reactions. It is transmitted to the earth through space.

Energy from sun has many features that makes it an attractive option. These are its wide spread distribution, pollution free nature and virtually inexhaustible supply. In-dia receives solar energy equivalent to over 5,000 trillion KWh/year (5×10^{15} KWh/yr.) which is far more than the total energy consumption of the country. On an average there are 250-300 sunny days in most part of our country. The daily average solar energy incident varies from 4-7 KWh/Mz depending upon the location.

The solar photovolatic (SPV) technology converts sun light directly into electricity in an environmentally clean and reliable manner. Photovoltaic technology has emerged not only as a power source for small applications such as lighting, water pumping, telecommunication etc., but also as a medium size power source for applications at the village level. The SPV program has been a major technological development and a wide spread field demonstration of various applications in India. The country has developed a strong research base as well as indigenous production capabilities in the entire area, starting from silicon material to solar cells, photovolatic modules and complete systems for various applications.

Advantages of photovoltaics are listed below :

Long life

Low maintenance

High reliability

Modularity in operation

Pollution-free construction

Non-conventional renewable energy source.

Photovoltaics is relatively unique among electricity generation technologies because it can provide reliable power in desired quanta for a large number of different applications, in many sizes across a broad range of environments to locations where it was previously not feasible. System modularity allows users to start with small systems for single applications (lights, water pumps etc.,) and add on to their systems as per their needs (hospitals, rural electrification systems, and mini utility networks).

Market

Streetlights in cities consume a lot of energy, which can be saved by using Solar Street Lighting systems. In India there are three major manufacturers of Solar lighting systems which are not able to satisfy the demand requirements of the country. The industry is also marked by a 45 percent growth rate.

As per the reports received from the various state implementing agencies, 680 street lighting systems, 7,470 domestic lighting systems, 44,938 solar lanterns and power plants of an aggregate capacity of 89 KWs were installed during 1997-98. The SPV power plants include a 26 KWs centralized plant commissioned in Sagar Island in West Bengal, implemented by the West Bengal Renewable Energy Development Agency, Calcutta.

About 75 companies are involved in the manufacture of solar cells, modules and photovolatic systems. Thirteen manufacturing companies are in regular production of solar cells and modules. The production of solar cells and modules by different firms in the country till 31 March, 1998 was estimated to be 40 MW.

Important Photovoltaic System Manufacturer

Manufacturer	City
Tata BP Solar India Ltd.	Bangalore
Bharat Heavy Electrical Ltd.	Bangalore
Crompton Greaves Ltd.	Nasik
Siemens Ltd.	New Delhi
Sun Source (India) Ltd.	Ahmedabad
Rajasthan Electronics & Instruments Ltd.	Jaipur
Premier Solar Systems	Hyderabad

GOVERNMENT POLICIES

Incentives for Setting Up Solar Lighting System Plant

Ministry of Non-conventional Energy sources has moved to a liberalised policy regime, allowing the market forces to play a major role. Direct cash subsidies have been phased out by a package of incentive and financing arrangements.

Steps Taken by the Ministry for Promoting Renewal Energy Sector

- Promoting private investment through fiscal and tax holidays, depreciation allowance, facilities for wheeling, banking and third party sale of grid power, and a remunerative price for the power generated.
- Extending institutional finance from Indian Renewable Energy Development Agency and other financial institutions for commercially viable projects, with private sector participation and external assistance from World Bank, global environment facility and bilateral programmes.
- Providing budgetary support to selected projects.

The ministry is implementing the SPV program through socially and market-oriented schemes. Under socially oriented scheme SPV systems like portable lanterns, fixed type domestic systems, street lighting system, community lighting TV systems and small village level power plants are being installed through state nodal agencies. Subsidy up to 50 percent is also provided for installing these systems. The market-oriented schemes are implemented through IREDA by soft loan assistance for SPV systems. In addition, IREDA is implementing the World Bank assisted SPV market development project.

The import and export policy, in force since April 1993, removed all restrictions on import of silicon material, solar cells, photovoltaic modules and systems. During the year, the custom duty rates were rationalised and anomalies in the duty structure were removed. Lowering of duties, expansion of programmes, competitive market and high volume of production have enabled reduction in the price of photovoltaic cells, modules and systems.

CONVERSION OF SOLAR ENERGY INTO ELECTRICAL ENERGY

Sunlight can be converted directly to electricity in solar cells. The process is known as photovoltaic conversion. The chief components of the cell are silicon semiconductors, which are very pure silicon wafers that have been carefully doped with small amounts of an element such as gallium (p-type) or with small amounts of an element such as arsenic (n-type). These two are placed in contact such that the junction between them is close to surface of the cell. Radiation from the sunlight releases the electrons in the other p-type layer, which acquires sufficient energy to jump across the p-n junction. This creates a potential difference between the layers that is proportional to the incident light. Terminals are attached to the two semiconductors and connected to an external circuit that produces electric current.

A single photovoltaic cell provides relatively small amount of power. With a silica cell of 100 square inch area, a current of 3 amp. at 0.5 volt is obtained in full sun light. Since this voltage level is too low for most applications, several cells are usually connected together to increase the voltage. The connected cells form a module typically containing 306-cells in series. Modules are usually designed to deliver about 15 volts under reasonable sunlight conditions. Such modules provide good mechanical strength and protection from damage from moisture or pollutants. They have an expected life of 20 years. A typical module will give a power output of 30 to 50 watts under good sunlight conditions. When more power is required, a number of modules can be connected to form an array. The current produced is DC, which can be converted to AC through an inverter.

How a Solar Cell Works

The key process of a solar cells is to convert sunlight into electricity. These light generated free carriers are then driven in opposite directions by the force of the built-in electric field. As light shines on the cell, an increasing number of positive charges are pushed to the top of the cell and negative ones to the bottom, or vice versa depending on the type of the cell. If a conductor is attached to the both the top and the bottom, the free charges will flow through it as electricity will flow continuously as direct current for as long as the cell is exposed to light.

Designing a Photovotaic System

Almost all-photovoltaic systems consist of a power source (the PV array), storage unit (usually a battery), controls (voltage regular, meters, and alarms) and a load (device consuming the electric power). The system design essentially involves selection of the PV array size and battery capacity to meet the requirements of the load after considering system losses.

A typical photovoltaic system's design includes :

System Sizing

Calculating the module output

The amount of energy a photovolatic module will produce depends on local sunlight and temperature conditions. Weather data, unique to the proposed site, is used to determine how much power a module will produce in that area. The amount of sunlight that falls on the solar cells can be expressed as the number of "peak hours" (KWh/sq mt. per day). The ampere-hours per day a module can produce (AH/day) is the number of peak hours per day times the module's current rating at a specified voltage (say 12 V). Hence a module generating 1.8 Amperes at a 12 V would generate 9 AH per day for a location where the insolation is 5 peak hours per day. This is typical for a 30 WP module.

Calculating the losses

There will be energy losses in the charge controller battery and inverter and hence the input power required from the PV array is inceased to compensate for these losses. The loss of power in the charge controller and battery may total up to 20 percent and the inverter could further cause losses up to another 20 percent of the input power.

Choosing a controller

To prevent overcharging and deep discharged of the battery an electronic charge controller is used between the PV array, the load and the battery. Its maximum ratings must exceed the maximum expected system voltage and current.

Sizing the storage capacity

The electrical requirements of the system and its geographic location will dictate the energy storage requirements. Storage of photovoltaic generated energy is usually required to provide an energy buffer between the time varying output of the solar array and the constant power demand of the load. To date, the most economical form of energy storage for photovoltaic applications is the lead acid battery. The required size of the battery, or its capacity, expressed in ampere-hours (AH) is based on the daily load plus losses and the number of consecutive no-sun (heavily overcast) days typical at the installation site selected.

The projects on technological assessment of Photovoltaic cells at TERI (Tata Energy Research Institute) and BHEL (Bharat Heavy Electrical Ltd.) has been successful in designing 5 KW photovoltaic system. Ministry of Non-Conventional Energy is supporting projects on reducing cost of silicon solar cells. The project will buy the technological know-how form TERI at a cost of Rs. 2.5 lakh.

Process of Manufacture

Solar Module

Although solar cells are the basic building blocks of SPV power generating systems, it is the solar photovoltaic modules and not the solar cells, with which system designer's work. A suitably interconnected combination of solar cells, when sealed hermetically with a transparent front glass cover form an SPV module. Modules are made through following process .

Solar cell testing

The procured solar cells are tested and sorted according to their current ranges, using a computerised automatic cell tester and sorter.

Lead Attachment and Stringing

Leads are attached to each solar cells by a soldering process. The lead attachment is done either manually or through a semi-automatic tabbing machine. After lead attachment, a definite number of cells are interconnected in series to form a string of solar cells, in a defined pattern, to give a sizeable power output.

Lay-ups and Encapsulation

The string of solar cell are then chemically cleaned (fluxes are removed using various chemicals like methanol; benzene etc.) and placed between a sheet of special soft polymer called ethyl vinyl acetate (EVA) and a sheet of Polyviny 1 fluoride (PVF) which act as encapsulate substrate for the strings. A sheet of high transmission toughened glass is used as the substrate. The complete lay-up is then put is an encapsulating equipment called a laminator in which it is subjected to a specific time temperature duration cycle to form the laminated module. The solar cell module interconnected with the glass sheets ethyl vinyl acetate and plastic film is laminated under high vacuum at 100°C tempera-ture in the laminator. It is cured at 150°C without vacuum. In this process the interconnected solar voltaic cells are incapsulated to protect them from atmospheric humidity, dust, wind and other mechanical stresses. While the lamination process was being carried out using imported machines earlier indigenous laminations using state-of-art features including microprocessor control have now become available.

Current Voltage Characterisation

The laminated module then tested in a sun simulator in which the module is exposed to a uniform illumination simulating the sun's insolation on a standard day (normally desginated as one sun, *i.e.,* 100 mw/cm^2). Through electrodes attached to the module the voltage across the module (V) are measured at different loads conditions, from open circuit (OC) condition to the short circuit (SC) condition, and the complete I-C curve for each module is plotted automatically using a computer. Each such I-V curve is stored in the computer memory after suitably tagging it with the module number and other batch data.

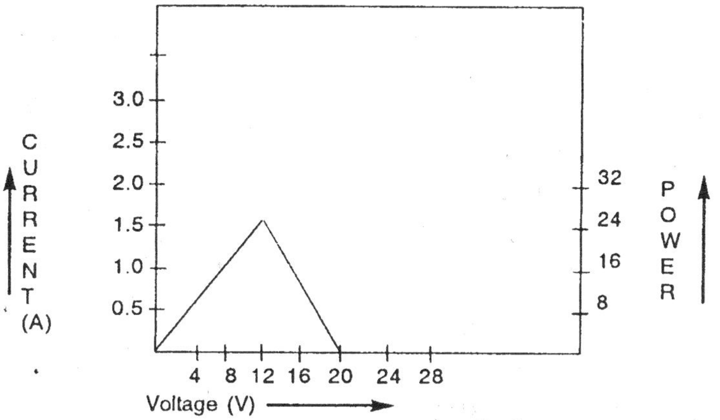

Fig. 1:1. C Curve

Framing and Termination

The encapsulated module is framed using aluminium channels of special design to protect the module from mechanical damage and for mounting it on suitable structures to form a panel. A nylon terminal box is then fixed to provide electrical terminals to extract electrical current from the module.

The output terminals from the solar cell string shall be terminated in two marked terminal posts inside this box.

Quality assurance

Statistically selected batchs are then subjected to a number of quality assurance tests as also environmental tests.

Quality control tests

Hot water immersion test

Hot/cold chamber test

Heat cycle test, etc.

The modules are now ready for use as a power generating source either individually or formed into a panel or an array depending upon the specific system design requirements.

Inverter-Gum -Charge Controller

The equipment is of compact design consisting of inverter and battery charge regulator. As per requirement it controls and current, converts DC to AC. In the period of peak sun ray, the instrument works as battery. It also protect battery from over/under charge, prevents reverse flow of current to the solar photovoltaic panel, acts as protective interface between the SPV panel and the battery. As per requirement and design, the parts like PCB, transistor, transformer, relay etc. are assembled by simple method of soldering, drilling etc. The whole assembly in setup in a special quality steel box. Terminals are joined in position.

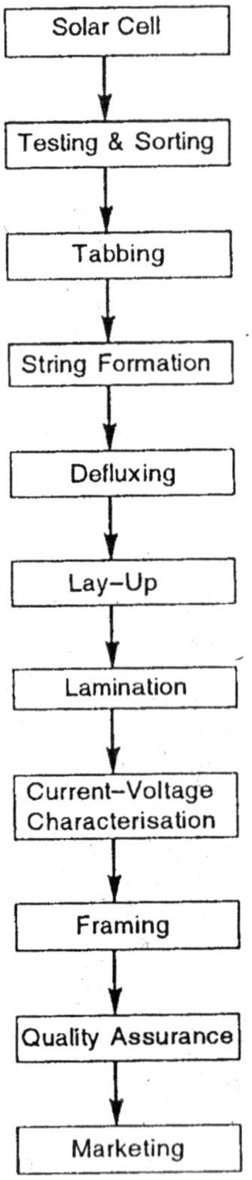

Fig. 2. Process Flow Chart

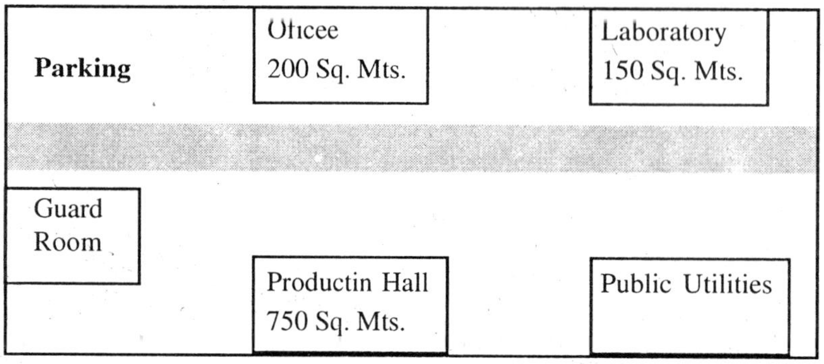

Fig. 3. Plant Layout

FINANCIAL VIABILITY

Plant Statistic

Plant Capacity	:	13,500 units of Solar Ligthing Systems
Working Days	:	25 days per month 300 days per annum
No. of Shifts	:	1 per day
No. of hours in one shift	:	7 hours

Production Capacity

Product	Production Per day	Production Per Annum
Solar Modules (35 watt each)	40 units	12,000 units
Controller (Charger-Cum Inverter)	5 units	1,500

Balance Sheet at the Beginning of 1st year.

Particulars	Amount (in Rs.)
Liabilities	
Equity Share Capital ... Schedule A	70,00,000
Debts .... Schedule B	69,01,700
Total Liabilities	**1,39,01,700**
Assets	
Fixed Assets	
Land & Building .... Schedule C	22,70,000
Plant & Machinery .... Schedule D	31,40,000
Other Fixed Assets.............. Schedule E	19,00,000
Pre-operative and Peliminery Expenses	8,00,000
Tech. Know-how fee	4,00,000
Current Assets	
Raw Materials .... Schedule F	58,25,500
Cash	7,66,200
Total Assets	**1,39,01,700**

Schedule A : Promoters Equity Capital

1.	Promoters Contribution	Rs. 40,00,000
2.	30,000 common stock shares with other members of Rs. 10 each	Rs. 30,00,000
	Total Owners Funds	Rs. 70,00,000

Schedule B : Long Term Funds

1.	7 years term loan from ICICI @ interest: 13% p.a.	Rs. 40,00,000
2.	4 years term loan from SBI for working capital © 12.5% p. a. interest	Rs. 30,00,000
	Total	**Rs. 70,00,000**

N.B. : *1 Term Loan form ICICI has a moratorium period of 3 years.*

Schedule C: Land & Building

S.No.	Particulars	Cost (Rs.)
1.	Land Area : 3000 Sq. Mtrs. (Family Owned Land)	
2.	Production Hall : 750 Sq. Mtrs. @ Rs. 1500 per Sq. Mtrs.	Rs. 11,25,000
3.	Raw Material & Finished goods Room : 300 Sq. Mtrs. @Rs. 1 000 per Sq. Mtrs.	Rs. 3,00,000
4.	Office : 200 Sq. Mtrs. @ Rs. 1500 per Sq. Mtrs.	Rs. 3,00,000
5.	Lab : 150 Sq. Mtrs. @ Rs. 1500 per Sq. Mtrs.	Rs. 2,25,000
6.	Guard Room : 20 Sq. Mtrs. @ Rs. 1000 per Sq. Mtrs.	Rs. 20,000
7.	Boundary wall & Gate	Rs. 1,00,000
8.	Internal Road, Writing, Water Supply & Fittings Drainage etc.	Rs. 2,00,000
	Total	**Rs. 22,70,000**

Schedule D: Plant and Machinery

S.No.	Particulars	No. of Machines	Cost (Rs.)
1.	Automatic Solar Cell Tester Cum Sorter	1	Rs. 2,50,000
2.	Laminator : microprocessor controlled, electric heating system and vacuum pump	1	Rs. 20,00,000
3.	Module tester	1	Rs. 2,00,000
4.	Drilling Machine	1	Rs. 10,000
5.	Cathode ray Oscilloscope (for testing inverter and charge controller)	1	Rs. 75,000
6.	Soldering Work Station	1	Rs. 40,000
7.	Diesel Generating Set (50 KVA)	1	Rs. 2,50,000
8.	D.C Power Shifter	1	Rs. 15,000
9.	Misc. Equipment		Rs. 1,50,000
10.	Cost of Machines Installation & Classification		Rs. 1,50,000
	Total		**Rs. 31,40,000**

Schedule E: Other Fixed Assets

S.No.	Particulars	Cost (Rs.)
1.	Office Equipment, Furniture, Accessories	Rs. 3,00,000
2.	Pre-operative & Preliminary Expenses	Rs. 8,00,000
3.	Technical know-how & General Consultancy	Rs. 4,00,000
4.	Weighing Equipment	Rs. 50,000
5.	Fire Fighting Equipment	Rs. 50,000
6.	Misc. Expenses	Rs. 3,00,000
	Total	**Rs. 19,00,000**

Schedule F: Raw Material Stock

S.No.	Particulars	Cost (Rs.)
1.	Module : 35,000 pcs. (Solar Cells of 35 watt) @ Rs. 110 Per Piece	Rs. 38,50,000
2.	Inverter-Controller : PCBs	Rs. 1,25,000
3.	Toughened Glass	Rs. 5,00,000
4.	Aluminum Channels	Rs. 4,00,000
5.	Transformers	Rs. 2,50,000
6.	Special Iron Boxes	Rs. 1,00,000
7.	Teddlar Sheet	Rs. 1,00,000
8.	Transistors/IC's	Rs. 1,00,000
9.	Lead Wire	Rs. 1,50,000
10.	Ethyl vinyl Acetate	Rs. 50,000
11.	Special Paper	Rs. 50,000
12.	Relay Systems	Rs. 50,000
13.	Miscellaneous	Rs. 1,00,000
	Total	**Rs. 58,25,500**

Estimation of Working Capital
(For One Month)

(I) Estimation of Current Assets :	
(i) Minimum Desired Cash/Bank Balance	Rs. 3,00,000
(ii) Raw Material	Rs. 58,25,500
(iii) Utilities and Overheads (A1)	Rs. 2,70,000
(iv) Salary & Wages (A2)	Rs. 1,96,200
Total Current Asset	Rs. 65,91,700
(II) Estimation of Current Liabilities	Rs. 0
(III) Net working capital required (I-II)	Rs. 65,91,700
Working Capital for one month	Rs. 65,91,700

Funding of Working Capital

Long Term Funds	Rs. 36,90,000
Working Capital Loan	Rs. 29,01,700
Total	Rs. 65,91,700

A-1 Utilities & Overheads

S.No.	Particulars	Cost
1.	Power Consumption	Rs. 30,000
2.	Advertising & Sales Promotion	Rs. 2,00,000
3.	Insurance	Rs. 2,000
4.	Administrative Expenses	Rs. 8,000
5.	Diesel	Rs. 8,000
6.	Repair & Maintenance	Rs. 10,000
7.	Miscellaneous including Salary/Wage	Rs. 10,000
	Total	**Rs. 2,70,000**

A-2 Wages & Salary

Sr. No.	Designation	No. of Employee	Salary/Wage
1.	Works Manager	1	Rs. 12,000
2.	Marketing Manager	1	Rs. 12,000
3.	Production Supervisor	2	Rs. 14,000
4.	Quality Controller	1	Rs. 25,000
6.	Accountant/Cashier	1	Rs. 5,000
7.	Lab Incharge	1	Rs. 8,000
8.	Lab Assistant	1	Rs. 4,000
9.	Skilled Workers	10	Rs. 35,000
10.	Unskilled Workers	15	Rs. 30,000
11.	Steno-Typist	1	Rs. 3,500
12.	Store Keeper	1	Rs. 3,000
13.	Peon/Darwan	3	Rs. 6,000
	Total	43	Rs. 1,63,500
	Perks @ 20 % Per Annum		Rs. 32,700
	Total Salary/Wages Per Month		**Rs. 1,96,200**

Cost of Production (Per Annum)

S.No.	Particulars	Amount (in Rs.)
1.	Raw Materials (Schedule F)	699,06,000
2.	Salary & Wages (A2)	23,54,400
3.	Direct & Indirect Overheads (Al)	32,40,000
4.	Interest (Bl)	10,07,713
5.	Depreciation (B2)	12,32,550
	Total	**7,77,40,663**

B 1: Interest Payable for 3 years

(Amount in Rs.)

Year	ICICI	To SBI	Total
1st Year	5,20,000	4,87,713	10,07,713
2nd Year	5,20,000	3,65,784	8,85,789
5rd Year	5,20,000	2,43,856	7,63,856

B 2: Depreciation Chart for 3 years

(Amount in Rs.)

Year	Building	Plant & Machinery	Furniture & Office Equipment	Total
1st Year	1,47,550	7,85,000	3,00,000	12,32,550
2nd Year	1,37,959	5,88,750	2,40,000	9,66,709
3rd Year	1,28,992	4,41,563	1,92,000	7,62,559

N.B. 1. Written down value method is used.

2. Rate of Depreciation : Building 6.5%

Plant & Machinery 25%

Office Equipment 20%

Sales Revenue Per Annum

Product	No. of Unit	Per Unit Cost	Revenue
Solar Modules	12,000	Rs. 6,000	Rs. 7,20,00,000
Inverter-cum Charge Controller	1,500	Rs. 8,000	Rs. 1,20,00,000
Total			**Rs. 8,40,00,000**

Income Statement

(100% capacity Utilization)

Particulars	**Amount (in Rs.)**
Sales Revenue	8,40,00,000
Total Expenditure	7,55,00,400
Gross Profit	84,99,600
Interest	10,07,713
Depreciation	12,32,550
Profit Before Tax	64,84,174
Tax	0
Net Profit	64,84,174

Note: Five year tax holiday for renewal energy projects.

Profit Analysis for 3 years

Particulars	**2000**	**2001**	**2002**
Capacity Utilization	80%	90%	100%
Sales (in Rs.)	6,72,00,000	7,56,00,000	8,40,00,000
Manufacturing Expenses (in Rs.)	6,04,00,320	6,79,50,360	7,55,00,400
Profits (in Rs.)	67,99,680	76,49,640	84,99,600
Depreciations (in Rs.)	12,32,550	9,66,710	7,62,555
Interest (in Rs.)	10,07,713	8,85,785	7,63,856
Net Profit (in Rs.)	45,59,417	57,97,145	69,73,189
Earning per share (EPS) (Rs.)	Rs. 65	Rs. 82	Rs. 98
ROCE	32%	41%	49%

EPS = Net Profit/No, of Outstanding Shares

Return on Capital Employed (ROCE) = Net Profit / Capital Employed

Discounted Cash Flow Statement for 5 years
(Amount in Rs.)

Particulars	1st	2nd year	3rd year	4th year	5th year
Capacity Utilization	80%	90%	100%	100%	100%
Profit after Tax	45,59,417	57,97,145	69,73,189	72,52,290	76,25,570
Add:					
Depreciation	12,32,550	9,66,710	7,62,555	6,05,380	4,84,030
Cash from Operations	57,91,967	67,63,855	77,35,744	78,57,670	81,09,600
Repayment of Loan	9,75,425	9,75,425	9,75,425	19,75,425	19,75,425
Net Cash Flow	48,16,542	57,88,430	67,60,319	58,82,245	61,34,175
Discount Factor	0.885	0.783	0.693	0.613	0.543
PV of Cash Flow	42,62,640	45,32,341	46,84,901	36,05,816	33,30,857

Net Present Value = (Present Value of Cash Inflow) – (Present Value of Cash Outflow)

= (42,62,640 + 45,32,321 + 46,84,901 + 36,05,816 + 33,30,857) – (1,39,01,700)

Net Present Value = Rs. 65,14, 855

- The project is viable, as the NPV is positive.
- Net present value is calculated with an assumption that the life of plant is 5 years.

Per Back Period = Investment / Annual Cash flows

= 1,39,01,700/(48,16,542 + 57,88,430 + 67,60,319)

Pay Back Period = 2 years 6 months.

Discounted Pay Back Period = 3 years 1 month.

Hence the project is financially viable.

Projected Balance Sheet **(Amount in Rs.)**

Particulars	Construction	1 year	2 year	3 Year
Liabilities				
Equity Capital	70,00,000	70,00,000	70,00,000	70,00,000
Reserve & Surplus		45,59,417	1,03,56,562	1,73,29,751
Term Loan	40,00,000	40,00,000	40,00,000	40,00,000
Working Capital Loan	29,01,700	21,76,275	14,50,850	7,25,425
Total Liabilities	1,39,01,700	1,77,35,692	2,28,07,412	2,90,55,176
Assets				
Fixes Assets	73,10,000	73,10,000	73,10,000	73,10,000
Less Dep.	12,32,550	9,66,710	7,62,555	
Net Fixed Assets	60,77,470	53,77,740	46,15,185	
Working Capital in Block	58,25,500	70,00,000	75,00,000	90,00,000
Surplus Funds	7,66,200	21,92,142	71,30,702	119,92,621
Total Assets	**1,39,01,700**	**1,77,35,692**	**2,28,07,412**	**2,90,55,176**

2

Feasibility Report Integrated Mineral Water and Bottle Plant

PROJECT AT A GLANCE

1.	PROJECT	Integrated mineral water and bottle making plant
2.	CAPACITY	4800 KL per /annum
3.	RAW MATERIALS	PVC compounds, Water, other Chemicals, and other Miscellaneous Consumables etc.
4.	LAND	500 sq.m.
5.	COVERED AREA	400 sq.m.
6.	PLANT & MACHINERY	Rs. 33.00 lakhs
7.	CONNECTED POWER LOAD	65 KW
8.	EMPLOYMENT POTENTIAL	60 Nos.
9.	ENVIRONMENTAL POLLUTION	None
10.	SOURCE OF KNOW-HOW	Indigenous
11.	LOCATION	Noida, U.P.
12.	FOREIGN EXCHANGE REQUIREMENT FOR IMPORT OF RAW MATERIAL	Nil
13.	DEBT TO EQUITY RATIO	1.18
14.	PAY-BACK PERIOD	3.05 Years
15.	BREAK-EVEN EFFICIENCY	49.46%

CAPITAL OUTLAY OF THE PROJECT

Project Cost

(a) LAND, BUILDING AND OTHER CIVIL WORK	Rs. 34.50 lakhs
(b) PLANT, EQUIPMENT & MACHINERY	Rs. 33.00 lakhs
(c) OTHER MISCELLANEOUS ASSESTS	Rs. 10.00 lakhs
(d) PRELIMIMARY & PRE-OPERATIVE EXPENSES	Rs. 11.10 lakhs
(e) MARGIN MONEY FOR WORKING CAPITAL	Rs. 12.05 lakhs
(f) CONTINGENCIES	Rs. 4.36 lakhs
TOTAL	**Rs. 105.00 lakhs**

Means of Finacing

(a)	LONG TERM LOANS FROM FINANCIAL INSTITUTIONS	Rs.57.00 lakhs
(b)	EQUITY CAPTIAL FROM PROMOTERS, THEIR FRIENDS, ASSOCIATES & RELATIVES	Rs.48.00 lakhs
	TOTAL	**Rs. 105 lakhs**

INTRODUCTION

Water is essential for sustenance of living organisms. In a human body system water and is necessity for keeping the system functioning. Humans need clean, tasty and safe drinking water free from any micro-organism and are willing to pay substantially if need be.

Mineral water originally meant water from various springs, which are thought to be having medicinal and curative value. These spring waters although contained dissolved chemicals of medicinal properties were also containing harmful micro-organism. Mineral water nowadays is a bottled drinking water, which is safe and hygienic to drink. The source can be natural mineral spring, borewell or municipal water supply, which is then processed and bottled. The former is called natural mineral water and the latter fortified mineral water.

Bureau of Indian Standards defined two types of mineral water :

(a) **Type 1:** Natural mineral water which is the water obtained directly from potable natural or drilled sources like spring, artesian well, drilled well or from an underground formation and not derived from a municipal system or public water supply.

(b) **Type 2:** Fortified mineral water characterised by its content of non-adverse health related mineral salts and their relative proportions and the presence of non-toxic trace elements or of other constituents in conformity to all provisions laid down in the specification of mineral water (15:13428-1992).

There is a large scope of exporting the mineral water as well as there is growing domestic market and as such the project is considered as an export oriented project.

PRODUCT SPECIFICATION AND STANDARDS

Pure water however is not fit for drinking. The presence of minerals and salts dissolved in potable water are beneficial to health. Pure water is tasteless. The presence of mineral and dissolved salts and gases impart the taste to water.

Drinking water should not contain substances that harm human system. World Health Organisation has specified properties and contents of drinking water.

Bureau of Indian Standards has specified both mineral water in bottle and drinking water. IS-13428-1992 stipulates the specification of mineral water. The stipulations are described below :

(a) Natural mineral water shall not be transported in bulk containers for packaging or for any other processing before packaging.

(b) Mineral water shall be manufactured and packed under hygienic conditions.

(c) Yeasts or moulds shall be absent in the water when tested as per prescribed methods.

(d) After bottling the total viable colony count shall not exceed 100 per ml at 20-22°C in 72 hours on agar gelatin mixture and 20% at 37°C in 24 hours on agar. The total viable colony count shall be measured within 12 hours after bottling, the water being maintained at 4°C+(–) 1°C during the period.

(e) Coli, other coliform bacteria and faecal streptococci shall be absent in any 250 ml sample.

Chemical and physical requirements of bottled mineral water as per 15:13428-1992

Number		Description	Unit	Limit Tested as per
1.	Colour	Hazen	5 Hazen	IS:3025 pt4-1983
2.	Odour		Agreeable	15:3025 pt5-1983
3.	Taste		Do	IS:3025 pt7 & 8-1984
4.	Turbidity	NTU	5 NTU	IS:3025 pt10-1984
5.	Total dissolved solids	Mg/1	1500 Mg/1 max	IS:3025 pt16-1984
6.	PH		6.5-8.5	IS:3025 pt11-1983
7.	Barium as Ba	Mg/1	1.0 Mg/1 max	IS:13428-1992
8.	Copper as Cu	-Do-	1.0 Mg/1 max	IS:3025-1964
9.	Iron as Fe	-Do-	0.3 Mg/1 max	-Do-
10.	Manganese as Mn	-Do-	0.5 Mg/1 max	-Do-
11.	Boron as B	-Do-	1.0 Mg/1 max	-Do-
12.	Nitrate as NO_3	-Do-	45 Mg/1 max	IS:3024 pt4-1988
13.	Free chlorine	-Do-	0.2 Mg/1 max	IS:3025 pt26-1986
14.	Fluoride as F	-Do-	1.5 Mg/1 max	IS:3025-1964
15.	Aluminium as Al	-Do-	0.03 Mg/1 max	-Do-
16.	Phenolic compound as phenol		Nil max	-Do-
17.	Mercury as Hg	-Do-	0.001 Mg/1 max	
18.	Cadmium as Cd	-Do-	0.01 max	IS:3025-1964
19.	Selenium	-Do-	0.01 max	IS:3025-1964
20.	Arsenic as As	-Do-	0.05 max	IS:3025 pt37-1988
21.	Cyanides as CN	-Do-	0.01 max	IS:3025 pt27-1988
22.	Lead as Pb	-Do-	0.05 max	
23.	Zinc as Zn	-Do-	5.0 max	
24.	Silver as Ag	-Do-	0.01 max	
25.	Mineral oil	-Do-	Absent	IS:3025 pt40-1992
26.	Chromium	-Do-	0.05 max	IS:13428-1992
27.	Chloride as Cl	-Do-	200 max	IS:3025 pt32-1988
28.	Sulphate as SO_4	-Do-	250 max	-Do-
29.	Alkalinity as HCO_3	-Do-	600 max	IS:3025-1964
30.	Radioactive material			
30. (a)	Alpha emitters	UC/ml	10^{-9} max	
30. (b)	Beta emitters	UC/ml	10^{-7} max	

Mineral water shall be packed in clean and sterile container made of polyethylene comforming to IS:1046-1982 or PVC conforming to IS:10148-1982 or PET conforming to IS:12252-1987 (PET&PBT). Mineral water may also be packed in glass or other suitable containers.

The following particulars shall be marked legibly and indelibly on the label of the container of the mineral water:

- Type of mineral water (natural or fortified).
- Name of manufacturer.
- Manner of disinfecting.
- Batch or code number of production.
- Date of bottling.
- Expiry date (best before.........).
- Net volume in ml.
- Source of water only in case of natural mineral water.

Although the total dissolved solids limit specified in IS:13428-1992 is 1500 mg/1, the taste of water is optimum if the total dissolved solid is between 150-500 mg/1. Higher the dissolved solids brackish is the taste of the water.

The method of sterilisation of water effects its taste. Chlorination gives a bad odour of residual chlorine unless removed, hydrogen peroxide makes it bitter because of residual peroxide, boiling makes the water tasteless and so on. Then there is the question of cost. Ozone treatment and UV treatment however, does not adversely affects the water taste.

Thus export packaging should preferably be done in glass containers. Many a customers intend to buy flavoured mineral water and in many a cases the users stipulate that the analysis and content of the water should be printed on the bottle.

MARKET SURVEY

Mineral water industry has grown many folds in all the developed economies of the world. The product is targeted especially at touring and travelling market segments. The market is also growing due to contamination/shortage of water supply in the metros.

Natural mineral water with certain dissolved solids/pH value from a single source, distilled water and processed pure water are the different types of water that are being marketed the world over. However, natural mineral water always has a separate market for itself and commands a premium. At present the Indian market is dominated by processed water. The demand for consumption of mineral water in India has been estimated at approx. 1.80 million litres of pure mineral water bottles in 1995 and the market is expected to grow at a rate of 25-35 per cent per annum. The domestic market of mineral water is mainly derived from the tourism sector. Further, the demand may also be from institutional sector as well as from higher income bracket group in urban areas.

Presently, the mineral water market is being dominated by Bisleri and Bailley who are packing the water in various sizes of containers. There are also other minor players with the brand names like Dew Drops, Penguin, Yes, Ice, Him Aqua, Hello etc., of late Papsi and Coke have come up with their brands of mineral water. Apart from the local, market there is a huge demand for mineral water in the Gulf as well as the East Euro-pean countries, particularly Russia.

There is a perceptible shift towards the consumption of mineral water due to boost in tourism and the concept of hygiene and shift to consumption of bacteria free water.

The regional share of bottled mineral water is as under :

Region	Market	States covered	Major cities
North	30%	Delhi, Haryana, Rajasthan, UP, Himachal Piadesh, J&K.	New Delhi, Jaipur, Udaipur, Lucknow, Allahabad, Agra, Kullu, Manali, Shimla, Srinagar, Chandigarh
West	35%	Maharashtra, Goa, Gujarat.	Mumbai, Nasik, Nagpur, Aurangabad, Baroda, Ahmedabad, Jamrnnagar, Panjim.
South	20%	Karnataka, Tamil Nadu, Kerela.	Bangalore, Mysore, Mangalore, Madras, Madurai, Pondicheery, Trivandrum, Coimbatore, Cochin
East and Central	15%	Bihar, West Bengal, Orissa, A.P., Madhya Pradesh and Far North East States.	Patna, Calcutta, Bhubaneshwar, Cuttack, Hyderabad, Guntur, Tirupati, Bhopal, Indore, Gwalior

The market for mineral water could be broadly classified as :

(a) Institutional — Five and four star hotels, airlines, shipping, industry, railways etc.

(b) Open market — Non star hotels, restaurants, chemists, hospitals, tourist spots, retail stores etc.

At present exports of mineral water is very limited. This is basically due to quality standards and high cost of transport. Through the 70s and the 80s, the mineral waiter category was a virtual shell, largely limited to travellers and the more affluent consumers. (Travellers constituted as much as 60 per cent of the total market, volume). Research showed that people equated the consumption of mineral water with foreigners wary of contamination.

Sale and production of mineral water in India for domestic and international market is relatively a new development. The bottled mineral water is fast gaining popularity despite its relatively high price compared to buying capacity of average middle class Indian. This is mainly because of high packaging cost, which constitutes more than 75 per cent of the mineral water cost structure. A few years back there were only two well-known companies manufacturing bottled mineral water. They are: (a) Parle beverages Pvt. Ltd., (b) Mohan Meakin Breweries Ltd. Besides these two companies there are other small companies also making bottled mineral water such as: Parle Agro, Mumbai (Brand - Bailley), Amrit Ganga, UP (Brand - Dew Drops), Himland Industries, (Brand - Him Aqua), Oasjs, Yes, Ice, Hello, Penguin etc.

The domestic market of mineral water is usually because of foreign tourists. They consume about 80 per cent of the domestic market product. The tourist influx has considerably increased in recent years. In 1996, thirteen lakhs foreign tourists visited India. This figure excludes the visitors from Pakistan and Bangladesh.

The earning in foreign exchange was Rs. 3000 crores. It is expected that at least 5-6 per cent growth rate will be there in the tourist arrivals of India. The estimated tourist arrivals in India in 2000 will be 16 lakh.

On an average a full-grown man or a woman is expected to drink about at least six litres of water in summer and four litres in winter. An average five litres per person. Thus the total mineral water consumed in 1995 was 8 million litre.

Even if 20 per cent of this is provided at the hotel through piped drinking water about seven million litre of mineral water was consumed in 1995 for domestic market. It is estimated that Indians consumed an equal amount of mineral water. Thus the total consumption of mineral water was 14 million litre in 1995.

The installed capacity of the sector to the tune of (30,000 Kl per year for organised sector and about additional 30,000 Kl per year in SSI sector). Although the market is still dominated by Bisleri, many regional brands have come up over the last three years. People do not mind coughing up Rs. 10 to 12 for a litre of mineral water.

The popularity of the drink is reflected in the kinds of health hazards has been growing and people are becoming careful about drinking only safe water. A few years ago, mineral water was available only at chemists and 5 star hotels. But now, one can buy it at railway stations, state transport halts, grocery stores and even paan shops.

Over the last three years, awareness of health hazards has been growing and people are becoming careful about drinking only safe water. Often, a travelling middle class family buys mineral water. Besides, drinking or serving mineral water is considered "up-market" and it is now served at social gatherings, like wedding receptions.

The national market is currently estimated at 60 million litres worth Rs 20 crore. It has been growing at around 25-30 per cent a year over the last three years.

MANUFACTURING PROCESS

The manufacturing process comprises of following operations.

— Water Treatment and Purification

— Bottle making

— Cap making

— Bottle Filling and Sealing

Water Treatment and Purification

Raw water is treated with chemicals which co-agulate the impurities. The sediments are settled and odours are removed. The supernatant water is filtered through sand filters to remove suspended impurities. This cleared water is passed through R.O. system to remove excess dissolved salts to soften the hard water. The softened water is passed through a series of micron filters comprising of cartridges having pore sizes 100 microns, 0.5 microns and 0.1 microns to make it sparkling clear. This sparkling clear water is passed through ultra violet lights and subsequently ozonised to make it completely free from harmful bacteria.

The pure, bacteria free water is transferred to filling units.

Bottle Making

PET compound is fed to the hopper of blow moulding machine.

Blow moulded bottles are automatically discharged from the mould and chopped of extra plastics, manually and kept in corrugated cartons.

The filled bottles are inspected for any defects and packed in the cartons.

PET Bottles

PET bottles are fairly established in India particularly for packing of cosmetics/toiletries. PET containers of one to six litre capacity are also manufactured for general purpose packing. Such containers are used in place of glass as they offer the system which shows better resistance to impact and also do not shatter like glass.

Some of the manufacturers of squashs and edible oils have carried out the compatibility study with PET bottles and have found that the results are very satisfactory.

PET bottles can be manufactured by extrusion blow moulding and injection blow moulding. Extrusion blow moulding which produces tubes/parison on continuous basis is more widely used due to simplicity and comparatively lower cost of the process.

PROCESS FLOW SHEET

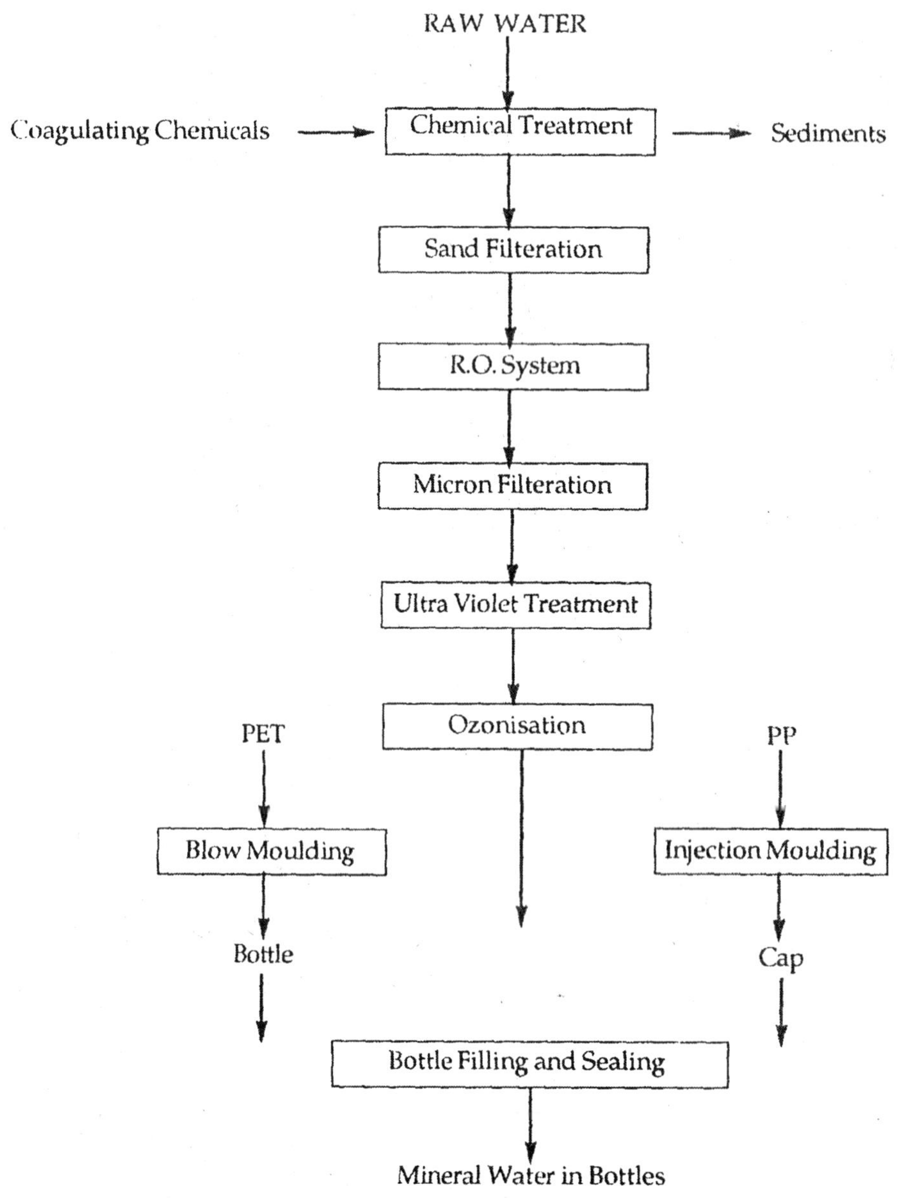

PET bottles are used as replacement of glass and metal containers and hence are expected to fulfill the requirements of packaging as described below :

1. Pilfer proof capping
2. Vacuum filling
3. Lablling
4. High speed packing

It has been observed that pilfer proof capping of PET bottles on manual as well as automatic packing line can be carried out provided that necks of the bottles as-well as capping machines are modified to transfer the capping pressure from the bottlenecks to some other convenient place. It is also necessary to have closer control on dimensions of necks of PET bottles.

Vacuum Filling

Vacuum filling of PET bottles depends upon the shape and design of the bottles. Cylindrical bottles offer the maximum advantage in respect of vacuum filling.

Labelling

Labelling with paper on PET containers requires special types of adhesives which can bound PET to paper. The viscosity of such adhesive can be adjusted so that labeling can be carried out on automatic high-speed packing line. While comparing cost of PET bottles against glass and tin, it is necessary to consider the overall cost of the packaging system rather than the cost of the basic bottles. PET bottles offer the following savings due to their inherent properties:

1. Lower freight due to lighter weight and less volume of PET bottles.
2. Lower cost of packaging due to lighter weight and higher impact strength.
3. Less loss of valuable packing product due to lower breakage.

It may be worthwhile to note here that although the basic cost of PET bottles is about 15-20 per cent higher than glass bottles, the overall cost of PET bottles comes out lower than the glass bottles.

Raw Materials

The main raw materials required for the manufacture of mineral water are: ground water chemicals and packaging material. The requirement of water will be met from bore-wells. Treatment chemicals like alum etc. are readily available from indigenous sources.

The project is proposed to be set up in Noida, U.P. which falls between River Ganges and Yamuna. Subsoil water in between these two Rivers is generally good, however it varies in quality from place to place as well as depends upon the depth of Bore-well. The raw water in this area has total dissolved solids varying from 500 to 1000 ppm.

Packaging Material

In this project one liter PET bottle packaging is proposed. One-litre food grade PET bottles sealed by PP caps. The bottles are subsequently packed in corrugated box cartons. For in-house production of bottles and caps compounded food grade PET and HOPE granules will be used respectively.

The properties of PET compound are as under :

Inherent Viscosity	:	0.68
'K' Value	:	57
Apparne Bulk Density	:	0.53
Porosity	:	0.19–0.29
Heat Loss	:	0.3 max
Flow Time	:	15-30 seconds
Residuel Monomer	:	Below 2 PPM

PROJECT MANAGEMENT AND CONSTRUCTION SCHEDULE

Project Scheduling

The management will be scheduling these activities so as to complete the job in an acceptable time span. In matters of planning, the management will consider the requirement, availability and employment of necessary manpower and facilities for carrying out the work as it progresses with time. The aim of the management will be to plan and conduct the work in such a manner that cost and time required are properly balanced.

Project Construction Schedule

A detailed programme in the form of CPM network has been prepared covering all the key contracts. The detailed programme highlights the dates for invitation of tenders, receipt of quotations, scrutiny of bids, placement of orders, receipt of materials and equipment and machinery etc. taking into consideration, the time required for preparation of bids and delivery periods of various purchased items.

Time Schedule

A time span of 12 months for project completion defined by erection and commissioning of the plant is estimated. The following table gives the time schedule for major works carried out in the implementation of the project.

	Project Work	**Period in Months**
1.	Preliminary and Promotional work such as registration of the company	0 to 1
2.	Procurement of Land and site development	2 to 4
3.	Construction of buildings and structures	4 to 7
4.	Design and engineering of the plant	2 to 3
5.	Ordering and procurement of equipment	4 to 8
6.	Erection and commissioning	8 to 11
7.	Start up of production	12

ESTIMATION OF PROJECT COST

Land and Site Development

The total covered area of the plant is estimated at 400 square metres. This includes the area required for the main production plant, utility section, laboratory, administrative office, godown, public conveniences etc., with a provision for roads and future ex-pansion, the land requirements for the proposed plant has been estimated at 500 square metres. The cost of land is estimated at Rs 16.00 lakhs.

Cost of Land and Site Development

1. Land 500 sq. m. @ Rs. 3200.00 per sq. m. including registration charges	:	16.00
2. Site clearing and leveling expenses	:	1.00
3. Internal roads and gate	:	1.00
TOTAL		**Rs. 18.00 lakhs**

Buildings and Structures

The cost of buildings and structures is estimated on the basis of area and volume and also on the type of foundation to be adopted for various items of equipment. The cost estimates have been worked out considering market prices of building materials prevailing in the market.

Cost of Building and Structures

A. Factory Building

1. Factory house with brickwall construction area of 200 sq.m. @ Rs. 4000 per sq.m. : 8.00
2. Store house area of 150 sq.m. @ Rs. 4000 per sq.m. : 6.00

Sub-total A Rs.14.00 lakhs

B. Non-factory Building

2. Administrative Block with brickwall construction area of 50 sq.m. @ Rs. 5000 sq.m. : 2.50

Sub-total B Rs.2.50 lakhs

TOTAL (sub-total A + sub-total B) **Rs. 16.50 lakhs**

Cost of Plant and Machinery

S.No.	Description	(Rs. Lakhs) **Estimated Cost**
A.	**Water Treatment**	
	(a) Borewell and pumps	3.00
	(b) Water storage tanks (plastics)	0.50
	(c) 2000 LPH Absorption (sand) Filters with M.S. frontal pipe line	0.68
	(d) R.O.system for 2000 LPH	8.50
	(e) 2000 LPH, 100 Micron T.S.S. filter with M.S. frontal pipe line	0.60
	(f) 0.5 Micron filter	0.62
	(g) 0.1 Micron Filter	0.70
	(h) Ultraviolet water disinfector system	0.36
	(i) Ozonator 2000 LPH	1.54
	(j) Installation	1.40
B.	**Packaging**	
	(a) PET moulding machine	4.67
	(b) Hand cutter	0.05
	(c) 1 Ltr S.S. Blow Mould	0.48
	(d) Screen printing machine	0.20
	(e) Natural cooling tower	0.40
	(f) Injection moulding machine for caps	2.80
C.	**Filling machine**	
	Automatic bottling system (24 BPM)	6.50
	Total	**33.00**

OTHER MISCELLANEOUS FIXED ASSETS

A. Electrical and Workshop Equipment

1. Switchgear, cables and cable trays : 1.00
2. Workshop Equipment including maintenance and Erection tools and tackles : 1.00

sub-total Rs. 2.00 lakhs

B. Office Furniture, fixtures and equipment

1. Executive tables and chairs :
2. Tables and chairs for clerks/typists :

3. Steel almirahs, filing cabinet and cash box	:	
4. Typewriter, telephone, intercome and wall clock etc.	:	
sub-total B		Rs. 2.00 lakhs
C. Vechicles		
1. Three wheeler and scooter	:	2.00
sub-total C	:	Rs. 2.00 Lakhs
D. Other Assets		
1. Platform type weighing machines	:	
2. Laboratory Equipment	:	
3. Fire fighting Equipment	:	
4. Generator sets	:	
5. Installation Expenses	:	
sub-total D		Rs. 4.00 lakhs
Total (A+B+C+D)		**Rs. 10.00 lakhs**

Preliminary and Pre-operative Expenses

The preliminary and pre-operative expenses for this project are estimated as follows :

Preliminary Expenses

1.	Drafting charges payable to Chartered Accountant for drafting the Memorandum and Articles of Association	:	15,000
2.	Printing charges for Memorandum and Articles of Association	:	15,000
3.	Registration Fee payable to the Registrar of companies for registration	:	18,000
	Total		**Rs. 48,000**

Pre-operative Expenses

1.	Salaries, wages and staff welfare expenses	1,20,000
2.	Printing, stationary and postage	60,000
3.	Rent, rates and taxes	60,000
4.	Travelling and conveyance expenses	60,000
5.	Auditor's remuneration	15,000
6.	Insurance premium	11,000
7.	Interest	4,46,000
8.	Bank charges and commission	7,000
9.	Recruitment of personnels	20,000
10.	Legal and professional fees	50,000
11.	Other Miscellaneous expenses	2,12,000
	Total	**Rs.10,61,000**

Working Capital and Margin Money

Estimates of working capital requirements have been worked out on the basis of following cycles of expenditures involving cash liabilities and other recurring requirements.

1. Stock of raw materials in store	:	0.5 months
2. Packing materials	:	0.5 months
3. Work-in-progress	:	0.25 months

4. Stock of finished goods in store	:	0.25 months
5. Accounts receivable	:	1 month
6. Other recurring expenses	:	1 month
7. Electricity deposit	:	Rs. 1.88 lakhs

1. Work-in-progress covers the cost of raw materials, utilities and labour and staff wages.
2. The value of finished goods for sale is arrived at by taking into consideration, the cost of raw materials, packaging materials, utilities, labour and staff wages, administrative overheads, maintenance and repairs and insurance.
3. Other recurring expenses cover utilities, labour and staff wages, maintenance and repairs, insurance, administrative overheads and sales expenses.
4. For calculating the accounts receivable, the sales price of mineral water is taken at Rs. 5600 per KL into consideration (exclusive of excise duty if any).

The requirements of margin money for working capital requirements are made on the basis of the following norms adopted by all nationalized banks in India.

Margin on Raw Materials in store	20%
Margin on packing materials	20%
Margin on work-in-progress	30%
Margin on finished goods in store	30%
Margin on accounts receivable	20%
Margin on other recurring expenses	100%
Margin on electricity deposit	100%

The requirement of total capital, bank borrowings and margin money during the first, second and third and subsequent years of plant operation are estimated.

MANUFACTURING INPUTS AND COSTS

Raw Materials and Consumables

For producing 4800 KL Mineral Water per annum at 100 per cent capacity utilization, the raw materials required is given in below and the cost estimates to Rs. 105.60 lakhs.

1 Liter bottle 48 lakh

= 192 MT PET compound/ PP @ Rs. 55/- Kg	Rs. 105.60 lakh

Annual Cost of Packing Materials

1. The annual cost of cartons (estimated)	Rs. 24.00 lakh

Utilities

The main utilities required for the plant are water and electricity.

Water: Water is required for process and bottle rinsing. Small quantity of water is also required for consumption by personnel and for cleaning and washing purposes. At 100 per cent capacity utilization is estimated at 18,000 K ltrs. As all the water is generated at the plant, the cost of water is covered in electricity costs.

Electricity: The unit will need a total connected power connection for 65 KW. The annual consumption of electricity at 100 per cent capacity utilisation is estimated at 3.00 lakhs units;. Considering a unit rate of Rs. 2.50 per KW h of electricity, the annual cost of electricity is estimated at Rs.7.50 lakh.

Annual Cost of Utilities

The annual cost of utilities is thus estimated as follows :

Annual cost of water	Rs. 0.00 lakh
Annual cost of electricity	Rs. 7.50 lakh
Total	Rs. 7.50 lakh

Manpower Requirements

The requirement of personnel has been worked out by taking into consideration the anticipated workload, degree of skill required and the productivity of the workers on similar jobs.

Designation	Nos.	Monthly Salary (Rs.)	Annual Wages (Rs. Lakh)
Factory Supervision			
1. Works manager	1	10,000	1.20
2. Chemist	1	6,000	0.72
3. Lab analyst	1	2,500	1.20
Administrative & Sales			
1. Admn. manager	1	8,000	0.96
2. Finance manager	1	8,000	0.96
3. Marketing manager	1	8,000	0.96
4. Sales executives	2	6,000	1.44
5. Accounts officer	1	5,000	0.60
6. Clerks/Typist	6	2,500	1.80
7. Peons	2	1,800	0.43
Labour & Watch & Ward			
1. Skilled workers	10	3,000	3.60
2. Semi-skilled workers	25	2,000	6.00
3. Unskilled workers	4	1,800	0.86
4. Security officer	1	5,000	0.60
		Total	21.33
		Other benefits	5.67
		Grand total	**27.00**

Administrative Overheads

Administrative overheads include administrative and office expenses such as staff travelling, office stationery and postage, telephone bills, audit fee, bank charges and other sundry expenses.

	Item	Expenditure in lakh
1.	Rent, rates & taxes	1.20
2.	Travelling & conveyance	1.20
3.	Postage, telegram, telephones	0.60
4.	Printing and stationery	1.00
5.	Vehicle expenses	1.00
6.	Advertisement & publicity	13.44
7.	Legal and professional expenses	0.30
8.	Directors sitting fees and expenses	0.06
9.	Bank charges, guarantee, commissions etc.	0.27
10.	Auditors fee and expenses	0.06
11.	Other miscellaneous expenses	4.78

Maintenance and Repairs

On the basis of norms available from similar plants in actual operation, provision has been made for annual cost of maintenance and repairs. The maintenance and the repair expenses are estimated at 1 per cent of the cost of the building and structures and 2 per cent of the erected cost of plant and machinery and other miscellaneous fixed assets. The cost of maintenance and repairs is estimated as follows:

		Rs. in lakh
1.	Cost of maintenance of building and structure @ 1% of Rs. 16.50 lakh	0.17
2.	Cost of maintenance of Plant and Machinery @ 2% of Rs. 33.00 lakh	0.66
3.	Cost of maintenance of other miscellaneous fixed assets @ 2% of Rs. 10.00 lakhs	0.20
	Total	**1.03**

Insurance

The building and structure, plant and machinery and other miscellaneous fixed assets of the plant will be insured against all types of risks. The annual insurance premium payable is estimated at 0.6 per cent on Rs. 59.50 lakh, which works out to Rs. 0.337 lakh.

Sales Expenses

The sales expenses generally cover commission, brokerage, discount etc. The annual sales expenses at 100 per cent capacity utilization are estimated at 5 per cent of the annual sales revenue of Rs. 286.86 lakhs which works out to Rs. 13.44 lakhs.

Sales Revenue

Sales revenue of Rs. 288 lakhs per annum will be generally at 100% capacity utilisation.

No. of one liter bottles	=	48 lakhs
Sales price	=	Rs. 6.00 per bottle
Total Revenue	=	Rs. 288 lakhs

FINANCIAL ANALYSIS

INTEREST ON TERM LOAN

Year	Loan o/s at the beginning	Loan o/s at the end of the first half year	Loan o/s at the end of the second half year	Interest for the first half year	Interest for the second half year	Total interest for the term loan
1	57	57	57	4.56	4.56	9.12
2	57	57	53.65	4.56	4.56	9.12
3	53.65	50.3	46.94	4.292	4.024	8.316
4	46.94	43.6	40.24	3.7552	3.488	7.2432
5	40.24	36.9	33.53	3.2192	2.952	6.1712
6	33.53	30.2	26.82	2.6824	2.416	5.0984
7	26.82	23.5	20.12	2.1456	1.88	4.0256
8	20.12	16.8	13.41	1.6096	1.344	2.9536
9	13.41	10.1	6.71	1.0728	0.808	1.8808
10	6.71	3.4	0.05	0.5368	0.272	0.8088

Note: A sum of Rs. 57 lakhs is proposed to be raised as long-term loan from financial institutions to meet the capital cost of the project.

The rate of interest to be charged by the financial institutions is taken as 16 per cent.

The loan is to be paid in 17 half yearly installments. The first installment of Rs. 3.35 lakh will be paid at the end of completion of second year of the working of the unit and the balance 16 half yearly installments each will be payable at half yearly intervals from the date of payment of first installment.

Interest on short-term loan (in Rs. Lakhs)

Year of Operation	Bank Borrowings	Interest Payable
First Year	16.69	3.0042
Second Year	19.28	3.4704
Third Year	21.87	3.9366

Note: for the purpose of calculating the interest on short term loan the interest rate is taken as 18 per cent.

WORKING CAPITAL AND MARGIN MONEY REQUIREMENTS

Assessment of Working Capital and Margin Money Requirements

Description	Norms in months	Margin money (%)	1st year 60%	Plant efficiency		2nd year 70%	plant efficiency		3rd year 80%	Plant efficiency	
			Working capital	Margin money	Bank finance	Working capital	Margin money	Bank finance	Working capital	Margin money	Back capital
1. Raw materials in store	0.5	20	2.64	0.528	2.112	3.08	0.616	2.464	3.52	0.704	2.816
2. Packing materials	0.5	20	0.6	0.12	0.48	0.7	0.14	0.56	0.8	0.16	0.64
3. Work-in-progress	0.25	30	1.98	0.594	1.386	2.21	0.663	1.547	2.45	0.735	1.715
4. Finished goods	0.25	30	2.8	0.84	1.96	3.09	0.927	2.163	3.37	1.011	2.359
5. Accounts receivable	1	20	13.44	2.688	10.752	15.68	3.136	12.544	17.92	3.584	14.336
6. Other recurring expenses	1	100	5.41	5.41	0	5.58	5.58	0	5.75	5.75	0
7. Electricity deposit		100	1.88	1.88	0	1.88	1.88	0	1.88	1.88	0
Total			**28.75**	**12.06**	**16.69**	**32.22**	**12.94**	**19.28**	**35.7**	**13.82**	**21.876**

DEPRECIATION SCHEDULE

A. Asset Valuation for Depreciation Purposes (in lakhs)

Asset	Basic cost	Share of preoperative expenses	Share of contingency margin	Total cost
1. Land & site development	18.00	2.46	1.01	21.47
2. Factory building	14.00	1.92	0.79	16.71
3. Non-factory building	2.5	0.34	0.14	2.98
4. Plant & machinery	33.00	4.52	1.86	39.38
5. Electricity & workshop equipment	2.00	0.27	0.11	2.38
6. Office furniture & fixtures	2.00	0.27	0.11	2.38
7. Vehicles	2.00	0.27	0.11	2.38
8. Other assets	4.00	0.55	0.23	4.78
9. TOTAL	**77.50**	**10.6**	**4.36**	**92.46**

B. Depreciation Schedule for Company Law Purposes by Straight-Line method (in lakhs)

	Depreciation on	Total cost	Rate of depreciation	Annual depreciation
1.	Land & site development	21.47	Nil	
2.	Factory building	16.71	3.39%	0.57
3.	Non-factory building	2.98	1.64%	0.05
4.	Plant & machinery	39.38	9.50%	3.74
5.	Electricity & workshop Equipment	2.38	9.50%	0.23
6.	Office furniture & fixtures	2.38	3.39%	0.08
7.	Vehicles	2.38	9.50%	0.23
8.	Other assets	4.78	5.28%	0.25
9.	**TOTAL**	**92.46**		**5.15**

C. Depreciation Schedule for Income Tax Purposes by Written Down Value method

	Depreciation on	Rate of depreciation	Year 1	Year 2	Year 3	Year 4	Year 5
1.	Land & site development	Nil					
2.	Factory building	10%	1.671	1.503	1.353	1.219	1.096
3.	Non-factory building	5%	0.15	0.141	0.134	0.128	0.121
4.	Plant & machinery	25%	9.845	7.383	5.538	4.154	3.115
5.	Electricity & workshop Equipment	25%	0.595	0.446	0.335	0.251	0.188
6.	Office furniture & fixtures	10%	0.238	0.214	0.193	0.173	0.156
7.	Vehicles	10%	0.238	0.214	0.193	0.173	0.156
8.	Other assets	15%	0.717	0.609	0.518	0.440	0.374
9.	**TOTAL**		**13.45**	**10.51**	**8.264**	**6.538**	**5.206**

TAX CALCULATION

Rs. lakh

	Year 1	Year 2	Year 3	Year 4	Year 5
Profit/loss before depreciation	12.85	26.13	40.21	41.29	42.36
Add: depreciation for company law purposes	5.15	5.15	5.15	5.15	5.15
Less: depreciation for tax purposes	13.45	10.51	8.26	6.54	5.21
Less: unabsorbed depreciation of earlier years	—	—	—	—	—
GROSS TOTAL INCOME	13.45	10.51	8.26	6.54	5.21
Less: deduction for newly set up industrial undertaking under Sec. 801 for 10 years @ 30% of gross total income	4.04	3.14	8.04	8.88	9.6
TOTAL INCOME	9.42	7.33	18.76	20.72	22.40
Income tax @ 45% of total income	4.24	3.29	8.44	9.32	10.08

PROFITABILTY ANALYSIS

	Year 1	Year 2	Year 3	Year 4	Year 5
Installed Capacity (KL)	4800	4800	4800	4800	4800
Production (KL)	2880	3360	3840	3840	3840
Capacity utilization	60%	70%	80%	80%	80%
A. Sales realisation	172.8	201.6	230.4	230.4	230.4
B. Cost of Production					
Raw materials	63.36	73.92	84.48	84.48	84.48
Utilities	4.50	5.25	6.00	6.00	6.00
Wages & Salaries	27.00	27.00	27.00	27.00	27.00
Maintenance & Repairs	1.03	1.03	1.03	1.03	1.03
Insurance	0.36	0.36	0.36	0.36	0.36
Packing materials	14.40	16.80	19.20	19.20	19.20
C. Administration & selling expenses					
Administration expenses	23.91	23.91	23.91	23.91	23.91
Selling expenses	8.07	9.41	10.75	10.75	10.75
D. Gross profit before interest	30.17	43.92	57.67	57.67	57.67
E. Total financial expenses					
Interest on term loan	9.12	9.12	8.32	7.24	6.17
Interest on bank borrowing	3.00	3.47	3.94	3.94	3.94
F. Depreciation	5.15	5.15	5.15	5.15	5.15
G. Operating profit	12.9	26.13	40.26	41.34	42.41
H. Preliminary expenses written off	0.05	0.05	0.05	0.05	0.05
I Profit /Loss Before Tax	12.85	26.13	40.21	41.29	42.36
J. Provision for Tax	4.24	3.29	8.44	9.32	10.08
K. Profit after Tax	8.61	22.84	31.77	31.97	32.28
M. Retained Profit	8.61	22.84	31.77	31.97	32.28
N. *Add*: Depreciation :	5.15	5.15	5.15	5.15	5.15
Preliminary expenses written off	0.05	0.05	0.05	0.05	0.05
O. Net cash accruals	**13.81**	**28.04**	**36.97**	**37.17**	**37.48**

PROJECTED CASH FLOW STATEMENT

Rs. lakh

	Construction period	Year 1	Year 2	Year 3	Year 4	Year 5
SOURCES						
Equity capital	48.00					
Profit before taxation with interest added back		24.97	38.72	52.47	52.47	52.47
Depreciation		5.15	5.15	5.15	5.15	5.15
Preliminary expenses written off		0.05	0.05	0.05	0.05	0.05
Increase in long term loans	57.00					
Increase in short term loans		16.69	2.59	2.59		
TOTAL A	**105.00**	**46.86**	**46.51**	**60.26**	**57.67**	**57.67**

APPLICATIONS						
Capital expenditure for the project	92.47					
Increase in working capital		28.75	3.47	3.47	0.00	0.00
Preliminary expenses	0.48					
Decrease in long term loans		0.00	3.35	6.70	6.70	6.70
Interest on term loans		9.12	9.12	8.32	7.24	6.17
Interest on short term loans		3	3.47	3.94	3.94	3.94
Taxation		4.24	3.29	8.44	9.32	10.08
TOTAL B	**92.95**	**45.11**	**22.70**	**30.87**	**27.20**	**26.89**
Opening balance of cash in hand and at bank	0.00	12.05	13.80	37.61	67.00	97.47
Surplus or (deficit)	12.05	1.75	23.81	29.39	30.47	30.76
Closing balance of cash in hand and at bank	12.05	13.80	37.61	67.00	97.47	128.30

PROJECTED BALANCE SHEET

Rs. Lakh

	At the end of the Construction period	Year 1	Year 2	Year 3	Year 4	Year 5
Liabilities						
Equity capital	48.00	48.00	48.00	48.00	48.00	48.00
Reserves and surplus		8.61	31.45	63.22	95.19	127.47
Term loan	57.00	57.00	53.65	46.94	40.24	33.53
Working capital adv.		16.69	19.28	21.87	21.87	21.87
TOTAL	**105.00**	**130.3**	**152.38**	**180.03**	**205.30**	**230.87**
Assets						
Fixed assets						
– Gross block		92.47	92.47	92.47	92.47	92.47
– Less accumulated depreciation		5.15	10.30	15.45	20.60	23.65
– Net fixed assets		87.32	82.17	77.02	71.87	63.82
Current assets, loans & advances						
– Raw materials		2.64	3.08	3.52	3.52	3.52
– Packing materials		0.6	0.7	0.8	0.8	0.8
– Work-in-progress		1.98	2.21	2.45	2.45	2.45
– Finished goods		2.8	3.09	3.37	3.37	3.37
– Other recurring expenses	1.88	5.41	5.58	5.75	5.75	5.75
– Electricity deposit		1.88	1.88	1.88	1.88	1.88
– Book debts		13.44	15.68	17.92	17.92	17.92
– Cash and bank balances	12.05	13.50	37.61	67.04	97.46	128.30
Preliminary expenses	0.48	0.43	0.38	0.33	0.28	0.23
TOTAL	**105.00**	**130.3**	**152.38**	**180.03**	**205.30**	**230.87**

PAY BACK PERIOD

The pay back period of the unit is estimated as follows:

	At the end of the year of operation		
Description	**First**	**Second**	**Third**
Net Profit Before Taxes	12.85	26.13	40.21
Depreciation	5.15	5.15	5.15
Interest on Long Term Loans	9.12	9.12	8.32
Gross Operating Surplus	27.12	40.40	53.68
Cummulative Operating Surplus	27.12	94.08	107.36

PAY BACK PERIOD = 3.05 years or 37 months

Debt-Service Coverage Ratio (Rs. Lakhs)

The following table shows the debt-service coverage ratio of the unit during the first five years of its operation.

		At the end of the year of operation				
	Description	**First**	**Second**	**Third**	**Fourth**	**Fifth**
A.	Debt servicing funds					
(1)	Net cash accruals	13.81	28.04	36.97	37.17	37.48
(2)	Interest on long term loans	9.12	9.12	8.13	7.24	6.17
	TOTAL A	22.93	37.16	45.10	44.41	43.65
B.	Debts					
(1)	Repayment of long term loans	0.00	3.35	6.70	6.70	6.70
(2)	Interest on long term loans	9.12	9.12	8.13	7.24	6.17
	TOTALS	9.12	12.47	14.83	13.94	12.87
(C)	**Debt-Service Coverage ratio (TOTAL A/TOTAL B)**	**2.51**	**2.98**	**3.04**	**3.19**	**3.39**

BREAK-EVEN POINT ANALYSIS

The Break-even point of the plant is determined from the assumed plant efficiency, fixed cost of sales, variable cost of sales and sales revenue using the following formula:

$$\text{Break-even point} = \frac{\text{Plant efficiency} \times \text{Fixed cost of sales}}{\text{Sales revenue} - \text{Variable cost of sales}}$$

Break-Even Point (in Rs. Lakhs)

	At the end of the year of operation				
Description	**First**	**Second**	**Third**	**Fourth**	**Fifth**
Capacity utilization (%)	60	70	80	80	80
Fixed cost of sales	66.81	66.81	65.91	64.70	63.49
Sales revenues	172.8	201.6	230.4	230.4	230.4
Variable cost of sales	93.33	108.85	124.37	124.37	124.37
Break-even efficiency (%)	50.44	50.42	49.73	48.82	47.90

Average break-even point = 49.46 per cent

BIBLIOGRAPHY

1. Davis H. Holt, "Entrepreneur—New Venture Creation", Printice Hall of India P. Ltd. N. Delhi 1998.
2. "The Facilitator's Hand book for Entrepreneurship Development among Rural Women" Asian and Pacific Centre for Transfer of Technology, New Delhi.
3. Akhowri MMP (Ed) "Training youth for Self. Employment/Entrepreneurship", Commonwealth youth Programme Asia Centre, Chandigarh 1989.
4. "Entrepreneur's Handbook", Technonet Asia and Institute for Small Scale Industries, Singapore 1981.
5. "Training Manual on Entrepreneurship Development", Technonet Asia, Singapore 1981.
6. Malhotra I. S. Gupta S.L., "Management of Small Scale Industries", Galgotia Publishing Co. New Delhi, 2000.
7. Richard Cantillon, "Essai surla nature du commerce en general, translated by H Higgs" Macmillon, London, 1931.
8. Carl Menger, "Principles of Economics", Free Press, 1950
9. Schumpeter, "Theory of Economic Development".
10. Peter F Drucker, "Managing for Results", Harper & Row, New York, 1964.
11. Welster's Third New International Dictionary, 1976.
12. Thomas J Peters and Robert H Water man Jr., "In Search of Excellence : Lessons from America's best–Run Companies", Harper & Row, New York, 1982.
13. Henry, Mintzberg 'Planning on the Lest Side and Managing on the Right." Harvard Business Review, July-Aug 1976.
14. Deloitte Haskins & Sells, "The Buy/Sell Decision : Small and Growing Business", 1987.
15. Donald F Kuratko and Richard M Hodgelts, "Entrepreneurship: A Contemporary Approach'. Dryden Press, New York, 1989.
16. James W Henderson, "Obtaining Venture Financing", Lexington, 1988.
17. Thomas J Martin, "Valuation Reference Manual", Thomar Publication NY, 1987.
18. Joel K Warley and Fess B green "Determinants of Risk Adjustment for Small Business Valuation in a growth Industry". Journal of Small Business Management Vol 27. No. 4 1989.
19. Arthur Lipper III, "Guide to Investing in Private Companies", Dow Jones-Irwin 1984.
20. David D Saitz, "How to get started in Your Own Franchise Business", Farnsworth 1980.
21. Russel M Knight, "The Independence of the Franchise Entrepreneur" Journal of Small Business Management Vol 23. No. 2, 1984.
22. "Franchise Opportunities Handbook", US Department of Commerce, Washington D.C.
23. Akkouri MMP, "Self Employment through Entrepreneurship Development Strategies, an experiment in Assam", National Labour Institute Bulletin, Jan-June, 1980.
24. Akkauri MMP and Vinod Gupta, "Sustaining Entrepreneurship", NIESBUD, New Delhi, 1990.
25. Alexender P.E "Industrial Estates in India", Asia Publishing House, New Delhi, 1963.
26. Bhatia B.S. "New Industrial Entrepreneur-Their Origins and Problems", Journal of General Management, Autumn 1974.
27. Bisht N.S. et al (Eds) "Entrepreneurship Reflections and Investigations", Chugh Publications, Allahabad, 1989.
28. Chandra P "Projects-Preparations, Appraisal and Implementation", Tata Mc Graw Hill, New Delhi, 1987.
29. Dasai A.N. "Entrepreneurship and Environments", Ashish Publishing House, New Delhi, 1990.
30. Desai V "Entrepreneur Development", Himalaya Publishing House, Bombay, 1990.

31. Drucker P.F, "Innovation and Entrepreneurship", Heinemann, London 1985.
32. Durand D.E. "Training and Development of Entrepreneurs -A Comparison of Mo-tivation and Skill Approaches", Journal of Small Business Management Vol 12,1974.
33. Gaikwad V.R. et al "Entrepreneurship Concept and Approaches", Indian Institute of Management, Abmedabad, 1974.
34. Ganguly S. "What Motivates Mr. Small Entrepreneur", Indian Management, May 1978,
35. Gautam V. "Enterprise and Society-Study of Some Aspects of Entrepreneurship and Management in India", Concept Publishing House, New Delhi, 1974.
36. Ghosh B. "Creating a Climate for Entrepreneurship", Capital, July 7, 1980.
37. "Entrepreneurship Development in Small Scale Industries", Ministry of Industry, Govt of India, New Delhi, 1977.
38. "Guidelines for the Preparation of Feasibility Reports", Planning Commission, Govt of India, New Delhi.
39. Hechansen H. "The Anatomy of Achievement Motivation", Academic Press, New Delhi, 1967.
40. Jain R "Planning a Small Scale Industry–A Guide to Entrepreneurs", S.S. Books Association, 1984.
41. Joshi A. and K. Singh "Lala Shri Ram—A Study in Entrepreneurship and Management"/ Orient Longman, New Delhi, 1975.
42. Kao J. "Entrepreneurship, Creativity and Organisation", Prentice Hall, New Jersey, 1989.
43. Kao J. and Stevenson H. (Eds) "Entrepreneurship—What it is and How to Teach It", Harvard University Press, 1989.
44. Kumar S.A. "Entrepreneurship in Small Industry", Discovery Publishing House, New Delhi, 1990.
45. Litt B "Why Entrepreneurs Succeed", Journal of General Management, 1974.
46. Mancuso J.R. "How to Start, Finance and Manage Your Own Small Business", Prentice Hall, New Delhi, 1978.
47. Meclelland D. "The Achieving Society", D.Van Nostrand & Co. New York, 1961.
48. Mishra D.N. "Entrepreneur and Entrepreneurship Development and Planning in India", Chugh Publications, Allahabad, 1990.
49. Newarlkar G.B. "Generation of Entrepreneurship in a Developing Economy", MSSIDE Bombay, 1979.
50. Pandey A.D et al "Developing the Entrepreneurial Spirit in India", SIET, Hyderabad, 1964.
51. Patel V.G. "Entrepreneurship Development Programme in India and its Relevance to Developing Countries", EDII, Ahmedabad, 1987.
52. Pathak H.N. "Entrepreneurial Tansition in Gujarat", Economic Scene, April, 1979.
53. Reddy T.S. and Murthy "Strategy for Development of Entrepreneurship in Backward Area—A Case Study", SEDME, 1979.
54. Rao. N.G. "Entrepreneurship and Growth of Enterprise in Industrial Estates", Deep and Deep, New Delhi, 1986.
55. Sharma K.L. "Entrepreneurial Growth and Industrial Development in North India", Abhinav, New Delhi, 1980.
56. Sharma R.A. "Entrepreneurial Performance in Indian Industry", Inter-India Publication, New Delhi, 1985.
57. Singh N. P. "Emerging Trends in Entrepreneurship Development—Theories and Practices", IFDM, New Delhi, 1985.
58. Srinivasan N.P. "Development Banking in India and Abroad", Kalyani Publishers, New Delhi, 1989.
59. Tandon B, "Environment and Entrepreneur", Chugh Publication Allahabad, 1975.
60. Timmons J.A. "New Venture Creation", Richard D Irwin, Illinois, 1985.
61. "UNIDO Manual for Preparation of Industrial Feasibility Study", New York, 1978.
62. "UNIDO Guide to Practical Project Appraisal", New York, 1978.

63. Vespar K. H. "New Venture Strategy", Prentice Hall, New Jersey, 1980.
64. Khanna S.S. "Entrepreneurial Development", S.Chand & Co. Ltd. New Delhi, 1999.
65. Gupta C.B. and Dr N.P. Srinivasan "Entrepreneurship Development in India", Sultan Chand & Sons, New Delhi, 1999.
66. Khanna S.S. "Entrepreneurship in Small-Scale Industries", Himalaya Publishing House, New Delhi, 1990.
67. Murthy Beveln "Entrepreneurship Development in India", Mittal Publication, New Delhi, 1989.
68. Siropolis Nicholas, "Entrepreneurship and Small Business Management", Houghton Mifflin Company, Boston, New York.
69. Irving Kristol "Business vs the Economy", The Wall Street Journal, June 1979.
70. Arnold C. Cooper "Entrepreneurship Starting a New Business", National Fedration of Independence Business, Washington DC, 1983.
71. Charles A. Scharf "Acquisitions, Mergers, Sales & Takeovers", Prentice Hall N.J., 1981.
72. Neilee Hing "Franchise Satisfaction : Contributors and Consequences", Journal of Small Business Management, April, 1995.
73. Ropert Jestin and Richard Judd "Franchising", South Western, 1989.
74. Timbothy Bates "Analysis of Survival Rates among Franchise and Independent Small Business Startups", Journal of Small Business Management, April 1995.
75. Andrew A. Caffee, "Understanding the UFOC", Entrepreneur, Jan. 1995.
76. US. Dept of Commerce "Franchise Opportunities Hand Book", US Govt. Printing Office, Washington DC, 1991.
77. Jamer Singh Saini "Entrepreneurship Development Programmes and Practices", Deep & Deep Publications, 1998.
79. Vasant Deasi "Small Scale Industries and Entrepreneurship". Himalaya Publishing House, 1999.
80. Pandey I.M. "Venture Capital—The Indian Experience", Prentice Hall of India Pvt. Ltd. New Delhi, 1996.
81. Verma J. C. "Venture Capital Financing in India", Response Books, Sage Publications Ltd., 1997.
82. Dilip M Sarwate, "Entrepreneurial Development; Concept and Practices", Everest Publishing House.
83. All India Management Association "Manaing Enterprises in the Era of Uncertainty", Amexcel Publishers Private Ltd.
84. Taneja Satish "Women Entrepreneurs Choice of Business", Indian Management, Vol. 38, No. 1/2, Jan/Feb 1999.
85. Taneja Satish "Franchising", Science Tech Entrepreneur, Vol 8, No. 3, May-June, 2000.
86. Prime Minister's Rozgar Yojana Instructors Manual–DC (SSI) Ministry of Industry, Govt. of India, 1994.
87. Taneja Satish "Venture Capital: Need of the Hours", Productivity Promotion, Vol. 3, No. 11, March, 1999.
88. Taneja Satish "Entrepreneurship & Management", Laghu Udyog Samachar (Monthly Journal of SIDO) Vol XV, No. 4, Nov. 90.
89. Taneja Satish "North East Women Show the Way", Laghu Udhog Samachar (Journal of SIDO) Vol. XV, No. 11, June 91.
90. Taneja Satish "Apparel Business A Preferred Choice by Women Entrepreneurs", Science Tech. Entrepreneur (Publication of NSTEDB-Govt. of India) Vol. VII, No. 5, Sep.-Oct. 99.
91. Varshney R.L. & Gupta S.L. "Marketing", Sultan Chand & Sons, 2000.
92. Gupta S.L. "Marketing Research", Excel Books, 1999.
93. Rampal M.K. & Gupta S.L. "Cases in Marketing Management", Galgotia Publishing Company, New Delhi, 2000.
94. Dr. Taneja Satish. "Venture Capital in India", Galgotia Publishing Company, New Delhi, 2002.